THE REFUGEE-DIPLOMAT

THE REFUGEE-DIPLOMAT

Venice, England, and the Reformation

DIEGO PIRILLO

CORNELL UNIVERSITY PRESS
ITHACA AND LONDON

First published 2018 by Cornell University Press

Printed in the United States of America

Library of Congress Cataloging-in-Publication Data

Names: Pirillo, Diego, author.
Title: The refugee-diplomat : Venice, England, and the Reformation /
   Diego Pirillo.
Description: Ithaca : Cornell University Press, 2018. | Includes bibliographical
   references and index.
Identifiers: LCCN 2018023439 (print) | LCCN 2018029335 (ebook) |
   ISBN 9781501715327 (epub/mobi) | ISBN 9781501715334 (pdf) |
   ISBN 9781501715310 | ISBN 9781501715310 (cloth ; alk. paper)
Subjects: LCSH: Venice (Italy)—Foreign relations—England. |
   England—Foreign relations—Italy—Venice. | Venice (Italy)—Foreign
   relations—1508–1797. | Religious refugees—Italy—Venice—
   History—16th century. | Protestants—Italy—Venice—History—
   16th century. | Diplomacy—History—16th century.
Classification: LCC DG676.97.G7 (ebook) | LCC DG676.97.G7 P57 2018
   (print) | DDC 327.45/31104209031—dc23
LC record available at https://lccn.loc.gov/2018023439

To Nestore, *dalla dolce parola*

Distraught, I understood the deeper meaning of a Somali
wisdom in which a high value is placed on owning one's own house,
as this affords a greater sense of privacy, of self-honour and
of dignity. . . . Having no home of one's own and no country
enjoying the luxury of peace, then perhaps one is a refugee

NURUDDIN FARAH, *YESTERDAY, TOMORROW:*
VOICES FROM THE SOMALI DIASPORA

CONTENTS

Illustrations

Acknowledgments

This book could never have been completed without the support of several institutions, colleagues, and friends. A first draft of the manuscript was written in 2015–16 during a wonderful year spent between the Fondazione Cini in Venice and Villa I Tatti, the Harvard University Center for Italian Renaissance Studies, in Florence. A special thanks to Alina Payne, the director of Villa I Tatti, for creating an ideal environment for intellectual exchange. The I Tatti community was in every respect crucial to the completion of the book. Many thanks also to Gino Benzoni and Marta Zoppetti of the Fondazione Cini. Spending an extended period of time on San Giorgio Maggiore, working in the library of the Fondazione and in close proximity to the Archivio di Stato and the Marciana, was a rare privilege. Grants from the Hellman Family, the Institute of International Studies at the University of California (UC), Berkeley, the Renaissance Society of America, and the Rare Book School at the University of Virginia provided me with additional support at several critical moments. A special thanks also to Mahinder Kingra of Cornell University Press for following all the stages of the book with expertise and attention, and to the two anonymous readers who provided me with essential feedback.

This book owes much also to many colleagues and friends who read the manuscripts, saving me from many mistakes and helping me to clarify the structure. Since I arrived at Berkeley, Timothy Hampton has been an invaluable interlocutor, and the book would have never been completed without his encouragement and friendship. Adriano Prosperi read the entire manuscript and with his typical depth and *sprezzatura* made many poignant observations. Isabella Lazzarini and John Watkins also kindly read the whole manuscript with great generosity and gave me several crucial suggestions. Before publication the manuscript was revised especially in response to the comments made during the manuscript workshop organized at UC Berkeley in November 2016 with the kind support of the Institute of International Studies and the Townsend Center for the Humanities. I am especially grateful to Kinch Hoekstra, Ethan Shagan, Nicholas Terpstra, and Stefano Villani for their generous participation and sharp comments.

I had the opportunity to present parts of the book at the European University Institute in Florence, at the Université de Strasbourg, at the University of Warwick in Venice, at the University of Oxford, at the University of Toronto, and at the Scuola Normale Superiore of Pisa. My thanks for their hospitality and feedback go to Michele Ciliberto, Joanna Craigwood, Emanuele Cutinelli Rendina, Jonathan Davies, Jorge Flores, Giuseppe Marcocci, Vincenza Perdichizzi, Lorenzo Pericolo, Natalie Rothman, Tracey Sowerby. The book also greatly benefited from conversations I had with colleagues and friends. Many thanks to Federico Barbierato, Simonetta Bassi, Ann Blair, Warren Boutcher, Abigail Brundin, Michele Campopiano, Giorgio Caravale, John Christopoulos, Filippo De Vivo, Lucia Felici, Massimo Firpo, Diletta Gamberini, Ingrid Houssaye Michienzi, Mario Infelise, Ioanna Iordanou, Andras Kiseri, Christian Kleinbub, Jill Kraye, Vincenzo Lavenia, Pamela Long, Armando Maggi, Hannah Markus, Ronald Martinez, Edward Muir, Stephen Orgel, Jessie Ann Owens, Chiara Petrolini, David Rosenthal, Carol Rutter, Silvana Seidel Menchi, William Sherman, Luka Špoljarić, Ramie Targoff, Pasquale Terracciano, Jane Tylus, Stefania Tutino, and Michael Wyatt.

Many thanks also to the archivists and librarians of the Archivio di Stato of Venice, the Bancroft and the Doe Libraries at Berkeley, the Berenson Library, the Butler Library at Columbia University, the Istituto Nazionale di Studi sul Rinascimento, Det Kongelige Bibliotek, the Newberry Library, the Trinity College Library at the University of Cambridge, and especially to Michela Del Borgo, Angela Dressen, Consuelo Dutschke, David Faulds, Paul Gehl, Sandy Paul, Claude Potts, Michael Rocke, Anders Toftgaard, and Vittorio Vasarri for comments and kind help with documentary resources.

Last but not least, I am very grateful to the intellectual community I had the privilege of joining at UC Berkeley. My colleagues in the department of Italian Studies, especially Albert Ascoli, Steven Botterill, Mia Fuller, and Barbara Spackman, provided me with rare warmth and mentorship. I benefited enormously from conversations with Déborah Blocker, Thomas Dandelet, Victoria Kahn, Abhishek Kaicker, Jennifer Mackenzie, David Marno, Maureen Miller, Harsha Ram, Jonathan Sheehan, and Randy Starn.

My greatest debt is to Danielle, whose wit, strength, and beauty is a constant source of inspiration, and to Nestore, to whom the book is dedicated.

THE REFUGEE-DIPLOMAT

Introduction

Who is a refugee? According to the 1951 United Nations Convention, a refugee is a person who, "owing to a well-founded fear of being persecuted for reasons of race, religion, nationality, membership of a particular social group or political opinion, is outside the country of his nationality and is unable or, owing to such fear, is unwilling to avail himself of the protection of that country."[1] Although this has been the word's standard legal definition since its adoption in the aftermath of the Second World War, the 1951 refugee convention has been subsequently expanded to come to terms with the new scenarios created by the Cold War and decolonization. More recently, the challenges posed by globalization have led to a further reappraisal of the 1951 convention, which no longer seems adequate for the reality of twenty-first-century international politics, when "most refugees are not fleeing a well-founded fear of being persecuted . . . but a well-founded fear of violent death in states torn apart by civil war."[2]

Precisely when the 1951 convention inserted the refugee into international law, the prominent German Jewish philosopher Hannah Arendt—who had herself fled to the United States to escape Nazi persecution—situated refugees at the center of political philosophy. In her classic work *The Origins of Totalitarianism*, published for the first time in English in 1951, Arendt carefully examined the condition of "stateless" people who, in losing their nationality status, were denied the very "right to have rights."[3] Since then, political philosophers have debated at length the moral obligations sovereign states have toward refugees, discussing whether political communities require closure to preserve the distinctiveness of cultures, or whether it is necessary to rethink the very distinction between citizens and aliens as well as the relationship between sovereignty and human rights.[4] In recent years, Arendt has remained a major point of reference for the discussion on refugees. The Italian philosopher Giorgio Agamben has regarded the figure of the refugee as "a limit concept that radically calls into question the fundamental categories of the nation-state," and that brings to light the separation between humanitarianism and politics, between the rights of man and the rights of the citizen.[5] On the other hand, the Turkish American philosopher Seyla Benhabib has pointed out the necessity of developing a new cosmopolitan theory and of imagining new forms of membership able to incorporate transnational political actors who transcend the territorially bounded state system.[6]

While political philosophy and international relations have been at the forefront of the growing field of refugee studies, history has remained at the fringe of scholarly debate and is often blamed for ignoring refugee movements.[7] As a result, refugee studies has largely developed as an ahistorical field that lacks a historical understanding of the many questions it confronts. Even today most historical overviews repeat conventional narratives following the rise of a European system of sovereign states with the peace of Westphalia to then concentrate almost exclusively on the twentieth century, as though the refugee question were an unprecedented phenomenon, born with the world wars and the United Nations.[8] Against this general trend, scholars have made a call to reinsert history at the center of refugee studies. Philip Marfleet has rightly pointed out "the need to know how today's movements are related to those of the past: how institutional actors responded to people displaced in earlier migration crises, how discourses of the refugee have emerged and how they have shaped policies for refugees and asylum." Indeed, against the policymakers' lack of interest in the migrations of the past, it is essential to emphasize that "denial of refugee histories is part of the process of denying refugee realities today."[9]

To be sure, our epoch is not the first to struggle with how to define the status of the refugee or how to treat and manage refugee flows. Refugees shaped European history well before the modern age, and only the "methodological nationalism" of nineteenth- and twentieth-century historians and social scientists failed to see it. In fact, the term "refugee" appears in English in the late seventeenth century as a translation from the French *refugié*, to indicate the Huguenots who had been expelled from France after the revocation of the Edict of Nantes in 1685.[10] Already in the previous century the Reformation had provoked a long-term process of religious migration. According to Heinz Schilling, the division of Europe into confessional churches changed the very notion of the "refugee" and forced religious minorities "to cope on a greater scale with the experience of being culturally and ideologically identified as *others* and *strangers*."[11]

More recently, Nicholas Terpstra has considered the Reformation the "first period in European and possibly global history when the religious refugee became a mass phenomenon."[12] Despite the fact that exile and persecution are not early modern inventions, the reform movements' growing concern with the purification and purgation of society created an unprecedented quantity of forced relocations, affecting not only Christian but also Jewish and Muslim minorities. In this respect, the Reformation was not simply an attempt to rediscover a purer faith in reaction to the corruption of the Catholic Church, it was also "Europe's first grand project in social purification."[13] Since purgation was such a central part of religious reform, Terpstra argues, scholars should challenge traditional periodizations and "include the expulsion of the Jews from Spain in 1492 as one of the critical events marking the start of the 'Reformation'—no less significant than Martin Luther's posting of the Ninety-Five Theses in 1517 or English king Henry VIII's divorce controversy of the 1520's and 30's."[14]

While also focusing on the Reformation, the current volume opens a new chapter in the historical study of refugees by demonstrating that in the early modern period they were not just passive recipients of assistance dispensed by states and churches, but were in fact dynamic actors in the transformation of European society. More specifically, the book recovers the agency of refugees in early modern diplomacy and shows that even as they were forced into exile they also contributed to shaping the new emerging system of international relations. During the early modern period, when diplomatic practices were not yet uniform or standardized, religious refugees served many different diplomatic functions and were employed as intelligencers, cultural brokers, translators, propagandists, and, at times, even as representatives and negotiators. Yet the goal of this book is not simply to add another group of intermediaries to the historical record, but rather to recover the figure of the "refugee-diplomat" in order to rethink early modern diplomacy beyond the state-centered paradigm that has long conditioned diplomatic studies. While maintaining that the growing power exercised by states is a central phenomenon of premodern diplomatic history, this book intends to explore the complex relationship between state and non-state agents, between formality and informality, that marked the Renaissance transformation of diplomatic practices.[15] As the following chapters demonstrate, refugees were not merely intermediaries between states or carriers of information for their patrons. On the contrary, in early modern Europe they functioned as a parallel and alternative diplomatic network outside of formal channels, reproducing the authority of states while also subverting it "through their appropriation of diplomatic practices for their own purposes."[16]

Situating religious refugees at the center of early modern diplomacy, this book builds on the new avenues of research opened by "new diplomatic history," which in recent years has challenged "the idol of origins" that for a long time regarded Renaissance Italy as the first step toward the emergence of modern diplomacy. Moving beyond the exclusive focus on the resident ambassador, "new diplomatic history" has succeeded in recovering the multifaceted world of agents, go-betweens, and intermediaries who engaged in diplomatic activity on the ground together with—or instead of—state representatives.[17] Although during the Renaissance and the early modern period states certainly wielded growing influence on international relations, they did not have exclusive control over them. Indeed, "formal political diplomacy was far from monopolizing diplomatic relationships: different diplomatic agents (and agencies) coexisted with formally qualified ambassadors . . . well into the modern age."[18] And yet, despite the fundamental attention devoted by scholars of the early modern Mediterranean to intermediaries such as converts, renegades, and dragomans, we still know very little about the diplomatic role that religious refugees played in Reformation Europe. As the several case studies examined in this book suggest, when the religious controversies undermined or suspended formal diplomatic channels between Catholic and Protestant states, refugees proved especially useful for facilitating cross-confessional exchanges.

More specifically, the book points out three overlapping and yet distinct areas of early modern diplomacy in which religious refugees were especially influential. First, information gathering: as scholars have pointed out, Renaissance diplomacy revolutionized the ways in which intelligence was collected and transmitted, marking a shift from a system in which the gathering of political information was not only relatively rare but also unsystematic and discontinuous, to a new one in which it became almost a daily business and in every respect crucial for an effective foreign policy.[19] Diplomacy increasingly became a business conducted by professionals of written communication, which in the eyes of contemporaries gave rise to a true "world of paper" (*mundo de carta*), as the bishop of Modena Giacomo Antonio della Torre wrote in 1448 to Marquis Leonello d'Este.[20] Famously, Niccolò Machiavelli argued that the first duty of the ambassador is to inform his government, as intelligence gathering shaped international politics and thus constituted a fundamental skill in order for the diplomat to be effective and to progress in his career.[21]

And yet the early modern "information society" was not centralized thus far, or "mediated by a dominant state or commercial communications sector," and "kings and their officials collected and deployed knowledge in unstandardized forms because what should be known was not yet determined by any dominant notion of a critical bureaucracy or public."[22] The sixteenth- and seventeenth-century "information society" consisted rather of "many overlapping groups of knowledge-rich communities" and knowledge was still "deeply embodied in the status of the particular informant or knowledge community."[23] Religious refugees functioned as just such a "knowledge community," navigating the perils of exile by offering intelligence in exchange for protection and remuneration. Taking advantage of their mobility and transnational connections, they were able to provide European states with the information they needed—collaborating or competing with, or even replacing, formal diplomatic representatives.

The second area of early modern diplomacy in which religious refugees were especially active was "cultural transfer." The role of diplomacy in putting cultures into contact has received growing attention in recent scholarship, especially as new diplomatic history has pushed to apply the methods of cultural and intellectual history to diplomatic studies. In addition to representing their princes, handling the negotiations on their behalf, and gathering intelligence, ambassadors were also used to gain access to a foreign country's cultural resources and to acquire rare editions or works of art.[24] New attention to material culture has also contributed to the revival of the study of cultural diplomacy. Indeed, early modern ambassadors were agents of "transculturation" not only through their words and reports but also through processes of gift giving, which, in enhancing the status of the giver and representing the person of the prince to another state, often conveyed complex political messages.[25] Moreover, ambassadorial reports have shed new light on the "connected histories" of the early modern Mediterranean, questioning the absolute dichotomy between Christianity and Islam, or between Europe and the Orient, while highlighting the complex strategies of cultural mediation employed by a variety of diplomatic agents.[26]

In this book, I study religious refugees as key intermediaries in the cultural exchanges between Italy and Northern Europe. Forced to leave their country and to go into exile, refugees brought to Protestant Europe the language and culture of Renaissance Italy and used their cultural capital to integrate in their host countries.[27] In this respect, they occupied a prominent place in the "cultural translation" of the Italian Renaissance outside of Italy, reminding us that "the migration of people" is essential for the diffusion of ideas and innovations.[28] Importantly, the cultural transfers facilitated by refugees did not move in a single direction from south to north, remaining limited to the export of Renaissance culture to Europe. They also imported Northern Protestantism into Italy, publishing, translating, and smuggling in authors of different confessions, such as Martin Luther, John Calvin, or James I. Thus, a substantial part of this book is dedicated to the influence of religious refugees on the early modern book world, considering their role in what Robert Darnton has called the "communications circuit" and examining their activity as editors, scribes, translators, readers, and literary agents.[29] Drawing on the methods of book history and the history of reading, I study the ways in which books were "differently apprehended, manipulated and comprehended," while moving across religious and linguistic borders and being adapted for new audiences.[30]

Finally, religious refugees became influential in early modern diplomacy because of their capacity to affect and manipulate communication. As has been noted, "The need to communicate is nowhere more apparent and normal than in diplomatic conversation."[31] Indeed, in Renaissance Italy diplomacy was created on the basis of a communication system that intended both to contain conflict through negotiation and to select the only legitimate powers by limiting access to the system.[32] At the same time, scholars have also pointed out that, despite their insistence on secrecy, early modern states did not have full control of political communication and that this was in fact "the object of mutual contexts by different political actors," while escaping the control of any of them.[33] Post-Reformation Europe was marked by a "quantitative increase of public discussion," forcing princes and governments, regardless of their official views, to develop new and more sophisticated communicative strategies, and bringing a wider array of people within the nexus of political communication.[34]

Religious refugees are a case in point. On the one hand they served their patrons as intelligencers and cultural intermediaries, but on the other they affected diplomatic communication with the aim of pressuring state agents and gaining influence over international affairs. In this respect, this book suggests that religious refugees be regarded as a "transnational advocacy network," a concept that political scientists and, more recently, also historians have used to bring to light the role played by nongovernmental entities in international society.[35] Functioning as a transnational advocacy network, refugees used information and books, in both manuscript and print form, to leverage more powerful patrons and to advance their own political and religious goals. In this way the book intends to show how the growing importance of communication in early modern diplomacy transformed the very relationship between formality and informality, and between state and nonstate agents, enabling a larger number of actors to participate in international affairs.

In considering the agency of refugees and their efforts to affect the course of diplomacy, the book also argues for the necessity of expanding diplomatic history to include not only the exchanges among states and the reports of formal representatives but also the echoes, hopes, and expectations that international affairs produced outside of courts and governments within a larger "public sphere," composed of individuals and groups excluded from active politics.[36] While the hopes studied in this book—namely the Italian Protestant refugees' goal of bringing the Reformation to Italy and transforming Venice into the "Italian Geneva"—could appear to be simply utopian dreams that arose within groups removed from the high spheres of politics, this study takes those expectations seriously and shows that they were in fact grounded in the unstable balance of power that existed in Reformation Europe, when confessional boundaries were not yet rigidly defined and clear-cut. In other words, the material examined in this book proposes a reconception of diplomatic history not merely as the study of the past "as it really was" but rather as "another present," with its hopes and expectations, without projecting onto the past the knowledge of what would happen only later.[37] To these "hopes, which never materialized" and to the traces that they left behind a large part of this book is dedicated.[38]

To bring to light the role played by religious refugees in early modern diplomacy, this book concentrates on one specific group, the Italian philo-Protestants who during the sixteenth century left Italy in several different waves beginning in 1542, when Pope Paul III created the congregation of the Holy Office in order to fight the spread of Protestantism on the peninsula. Though persecuted and defeated in early modern Italy, the Italian Protestant refugees had a lasting influence on other communities driven out of their homelands for religious reasons. It is worth noting that when crossing the Atlantic the Puritans brought with them several texts by Italian reformers, such as Pietro Martire Vermigli's epistle *De fuga in persecutione*, which provided them with arguments to justify their decision to flee to New England.[39] In North America the memory of the Italian Protestant refugees continued to arouse the curiosity of readers for years. The North American circulation of the life of the Neapolitan Calvinist Galeazzo Caracciolo, Marquis of Vico, included in John Harvard's library and republished in Boston in 1751 and again in 1794, is perhaps the best evidence of the reception of the Italian Protestant refugees across the Atlantic.[40]

The Italian Protestant diaspora has long been at the center of historical studies, especially after the publication of Delio Cantimori's classic *Eretici italiani del Cinquecento*, published in 1939.[41] *Eretici italiani* established a fundamental framework, a true paradigm, that opened a series of investigations into the contributions of the Italian heretics to the history of religious tolerance. At the center of *Eretici italiani* was an attempt to comprehend the legacy of the "Italian Reformation" in Northern Europe, from Poland to Switzerland and England, to shed light on the hidden connections between the Italian heretics and the radical Enlightenment. Thus, Cantimori's main focus was not directed toward the Italian followers of the magisterial Reformation but rather toward the Anabaptists and Antitrinitarians, those radical heretics—"rebels against every form of ecclesiastical organization"—who were often as much at odds with the new as with the old orthodoxies.[42] Despite the fact that it was never translated into English, *Eretici italiani* enjoyed a wide circulation in North America, where Cantimori found important interlocutors in Roland Bainton and Eric Cochrane, and where his ideas were discussed and reappraised by generations of scholars.[43]

Although it was not the first historical study on Protestantism in Renaissance Italy, Cantimori's *Eretici italiani* marked a decisive turning point in the history of the scholarship, moving away from the old debates on the absence of a religious reform in Italy that had marked the Risorgimento, and turning its gaze on the cultural underground of sixteenth-century Italy, composed of dissidents, prophets, and sects, many of whom hardly fit the confessional categories of the Protestant or Catholic Reformations. Thus, in opposition to the traditional view that reduced the religious crisis of sixteenth-century Italy to the reception of the northern reformers south of the Alps ("the Reformation in Italy"), Cantimori pointed out the impossibility of studying many figures and groups of the period along the rigid confessional identities that emerged only later, and underlined the original and complex answers that Renaissance Italy gave to the religious question ("Italian Reformation"). Successive scholarship has tested Cantimori's thesis and brought to light the ways with which sixteenth-century Italy appropriated and often radicalized the ideas of not only Protestant reformers but also other European authors, from Erasmus of Rotterdam to Juan de Valdés.[44] The systematic study of inquisitorial records has enabled scholars to further recover the complexity of the "Italian Reformation" and to trace the lives and ideas not of individuals who "passed . . . merely from Catholicism to a form of Protestantism or evangelism" but rather of "individuals whose religious identities were never fixed, never completed." As it has been argued, "There was, in short, something extremely malleable, or restless and individualistic, about many of the reformers and heretics in Italy" and in fact "the prominence of these figures in the Italian reform was one of its defining characteristics."[45]

Cantimori did not have much interest, however, in diplomatic history. Explaining the thinking behind his work, Cantimori regarded the decision to focus on the Italian heretics as a reaction against the "traditionalist turn toward national history in the sense of the history of politics, the state, diplomacy, and military affairs."[46] Rarely have scholars noted that the *Eretici italiani* was crafted out of an intense debate over diplomatic history that took place in Italy in the interwar period. During the 1920s and 1930s the rise of fascism led the most prominent Italian historians of the period, from

Benedetto Croce to Gaetano Salvemini and from Gioacchino Volpe to Federico Chabod, to reevaluate the status and methods of the history of international relations.[47] In the background there was a critical dialogue with German Historicism and with the "founding father" of diplomatic history, Leopold von Ranke. While Croce polemically labeled Ranke "a historian without a historical problem" (*uno storico senza problema storico*), Cantimori blamed the German historian for his ties with Prussian nationalism.[48] Despite the fact that Ranke had inaugurated "a new historiographical style, in which the critical philological lens was infused with narrative and reflection," Cantimori argued that his close relationship with the Prussian state led him to believe that historical truth could be found only in the reports of high officials, ministers, and sovereigns, "the only [sources] that can tell us how things had really happened" (*che sole possono dirci come le cose sono andate in realtà*).[49]

Thus, *Eretici italiani* dismissed diplomatic history as the study of political and military events, moving from the conviction that politics was not the "relationships among states" (*rapporti fra potentati*) but rather "men's battle for the institutions that must regulate their life together" (*lotta degli uomini per le istituzioni che debbono regolare la loro convivenza*).[50] Therefore, while *Eretici italiani* reshaped the study of the Renaissance and the Reformation, placing the "Italian heretics" at the forefront of early modern studies, it also contributed to a long-term separation between religious and political history. Indeed, as Silvana Seidel Menchi has noted, Italian scholarship on the Reformation and the Counter-Reformation has long been divided into "two independent trajectories of the history of power and the history of conscience," with the consequence that those scholars who "studied the institutional realities of Italy and Europe—the papacy, the Church, the modern state and its origins, justice and structures" did not communicate with those working on the "archeology of the conscience," who studied the history of religious dissent expressed in "individual cases, or tiny groups at the level of individual experience."[51]

This book thus situates itself at the intersection of religious and political history and aims to close the gap between these different fields. While scholars have significantly revised the "Cantimori paradigm," moving beyond the separation between the "history of power" and the "history of conscience," very little attention has been dedicated to the relationship between the Italian Protestant refugees and European diplomacy.[52] This is striking, given the fact that during the early modern period embassies played a crucial role in the practice of religious tolerance, offering a safe space to refugees and turning their chapels into clandestine churches, even before the legal principle of extraterritoriality was officially formulated. As has been noted, it was through these "fictions of privacy" that early modern European states were able to accommodate religious dissent and to unofficially allow a certain degree of tolerance to religious minorities while officially maintaining their commitment to confessional uniformity.[53] *The Refugee-Diplomat* fills this lacuna and investigates the many ways in which Italian Protestant refugees facilitated the exchanges among states that could not officially communicate, even after formal diplomatic channels had been suspended.

A problem that every scholar of early modern diplomacy must face is the overabundance of sources. The historian has at his or her disposal not only letters, dispatches, instructions, and final reports—often in multiple drafts—but also a broad range of different documents regarding both the content of the embassy and the daily life of the ambassadors and its servants. Closer contacts between states and the growing quantity of correspondence exchanged between governments and their representatives abroad multiplied the amount of diplomatic sources to an unprecedented quantity. It is not a coincidence that the early modern period saw the emergence of new needs for ordering and storing information and the transformation of archives into "hearts of the state"—spaces that stocked documents but that also organized them according to the needs of the emerging sovereign states or of competing political factions within them.[54]

In writing *The Refugee-Diplomat* I essentially relied on four main groups of sources: first, on the records contained in the London and Venetian state archives. To be sure, the starting point for the study of Anglo-Venetian diplomacy during the early modern period cannot but be constituted by the volumes of the Calendar of State Papers relating to English Affairs in the Archives of Venice, commissioned by the British government in 1861 from Rawdon Brown—an "Italianate Englishman" like his friend John Ruskin, and yet not a sympathizer of Italian unification—as part of a larger project with the intention of ordering the country's history preserved in foreign archives.[55] Whenever possible I used the Calendar of State Papers (CSP) to retrieve the original archival records, as many of them have never been transcribed or translated into English. At the National Archives in London, research in the State Papers (SP), especially SP 70—the general series on

foreign affairs during the first decades of Elizabeth's reign (1558 to 1577)—
and SP 99—the series relating to England's interaction with the Venetian
Republic (along with SP 1, 78, 83, 85), has revealed dozens of letters from
religious refugees and their associates that uncover the unofficial diplomatic
networks created by the Tudors in Italy after Henry VIII's break with Rome
throughout the Elizabethan period. In the Archivio di Stato in Venice the
series *Senato, Dispacci ambasciatori e residenti, Inghilterra* (along with *Collegio, Esposizioni principi—Collegio, Esposizioni Roma—Capi del Consiglio di
Dieci, Dispacci degli ambasciatori—Consiglio di Dieci, Deliberazioni, Secrete*)
has been extremely valuable for clarifying the interruption and the reopening of formal diplomatic contact between Venice and England.

As the book focuses on a long diplomatic crisis in which formal exchanges
were suspended for decades, it was necessary to complement official govern-
mental records and to expand the sources traditionally used by diplomatic
historians. While at times the records of National Archives in London and
the Archivio di Stato in Venice suffice to uncover the existence of unofficial
diplomatic networks, on some occasions it was necessary to turn to other
sources not included in the Calendar of State Papers. Thus, I made extensive use of manuscript copies of diplomatic reports and other political writings contained not in state archives but in private libraries. Through material gathered in particular at the Newberry Library in Chicago and the
Trinity College Library in Cambridge, and to a lesser extent at the British
Library in London, the Butler Library in New York, the Folger Library in
Washington, DC, and the Royal Library in Copenhagen, I was able to examine the copies of diplomatic reports made, circulated, and annotated by
Italian refugees. Drawing on the methods of bibliographers and book historians I have examined the marginalia and other material traces to bring to
light the ways in which the Italian refugees used their books.[56] In this respect, I benefited from the suggestions of those scholars who have recently
shifted attention from the writing of diplomatic texts and their governmen-
tal use to their circulation into a wider information system beyond the European elite.[57] Moreover, following the golden rule that "books are not simply what is printed in them," I studied the material form in which books
circulated, and examined how printed and manuscript texts were used by
Italian refugees as tools of community formation employed to strengthen the
bonds among like-minded individuals.[58]

I next drew on inquisitorial records, a source which is well-known to religious historians but less to diplomatic historians. And yet diplomatic and inquisitorial sources are often in dialogue and complement each other. This is especially true in the case of sixteenth-century Italy, where the clash between *spirituali* and *intransigenti* within the Catholic Church corresponded to a confrontation between Imperial and French diplomacy.[59] The records of the Venetian and Roman Inquisition have been especially crucial for this book, as they are essential for following the movements and activities of the Italian Protestant refugees. I relied on the series Fondo Sant'Uffizio, created in 1547 and preserved in the Archivio di Stato in Venice, as well as on other inquisitorial records, such as the trials against the apostolic protonotary Pietro Carnesecchi and the bishop of Bergamo Vittore Soranzo, that have recently been published by Massimo Firpo, Dario Marcatto, and Sergio Pagano.[60] Inquisitorial records contain evidence of the diplomatic activity of the Italian refugees and on their role as intermediaries between Venice and Protestant Europe, but they also point to the growing power of the Roman Inquisition in international affairs. While the book focuses on the diplomatic exchanges between Venice and England, any study of Anglo-Venetian diplomacy during the early modern period would be incomplete without taking into account the third party constituted by Papal Rome, which after the Council of Trent strengthened its diplomatic presence in Europe.

Finally, I made use of literary sources and took advantage of the new methods introduced by literary scholars in the study of early modern diplomacy. The collaboration between historical and literary methodologies has shown that literary texts are fundamental to the understanding of early modern diplomacy, as they did not simply reflect but also contributed to the conception of new diplomatic practices.[61] The new wave of studies on William Shakespeare is a case in point in this respect. While *Hamlet* has been read as a drama about Elizabethan state building that through the stage allowed theatergoers a glimpse into the world of ministers, diplomats, and secretaries, *The Merchant of Venice* is seen as a play that comments on the shifting mercantile and diplomatic relations between Venice and England at the end of the sixteenth century.[62] While the relationship that literature and diplomacy established during the early modern period has been the focus of numerous studies, much less attention has been dedicated to examining how literary texts were read within embassies or the role of ambassadors as patrons of letters. For this reason the second chapter considers the English embassy in Venice during the 1540s as a center of literary activity whereas the fifth chapter discusses the reception of the Italian Renaissance poet Torquato Tasso in Elizabethan England, bringing to light how the *Gerusalemme liberata* (Jerusalem Delivered) became relevant for the late sixteenth-century discussion on the confessionalization of European diplomacy.

Focusing on several specific case studies, the seven chapters of the book track the many different functions of Italian Protestant refugees in the diplomatic exchanges between Venice and England during the sixteenth and early seventeenth centuries. Chapter 1, "When Diplomacy Fails," provides the reader with an overview of the diplomatic contacts between Venice and England during the sixteenth century. It explains why the Reformation was at the heart of the diplomatic crisis between the two states and the reasons that the exchange of resident ambassadors was suspended during the entire reign of Elizabeth I (1558–1603). The chapter also argues that the exchanges between Venice and England cannot be fully understood without taking into account Papal Rome, which strongly influenced the relationship between the two states. It was not a coincidence that the crisis of Anglo-Venetian diplomacy took place when the election of Pope Paul IV and the strengthening of the Roman Inquisition over the Italian states introduced into European diplomacy language and practices taken from the contemporary fight of the Catholic Church against Protestant heresy.

Chapter 2, "*Tudor Diplomacy and Italian Heterodoxy*," reconstructs how and when Tudor diplomacy and Italian heterodoxy met. I study this encounter by examining the career of the English ambassador in Venice, Edmund Harvel, and reveal how Henry VIII's rupture with Rome (1534) led English diplomacy to forge an alliance with the Italian Protestant movement. I draw attention to Harvel's encounter with Italian heterodoxy through his relationship with Reginald Pole, the future cardinal who was also a cousin of Henry VIII, and with Pietro Aretino, the famous Renaissance writer who sought the patronage of the English king. In addition, I retrace the role played by Harvel's secretary, the Italian reformer Baldassarre Altieri, correspondent of Luther and Calvin. Through Harvel and Altieri the English embassy in Venice became a hub of Protestant propaganda in Italy, at the center of a transnational network that included not only Tudor England but also the heads of the Reformation in Germany, from Luther to the leaders of the League of Schmalkalden. The chapter then follows the activities of the English embassy in Venice until its closure in January 1557, driving Anglo-Venetian diplomacy from that moment forward out of formal channels.

Chapters 3 and 4, "*Spying on the Council of Trent*" and "*The Merchant, the Queen, and the Refugees*," bring to light the information flow between Venice and England during the 1560s, after the closure of the embassies. By analyzing a large number of never before transcribed letters sent by the Italian refugee Guido Giannetti to Elizabeth I and her secretary William Cecil, chapter 3 presents in detail the knowledge the Tudors had of the Council of Trent and how they evaluated its religious and political consequences. The fourth chapter investigates the channels of communication that the Italian refugees used to transmit information to their English patrons and recovers their relations with the prominent Venetian merchant Giacomo Ragazzoni.

Chapters 5 and 6, "*Reading Tasso*" and "*Reading Venetian Relazioni*," discuss the role of the Italian refugees as readers and cultural brokers and show how their influence on English diplomacy was also reliant on their capacity to bring to England the culture and literature of their homeland. Chapter 5 reconstructs the reading practices of Alberico and Scipione Gentili, examining their annotations and commentaries on Torquato Tasso's epic poem, *Gerusalemme liberata* (Jerusalem Delivered). Chapter 6 elaborates on the diplomatic culture of the Italian religious refugees by studying their use of the famous Venetian ambassadorial *relazioni* (the comprehensive reports presented to the senate by Venetian ambassadors at the end of their missions). Using the rich collection of manuscripts assembled by Giacomo Castelvetro, especially those held at the Newberry Library in Chicago, the chapter examines for the first time numerous annotations made by the Italian refugees on Venetian diplomatic reports.

Chapter 7, "*Great Expectations*," considers the hopes that the reopening of the English embassy in Venice in 1603 stirred among the Italian Protestant refugees. James I's clash with Rome over the oath of allegiance (1606) and the support he gave to Venice during the Interdict (1606–7) convinced them that the Protestant cause in Italy was still supported by England. This chapter first elucidates the relationship between the Italian refugees and the English ambassador Henry Wotton and their plan to transform Venice into an "Italian Geneva." It then draws on Giacomo Castelvetro's manuscript collection (held in the library of Trinity College, Cambridge) to demonstrate the role of the Italian refugees in the "war of words" that erupted with the

Interdict. Protected by the English embassy, they circulated prohibited texts in manuscript form in order to bond with the Venetian patricians and to convince them to break off relations with Rome. Despite the fact that the attempt to transform the Interdict controversy into an open rebellion against Rome was ultimately unsuccessful, the chapter proposes new evidence suggesting that, in the early seventeenth century, the relationship between Italian Protestant refugees and English diplomacy seemed to acquire fresh strength. Not until the second decade of the century would James I's philo-Hispanic policy ultimately undermine this relationship that had grown under the Tudors, inflicting a fatal blow to the Italian refugees' dream of introducing the Reformation into Italy.

To conclude, the chapters in this book offer an alternative history of Renaissance and early modern diplomacy, centered not around the resident ambassador but around "the refugee-diplomat." While the establishment of permanent embassies in fifteenth-century Italy has traditionally been regarded as the moment of transition between medieval and modern diplomacy, this book tells a different story. Concentrating on apparently marginal figures like Italian philo-Protestant refugees, the book intends to rediscover how diplomacy worked not only within but also outside of formal channels, through underground networks and individuals without a formal appointment who were able to move across religious and linguistic borders, often adapting their own identities to the changing political conditions they encountered. In recovering the agency of religious refugees, the following chapters do not simply present another group of intermediaries but in fact reveal their capacity to influence international affairs and to shape the transformation of early modern diplomatic culture and practice. In the end, this book is an attempt to recover the tension between state and network diplomacy in an age in which, not unlike ours, states were not the exclusive actors of international relations.

Chapter 1

When Diplomacy Fails

In the *History of Italy*, published in London in 1549 and destined to become the most influential guidebook to Italy available in Tudor England, the Welsh scholar William Thomas pondered over the "marvelous situation of the city of Venice," which, despite standing "open upon the main sea, four miles from the nearest mainland . . . is now not only exceeding full of people and rich of treasure and buildings but so wholesome withal" that "no place of all Europe [is] able at this day to compare with that city."[1] It was not only the wealth and the beauty of Venice that impressed Thomas. Appropriating the "myth of Venice" and reformulating it for his English readers, the author of the *History of Italy* expressed his admiration for the cosmopolitanism of the Italian Republic, celebrating the tolerance granted by the Venetian government to the many religious minorities along with the freedom enjoyed by foreigners with regard to sexual and dietary habits:[2]

For no man there marketh another's doings, or that meddleth with another man's living. If thou be a papist, there shalt thou want no kind of superstition to feed upon. If thou be a gospeler, no man shall ask why thou comest not to church. If thou be a Jew, a Turk, or believest in the devil (so thou spread not thine opinions abroad), thou art free from all controlment. To live married or unmarried, no ma shall ask thee why. For eating of flesh in thine own house, what day soever it be, it maketh no matter. And generally of all other things, so thou offend no man privately, no man shall offend thee, which undoubtedly is one principal cause that draweth so many strangers thither.

The epitome of the "Italianate Englishman"—as is suggested by his many other writings, from the *Pellegrino inglese* written in defense of Henry VIII's religious policy to the *Principal Rules of the Italian Grammar, with a Dictionarie for the better understandyng of Boccace, Petrarcha, and Dante*—Thomas ensured that the "myth of Venice" had a powerful echo in early modern England. The English fascination with Venice is well-known, and yet, this very fascination has obscured the paradox that lay at the heart of Tudor England's relationship with the Italian Republic. Even as Venice occupied a prominent place in the minds of many English playwrights, from William Shakespeare to Ben Jonson, and its republican institutions were examined in several treatises available to English readers, from Thomas's *History of Italy* to Gasparo Contarini's *The Commonwealth and Government of Venice*, formal diplomatic exchanges between the two states were reduced to a minimum or suspended for most of the Tudor period.

Though formal diplomatic contacts between Venice and England dated back to the early years of the Italian wars, when Henry VII offered the Italian Republic support against the League of Cambrai, Henry VIII's divorce controversy triggered a long diplomatic crisis between the two states.[3] While in 1531 the Venetian ambassador to England Ludovico Falier warned his government that Henry VIII "might easily swerve [from his friendship with the Republic], because you did not assent to his request about the divorce," in 1534 the English king's break with Rome led Venice to call back its ambassadors entirely and to leave in London only nonpatrician representatives, selected from among the *cittadini originari* (native-born citizens) who occupied the high ranks of Venetian bureaucracy.[4] In the following years diplomatic exchanges between Venice and England continued mostly undisturbed despite the absence of patrician envoys, but Elizabeth I's accession to the English throne marked a point of no return. On May 30, 1559, the Venetian senate debated over whether or not an ambassador should be sent to England

and concluded that they would put off the decision "until it might be seen how things were proceeding in that kingdom" (*fino che si veda come passavano le cose in quel regno*).[5] The deferral lasted forty-four years. No Venetian resident ambassador was sent to England until James I succeeded Elizabeth in 1603, and the unwillingness of the Venetian patriciate to reestablish the exchange of formal representatives deprived England of what was at the time its only embassy in Italy and contributed to its isolation in Europe.

This chapter examines the unfolding of the diplomatic crisis between Venice and England and singles out its two principle causes: first, the Venetian government's fearful reaction to the Protestant Reformation and its conviction that religious change would inevitably undermine social order; and second, Papal Rome's pressure on Venetian diplomacy and its intention to isolate England in Europe. Indeed, the diplomatic crisis between Venice and England took place precisely when the pontificate of Paul IV (1555–59) and the Holy Office's "grip on power" at the top of the Roman curia contributed to the division of European diplomacy along confessional lines, troubling also Venice's exchanges with Protestant Europe.[6]

Venice, England, and the Reformation

In March 1603, while in London to reopen formal diplomatic contact between Venice and England, the Venetian secretary Giovanni Carlo Scaramelli did not hide his disdain for the piracy practiced by English merchants, accusing them of being "greedy and cruel" and "hated by all other nations" because "under the guise of mercantile ships they go about indifferently in the bowels of other nations pillaging all the ships and all the men."[7] The following October, at Scaramelli's insistence, James I announced "A Proclamation to represse all Piracies and Depredations upon the Sea," which after being printed in London was soon sent to Venice.[8] To be sure, Scaramelli's protest and the reopening of diplomatic contact under James I did not change the new power dynamics between the two states that progressively led to Venice's decline and to the rise of England as a maritime empire. The late-sixteenth and seventeenth centuries coincided with what Fernand Braudel famously labeled the "Northern Invasion," referring to the period in which English ships began to trade in the Mediterranean and thereby challenge the dominion of the traditional powers in the region, starting with the Italian

Republic.[9] While Venice continued to act as a "territorial" rather than a "commercial" empire, considering itself "as the centre of all commercial activity, not as the hub coordinating a growingly multifaceted imperial economic strategy," the superior commercial organization of the English Levant Company allowed English merchants to challenge Venice's dominance of trade in the eastern Mediterranean.[10]

If the growing English presence in the Mediterranean complicated Anglo-Venetian exchanges, in reality the primary reason for the interruption of formal diplomatic ties between the two states during the Elizabethan period lay in the ambivalent reaction of the Venetian ruling class to the Protestant Reformation. On the one hand, Venice appeared to many to be "the gateway" of the Reformation in Italy.[11] Its commercial ties with Germany and its flourishing book trade allowed Protestant texts to enjoy a vast diffusion in Venice. In 1520 Luther's works were already available for sale in the city, and the *Diaries* of Marin Sanudo confirm the attention with which the patriciate followed the eruption of the Reformation.[12] More than agents, however, the northern reformers served as the catalysts of an already existing religious crisis, which in Venice had not waited for the Reformation. The consequences of the Battle of Agnadello (May 14, 1509), in which the Venetians were defeated by the League of Cambrai—losing "in one day's battle . . . what they had laboriously acquired over the course of eight hundred years"—created a crisis of confidence and civic identity that had a powerful impact on the religious restlessness of the following decades.[13] The religious crisis of the young Gasparo Contarini was only the most famous episode of a general crisis that tore through the Venetian patriciate in the years of the Italian wars.[14]

On the other hand, the widespread religious restlessness never led the Venetian patriciate to break off from Rome. Catholicism was too deeply ingrained in the Venetian "civic religion," as it allowed the patricians to justify their rule precisely "because it was based on Christianity and was concerned with creating a truly Christian and moral society."[15] Throughout the sixteenth century, Venice's jurisdictional autonomy was grounded in its special relationship with the Holy See, which was traced back to the *trionfi* granted by Pope Alexander III to Doge Sebastiano Ziani in 1177 as repayment for his assistance in fighting Emperor Frederick Barbarossa.[16] As Gaetano Cozzi famously put it, while the new Protestant doctrines did spark the interest of the Venetian elite, the Reformation did not manage to fracture the bond between the Venetian patricians and "the religion of their fathers" (*religione dei padri*): "Catholicism, in addition to being a group of dogmas and traditions that they accepted, perhaps with some reservation and some impatience . . . constituted a fundamental element of their society. It ensured respect for hierarchy, for authority; it provided the people with moral rules that were indispensable for a healthy coexistence within the state."[17]

More recent work has confirmed Cozzi's argument, showing that even those patricians who pondered the new Protestant doctrines never publicly voiced their religious views, prudently deciding instead to hide them under a veil of religious simulation and thereby to respect the system of social relations and family obligations in which they were embedded.[18] Examining the production of sacred images in Venice during the sixteenth century, Fabrizio Biferali and Massimo Firpo have reached similar conclusions, showing that the broad diffusion of heterodox positions produced only scarce echoes in the figurative arts, and that these were limited to artists who, like Lorenzo Lotto, were at the margins of the primary circuits of artistic patronage.[19] The diffusion of Protestant heresy in Venice thus never managed to put Catholicism into question within the Venetian patriciate. There was no clearer sign of the republic's will to fight heresy than the establishment in April 1547 of the Savi all'Eresia, the lay magistracy that assisted the ecclesiastical body in the repression of heresy and at the same time preserved the jurisdiction of the secular government over religious affairs.[20] While the "myth of Venice" as an open and tolerant city continued to circulate and to influence European scholars—to the point that Jean Bodin set in the lagoon his famous *Colloquium Heptaplomeres*, a dialogue among representatives of seven different faiths—the introduction of the Inquisition intensified the repression of religious dissent and in the second half of the sixteenth century erased the Italian philo-Protestant movement from the republic.[21]

In this sense the Reformation not only failed to fracture the Venetian patriciate's bond with the "religion of their fathers," but in fact incidentally reinforced it. As the reports of the Venetian ambassadors suggest, the Reformation was regarded by large sectors of the Venetian elite as an essentially political phenomenon that inspired fear because of its potential to disrupt the social order.[22] The echo of the German Peasants' War, amplified by the arrival in Padua of Michael Gaismair who had led the revolt in Tyrol, and the spread of Anabaptism in the republic convinced the patriciate that religious innovation posed a danger to the stability of the state. In 1532, the Venetian ambassador Niccolò Tiepolo voiced his concern about the recent events in Germany, where the Reformation had led the popular classes to turn the social order upside down, deposing "the nobles, or the traditional governing citizens of the territory, and replacing them with tailors, shoemakers, and other craftsmen," who were convinced that "no one should accumulate personal wealth, and all goods should be shared communally" (*niun dee possedere alcuna ricchezza propria, ma tutti li beni si devon mettere in comune*).[23]

In the same way, the reports of the Venetian ambassadors on the English Reformation also illustrate the patriciate's fears of the social consequences of heresy. According to Giacomo Soranzo, the continuous religious changes imposed by the Tudors had led England into a state of confusion and disorder "with so many variations and transformations the people no longer knew what to believe or where they could ground themselves."[24] Among the English, Daniele Barbaro remarked, "Nothing is more inconstant than their decrees concerning religion, as today they do one thing and tomorrow another" (*nessuna cosa è più incostante dei decreti loro circa la religione, perché oggi fanno una cosa e dimani l'altra*).[25] The diversity of beliefs "as much on the Holiest Trinity and the angels, as regarding the creation of the world, the humanity of Christ, and the virtue of the sacraments" was so extreme that "the chaos of languages" (*la confusione delle lingue*) reigned in England.[26] In 1559 the ambassador Michele Suriano distilled the Venetian fears about the Reformation to their essence, arguing that "the transformation of faith . . . is the most serious change that can arise in a kingdom [*la mutazione della fede . . . è la maggiore alterazione che possa nascere in un regno*], because in addition to the offense against our Lord God, there follows the change of customs, laws, loyalty, and, finally, of the government."[27] Thus, in the eyes of the Venetian ambassadors the turmoil England was experiencing confirmed that religious change inevitably undermined social order, threatening the authority of both the church and the state. Also in this respect, the Venetian *relazioni* tell more about the mentality of their authors than about the states and societies that they describe.[28]

Moreover, by looking at England, the Venetian ambassadors concluded that once initiated, religious change could hardly be stopped. In their view, the conflicts unleashed by the Reformation were barely under the control of the monarchy and even Mary Tudor's restoration was only an illusion of bringing England back to its Catholic past. According to Giovanni Michiel, who carefully ciphered many of his dispatches dealing with English religious affairs, Mary Tudor's policy had in fact encountered violent opposition. In London public authorities struggled with prohibiting the circulation of Lutheran and subversive publications, and iconoclasm targeted Catholic devotional objects on a daily basis.[29] Religious tensions often led to social unrest, as was evident from the popular classes, who "due to religion . . . often wish to see change and innovation."[30] According to Michiel, while in Essex the crowd attending the public executions of Protestants sided with the victims, threatening the local government, and on Easter of 1555 the mass in the church of St. Margaret in Westminster was interrupted by a plebeian (*persona populare*) attacking the priest with a sword.[31] After the death of the chancellor, Stephen Gardiner, in November 1555, Mary Tudor was forced to confront a harsh opposition in a Parliament "full of knights and noblemen for the most part suspicious because of their faith, and for that reason bold and licentious."[32] For the Venetian ambassador, the religious unrest in England had reached such a point that several cities such as Ipswich and Cambridge were raising armies "not only to conspire against the faithful Catholics, whom they call papists, but also against their rulers," creating "as much disruption and confusion in the kingdom as they can to damage and perhaps even to place in mortal danger those sovereigns, as the instigators of the religious change."[33]

Papal Rome as a "Third Party"

The fear of the social and political consequences of the Reformation was thus a primary factor behind the Venetian government's unwillingness to reestablish the exchange of resident ambassadors with England. And yet the diplomatic crisis cannot be fully understood without taking into consideration the third party constituted by Papal Rome, whose influence over international affairs strongly conditioned Venice's relationship with Protestant Europe. It was not a coincidence that the relationship between Venice and England was interrupted in the years of the pontificate of Paul IV (1555–59), who imposed in Rome the logic of the "spiritual war" against heretics and situated the Holy Office at the top of the Roman curia.[34] While the impact of the Roman Inquisition on the Italian states has been thoroughly investigated, much less attention has been dedicated to its effect on early modern diplomacy. In the second half of the sixteenth century the election of popes from the ranks of the Inquisition, including Paul IV, Pius V, and Sixtus V, reshaped Roman diplomacy, forcing papal representatives to come to terms with inquisitorial principles and undermining any attempt to negotiate with heretics.[35] When in 1571 Cardinal Cristoforo Madruzzo pointed out that the Bible did not forbid the Jews from having relations with heretics and infidels, and thus Rome could send representatives to the Lutheran princes, Pius V replied vigorously that no dealings with heretical sovereigns were permissible.[36]

The diplomatic crisis between Venice and England resulted therefore no less from the Venetian fear of the Reformation than from the new direction taken by Roman diplomacy in the years of the Council of Trent. This turning point had important repercussions in Venice, in that very moment engaged in defending from the Inquisition various members of the patriciate accused of heresy, including the patriarch of Aquileia Giovanni Grimani, the bishop of Bergamo Vittore Soranzo, and Reginald Pole's friend Andrea Priuli.[37] In August 1555, a few months after the election of Paul IV, the Venetian ambassador in Rome, Domenico Morosini, was forced to concede to the pope that the Reformation had found sympathizers among the Venetian elite. Having responded defensively that even among the apostles "one was a rogue and unfaithful" (*uno vi fu ribaldo et infedele*), Morosini nonetheless reassured the pope that the Venetian government had no hesitation in repressing heresy and declared that if someone were discovered deviating from Catholic orthodoxy, he "would not be tolerated but punished" (*non sarebbe sopportato ma castigato*).[38]

The defensive position that Venetian diplomacy held in those years to minimize the spread of heresy within the patriciate helps to explain why the republic yielded to papal pressures with regard to its relationship with Protestant states. Rome's capacity to influence Anglo-Venetian relations appeared clearly even before Elizabeth's succession. Indeed, in 1557 Paul IV revoked the English legation of Cardinal Reginald Pole, Henry VIII's cousin, who was at that time in England to guide the country's return to Catholicism.[39] In Pole the pope saw a dangerous heretic, the leader of the spirituali, who, following the teaching of the Spanish mystic Juan de Valdés, accepted the theological premises of the Protestant reformers "while carefully avoiding any hint of polemic and rejecting their break with the Church."[40] As the apostolic protonotary and prominent member of the spirituali Pietro Carnesecchi pointed out, Pole had become the target of convergent attacks in Protestant and Catholic Europe and was by then considered "a Lutheran in the opinion of Rome and a papist in Germany."[41] Only the protection of Mary Tudor and Philip II allowed Pole to avoid being recalled by Paul IV and to conclude his life in England rather than in the prison of Castel Sant'Angelo.

No single event, however, demonstrated the extent to which Rome could condition Anglo-Venetian diplomacy better than Pius V's excommunication of Elizabeth in February 1570. The excommunication echoed powerfully throughout Venice, and shaped the relationship between the republic and the English queen. Despite the fact that some patricians continued to sympathize with Elizabeth, recognizing her capacity to give "balance to the world" by fighting Spain and the papacy, few were willing to embrace the myth of the English queen as the Virgin Astraea, which Giordano Bruno worked to disseminate in the lagoon at the end of the sixteenth century.[42] Instead, the anti-myth of Elizabeth as a heretic and illegitimate sovereign, cruel persecutor of her Catholic subjects, enjoyed a vast circulation in Venice, especially through the works of English Catholic writers such as Nicholas Sanders's *De origine ac progressu schismatis Anglicani* (On the Origin and Growth of the Anglican Schism).[43] In 1587, having been appointed cardinal in August of that year, William Allen donated a copy of Sanders's work to the Venetian ambassador in Rome, Giovanni Gritti, in exchange for his effort to support English Catholic exiles.[44]

The excommunication also shined a light on Venice's limited political autonomy with respect to Rome. As the Venetian ambassador to France noted in April 1571, the Elizabethan court believed that Venice did not want to send a resident ambassador to England because the republic was dominated by Rome's intransigence.[45] The Venetian attempts to claim some political autonomy from the confessional strife amounted to little. In November 1578, when the Venetian government pointed out that many Catholic states such as Spain, Portugal, and France had representatives in England, the papal nuncio replied that "it would be better if those were removed as well, rather than that others be sent," arguing that the republic had to respect the will of Rome, "from which the entire world draws its morality, and example of the true faith."[46]

Pius V's excommunication also had some unintended consequences, however. As has been noted, the excommunication led Elizabeth to look for new partners in the Mediterranean and to establish closer diplomatic and commercial relations with the Ottoman Empire.[47] This situation seriously damaged Venice's economic interests, as England's new relationship with the

Figure 1. Elizabeth I to the Venetian doge Niccolò da Ponte, Greenwich,
March, 15, 1582 (Archivio di stato di Venezia).

Ottomans challenged Venice's traditional role of European gateway to the
East.[48] In the early 1580s Elizabeth wrote directly to the Venetian government, primarily to demand fiscal privileges for English merchants and to defend the currant trade between England and the Ionian Islands.[49]

In her letters Elizabeth also expressed her wish to resume "the ancient,
intimate friendship between our two kingdoms" and her expectation that
Venice would reciprocate the "affection, that we hold generally for the whole
nation of Italy, and particularly for your Glorious Republic."[50] Nonetheless,
Elizabeth's attempt to reestablish diplomatic relations with Venice did not
come to pass. As late as February 1603, when the diplomatic crisis was nearly
resolved, the English Queen maliciously asked the Venetian secretary Scaramelli whether the lack of a resident ambassador during the decades of her

Figure 2. Elizabeth I to the Venetian doge Niccolò da Ponte, Westminster,
April 20, 1584 (Archivio di stato di Venezia).

reign was a result of her gender or rather—alluding to Rome's pressures—
of the fact that Venice was "not able to obtain the permission of certain
princes" (*non ha potuto haver licentia da certi Principi*).[51]

As this chapter has suggested, the diplomatic crisis that interrupted the exchange of resident ambassadors between Venice and England for the entire
reign of Elizabeth I was caused by the confessionalization of European politics. The Venetian government hesitated to reopen formal ties with
England because it feared the political and social consequences of the Reformation, considering heresy as a risk for both the civil and the religious order. In the eyes of the Venetian ambassadors the many reforms imposed by
the Tudors had thrown England into a state of disorder, confirming that religious change inevitably affected the social hierarchy. At the same time, the
study of the diplomatic crisis between Venice and England demonstrates the
growing influence of the Roman Inquisition over papal diplomacy as well as
over the Italian states.[52] In the second half of the sixteenth century the election of several popes from the ranks of the Inquisition, such as Paul IV and

Pius V, brought into international affairs values and practices that derived from the mendicant orders' fight against heresy, also undermining the Anglo-Venetian attempts to negotiate across confessional lines.

And yet, despite England's isolation after the break with Rome, it is important to remember that "no island is an island."[53] Indeed, the diplomatic crisis led England to seek alternative channels of communication. Recruiting the Italian Protestant refugees into "patronage networks," English sovereigns, ministers, and powerful courtiers formed interstitial and parallel structures, supplementing formal diplomacy when the latter was uncertain or too weak.[54] As the following chapters demonstrate, starting in the 1540s England's relationship with the Italian refugees grew stronger, as it was grounded simultaneously in the Tudors' ideological commitment to defending the Protestant cause on the continent, and in the pragmatic need to keep communications open with Counter-Reformation Italy in the absence of formal diplomatic channels.

Chapter 2

TUDOR DIPLOMACY AND
ITALIAN HETERODOXY

As a gift for the New Year of 1548 the young princess Elizabeth Tudor
presented her brother Edward VI with a Latin translation of *Che cosa è
Christo* (What Is Christ), a sermon by the Italian reformer Bernardino Ochino,
the former general of the Capuchin order and one of the most famous preach-
ers in sixteenth-century Italy. Introducing the author of the sermon, Elizabeth reminded Edward VI of the fame that surrounded Ochino, a religious
refugee whose Protestant sympathies had brought him to England: "If nothing else commended the work, the reputation of the writer would adorn it
enough: who, expelled from his homeland on account of religion and Christ,
is driven to lead his life in foreign places and among unknown men."[1] Ochino
had arrived in England on December 20, 1547, taking advantage of the in-
vitation the Archbishop of Canterbury Thomas Cranmer had extended to
several continental reformers in an effort to organize a Protestant council in
opposition to Trent.[2] The English court gave Ochino a warm welcome. He
was granted both a royal pension and a nonresidentiary prebend at Canterbury, while his writings were published in English translations. Ochino's

relationship with Elizabeth continued even after he moved back to the continent following Mary Tudor's Catholic restoration. Indeed, in 1561, having found refuge in Switzerland, Ochino dedicated his *Laberinti del libero arbitrio* to Elizabeth, recalling the discussions they had had in England on predestination and free will.[3]

The encounter between Elizabeth and Ochino is only one example of the interest that early modern England had in the Italian reformers. Whereas in Italy the Counter-Reformation and the strengthening of the Roman Inquisition progressively suppressed the spread of Protestantism, the Italian Reformation was given new life—and a physical home—in Tudor England. In 1550, the creation of an Italian Protestant church in London at Austin Friars gave the Italian Protestant refugees a place to congregate and worship, and officially recognized them alongside the other stranger churches hosted in the city.[4] However, as this chapter shows, the first encounter between Tudor diplomacy and Italian philo-Protestants occurred much earlier—and not in London, but in Venice, at the English embassy.[5] Henry VIII's clash with the papacy prompted English ambassadors to enlist Italian Protestants as diplomatic agents in order to defend English interests on the peninsula and to ensure that the flow of information between Italy and England was not interrupted. To reconstruct the first encounter between the Tudors and the Italian reformers, this chapter concentrates on the English ambassador Edmund Harvel and his secretary Baldassare Altieri, the spokesman of the Protestant community in the Veneto. The following pages demonstrate how during the 1540s the English embassy in Venice became a center of Protestant propaganda that spread heretical texts across different social groups with the intention of creating a clandestine Evangelical church in the Veneto. While working toward this goal, Altieri also corresponded with Martin Luther and with the League of Schmalkalden, transforming the English embassy into a "contact zone" between Italy and Protestant Europe.

Becoming an Ambassador

On January 21, 1539, as part of an effort to bring England out of the diplomatic isolation that had resulted from both Henry VIII's break with Rome and the temporary reconciliation between Francis I and Charles V with the treaty of Aigues Mortes (1538), the secretary of state Thomas Cromwell sent instructions to his agent in Venice, Edmund Harvel, ordering him to gather information on the Italian princes in Urbino, Ferrara, and Mantua, and to further verify "the inclinacion of the Venecians towardes the Bishop of Rome."[6] Cromwell directed his agent to use "all wayes and meanes to hym possible" in order to "diligently enserche, investigate, and inquire" not only "the Bishop of Romes behaviour, practises, or any entreprises agenst the Kinges Majesty" but especially to determine the tenor of the pope's dealings with Cardinal Reginald Pole, cousin of Henry VIII, who by the late 1530s had become the most authoritative voice in the opposition against the English king.[7] In addition, Cromwell told Harvel to create support in Italy for Henry VIII, specifically by spreading antipapal sentiments and looking for sympathizers of the Reformation:[8]

> that in all places where the said shall perceive any notable and honest persons, apte to here and to lerne the truthe, and that be like to have a sincere zeale to the truthe, or beire some hatred to the Bishop of Rome, [*he then*] shall soberly, and with no rayling wordes, endevour hym self circumspectely to fele thair veray myndes and disposicion, and so employe his witt, to powre in some smak of the pure lernyng of Cristes doctrine amonges them, and to open them the sight to perceyve the abuses of pardons, reliques, and other supersticions of the Bishop of Romes See, contrary to the Gospell, not forgetting to declare his usurped power upon his neiburs and Princes, to the detriment of thair supremacye graunted to them by the Holy Scripture.

Cromwell's instructions to Harvel reshaped Henry VIII's foreign policy in the difficult years that followed the break with Rome, and laid the foundation for an alliance between English diplomacy and Italian philo-Protestants that continued well into the seventeenth century. The crisis triggered by Henry VIII's divorce and the isolation into which England fell as a result have led scholars to forget the tenacity with which the Tudors defended their interests in Italy after the rupture of relations with the papacy. And it was by recruiting the Italian reformers as diplomatic intermediaries that Cromwell ensured that the information flow continued and England was not cut off from Italian affairs. Through their agents in Venice, one of the most important centers for news in sixteenth-century Europe, the Tudors were able to stay up-to-date on international politics even after they had called back their diplomatic representatives from Rome.[9]

In his instructions, Cromwell told Harvel to use absolute discretion on his mission and to keep "this commission secrete from al men," adding that "for his costes and expences his Lordship sendeth unto hym at this tyme the somme of 200 merkes, to be received by exchaunge ther, shal under the colour of his feate and trade of merchandise."[10] Edmund Harvel, the recipient of Cromwell's instructions, was an English merchant who entered the service of Tudor diplomacy in the spring of 1535 and led the English embassy in Venice until his death in 1550.[11] Despite Harvel's close ties with Cromwell and Henry VIII and the influential role that he played in Tudor diplomacy in the mid-sixteenth century, his career has largely escaped scholarly attention.[12] One reason for this neglect is the fact that Harvel's diplomatic status remained ambiguous in Venice, where his role oscillated between merchant, intelligencer, envoy, and ambassador. While in 1537 he was simply referred to as a "mercadante," in 1540 the republic recognized him as "minister of the Most Serene King of England" (*ministro del Serenissimo Re d'Inghilterra*), and granted his four servants permission to carry arms.[13] Only in 1545, however, did the senate exempt him from taxes, finally recognizing that "the magnificent Lord Edmund Harvel, orator of the Most Serene King of England, has been in the city for a long time, partly conducting business as a private man, and then being appointed to a public office" and therefore "as long as he continues to occupy that office, he shall not be obliged to pay any tax and shall be absolved of any debt."[14] At his death in 1550, the republic paid only partially for the funeral, considering Harvel more of an "envoy" than a full ambassador.[15]

Harvel had been in Venice long before becoming Cromwell's agent. The first evidence of his presence in the Veneto dates back to August 1524, when he corresponded with the Venetian scholar Niccolò Leonico Tomeo, a prominent humanist at the forefront of the Hellenic Renaissance in Padua, who had many English visitors among his students.[16] Within the English community in the Veneto Harvel not only pursued the study of ancient learning but also followed attentively the political turmoil caused by Henry VIII's divorce controversy. In 1530 he provided financial assistance to the English scholar Richard Croke, who had been sent to Padua to solicit a favorable pronouncement from the university on the annulment of Henry's marriage.[17] Through Leonico Harvel also established a close connection with Henry's cousin Reginald Pole, the future cardinal, who was at that time in Italy to complete his humanist education.[18] During the 1530s Harvel became a prominent member of Pole's circle, accompanying him on his travels while also acting as his courier. In the summer and fall of 1535 he traveled between Venice and Palermo to handle the correspondence between Pole and Charles V.[19] Harvel's initiation into European diplomacy can thus be traced to this period, when the future English cardinal was on the verge of ending his relationship with Henry VIII.

In November 1534 Henry VIII's Act of Supremacy split the English community in the Veneto, with serious consequences for Harvel's connection to Pole. Harvel was still aligned with his patron between 1535 and 1536, while Pole was writing the *De unitate*, the text that condemned England's separation from the church of Rome and urged Charles V to repel the Anglican schism, asking him to divert his attention from the Turks to focus on the heretics within Christianity.[20] Despite his familiarity with Pole, Harvel did not anticipate his definitive estrangement from Henry VIII, and in January 1536 Harvel still believed that Pole's work would be well-received by the English court.[21] After the *De unitate* reached England, Harvel's relationship with Pole deteriorated and their paths took opposite directions. While Pole dedicated his efforts to bringing England back to Catholicism, from 1535 on, Harvel entered the service of Henry VIII, defending the Tudors' interests in Italy and later turning his embassy into a center of Protestant propaganda.

And yet, despite the fact that they ultimately found themselves on opposing sides, while his relationship with Pole was still intact, Harvel had witnessed not only Henry VIII's clash with Rome but also the religious crisis of sixteenth-century Italy. Venice was in this respect a privileged observatory. As scholars have pointed out, the city was the "gateway" of the Reformation on the peninsula.[22] In the fluid religious situation preceding the Council of Trent, when no clear barriers existed between confessions, it was still possible to agree with some Protestant doctrines while remaining obedient to the Catholic Church. These circles of reformers, who found their leader in Pole, became known as the spirituali, because of their insistence on individual faith as opposed to the institutional church and its dogmatic apparatus.[23] Frequenting Pole's circle during the 1530s, Harvel entered into contact with several of them, including Alvise Priuli, Donato Rullo, and Bernardino Sandro.[24]

After abandoning Pole, Harvel began serving Henry VIII from Venice as an intelligencer and later as ambassador. Harvel's first goal was to facilitate the contact between the republic and England that had been troubled by Henry VIII's rupture with Rome. After the Act of Supremacy, relations between the two states continued, but Venice called its patrician ambassadors back and replaced them with secretaries selected from among the *cittadini originari* who occupied the high ranks of Venetian bureaucracy. In the following years exchanges proceeded smoothly, a few incidents notwithstanding. In April 1544 Harvel was ordered by London to complain to the Venetian government about the behavior of the secretary Gerolamo Zuccato, who, having fallen out of grace with Henry VIII, was forced to move back to Venice.[25] Having insisted repeatedly before the Venetian government that they send a new patrician ambassador to England, in December 1546 Harvel seemed close to solving the diplomatic crisis, as the senate appointed Bernardo Navagero to the role.[26] In the end, however, Navagero's appointment was never enacted because of Henry VIII's death on January 28, 1547. Only in March of that year, after Harvel presented his new credential from Edward VI to the Venetian government, did Venice reopen the exchange of resident ambassadors, sending first an extraordinary envoy to offer its condolences on the death of Henry VIII and one year later the humanist Daniele Barbaro as its representative to England.[27]

Until the end of his life in 1550 Harvel was the "eyes and ears" of the Tudors in Italy, providing the English court with fresh information on Italian and continental affairs. Harvel's letters show the breadth of information that he was able to gather in the lagoon. In the mid-sixteenth century, Harvel kept his patrons up-to-date on the conflicts between Charles V and Francis I as well as on the changing attitudes of the Italian states toward foreign powers. Venice was in this respect a case in point. While in the summer of 1537 the incursions of the Ottoman fleet had pushed the republic to enter into an alliance with the empire, the strength of Charles V had then raised fears among the Venetian patricians, leading them to negotiate secretly with France and the Ottomans.[28] As Harvel wrote to Cromwell on November 25, 1537, Venice and the other Italian states intended to preserve the balance of power on the peninsula and for this reason they secretly favored France, even if they did not openly admit it.[29] According to Harvel, Venice's distrust of the emperor and its negotiations with Constantinople were a sign that the Italian wars were not over and that Italy was about to experience a new phase of political instability.[30]

In addition to forwarding his intelligence on the Italian wars, Harvel also informed the English court on the Italian religious crisis and on the papacy's reactions to the Protestant Reformation. On December 28, 1535, Harvel informed Thomas Starkey that the papal nunzio Pier Paolo Vergerio had been sent to the emperor and to the German princes to discuss a future general council with them.[31] In his letters Harvel also warned Henry VIII of the possible repercussions of the Council of Trent on European politics. Forced by the spread of heresy in Italy to open the council against his will, Paul III risked uniting France and the empire against England.[32] While following the preparations for the Council of Trent, Harvel carefully tracked his former patron Pole, now cardinal and papal legate to the Tridentine assembly.[33] On March 1, 1545, Harvel informed Henry VIII that Pole, fearing an English plot against him, refused to go to Trent.[34] In fact, Henry VIII had long been trying to infiltrate Pole's households. In 1542 Harvel had already helped English agents who attempted to get close to Pole in Viterbo.[35]

The dispatches that Harvel sent to the English court during the 1530s and 1540s illustrate well the increasing amount of political information that the ambassador was required to handle in the age of resident embassies. As a number of scholars have pointed out, Renaissance diplomacy contributed no less than the "printing revolution" to a shift in the ways in which political information was collected and transmitted, leading to a transition from a system in which intelligence gathering was relatively rare, and above all unsystematic and discontinuous, to a new one in which it became bloated and almost a daily business.[36] At the same time, Harvel's dispatches also show how crucial intelligence gathering had become to the careers of Renaissance ambassadors. It was by serving Cromwell as informant that Harvel was able to break away from his mercantile past and to enter the ranks of Tudor diplomacy, becoming Henry VIII's only resident ambassador in Italy.[37] By the early sixteenth century, the idea that the ambassador needed to be above all else a skillful intelligencer was already a commonplace. As Niccolò Machiavelli famously observed, the ability to ensure a regular flow of information between the embassy abroad and the government at home was crucial not only for preserving the prince's power but also for advancing the ambassador's career.[38]

The Ambassador and the Poligrafi

After the break with Rome the English embassy in Venice became Henry VIII's outpost in Italy, serving as a center of information on Italian and continental affairs. Having been educated in the circles of Leonico and Pole, Harvel was not only a talented intelligencer but also possessed a very keen understanding of the role that scholarship could play in international affairs. During a time in which foreign ambassadors in Venice counted among their ranks sophisticated humanists and bibliophiles such as Diego Hurtado de Mendoza and Giovanni della Casa, Harvel also turned his embassy into a cultural hub, hosting distinguished English visitors during their grand tour of Italy. Among them was Thomas Hoby, the future translator of Baldesar Castiglione's *Cortegiano*, who visited Venice in 1548.[39] Harvel also prudently maintained his contacts with Venetian literary circles and fashioned himself as a patron of letters. During the late 1530s and the 1540s Harvel's embassy opened its doors to many *poligrafi*, who had moved to Venice to take advantage of the new career opportunities created by the printing industry and by the growing market for vernacular literature. Through them Harvel was able not only to enhance his reputation in the lagoon but also to establish close contact with the Italian philo-Protestants.

Harvel's contact with the restless world of the poligrafi dates back to his exchange with Antonio Brucioli, a Florentine philo-Protestant who had moved to Venice in 1522 because of his anti-Medicean convictions and had gained visibility in the lagoon after publishing a new vernacular translation of the Bible in 1532.[40] The translation was republished in August 1539, just before Harvel approached Brucioli in the effort to recruit him as an intelligencer.[41] In the following years several other poligrafi benefited from the patronage of the English ambassador. In 1545 Harvel figured in *I segni de la natura ne l'huomo* by Antonio Pellegrini, already known as the translator of Erasmus's *Encomium moriae*.[42] Pellegrini's work consisted of a dialogue set "in the church of the Baptist in Murano" (*ne la chiesa del Battista a Murano*) and included among its interlocutors also "Messer Gismondo Harrvel, an Englishman, who is now commissioner and his King's ambassador to this Republic" (*Messer Gismondo Harrvel Inglese, che hora è Commissario e Ambasciadore del suo Re presso a questa Repubblica*).[43] From the beginning of the work, Pellegrini does not hesitate to engage with contemporary religious conflicts, and in the first pages, having introduced Harvel and the other characters, he contrasts the greatness of ancient Rome with the corruption of the papal court.[44] The antipapal polemic facilitated exchanges between the English ambassador and the Venetian poligrafi, who did not simply rebel against humanist literary conventions, but in their criticism of Italian society also embraced ideas of religious reform.[45] Indeed, in their works they often emphasized the centrality of the Scripture, contrasting contemporary ecclesiastical corruption with the purity of the primitive Church.

In 1548, Harvel's patronage was celebrated again by the humanist Ortensio Lando, who in the same years was completing his Italian translation of Thomas More's *Utopia*.[46] Lando dedicated to Harvel the *Lettere di molte valorose donne, nelle quali chiaramente appare non essere né di eloquentia né di dottrina alli huomini inferiori* (Letters of Many Talented Women, in which they appear clearly to not be inferior to men either in eloquence or in learning), the first book of women's letters and the only anthology of the period consisting entirely of letters exchanged by women.[47] In the dedication, Lando praised Harvel as the ideal recipient of his volume, declaring that "he did not currently know whom better to turn to than you, who, because of your courtesy and loyalty can compete with the most honored knight that the sun sees, or that walks upon earth."[48] Lando also included in his collection letters by Harvel's German wife Apollonia Huttinger.[49] Situating himself under the protection of the English ambassador, Lando entered the contemporary debate on the literary merits of women, and he moreover examined the current religious controversies, praising the German faith and its holy simplicity, attacking the chastity imposed on nuns, justifying the use of simulation, and also dealing with the relationship between Christianity and Judaism.[50]

Without doubt, the most important relationship Harvel developed with Venetian *poligrafi* was the one he secured with Pietro Aretino, "the scourge of princes," the scandalous writer who became the icon of Renaissance erotic literature. Aretino was well-known to Tudor diplomacy for having taken Henry VIII's side against Rome, labeling Clement VII as a "second Lucifer."[51] After being financially rewarded by Cromwell in 1534, Aretino carefully cultivated his English contacts. In June 1538 he wrote to Harvel in an effort to become his client, and in the following years he repeatedly tried to obtain a stipend, offering his pen to defend the reputation of Henry VIII in Italy.[52] Having lost a generous patron after Cromwell's execution, Aretino decided to address Henry VIII directly, dedicating the second book of the *Lettere* to him in 1542. The English king was praised for having defeated the tyranny of the popes, thus establishing his sovereignty in spiritual as well as civil affairs: "Just as he [King Arthur] freed the bodies of the English nations from the tyranny of the Romans, so you have freed their souls from the tyranny of the pontiffs. Wherefore you reign within the heart of the consciences of your peoples, with absolute preeminence."[53] Aretino's capacity to navigate Renaissance politics and to cultivate his relations with ambassadors and princes was certainly exceptional, but it also illustrates a more general phenomenon regarding the growing influence of Italian Renaissance culture on Tudor diplomacy.[54] This was especially true for a court as profoundly shaped by Italian humanism as that of Henry VIII, which had welcomed such distinguished visitors as Baldassarre Castiglione and Polydore Vergil.[55]

Harvel clearly understood that, because of his exceptional rhetorical skills, Aretino was a formidable ally for English diplomacy in Italy. For this reason, in September 1542 Harvel sent the second volume of Aretino's *Lettere* to Henry VIII, inviting him to reward the author and to consider how far the "powar of his penne can extend, in angar and spite of the Romayn prelates," "whose detestable vices he hath not only scorgid, with his vehement and sharpe stile, most bitterly, but also drawen them in note of perpetual infamye."[56] To be sure, their relationship was not always peaceful, and in 1548 became tense due to a payment that Aretino never received from Harvel for the second book of the *Lettere*.[57] And yet, through Aretino, Harvel was able to further expand his web of contacts in Venice and to establish close relationships with the Italian philo-Protestants. Indeed, in March 1542, Harvel hired as his secretary Aretino's protégé Baldassarre Altieri, a humanist scholar with strong Protestant sympathies who in the late 1530s had already served the count of Modena Claudio Rangoni in the same capacity.[58] In August of that year, Aretino congratulated Altieri for his new appointment and invited him not to forget his humanist "studies" (*studi*) while taking care of Harvel's "important business" (*alti negozii*):[59]

> And behold God, after all your wanderings, placed you where your virtues and customs are honored and praised. Seeing you stationed in the service of Sir Edmund Harvel, dignified and wise ambassador of the merciful and solemn King of England, most assuredly keeps my entire soul at peace.... Be attentive thus in writing the secrets of his important business, taking care to interpret his mind with the care of your usual prudence. In the meantime do not forget to use part of the hours that remain to devote yourself to those studies through which you earned your reputation.

As the following pages demonstrate, the appointment of Altieri as secretary of the English embassy had significant consequences, turning Harvel's household into a center of Protestant propaganda, in touch not only with the Tudor court but also with German and Swiss Protestantism. Most important, it marked the spring of 1542 as the moment when the alliance between Tudor diplomacy and Italian philo-Protestants envisioned by Cromwell three years earlier was officially established.

The Embassy, the Secretary, and the Clandestine Book Trade

During the Renaissance the intensification of diplomatic exchanges required that the ambassador be assisted by many helpers, such as servants, agents, and above all secretaries, to aid him in the performance of his many tasks. Secretarial support was crucial for dealing with the growing amount of correspondence that the ambassador dealt with on a daily basis. Letters needed to be written, transmitted, recorded, copied, and of course ciphered when they contained classified information. Renaissance treatises agreed, portraying the perfect secretary as a simple servant of his master, an executor of the will of his employer, who "disappeared in the message that he transmitted in a letter: it was not his I that spoke in the correspondence but the person of his patron."[60] Renaissance portraits often mirrored this commonplace, as is clear in Sebastiano del Piombo's portrait of Ferry Carondelet, Margaret of Austria's envoy to Rome (1511–12). The secretary's cramped position in the right corner of the canvas underlines his marginality with regard to the ambassador. Pen poised over his paper and eyes on his patron's mouth, his role is to be an instrument of his patron's will, to record rather than to counsel.[61] And yet, despite the marginal role to which contemporary treatises and portraits relegated them, in the age of permanent embassies secretaries occupied an important position and often enjoyed a high degree of autonomy from the resident ambassador. This is evident in the relationship between Edmund Harvel and his secretary Baldassarre Altieri. During the 1540s Altieri took advantage of his position at the English embassy in Venice to advance his own personal goals and to situate himself at the head of the Italian Protestant movement. While in 1545 Harvel lost the trust of Henry VIII and was suspected of being too close to Charles V, Altieri and his associates became more and more influential, acting as intermediaries between Venice, England, and Protestant Europe.[62]

In 1542, precisely when the flight of Bernardino Ochino and the death of Gasparo Contarini deprived the Italian reformers of their leaders, the appointment of Altieri as the secretary of the English embassy provided the philo-Protestant movement with a new spokesman. Taking advantage of the protection that he enjoyed at the English embassy, Altieri played an essential role in the history of the Italian Reformation. During the 1540s he brought religious dissent out of the closed circles of the spirituali and adopted a more decidedly Protestant stance able to reach a wider section of the population, from artisans to professionals and merchants. The medium of communication that enabled Altieri to expand the philo-Protestant movement in Italy was the printed book, which reached a large group of readers because of the loose censorship system that existed in Venice in the 1540s. Despite the fact that in 1527 the heads of the Council of Ten introduced restrictions for all books published in the lagoon as well as for those imported from abroad, censorship was only lightly enforced and Protestant books continued to circulate freely. It was only in the spring of 1547, with the arrival of the Inquisition and the creation of the Savi all'eresia, the lay magistracy that assisted the ecclesiastical body in the repression of heresy, that the procedure for issuing licenses was made official and heretical texts began to be confiscated and burned.[63] Until that time, as inquisitorial records suggest, "everyone felt free to read every book" (*ogni uno si faceva licito il legger ogni libro*) and at times texts identifying the papacy with the Antichrist were read "publicly" in the city.[64]

To be sure, what was new and innovative in Altieri's strategy was not simply the use of print to spread religious dissent but rather the awareness that books could be formidable tools for shaping a collective identity, and the intuition that a print community could constitute the initial stage of a clandestine evangelical church. In sixteenth-century Italy it was precisely the practice of gathering around the same books and reading them aloud that permitted scattered communities of religious dissidents to bond and to regard themselves as members of the same ecclesiastical organization.[65] In other words, Altieri knew well that "reading can itself create a social bond" and "foster convivial social relations."[66] Borrowing the category of the "mystical reader" from Michel de Certeau and Roger Chartier, it might be argued that for Altieri too the book took "the place of the lacking or decadent institution," playing its role and becoming "itself the major institution."[67] Thus, in circulating prohibited books, Alteri intended not only to spread Protestant doctrines but also to unify different dissident communities, providing them with a common set of readings and beliefs. As the following pages explain, this attempt had to confront multiple opponents. If Altieri's direct target was the papacy and Catholic practices, in the same years he was also to face the challenge posed by the Radical Reformation and by the spread of Anabaptism in the Veneto, which undermined his effort to create a common front among the Italian philo-Protestant groups.

In order to obtain copies of Protestant texts, Altieri turned to the leaders of the Reformation. On November 26, 1542, Altieri wrote from the English embassy in Venice to Martin Luther in Wittenberg signing on behalf of "the brothers of the church of Venice, Vicenza and Treviso."[68] Having praised Luther as the one sent by God to fight the Antichrist and to reform Christianity, Altieri pointed out the difficulties that the Italian reformers faced in the Venetian Republic, where persecution forced many into exile or imprisonment.[69] Altieri also requested that Luther send to Italy his writings, which were not easily available in Venice, not only because of the obstacles created by Catholic censorship but also because of the avarice of the booksellers, who took advantage of the situation, selling Protestant books for high prices:[70]

> Remember us, most kind Luther, not so much in your ardent prayers to God, that we successfully get to know Him through the spirit of Christ, as by means of your numerous, yet learned, delightful, and virtuous writings and letters, so that those, whom you have created through the word of truth, are more quickly shaped and mature into the perfect men of the age of Christ. For here we suffer from hunger and dire need for the word of God, not so much due to the cruelty and rigor of the Antichristians, but rather because of the utmost wickedness and barely believable greed of the booksellers, who bring your writings here, and deceitfully hide them until they can sell them at a higher price, not without inflicting great damage to the whole Church.

A few months later, on August 30, 1543, Altieri wrote again to Luther confirming the receipt of his writings and thanking him for having liberated the Protestants in the Veneto from "that cruel avarice of the booksellers" (*dira illa librariorum avaritia*).[71] It is important to note that Luther was not the only reformer who provided the Venetian Protestant community with books. Altieri was also in touch with Martin Bucer in Strasbourg and, albeit less directly, with John Calvin in Geneva.[72] In the summer of 1549, having already written to the church of Geneva, Altieri used his contacts to ask Calvin for copies of many of his works, including his biblical commentaries and fifty copies of the *De vitandis superstitionibus*, which collected several writings against the Nicodemites, the crypto-Protestants who compromised with Catholic orthodoxy and practiced simulation to hide their religious beliefs.[73]

Taking advantage of his role at the English embassy, Altieri imported a large number of Protestant books into Venice in order to spread religious dissent and to give to the different Protestant communities of the Veneto a shared set of beliefs. Inquisitorial records contain significant evidence of the central role that Altieri occupied in the clandestine book trade during the 1540s. During his trial the apostolic protonotary Pietro Carnesecchi admitted to having met in Venice "an ambassador from England called Edmund Harvel, held to be not simply suspicious but a rotten heretic" (*un ambasciatore d'Inghilterra chiamato Sigismundo Aroel, il quale era tenuto non solo sospetto ma heretico marcio*) and to have received prohibited books from his secretary Baldassarre Altieri, who "was not only suspicious but almost indeed a declared Lutheran, because he kept up an exchange of letters with many princes and theologians from Germany and nearly held a monopoly over heretical books" (*era non solamente sospetto, ma quasi anchora dechiarato lutherano, perché teneva commercio di lettere con molti principi et theologi d'Allemagna et faceva quasi monopolio de libri heretici*).[74] The deep roots of Altieri's clandestine network in the Veneto can be further measured by the depositions of the bishop of Bergamo Vittore Soranzo, who was brought to trial having attempted to reorganize his diocese in an Evangelical-Lutheran direction.[75] When asked by the inquisitors to explain the origins of the heretical books found in his possession, Soranzo revealed that he had "received many, many of these prohibited books from Venice through Messer Baldassare Altieri" (*Da Venetia ho havuto molti et molti di questi libri proibiti per mezo de misser Baldassare Altieri*), explaining, "I kept his friendship secret because, as he was of such ill repute, I did not want him to bring dishonor to me too, and I was a friend of his only for the desire I had to obtain books, that he trafficked and sold at very high prices."[76] Through Altieri, Soranzo was able to form an impressive library of Protestant texts, which included works by Luther, Melanchton, Zwingli, Karlstadt, Oecolampadius, and Brenz, as well as the letters that the German reformers sent to the Protestant communities in the Veneto and Italy.[77]

One of the most remarkable pieces of information on the books circulating behind the walls of the English embassy is contained in the trial against Harvel's physician Girolamo Donzellini, who taught medicine at the University of Padua and had several clients among the Venetian patriciate.[78] On November 26, 1560, Donzellini declared to the inquisitors that soon after he arrived in Venice in 1546 he was introduced to Harvel and Altieri, who "not only read books prohibited by law but also made an effort to have others read them." Donzellini also declared that he had received a copy of Philip Melanchton's *Loci communes* from Altieri:[79]

Through friends I was introduced to the house of Sir Edmund Harvel, at the time here as ambassador for the English crown, and frequenting it I had the chance to talk to his secretary, who was called Baldassar Altieri: a man of letters, but once I knew him better, also very greedy and ambitious, and twisted in his new opinions about religion. He did not only read books prohibited by law but he also made an effort to have others read them. When he understood that I had read the logic and natural and moral philosophy of Melanchthon— whose books, being secular and not dealing with religious matters, were publicly sold throughout Italy and were read even by Catholics—he tried to convince me that I should read also books by the same author on the subject of religion, arguing that he [Melanchthon] was moderate in his doctrine and that he only disagreed with the Roman church on a few things. And he gave me a book entitled *Theological Commonplaces* composed by the same Melanchthon, which I read despite the fact that I found many things that did not align with my faith. Nonetheless his arguments did not have any effect on me and did not lead me to change my faith. I remained the same as I had been before reading that book. And this was the first temptation that was presented to me.

Thanks to a sophisticated communication strategy, Altieri set up an extensive clandestine network that circulated books beyond scholars and ecclesiastical ministers to a diverse audience, thus spreading religious dissent among different social classes. This is suggested, for example, by the inquisitorial trial against the goldsmith Bartolomeo Carpan, probably portrayed in Lorenzo Lotto's *Triple Portrait*.[80] When interrogated by the inquisitors for having shipped Protestant books from Venice to his colleagues in Messina, Carpan confessed that he had received them from Altieri, who assured him that they were "holy books" (*libri santi*).[81] Carpan also revealed that his shop in Ruga degli Orefici next to the Rialto Bridge was a meeting point for the sympathizers of the Reformation, admitting that he had been a friend of Altieri, "as are some others, who come and patronize my shop" (*come sono anche degli altri, che vengano a servirsi alla mia bottega*).[82] As the example of Carpan indicates, the clandestine network set up by Altieri extended both socially and geographically, even outside of Venice. Indeed, Altieri was able to use his contacts to reach other cities in the territories of the republic, from Treviso to Brescia to Bergamo.[83] Even in small villages such as Portobuffolè, near Treviso, Altieri's associates diffused criticism of Catholic practices among "poor farmers and illiterate people, to whom they preached and managed to persuade that the images of the saints are worthless things and that a dog is more deserving of being revered than an image of our Lady or of any saint."[84]

Altieri regarded books as powerful tools of identity formation, and their clandestine circulation was intended to go beyond spreading religious dissent in order to ultimately transform a community of readers into an ecclesiastical organization. With the goal of creating a Protestant church in Venice Altieri again asked for the help of the German reformers. In his letters he urged Luther to use his influence over the German Protestant princes to intercede with the Venetian senate on behalf of the Italian Protestants, asking the patricians to grant freedom to their cult.[85] The plan was not limited to the Veneto exclusively, but rather extended to other Italian Protestant communities outside the republic. The philo-Protestants in Bologna, for example, also received books from Altieri. On June 18, 1545, Altieri recommended to the "magnificent and most observant brothers" (*magnifici et osservantissimi fratelli*) in Bologna the bookseller Pietro Perna, who at the time worked as an agent for the famous Basel printer Johannes Oporinus, and in this capacity was able to import large quantities of books from Switzerland into Italy. Altieri presented Perna as "my brother," who "came here to see if by selling books he can earn his daily bread."[86] Moreover, Altieri advised the "brothers" in Bologna to be patient and to trust that they would soon be able to worship God publicly:[87]

> Be firm then and do not lose the hope that you placed in the holy gospel that was preached and brought to you. . . . If you have patience, I promise you that in a short while you will see your whole city become Christian. Do you truly believe that God spread his seed here without hope of harvesting its fruit when it is ready? I say that he wants to found a church so that one might pay him

due thanks, honor, and adoration, publicly and without obstacle, as is appropriate to him in the congregation of the elect, and he will surely do it.

Altieri's plan to create a Protestant community in Venice and in other Italian cities was intently monitored by the reformers across the Alps. On February 15, 1544, the German physician Matthias Guttich wrote to Melanchthon, praising "Baldassarre," who "in such a difficult moment when the church cannot gather anywhere because of the papal legate . . . brings together the poor and provides for them. In sum, whatever happens in this poor church happens through his great labor. He leads and all the others follow."[88] Guttich told Melanchthon that in Venice the Reformation had found many followers and that if only the princes would allow it, a Protestant church would spring up with no difficulty.[89]

According to Altieri, the creation of a Protestant church in Italy was also necessary in order to contain the divisions at the heart of the Reformation born from the dispute between Luther and Zwingli on the doctrine of the Eucharist. While Luther maintained Jesus's real presence in the bread and wine, for Zwingli these were only symbols of Christ's body and blood and thus their presence was purely spiritual. As Altieri explained to Luther, the dispute had had worrisome repercussions in Italy, giving strength to radical positions:

> If in Germany, where there are so many properly established churches, and so many most holy men, fervent in spirit and distinguished in all fields of learning, this poison grew so strong . . . , how much more has this plague spread among us, to the point that it grows unchecked with each day! Here we do not have public churches, but everyone is a church unto himself. . . . All prefer to be seen as pedagogues rather than disciples, although they are not learned enough; all prefer to be seen as prophets, although they are utterly ignorant and are not driven by the sprit of God.[90]

The dispute about the sacraments nourished the radical wings of the Reformation, for which Altieri had no sympathy. Aware of the deep roots that religious radicalism had in the Veneto, he circulated among his associates copies of Melanchthon's writings against the Anabaptists.[91] Thus, smuggling Protestant texts could challenge the Catholic church while also unifying, through a common language, the different dissident communities that existed in the territories of the republic, thereby simultaneously fighting Catholic orthodoxy and the Radical Reformation.

"Italy's Ancient Freedom"

Immediately after his appointment as secretary of the English embassy in Venice in 1542, Altieri established close contact with the leaders of the Reformation in Germany and Switzerland and began receiving books and advice in order to create a Protestant church in Venice. Toward the end of 1545 Altieri's plan became even more ambitious, moving, so to speak, from defense to offense. He did not limit himself to requesting tolerance for the Italian philo-Protestants but actively tried to influence Venetian and European politics. Altieri's goal was to create an alliance among Venice, England, and the German Protestant princes of the League of Schmalkalden, which had been formed in 1531 to protect Lutheranism in the Holy Roman Empire. Thus, Altieri and his associates acted as intermediaries both between Venice and England and among different Protestant states, smoothing the relationship between Henry VIII and the German Protestants, whose exchanges were troubled because of differing religious views.[92] In expanding their capacities, Altieri and his associates competed directly with Harvel, whose loyalty Henry VIII began to question, suspecting his close ties with imperial diplomacy.[93] Three letters shed light on Altieri's political maneuvers. The first letter addressed the new doge Francesco Donà in December 1545, while the other two were sent to the German Protestant princes Philip, Landgrave of Hesse, and John Frederick of Saxony in June 1546. These documents clarify how the fluid political situation of the mid-1540s, marked by Charles V's confrontations with the League of Schmalkalden, encouraged Altieri's hopes for a Protestant Venice.

In December 1545, an anonymous letter was composed to congratulate the new doge Francesco Donà. The author was the bishop of Capodistria Pier Paolo Vergerio who, under the influence of new Protestant ideas, was destined to flee Italy in 1549 and become one of the most skillful pamphleteers in the history of the Italian Reformation.[94] Printed in Florence in 1547, a single manuscript copy of the letter survives—in Altieri's hand.[95]

Originally composed by Vergerio, the text was then copied by Altieri, who presumably intended to circulate it among a select audience within the

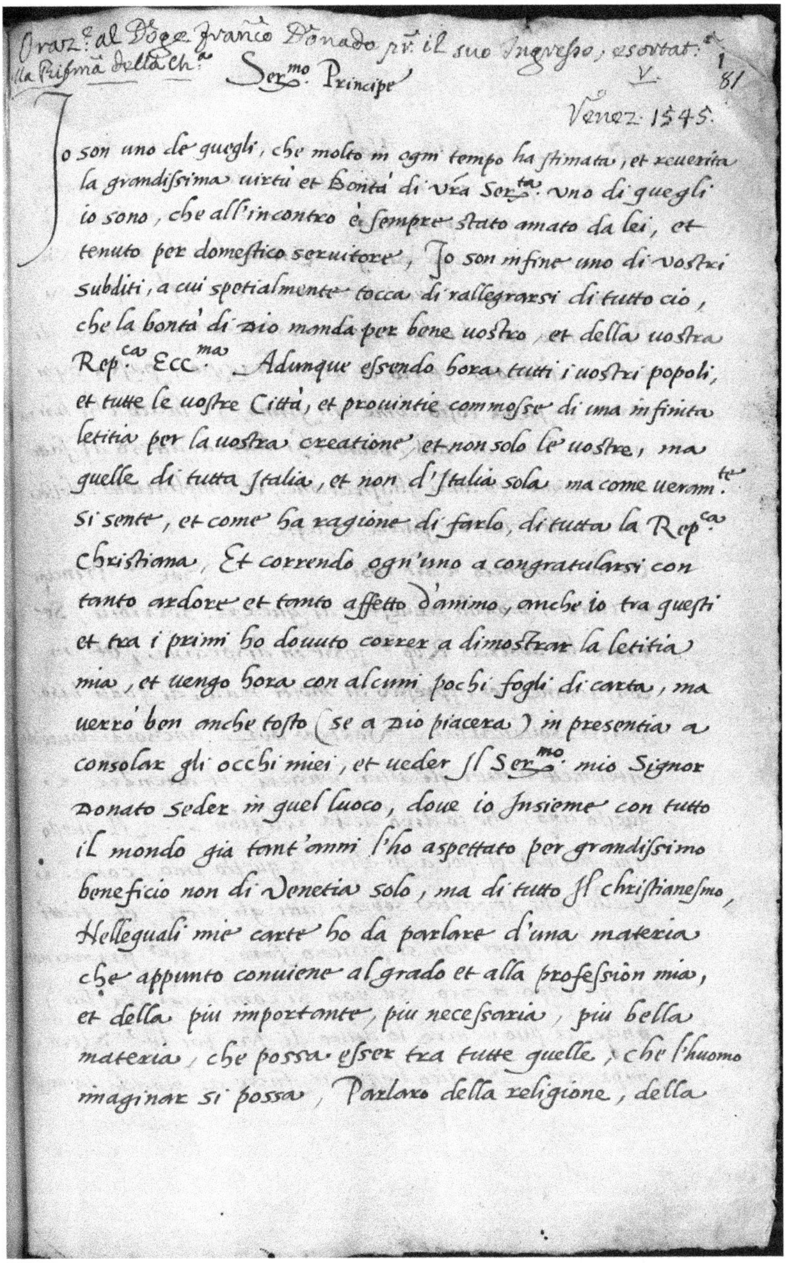

Orat.e al Doge Franco Donado p il suo Ingresso, esortat.e
lla Riforma della Ch.a   Ser.mo Principe   V.   1
                                    81

Venez. 1545.

Io son uno de quegli, che molto in ogni tempo ha stimata, et reveria
la grandissima virtù et bontà di vra Ser.tà, uno di quegli
io sono, che all'incontro è sempre stato amato da lei, et
tenuto per domestico servitore, Io son infine uno di vostri
subditi, a cui spetialmente tocca di rallegrarsi di tutto ciò,
che la bontà di Dio manda per bene uostro, et della uostra
Rep.ca Ecc.ma. Adunque essendo hora tutti i uostri popoli,
et tutte le uostre Città, et prouintie commosse di una infinita
letitia per la uostra creatione, et non solo le uostre, ma
quelle di tutta Italia, et non d'Italia sola, ma come ueram.te
si sente, et come ha ragione di farlo, di tutta la Rep.ca
christiana, Et correndo ogn'uno a congratularsi con
tanto ardore et tanto affetto d'animo, anche io tra questi
et tra i primi ho douuto correr a dimostrar la letitia
mia, et uengo hora con alcuni pochi fogli di carta, ma
uerrò ben anche tosto (se a Dio piacerà) in presentia a
consolar gli occhi miei, et ueder il Ser.mo mio Signor
Donato seder in quel luoco, doue io insieme con tutto
il mondo gia tant'anni l'ho aspettato per grandissimo
beneficio non di Venetia solo, ma di tutto il christianesimo,
Nelle quali mie carte ho da parlare d'una materia
che appunto conuiene al grado et alla professiòn mia,
et della piu importante, piu necessaria, piu bella
materia, che possa esser tra tutte quelle, che l'huomo
imaginar si possa, Parlaro della religione, della

Figure 3. Baldassarre Altieri's copy of Pier Paolo Vergerio's *Oratione al doge Francesco Donà per il suo ingresso, esortatione alla riforma della Chiesa*, Venice, 1545 (Biblioteca Universitaria, Padova: MS 1656, c. 81r).

Venetian elite. To persuade Donà and the patricians to grant tolerance to the Italian philo-Protestants and to advance the cause of religious reform, the letter used a skillful rhetorical strategy, one that praised the Venetian ruling class but also exploited its fears. On the one hand, having presented the Reformation as the last step of the Renaissance revival of antiquity, Vergerio praised the freedom that the book trade enjoyed in Venice, where "there are books printed regarding religious matters that are sold in public, and good people buy and read them."[96] Against the inquisitors' attempt to limit the circulation of books, Vergerio suggested showing "these books to trustworthy and loyal people, who are impartial, and if the books are good in every part, they should be allowed to circulate freely, and severe punishment should be used to prohibit anyone from writing against them," as had recently happened after the publication of the *Beneficio di Cristo*, published in 1543 and rebutted the following year by the Dominican Ambrogio Catarino Politi.[97]

On the other hand, the letter encouraged the Venetian doge to use his authority to pressure the papacy and to make sure that the Council of Trent—that had just begun in the very weeks the letter was drafted—would reform Christianity.[98] Taking advantage of the fears of the Venetian patricians, it suggested that if Donà did not intervene in the council and use his power to reform religion the people might act in his place, with the risk of producing social unrest. As Vergerio and Altieri knew well, the memory of the Peasants' War (1524–25) was still vivid in the imagination of the Venetian government, which remained extremely concerned by the possibility that German events might inspire analogous rebellions in the republic:[99]

> The people see that in this Church there are things that need to be fully reformed. They expected and still expect that a legitimate council will have this effect. After they have waited and waited, and see that nothing happens as a result of the council, they will want to take matters into their own hands, and this will lead to no good. What will the people, the multitude do? They could do things that will bring disgrace to God and great disturbance to public affairs. There is still time to consider and remedy this. As such, there is no time to sleep, most holy Prince; this is a matter for which your Most Serene self must go in person, not only through your orators, to the pontiffs, the emperors, the kings and to the Council itself, and there exhort, beg, supplicate everyone, that for the love of God they will leave behind every passion and interest and see to the reform and establishment of the Church, to the health and safety of the people, to the glory of God.

By reminding Donà that the prince's duty was to reform the Church, Vergerio and Altieri intended to draw a sharp distinction between the radicalism experienced in Germany through the Peasants' War and the moderate line of the Italian Protestant movement. As previously noted, Altieri felt no compassion for the Radical Reformation, considering it an enemy no less dangerous than the Roman Antichrist. According to the letter, while north of the Alps religious change led to social unrest, in Venice the reformers were loyal servants of the state. Thus, the religious reform would not have challenged but instead reinforced the government of the *Serenissima*, by giving the doge jurisdiction over spiritual as well as civil affairs. The Reformation was presented not as a dangerous innovation but rather as a harmonic development with the Venetian tradition for which the doge was *princeps in republica* as well as *princeps in ecclesia*, the head of both the state and the church:[100]

> You are the father of so many great gentlemen, so many citizens, who are under your power; they are your sons, not just your subjects. This was the custom of your holy Republic. Now, if fathers must nourish their children, must clothe them and guard them from the dangers of life, must acquire necessities for them, should they not all the more take care of the most important part, which is the soul? Indeed, they must concern themselves even more greatly with this, and it would be an impious father, a cruel father who said to his son: look, son, I give you all that you need to eat and to dress, I protect your earthly life, but with regard to your soul I do not care, not at all.

Whether Donà received the letter and what his reaction was to the plan outlined by Vergerio and Altieri remain matters of speculation. What is certain is that the Venetian government never came to support the Reformation, and the hopes of the Italian philo-Protestants soon met with resounding disappointment. Venice was often at odds with Rome but this did not mean that it favored a reform of the Church following Protestant beliefs. The anticlericalism diffused among Venetian patricians should not be confused with philo-Protestantism. As scholars have observed, Italian anticlericalism did not express a real need for change but was in fact a "control mechanism" to the total osmosis between Church and civil society, or, in other words, "a healthy blowing off of steam that served to reinforce the system which it claimed to challenge."[101]

While studying the demise of the Italian philo-Protestants, historians have often regarded their hopes as utopian visions that arose within groups far from high politics.[102] And yet, the letter that Vergerio and Altieri intended to deliver to Francesco Donà should not be dismissed as something irrelevant for the history of sixteenth-century diplomacy. Traditionally, diplomatic historians have not shown much interest in hopes and dreams, and have focused instead on ambassadorial reports in order to reconstruct the past "as it really was." Nonetheless, in the effort to write a "new diplomatic history of early modern Europe," it is perhaps more useful to study the past not "as it really happened," but rather as "another present," with "its baggage of expectations and projections, erasing from our perspective the knowledge of what was to happen shortly thereafter."[103] Instead of projecting onto the past the knowledge of what would later happen, it is necessary to understand the expectations of the Italian reformers on their own terms, situating them in the restless atmosphere of the mid-1540s, when the uncertain political situation in Europe led them to believe in the possibility of introducing the Reformation into Venice.

During the spring of 1546 Altieri tried actively to establish an alliance between Venice, England, and the German Protestant princes of the League of Schmalkalden. To achieve this goal Altieri wrote to the Lutheran ruler Philip, Landgrave of Hesse, asking to be officially appointed as the agent in Italy of the League of Schmalkalden: "I would require solemn letters showing that the Protestant princes appoint me as their agent, as they say, not only in the republic of Venice, but throughout Italy, and presenting me to all princes, republics, cities, and dominions of Italy."[104] Between May and June Altieri had already asked the Venetian government to recognize his new diplomatic role. The affair had created embarrassment in Venice, especially after the news arrived to the ears of both the papal nunzio Giovanni Della Casa and the imperial ambassador Diego Hurtado de Mendoza, who protested violently before the Council of Ten.[105] Altieri's request divided the Venetian patriciate. On June 8, 1546, the senate was torn between those who feared that admitting a Lutheran agent into Venice would create dissensions in the city and those who responded that "it was not a question of faith but of government [and] that these Princes are great Lords, and they represent nearly all of Germany, and their goal is to oppose the power of the Emperor." This second group of patricians pointed out that the League of Schmalkalden had redesigned the balance of power in Europe, to the point that England and

France were close to entering into an alliance with the German princes, and Venice needed to be on good terms with them.[106] Moreover, responding to those in the senate who opposed the alliance on religious grounds, some patricians argued that they should not condemn the Protestants but consider instead the abuses of the Church: "If they respect religion, they should react differently, and they should not encourage those who commit simony, which is to say the priests."[107]

Though in the end the senate denied the recognition, the rumor that Altieri was negotiating in Venice on behalf of the League of Schmalkalden traveled quickly through European diplomatic circles. In June 1546 Cardinal Alessandro Farnese ordered the papal nunzio Della Casa to use all his influence to prevent any further contact between Altieri and the Venetian government, expressing his irritation at the fact that the republic had given an audience to the secretary of the English embassy, who "procured and begged through different means credential letters by Protestants, not so that he could negotiate with them, but only as a pretext so that he would be able to live freely and write as he pleased about the affairs of that and other states, and to become the head of that sect, circumspectly."[108] In January 1547, Cardinal Marcello Cervini, at the time papal legate to Trent and future pope Marcellus II, was informed that Altieri, an "agent of the Protestants" (*agente di Protestanti*), "brought many of those books by Luther against the Roman papacy founded by Satan together with that work by Butzer against the Council of Trent."[109] A few months later Cervini received a new letter from one of his agents expressing his displeasure at seeing "that evil Baldassare Altieri . . . in Venice" (*quel tristo di Baldissera Altieri . . . in Venetia*), without "any way of getting him out."[110] The news that through Altieri Venice was secretly negotiating with the Lutherans was also received with alarm at the imperial court, which was involved in military confrontations with the League of Schmalkalden. According to the report of the Venetian ambassador in Germany, when Charles V heard of it, he became furious and declared that he would have hanged Altieri were it not for the protection that he enjoyed from Henry VIII.[111]

What preoccupied papal and imperial diplomacy was that through his post at the English embassy Altieri was able to facilitate exchanges between Venice and Protestant Europe and in that way to reopen the battle over the control of the peninsula that marked the Italian wars. They were right to be concerned, as in fact in his exchanges with the League of Schmalkalden

Altieri considered the possibility of a military insurrection in the papal state, one intended to bring Italy back to its "ancient freedom" (*althergebrachte Freiheit*).[112] In June 1546 Altieri's associate Guido Giannetti, an Italian philo-Protestant who had long served Tudor diplomacy, delivered a letter to John Frederick of Saxony, outlining the plan to stir a rebellion in the papal state to prevent the creation of a Catholic league against the German Protestant princes: "In the case that the situation . . . evolves in such a way that with the help of some lords and princes it is decided by the Council of Trent to militarily attack the princes and states of the German nation with the intention of depriving them of the pure Gospel and of the true confession of the Word of God . . . in that case one could put into action a plan to assault in his own dominion the pope, who is the head of this Council."[113]

The letter specified that the purpose of the plan was not to cause social unrest but simply to reconquer "the Fatherland's ancient freedom" (*des Vaterslannds althergebrachter Freiheit*) and to ensure that "the Gospel would be preached freely and publicly" (*das Evangelium frey unnd offentlich gepredigt*).[114] While in October 1546 Altieri, albeit unsuccessfully, asked the Council of Ten to lend the League of Schmalkalden 100,000 ducats, Altieri's associate Ludovico Dall'Armi, an Italian condottiere, had for months been recruiting troops in Italy on behalf of Henry VIII.[115] In September 1545 Dall'Armi had also participated in the London negotiations to formalize England's alliance with the League of Schmalkalden.[116]

The Venetian government had followed Altieri's maneuvers attentively. Already in September 1545 the Venetian secretary in England Giacomo Zambon gave its government an account of the diplomatic activities of the Italian philo-Protestants and concluded that "these Lords [the English] are currently working to promote to Your Serenity certain parties or to form a secret league together or a similar thing."[117] The republic was also aware that the alliance between Henry VIII and the League of Schmalkalden was troubled by theological dissensions. The disagreement went back to 1521, when Henry VIII had written the *Assertio semptem sacramentorum* against Luther earning the title of "Defender of the Faith." According to Zambon, while Henry VIII sought a political alliance founded solely on common military goals, the League of Schmalkalden wanted the alliance to be grounded on common religious principles and asked that the English king "declare himself a Protestant like them."[118] On September 20, 1545, however, the Venetian secretary noted that the negotiations proceeded and that Henry VIII now intended to find a common religious ground with the German Protestant princes.[119] In October of the following year Zambon noted that the forthcoming war between the League of Schmalkalden and Charles V had convinced even the "most Christian king" Francis I to put aside his disagreements with Henry VIII and to consider entering the anti-imperial league.[120] Seen in this light and situated in the uncertain political situation of the mid-1540s, Altieri's hopes appear to be not utopian desires, but, to a certain degree, plausible aspirations grounded in the widespread belief that a league among England, the League of Schmalkalden, and possibly France could question Charles V's hegemony over the continent.

What happened in the following months is well-known. Even before the defeat of the League of Schmalkalden in the Battle of Mühlberg (April 24, 1547), the death of Henry VIII (January 28, 1547) put a brusque end to Altieri's plans. The passing of the English king and the outcome at Mühlberg had immediate repercussions on the status of the Italian philo-Protestants gathered around the English embassy in Venice.[121] On May 14, 1547, the execution of Ludovico Dall'Armi between the columns of justice in Piazza San Marco was a clear signal of the new political and religious climate.[122] Through the execution of Dall'Armi, Venice tried to hide its previous contacts with Protestant Europe and to show its loyalty to Charles V, whose victory at Mühlberg would soon be celebrated by Titian's famous equestrian portrait. The republic's relations with the Habsburgs, but also those with Rome, soon changed radically. In the same weeks, the creation of the Savi all'eresia inflicted a harsh blow to the myth of Venice as the Italian Geneva. Shortly thereafter the discovery of how diffused Anabaptism was in the republic convinced the Venetian patriciate that heresy endangered not only the ecclesiastical institutions but also the civil authorities.[123]

The Battle of Mühlberg also had significant consequences for the personnel of the English embassy in Venice. Despite the fact that for some time Altieri continued to correspond with northern reformers and kept smuggling Protestant books into Italy, the defeat of the League of Schmalkalden irremediably weakened his position and forced him to leave Venice and ultimately Italy.[124] His relationship with Harvel deteriorated and the support of his old patron Pietro Aretino was not adequate to reestablish his connections with the English embassy.[125] Having tried to win the favor of other Italian princes, from Cosimo de Medici to Renée de France, Altieri fled Venice in April 1549 in secret. Only his closest friends were informed.[126] The following

May, Altieri was already in Switzerland, where he witnessed again the dissensions within the Italian Protestant community of exiles, torn between the moderate and the radical wings.[127] He died shortly thereafter.[128]

Though Altieri was forced to leave Venice, Harvel remained in the city. On March 2, 1547, while telling the Venetian government the news of Henry VIII's death, he also presented his new credentials from Edward VI.[129] From this moment on, however, his contact with the English court was limited and his influence in Venice diminished, also as a consequence of Dall'Armi's execution and Altieri's flight.[130] Nonetheless, Harvel continued to guide the English embassy until his death in 1550. On January 7 of that year he was buried in the church of Santi Giovanni e Paolo.[131] In May 1550 the new English ambassador, Pietro Vanni, an Italian from Lucca who made his career as Henry VIII's Latin secretary, arrived in Venice and in the following August was received by the Venetian Collegio.[132] Like his predecessor, Vanni was also regarded with suspicion by the inquisitors for his Protestant sympathies.[133] In the following years he served as representative to the republic not only for England but also for his Italian hometown, Lucca.[134] His role in Venice was, however, weakened by the instability of English foreign policy in the mid-sixteenth century caused by the death of Edward VI and the subsequent Catholic restoration under Mary Tudor.[135] In December 1555 Vanni was called back to England.[136] As the Venetian ambassador Giovanni Michel explained to the senate, recalling Vanni was a consequence of Mary's marriage to Philip II, which had led Spain to absorb English diplomacy, leaving abroad only Spanish representatives for both the king and the queen.[137]

In January 1557 the English embassy in Venice closed.[138] It reopened only in October 1604, when James I's ambassador Henry Wotton, the friend of the prominent Venetian scholar Paolo Sarpi, arrived in the lagoon and reorganized English diplomacy in Italy. Still, during the second half of the sixteenth century, the contact between Venice and England continued, albeit unofficially, through the Italian refugees who acted as go-betweens and facilitated cross-confessional exchanges. Indeed, the alliance between Tudor diplomacy and Italian heterodoxy established in the 1540s was destined to survive the death of Henry VIII and to gain new life under the reign of Elizabeth I.

By focusing on the English embassy in Venice during the 1540s, this chapter has clarified when and how the encounter between Italian heterodoxy and

Tudor diplomacy took place. Indeed, the appointment of Baldassarre Altieri as secretary of the English ambassador Edmund Harvel in 1542 can be considered the beginning of an alliance between Italian heterodoxy and English diplomacy that would last until the early seventeenth century. Such an alliance was conceived by Thomas Cromwell in the late 1530s to respond to the diplomatic crisis triggered by Henry VIII's break with Rome. After severing ties with the papal court, English diplomacy in Italy went through a period of crisis, and in the absence of formal diplomatic channels England risked becoming isolated from European politics. For this reason, the Tudors recruited the Italian philo-Protestants as agents and informers to ensure that the information flow between Italy and England continued. From Venice, one of the most important centers of information during the early modern period, England was able to gather information not only on Italian but also on continental and Mediterranean affairs and to play an active role in Europe between France and Spain.

The case of Altieri also underlines the high degree of autonomy that the Italian philo-Protestants enjoyed as diplomatic agents. From the English embassy Altieri was able to build a wide international network corresponding with the leaders of the Reformation in Germany and Switzerland and circulating Protestant books throughout the Veneto. The goal was not only to create a Protestant church in Venice but, more important, to influence European politics in order to undermine Charles V's hegemony and to bring Italy back to its "ancient freedom." Though the Battle of Mühlberg put an end to Altieri's plan, the dream of Venice as the Italian Geneva was destined to survive well into the seventeenth century.

Chapter 3

Spying on the Council of Trent

After the Council of Trent concluded in December 1563, the Roman curia carefully gathered the acts drafted by the secretary of the council Angelo Massarelli, but also, later on, the papers of Cardinals Giovanni Morone and Carlo Borromeo, protagonists of the third phase of the assembly. It has been remarked that "the safekeeping of the documents in the Vatican secret archive established itself as a guarantee of the control over and handling of the information" on the council.[1] For centuries, access to the documents on Trent remained a rare privilege, nourishing confessional controversies more than historical work. It was only in 1901, twenty years after Pope Leo XIII opened the Vatican Archive, that the publication of the acts of the council began.

No one in the early modern period expressed the desire to bring to light the secret history of the council better than its first historian, the Venetian scholar Paolo Sarpi, who famously labeled Trent the "Iliade of our age." In the opening of his *Istoria del Concilio Tridentino*, published in London in 1619, Sarpi described the various sources that he was able to consult, from the pub-

lic documents available in print and in manuscript to the diaries and correspondence of the participants:[2]

> For my selfe, so soone as I had understanding of the affaires of the world, I
> became exceeding curious to know the whole proceedings therof: and after I
> had diligently read whatsoever I found written, and the publique instructions,
> whether printed or divulged by pen, I betooke my selfe, without sparing either
> paines or care, to search in the remainder of the writings of the Prelates, and
> others who were present in the Councel, the Records which they left behind
> them, and the Suffrages or opinions delivered in publique, preserved by the
> Authors themselves, or by others, and the letter of advise written from that
> Citie; whereby I have had the favour to see even a whole register of Notes and
> Letters of those persons, who had a great part in those negotiations.

Only the controversy that followed the publication of *Historia del concilio
tridentino,* and the necessity of rebutting Sarpi's accusation that Trent did not
reform Christianity but reinforced the power of the papacy over the Church,
finally forced Rome to make the sources available to the Jesuit historian Pietro Sforza Pallavicino. The rigid control Rome exercised over the history of
the council has led scholars to neglect the fact that, in the early modern period, information on Trent nevertheless spread across confessional borders.
According to Hubert Jedin, the author of the most comprehensive history of
the council, Protestant Europe had only a meager knowledge of what happened in Trent and the leaders of the Reformation were not interested in a
council that they considered neither free, nor Christian, nor ecumenical.[3]
This chapter reappraises this thesis by revealing how sixteenth-century Italian Protestant refugees leaked information on the council, making it available to Protestant Europe and the Elizabethan court.[4] While the Tudors opposed the council from its beginning and tried to sabotage it by exacerbating
the rivalry between the Valois and the Habsburgs, they were also very keen
to be informed on Trent. For this reason, the Tudors kept agents and informants in Italy and, through them, gathered information on the Tridentine
debates. Their interest in Trent stemmed from the fact that the council was
regarded not only as an assembly of prelates dealing with theological matters
but first and foremost as a "seismograph" of international politics, through
which it was possible to follow the changing relationship between the papacy
and the European states.[5]

The following pages concentrate on the Italian philo-Protestant Guido Gi-annetti, who joined Tudor diplomacy in the 1520s, and spent his entire life working as a diplomatic agent for the English court. Though after Henry VIII's break with Rome Giannetti fled to England, he then moved back to Italy and was employed as an intelligencer in Venice, where he established close ties with the English ambassador and his secretary, Baldassarre Altieri. Giannetti's career stems from the same context explored in the previous chapter and offers a new perspective on the initial encounter between Tudor diplomacy and the Italian philo-Protestants. Moreover, by discussing Giannetti's letters, which have never been transcribed or translated, this chapter reconstructs in detail what knowledge the Tudors had of the council and how they evaluated its consequences. Instead of simply repeating the traditional Protestant arguments against the council, Giannetti's letters focused attentively on the Tridentine debates, enabling the Elizabethan court to follow them from a distance. In this respect, the letters shed light on England's complex relationship with the plural and conflictual Catholicism of the early modern period, a subject that has recently been the focus of scholars pushing beyond the classic paradigm set by Jedin.[6]

An Italian Heretic in the Service of English Diplomacy

On November 20, 1566, the former secretary of Clement VII and apostolic protonotary Pietro Carnesecchi, long suspected of heresy because of his close relationship with the circles of the spirituali, was interrogated by inquisitors to establish why he had such a precise knowledge of English affairs. Carne-secchi replied that he often conversed with foreign ambassadors "to learn the news of the world" (*per sapere delle nuove del mondo*). He admitted that with the English representatives he lingered "a little bit longer . . . than I normally would have because I was curious to know about English affairs and so I would be able to give information to the cardinal of England [Reginald Pole], who was at the time in Italy."[7] To downplay the suspicions of the inquisitors over his dealings with Pole and with English ambassadors, Carnesecchi tried to justify himself by saying that, since he lived in Venice, he naturally had easy access to news about every part of the world, not least from reading the reports of the Venetian ambassadors that circulated widely in the city, well beyond the senate.[8] He further added that in the morning "gentlemen, some

Venetian and some foreigners" were accustomed to meeting "under the loggia of San Marco and there they consider and argue about everything, each according to his view about the newsletters that he had of the affairs of the world."[9] In the end, however, Carnesecchi was forced to reveal that, in truth, his knowledge of English affairs came from his friend "messer Guido Giannetti": "I have said it a thousand times and I repeat it again that in Venice anyone can hear news about the whole world and with no difficulty at all, because those Lords have ambassadors everywhere and the letters that they write—especially those that do not concern the interest of their state—are read publicly in the senate, and from there they circulate throughout the city. And at times I received *avvisi* from messer Guido Giannetti, who was informed by his friends there."[10]

Who was Guido Giannetti, the informant who provided Carnesecchi with fresh intelligence about English affairs? Although his name occurs frequently in several inquisitorial and diplomatic sources, in which he is labeled an "utter Lutheran," "a very evil, and pernicious man," and "immersed in heresies,"[11] Guido Giannetti has received only meager attention from scholars.[12] His letters, almost completely unstudied, offer a new perspective on the history of the Italian Reformation, and especially on the Italian Protestant refugees' contribution to the information flow between sixteenth-century Italy and Tudor England.

Giannetti's relationship with English diplomacy was strong and long-lasting. In 1559, writing to the secretary of state William Cecil, Giannetti claimed to have been in the service of England for thirty-four years.[13] Certainly in 1528 he was already working as the secretary of ambassador Gregorio Casali, Henry VIII's representative in Italy, who had tried unsuccessfully to mediate between Rome and England during the divorce controversy.[14] In that year, Giannetti followed Casale to Viterbo, to which the papal court had relocated after the Sack of Rome.[15] In December 1532 Giannetti moved to England, where he was naturalized and appointed cathedral canon in the diocese of Salisbury.[16] His letters show that in 1538 he became a client of Thomas Cromwell, who took advantage of his knowledge of Italian affairs.[17] In addition to employing him as an informant in Italy, the Tudors also entrusted Giannetti with the task of communicating with other Protestant states. In June 1546, he participated in the plan organized by Baldassarre Altieri, the secretary of the English embassy in Venice, and traveled to Germany to outline before the leaders of the League of Schmalkalden the details of the insurrection that intended to bring Italy back to its "ancient freedom" (*althergebrachte Freiheit*) and to defend "the pure and just doctrine of the holy Gospel" (*die reine rechtschaffene Lehr des heiligenn Evangelii*).[18] Because of his long experience in the service of the Tudors and his close relationship to the Italian philo-Protestant movement, Giannetti was a crucial player in the establishment of the alliance between English diplomacy and Italian heterodoxy that resulted from Henry VIII's break with Rome, as reconstructed in the first chapter.

After the death of Henry VIII in 1547, Giannetti moved back to London, where he lived in the house of the Florentine merchant Bartolomeo Compagni.[19] In 1554, during the initial phase of Mary Tudor's reign, Giannetti was able to meet Reginald Pole, now papal legate to England, who, even as he was accused of heresy by the Roman Inquisition, had become the leader of the Catholic restoration across the channel.[20] In Pole's circle Giannetti had many friends, from Pietro Carnesecchi to Donato Rullo, who— despite their sympathy for the Reformation—never formally broke with the Catholic church. In fact, it was likely following the suggestion of Pole and his followers that Giannetti considered the possibility of reconciling himself with the Church.[21] His reconciliation, however, was not to be. Despite the fact that he followed Mary Tudor's ambassadors to Italy with the intention of reaching Rome, the 1555 election of Paul IV, the promoter of the Holy Office and the great opponent of the spirituali, convinced him to make a detour to Venice.[22] Giannetti spent the rest of his life working between Venice and Padua as an informant for the Elizabethan government. The letters that he sent to the English court during this period are not just collections of *avvisi*, the newsletters that circulated widely in Venice; rather, they are documents that reveal a sophisticated political informer with a solid humanist education.[23] Giannetti's library included a rich selection of humanist authors, among them Lorenzo Valla, Thomas More, Philip Melanchton, and Etienne Dolet, along with several vernacular works such as the *Alcorano di Macometto* (The Quran of Muhammed), the Italian version of the Quran published in Venice in 1547.[24] The two names that stand out most, however, are Erasmus of Rotterdam, of whose writings Giannetti owned the *Encomium Moriae*, the *Adagia*, and the edition of the New Testament, and Niccolò Machiavelli, whose *Principe* (The Prince), *Discorsi* (Discourses), and *Istorie fiorentine* (Florentine Histories) were also on Giannetti's shelf. Indeed, it was through reading Erasmus and Machiavelli that Giannetti interpreted sixteenth-century diplomacy and pondered Europe's division into confessional churches.

As his extensive reading suggests, Giannetti was not a simple newswriter but instead a "professional of intelligence," who fully inhabited the "political arena" of early modern Venice, a space situated between the authorities and the city and inhabited by "an elite that was politically, not socially, defined, distinguished not by birth but by access to information."[25] Giannetti's circle in Venice included members of the spirituali and foreign ambassadors as well as Venetian patricians, such as the cosmographer Livio Sanuto. In his *Geografia dell'Africa* (Geography of Africa), Sanuto thanked Giannetti, "a most erudite man" (*huomo eruditissimo*), for providing him with fresh knowledge on the voyages of Sebastian Cabot to the New World and especially on the magnetic declination of the compass.[26] Thus, Giannetti was at the center of an information network through which the Tudors continued to receive a constant stream of news from Italy, even after the closure of the English embassy in Venice—the last still open in Italy at that point—in January 1557.

The Council as "Seismograph" of European Politics

Giannetti's letters to the Elizabethan court convey news regarding a variety of topics concerning Europe and the wider Mediterranean. Working in Europe's most important center of information on the East allowed him to closely follow the confrontations between Spain and the Ottomans.[27] On September 7, 1560, for example, he informed Elizabeth that Spain had been "miserably defeated" (*miseramente sconfitta*), having allowed their fort on the island of Jerba, off the coast of Tripoli, and with it their navy, to fall "into the hands of the Turk, increasing his power in the Mediterranean sea, and his reputation over the might of such a great Christian Prince."[28] Nonetheless, despite the attention to Mediterranean affairs, the most recurrent subject in Giannetti's letters is the Council of Trent. Venice was not only the entrance to the Orient but also a privileged point of observation on the debates that took place in Trent, where the council had opened on December 13, 1545.

Earlier in his career Giannetti had already kept a close eye on Trent and on the long preparations that preceded its opening. As early as November 21, 1536, he wrote to the English ambassador Richard Pate that the pope had summoned Reginald Pole and other cardinals to discuss the matter of the council.[29] From his station in Rome during the 1540s, while serving as the secretary of the archbishop of Otranto Pietro Antonio di Capua, Giannetti was able to further observe the arrangements for the council made by Paul III. But it was especially the third and final part of the council (1561–63), marked by what Jedin called the "great crisis" around the debate over bishops' obligations of residence, that Giannetti followed in great detail.[30] His letters to the English court contained information on the participants in the different sessions as well as copies or summaries of official documents.[31] On December 21, 1560, for example, Giannetti furnished Elizabeth with a summary of *Ad ecclesiae regimen*, the bull issued by Pius IV that had reopened the council, and explained that "in that bull the Council was convened in the city of Trent, lifting the suspension implemented by Julius III. The day on which it will begin is next Easter, the day of the resurrection. The reasons for which it will be convened are stated: the desire to weed out heresies, remove the schism, correct behaviors."[32] On another occasion, in August 1562, Giannetti kept the English court up-to-date with the Tridentine debate on the Eucharist, sending to Secretary of State William Cecil a copy of the decree on Communion recently approved at Trent, in the twenty-first session.[33]

To be sure, Giannetti was not the only Italian reformer who took advantage of his contacts in Italy to leak information on the council. The former bishop of Capodistria Pier Paolo Vergerio, already mentioned in the first chapter as an associate of Altieri, also contributed to keeping the Tudors up-to-date. While serving as papal nuncio to Germany during the 1530s, Vergerio had closely followed the preparations for the council in his meetings with the emperor as well as with Luther, and also contributed to the drafting of Paul III's bull of convocation.[34] After fleeing Italy in May 1549 to embrace the Reformation, Vergerio used his inside knowledge as a weapon against the Catholic Church, publishing papal bulls, commissions, decrees, and other documents to which he added his own comments and new prefaces.[35] Among the dozens of pamphlets that he published, many were dedicated to English sovereigns, from Edward VI to Elizabeth I, and others to their ambassadors, such as Richard Morison, English representative to the court of Charles V.[36]

Despite their English dedicatees, Vergerio's pamphlets were in truth intended to reach primarily an Italian audience, especially those readers who remained undecided on whether to break off from the Roman Church and leave Italy, or stay and compromise with Catholic orthodoxy. A skillful pamphleteer, Vergerio understood that the purpose of "adversarial propaganda" was to create stereotypes, and that by contrasting a positive set of ideas with its negative antithesis he could target "uncommitted" readers situated between the two extremes.[37] Thus he outlined a sharp opposition between the supporters of the Reformation on one side and the Roman Antichrist on the other, aware that any third alternative would have undermined the efficacy of his communication strategy. This explains why he expended substantial energy attacking the Italian "Nicodemites," the crypto-Protestants who refused to pick a clear side, hiding their real beliefs under the veil of religious simulation while expecting that the council would settle the theological controversies.[38] Vergerio immediately understood that the hopes of religious reform spurred by the council seemed to legitimate the practice of religious simulation.[39] On several occasions, Vergerio cited his polemical targets by name, calling out Cardinal Reginald Pole, whom he accused of hiding an adherence to the doctrine of justification by faith alone and of not openly expressing his true religious views, and the Benedictine monk Giorgio Siculo, who taught "that Christians should be patient, and allow errors and idolatries, and not say a word, nor speak to the contrary, until the council has concluded."[40]

While Vergerio's pamphlets on Trent were tools of propaganda intended to reach and influence a wide Italian audience, Giannetti's letters were instead addressed to a select group of recipients at the Elizabethan court, to enable them to make sense of the council and understand its religious as well as its political consequences. Indeed, Giannetti presented Trent not only as an assembly of prelates dealing with the theological controversies of the time but more importantly as a "seismograph" of European politics.[41] By following the debates of the council, it was possible to trace the shifting balance of power between the papacy and the European states. In August 1560, informing Elizabeth of the reopening of the council, Giannetti argued that the uncertainties about the possibility of bringing the council back to Trent or moving it to a new city were the result of the disagreements among the Catholic rulers created by the death of Charles V. While in the first half of the century the emperor had been the driving force behind the council, the division of the Habsburg Empire between its Austrian and Spanish branches radically changed the balance of power in Europe with immediate repercussions for Trent:[42]

Most Serene and Most Merciful Highness. The pope has offered the general council to the Emperor, the king of France, the king of Spain, and the other princes; the king of Spain has accepted the offer. Regarding the place where it will be held, the city of Trent has been proposed, and it is now left to be seen what will please the Emperor and the king of France. The pope, or his counsel on the matter, hardly dares to give it to Trent, fearing the present power of Germany, and not trusting the protection of Ferdinand as much as he did that of Charles V, who beyond the Germanic Empire had many other realms, which rendered his power formidable.

According to Giannetti, while Spain had imposed on its territory "one faith and one king," the empire and France had allowed forms of confessional coexistence and had different expectations from the council. On the one hand, the Holy Roman Emperor Ferdinand I requested discontinuity with the past and pressured the papacy to convene a new and different council "more free, of a different nature than the previous Tridentine one" (*più libero, d'altra condizione del superiore Tridentino*)—one that would have also allowed Protestants to participate: "Seeing clearly that the Tridentine council had an effect contrary to its intention, given that as a result of it the Protestants have become more numerous and bolder. And he requests (I don't know with how much conviction) that it be in a free city of Germany."[43]

On the other hand, the spread of Calvinism in France had led the Valois to seek a compromise with the Huguenots and to oppose Rome, reasserting the Gallican tradition that regarded the council as "superior to the pope (and the Church of France never understood it differently) and free, and safe so the Germans could be heard: something the pope would never concede, if the Christian princes did not impose it by their authority."[44] As Giannetti pointed out in his letters, the whole conciliar discussion over sacraments was conditioned by the power relations between the papacy and the European princes. On July 11, 1562, informing Elizabeth about the requests presented at the council by the French ambassadors, Giannetti explained that France was requesting permission to allow Communion under both forms, but would not have obtained it if the same request had not also come from the empire.[45]

According to Giannetti, the profound disagreements between Rome and the European princes had unexpected consequences that put the papacy in serious jeopardy. Assembled with the intention of stopping the spread of Calvinism in France, the third phase of the council had in fact accelerated it.

Moreover, it had put a very difficult choice before Rome. By revoking the council, the papacy risked fomenting other schisms; in moving forward, it left open the possibility of questioning papal power and its relation to the authority of the council itself. In any case, Rome faced a dangerous situation, which Giannetti glossed with the Latin proverb *auribus lupum tenent* (they hold the wolf by the ears):[46]

> There is no man who believes that the papists are about to achieve what they want through the council. They believed that in calling the council to Trent they would obstruct the progress of the Reformation in France, and it seems that instead it has accelerated. They fear both moving forward with the council and halting it. Should they halt it, other regions would move ahead with church reform without hesitation—in which case things would go from bad to worse for Rome. If they go forward with it, even if the Protestants don't attend, the Spanish, French, and German bishops, through the Emperor, would easily come to the conclusion that holds that the pope is not superior to the council, but that he must submit to it. At which point the power of the pope would be under dispute. In this way, in fleeing danger, they would run into its arms. Thus, *they hold the wolf by the ears.*

These last words were a citation from Erasmus's *Adagia*, a text that was part of Giannetti's library.[47] Tracing the proverb back to Terence's comedy *Phormio*, Erasmus had explained that "it is said about people who become involved in some affair which it would not be honest to abandon, and yet cannot be borne," adding that "while the hare has very long ears and can easily be held by them, the wolf has ears which are short for its size, and there is no holding it in that way, but on the other hand it is most dangerous to let it escape from one's hands, since the beast has such a bite."[48] Interpreting the council through Erasmus, Giannetti thus imagined Trent as a wolf that the papacy had little hope of domesticating and directing to its purposes.

In addition to informing Elizabeth of the conflicts between the papacy and the European powers, Giannetti also reported on the politics of the Italian states present at Trent, from the Republic of Venice to Medici Florence to the Duchy of Savoy. In the 1540s, Giannetti had promoted the effort to bring the Italian aristocracy over to the side of the Reformation along with the other reformers grouped at the English embassy in Venice, but twenty years later the relationship between the Italian elite and the Catholic Church appeared stronger than ever. As Giannetti wrote to Elizabeth, the repression of heresy had become the foundation of an alliance between Rome and the Italian princes, who "abhor that preaching: and they would do anything to eliminate it from the world." Both the Church and the princes had become convinced, Giannetti explained, that heresy is dangerous for the state, and that it "leads to the path of disobedience of the magistrates, and to revolt and to the renewal of states and kingdoms."[49] In Savoy, where "everyday those who profess the Gospel become bolder," only the force of arms allowed Protestant communities to evade the duke's repression.[50] Even the Venetian patricians appeared to Giannetti to have sided for the most part with Rome, fearing "that because of Religion there might even be danger of the government changing, something that they would not want to see in Italy."[51]

Giannetti also gave special attention in his letters to the conciliar politics of Cosimo I de'Medici. While the Venetian ambassadors appeared to be merely spectators of the council, Cosimo was in fact regarded as a main actor in the Tridentine assembly.[52] Giannetti was well-informed on Cosimo thanks to his friendships with Pietro Carnesecchi, tied closely to the Medici, and Pietro Gelido, the Florentine ambassador to Venice with secret leanings toward Calvinism who in December 1561 fled Italy and moved to Geneva.[53] Through the letters sent by Giannetti, the Elizabethan court was able to decipher Cosimo's changing attitudes toward the council. In the 1540s, because of the dynastic rivalries with Paul III and the Farnese, Cosimo had been a strong supporter of religious reform as an instrument for questioning papal authority and putting pressure on Rome.[54] In the third phase of Trent, however, the relationship between Florence and Rome had radically changed, in part because of the election of another Medici, the Milanese Giovanni Angelo Medici, as Pope Pius IV. While initially Cosimo had protected sympathizers of the Reformation and nourished their hopes, he quickly became a close ally of the pope and his adviser on the matter of the council: "Thus he [Pius IV] insistently appealed to the Duke of Florence, wishing to have his advice regarding this matter, holding his friendship and his opinion in great esteem. He greatly revered him and coddled him, and hosted him and the duchess at his own expense in the papal palace. He consulted with him on his affairs, in particular with regard to this highly important matter of the council for which he stated he had the duke in place as his adviser."[55]

As Giannetti explained, Cosimo's alliance with the papacy had a precise political goal. Cosimo needed the support of Rome in order to obtain the title of grand duke and temper the opposition of the emperor: "But that which matters most is that the duke of Florence would like to have the pope and the emperor, or at least the pope with the emperor's consent, create him king of Tuscany: and the pope would like to do it. But the emperor vigorously refused . . . saying that as he was king of the Romans there was no need of another king in Italy."[56] While none of the Italian states doubted the importance of their relationship with Rome, for the Medici the cultivation of that relationship was essential, all the more for a "new prince" like Cosimo, in search of legitimating his authority and enlarging his state.[57] As the final section of this chapter shows, the growing affinity between Florence and Rome that ultimately resulted in the granting of the grand-ducal title on August 27, 1569, marked a decisive turning point in the history of the spirituali, with a correspondingly decisive impact on Giannetti's inquisitorial vicissitudes.

Giannetti's Information Network

The microscopic analysis of the council that Giannetti offered in his letters to the Elizabethan court begs a verification of what channels he used to gather information on the Tridentine assembly. After almost forty years spent serving English diplomacy, Giannetti could count on an impressive web of contacts that included members of the spirituali and foreign ambassadors, as well as members of the Venetian elite. One of the most decisive sources of information for Giannetti was unquestionably the circle around the apostolic protonotary Pietro Carnesecchi. Carnesecchi's home was a meeting point for several dissidents and restless spirits, many of them associated with Giannetti, including Cosimo's ambassador to Venice Pietro Gelido, Reginald Pole's chaplain Apollonio Merenda, and Cardinal Ercole Gonzaga's former secretary Endimio Calandra. Giannetti met with them regularly, debating over the religious crisis and the proceedings of the council, at times by reading aloud Johannes Sleidanus's *Commentarii de statu religionis et reipublicae Carolo Quinto Caesare* (Commentaries on the Condition of Religion and the State under the Emperor Charles V), translated into Italian in 1557 and eventually becoming one of Sarpi's most important sources for the *Istoria del concilio tridentino*. As Calandra revealed to the inquisitor during his trial, "In the house of Monsignor Carnesecchi . . . at times we read the *Histories* of

Sleidanus. . . . I remember well that Sir Guido Giannetti then came often and acted very much at home there: and it might be that I even heard him read because at times he came to eat, and after eating we read."[58]

Trent had kindled great expectations in Carnesecchi's circle by fostering hopes for a conciliar solution to the confessional strife. Indeed, the council and its consequences were at the center of Carnesecchi's correspondence with his patron Giulia Gonzaga.[59] Writing to Gonzaga on October 7, 1559, Carnesecchi argued that instead of fleeing Italy for religious reasons it was better to stay and wait for the end of theological controversies. In his opinion an angelic pope would soon arrive, and with him the conversion of the Jews and the reunification of the Church:[60]

> at the time when it pleases God to unite all of us as one flock under one shepherd, and it looks as if the time is growing near when He will do so, as many Jews have been enlightened, but they have not yet chosen to be baptized, because they prefer to wait until the controversies they see concerning the faith among us Christians have reached an end. Now we must wait to see what God will do, setting ourselves to praying to His Divine Majesty that he give us a pastor who is capable of gathering and uniting the poor lost sheep, of bringing in those who are still outside into the good pastures of salvation, and bringing back those who have left them.

Grounded in medieval apocalypticism, the myth of the angelic pope remained very much alive in sixteenth-century Italy.[61] As Delio Cantimori famously observed, "The hope that the council, however it might be assembled, would resolve the conflicts, let the 'true faith' win, or at least put an end to the persecutions" did not vanish after the first sessions and not even after the end of the council.[62] On the contrary, the expectations triggered by Trent survived and continued to give life to religious utopias well into the age of confessions, confirming that at times in history "hopes are perhaps as important as the events."[63] Even as late as March 1562, having recently fled Italy for religious reasons, the Florentine ambassador Gelido wrote to Cosimo suggesting that he persuade the pope to set apart "every ambition and every private interest" (*ogni ambizione ed ogni interesse*) and to gather "a legitimate council in the middle of Germany" (*un concilio legittimo nel mezzo di Germania*) so that "the Church would truly be reformed" (*davvero si riformasse la Chiesa*).[64] Just as for Carnesecchi, Gelido's hopes were also rooted in

a millenarian reading of history. As he declared to Cosimo in the same letter, sooner or later such a council would have in fact been held regardless of
princes' wills: "And despite everything this will be achieved against the will
and the power of all the princes, because as Gamaliel said, if this plan comes
from God it will not be undone."[65]

Through Carnesecchi, Giannetti also managed to encounter in Venice his
old patron Pietro Antonio Di Capua, the archbishop of Otranto and a prominent member of the spirituali, who in October 1565 had been appointed
papal nuncio to the republic.[66] Giannetti knew him from his time in Rome
in the 1540s, when he had served as Di Capua's secretary and taken advantage of his protection to circulate Lutheran texts, including the *Loci communes* by Melanchton.[67] It was during this period, in the spring of 1541, that
Giannetti read the *Beneficio di Cristo* and contributed to its clandestine circulation.[68] When Giannetti was forced to flee Rome at the end of 1545, his
relationship with his old patron was interrupted but did not cease completely,
and in the winter of 1565 they met again in Venice. According to Carnesecchi, who acted as intermediary, this meeting was kept secret because Giannetti was being carefully watched by the Inquisition.[69] Di Capua's efforts
to rehabilitate himself in the eyes of the papal curia by hiding his previous
ties with the spirituali complicated the exchange of information between him
and his former secretary, now openly Protestant and in the service of Elizabeth I. It is nonetheless possible to suppose that Giannetti's knowledge of the
council came at least in part from Di Capua. As it happens, the archbishop
of Otranto had participated in the Tridentine assembly from its beginning
to its final phase, playing an integral role alongside the papal legates as intermediary between Rome and the council.[70]

Giannetti's other crucial source of information on Trent was the French
ambassador Arnaud du Ferrier, who represented Charles IX in the last phase
of the council, moving then to Venice, where he led the French embassy for
almost twenty years until 1582.[71] In Trent, Du Ferrier defended the independence of the Gallican Church against Rome, which made him suspicious
in the eyes of papal diplomacy.[72] The nuncio in Venice argued that while he
publicly "behaves like a Catholic" (*si mostra catholico*), in truth he rarely went
to mass and "is regarded more as a Lutheran than as a Catholic" (*è più tosto
in opinione di luterano che di cattolico*).[73] Du Ferrier's secret sympathies for
Calvinism were later corroborated by Michel de Montaigne, who wrote about
his meeting with the French ambassador in the *Journal de voyage*.[74] A close

friend of the French chancellor Michel de l'Hospital, Du Ferrier was in fact a prominent member of the *politiques*, who sought a diplomatic solution to the confessional strife by defending the power of the French sovereigns over ecclesiastical matters. Though in France the Gallican model was in the midst of a serious crisis, Du Ferrier believed that it thrived in Venice, which he considered an ideal state, because of the strict control the republic exercised over spiritual affairs. In his correspondence with Charles IX, Du Ferrier encouraged the French king to follow the wisdom of the Venetian senators who guaranteed the stability of the state and avoided the risk of civil wars by granting religious tolerance.[75] The relationship between Du Ferrier and Giannetti was soon noticed by the papal nuncio in Venice.[76] Inquisitorial sources later confirmed that Giannetti used to frequent the house of the French ambassador in Venice, where discussions were stimulated by the reading of the *avvisi* on the wars of religion. As Endimio Calandra told the inquisitors on April 8, 1568:[77]

> I had exchanges with Messer Guido da Fano in the house of the French ambassadors, where these religious issues of the Huguenots were discussed in light of the newsletters that came and the people who arrived from France. And I remember specifically that Ambassador Du Ferrier came, and that he had been in Rome, having been sent there by France, and he discussed at length the business that he had handled in Rome . . . and the conclusion was that in Rome they would never do anything good if not by force. And Guido Giannetti was present for all of this. I also found myself other times in places where, as I said above, French religious matters were discussed according to the people and newsletters that arrived, and everyone, both Italian and French, seemed to me to be of one opinion, and most of the time Messer Guido was there. I also talked with him under the loggias of San Marco about the newsletters that he had received from a Messer Bartholomeo Compagno, if I recall correctly, which he had written to Messer Giannetti from England, and we argued about them and at times we argued in favor of the Huguenots.

The familiarity between Italian reformers like Giannetti and the ambassadors of the "most Christian king" was not without parallels in sixteenth-century Italy. As has been noted, a close relationship existed between the Italian philo-Protestant movement and the Valois, who, like the Tudors, also used the Italian reformers as agents to defend their claims on the peninsula during and even after the Italian wars.[78] Thanks to his connections with Du Ferrier, Giannetti was able to provide his English patrons with detailed information about the confrontations in Trent between the Valois and the papacy. On January 16, 1563, for example, Giannetti sent Elizabeth and Cecil the text of thirty-four articles that the French ambassadors had presented at Trent twelve days before, a plan of religious reform in which the Valois pressured Rome on several issues, including requesting Communion under both forms and the use of the vernacular in the liturgy, as well as a reorganization of the benefice system.[79] Again, on March 25, 1564, a few months after the conclusion of the council, Giannetti informed the English queen of the firm opposition that the Tridentine decrees had encountered in France, reporting on the clash at court between the Cardinal of Lorraine on the one hand and Catherine de'Medici and Michel de l'Hospital on the other.[80] While Lorraine tried to persuade the king to accept the council and to send its decrees to all the parishes, l'Hospital advised the king not to do so, adding that Trent was not a "true Council" (*vero Concilio*).[81] As Giannetti further explained, despite Lorraine's efforts, the Parliament of Paris declared that the council "could be, in the kingdom of France, declared worthless, for four reasons: the first being that it was not legitimately convened; the second, that it should be reconvened and without following the path of the previous one; the third, that the pope had allowed the Spanish ambassador to sit in such a way as to show prejudice against His Highness the King of France; the fourth, that the pope remained above the council, and not the council above the pope, and this was against the ancient designation of the Theological University of Paris."[82]

Between the Council and the Inquisition

Thus, by observing the council, Giannetti highlighted the disagreements between the papacy and the European states, and the resistance that the empire and especially France put up against Trent. At the same time, Giannetti did not fail to see the divisions within the Catholic Church and the different strategies for responding to the religious crisis under discussion in the college of cardinals. Through his letters he enabled the English court to understand that the Tridentine debates were heavily influenced by the growing power of the recently founded Roman Inquisition. Created by Paul III on May 22, 1542, as a temporary remedy to deal with the religious matters that were to be settled at the council, the Inquisition survived Trent and determined its outcome.[83] Giannetti's letters show not only how well-informed the Elizabethan court was on the council but also how detailed its knowledge was of the conflicts within the college of cardinals, divided between the irenic tendencies of the spirituali, including Reginald Pole and Giovanni Morone, and the intransigent line of Gian Pietro Carafa and Michele Ghislieri. In this respect, Giannetti's dispatches further bring to light the plural and conflictual nature of the period commonly called the "Counter-Reformation," revealing the harsh disputes that were fought not only among but also within Christian confessions.[84]

During the third phase of Trent, the friction between the council and the Inquisition was made plain in the vicissitudes of the leader of the spirituali Cardinal Morone. Tried for heresy under Paul IV, Morone was rehabilitated under his successor Pius IV and subsequently made papal legate to Trent on March 7, 1563.[85] As Giannetti explained to Cecil, Pius IV did not have sympathy for the Inquisition and tried to reduce its power by reopening the council and reinstating Morone: "The pope counted first among his advisers Cardinal Morone, that friend of Cardinal Pole, whom his predecessor Paul IV held in prison as a heretic."[86] A man of exceptional political skills and diplomatic experience, Morone was soon sent to the emperor to deal with his requests for Communion under both forms and the marriage of priests.[87] Morone had a keen knowledge of the religious situation of the empire, where he had served as papal nuncio, participating in 1541 in the colloquy of Regensburg, which tried to preserve the unity of the Church. Convinced that "with these modern heretics it was much better to proceed with leniency than to irritate them with insults," Morone perfectly represents that vein of sixteenth-century irenicism that regarded diplomacy as a tool for governing confessional strife.[88]

In March 1563, the appointment of Morone as papal legate to Trent momentarily reactivated the hopes of the spirituali. It seemed that a reform of the Church and perhaps even an agreement with the Protestants were within reach. These were, however, expectations destined to meet with disappointment.[89] According to Giannetti the growing power of the Roman Inquisition not only made Morone's position precarious but ultimately undermined the whole conciliar plan of reform "in head and members" discussed in Trent. On March 13, 1563, Giannetti wrote a disenchanted dispatch to Elizabeth declaring that "the Italian Prelates in Trent do not want to attempt to reform the pope, the cardinals or the Roman court . . . therefore, while they ought to heal the head and the vital organs, they barely manage to manicure the nails."[90] Again, on December 18, 1563, updating the English court on the sudden closure of the Tridentine assembly due to the illness of the pope and the "danger of a council opened while the seat was vacant" (*pericolo di Concilio aperto in sede vacante*), Giannetti proffered an unimpressed review of the council, criticizing not only the papacy but especially the European princes who, "while they could have done anything they wanted to, through a council they convened themselves," in the end "did not want to do much at all."[91]

As Giannetti knew well, the conflict between the council and the Inquisition had considerably influenced the fate of Italian philo-Protestants. In the spring of 1561, having already been in exile for twelve years, Pier Paolo Vergerio still discussed with the papal nuncio in Germany the possibility of being heard by the council and readmitted to the Catholic Church.[92] The same unsuccessful attempt was made in September 1561 by the prominent Italian scholar Ludovico Castelvetro, who fled to Switzerland in the spring of that year to escape the Inquisition.[93] From his Venetian observatory Giannetti also watched closely the misadventures of Giovanni Grimani, the patriarch of Aquileia, who had long been accused of heresy. In September 1561, when the Inquisition established that his opinions were heretical and therefore he had to be brought to trial, Grimani fled to Venice and asked to be judged in Trent by the council.[94] After months of negotiations, on September 5, 1563, the special commission absolved him, reversing the verdict of the Inquisition and declaring that no evidence of heresy was found in his writings.[95] In the midst of the controversy, on June 20, 1562, Giannetti informed Cecil that Grimani, "a man of great virtue, withdrew from Rome without the pope's knowledge, as the pope was about to hand him over to the Inquisition, because sixteen years previously he had written a letter in which he affirmed it to be sound doctrine that those whom God predestines to eternal life cannot fall from it, and those who are foredoomed cannot be saved."[96]

While under Pius IV the Tridentine assembly had been reconvened and brought to its conclusion, the conflict between the council and the Inquisition exploded again with the election of his successor, the great inquisitor Michele Ghislieri, named Pope Pius V on January 7, 1566.[97] Shortly after the conclusion of the conclave, Giannetti sent Elizabeth a brief résumé of the new pope, a Dominican friar of humble origins who, after making his career in the Inquisition, now sat on the seat of Peter:[98]

> Most Holy and Merciful Queen, the reason for which I did not write to Your Majesty in the last months is that I have moved from Venice to Padua. It has already been several months that I no longer find myself in Venice, where one is able learn of many important things; hence why my letters are not what I wish they were, and worthy of being presented to Your Royal Highness. Nonetheless . . . I take the present opportunity to speak of the new Roman pontiff. . . . Next March it will be nine years since Paul IV created him cardinal, with the name Alessandrino, having previously been known as friar Michele, Inquisitor of heresy in Rome, and moreover a simple and poor friar of the Dominican order. But as cardinal under that pope he became Inquisitor General, and then under Pius IV he became one of the Cardinal Presidents of the Inquisition. And now he has risen so high that his princes and monarchs would genuflect before him in reverence.

Upon his election, Pius V, who as head of the Holy Office had arrested Morone and brought him to trial during the late 1550s, launched a new offensive against the spirituali that was ultimately devastating also for Giannetti. The diplomatic dispatches between Venice and Rome in the summer of 1566 show the tenacity with which the new pope pursued Giannetti's arrest and extradition. As the Venetian ambassador wrote to the heads of the Council of Ten in July 1566, in Rome Giannetti was considered "a very wicked and most pernicious man, on whom the pope had had his eye for a long time."[99] At the same time, because of his relationship with the spirituali and with Protestant England, Giannetti was also considered a precious asset, since from him "one could gather more information than from anyone else."[100] Initially Venice tried to resist Rome's pressure for the extradition, arguing that "to send Guido to Rome would be to undermine the authority of the tribunal of the Holy Inquisition in Venice."[101] However, Pius V responded that the case fell under Rome's and not Venice's jurisdiction, declaring that "it would not be appropriate for this central tribunal of the Inquisition to allow that a case be tried by an inferior court," and restating that he "wished that Guido Giannetti would be arrested and sent here, as he was a man who hosted students in Padua, and further a man of weak doctrine and great scandal, as the Inquisition has proved."[102]

Within a few weeks Venice desisted from defending its sovereignty over religious affairs and complied with the pope's requests.[103] On August 24, 1566, the Elizabethan Privy Council was informed by one of its agents that Venice had granted the extradition and sent Giannetti to Rome: "Poor messer Guido Giannetti from Fano was finally brought to Rome, bound and in the hands of guards. . . . Oh God, who would have ever believed it! And it is indeed true . . . I know how much he loved your Lordship and I beg you to recommend him to Her Majesty in order to obtain some favor from the Venetian Lords, among whom many were surprised that they would ever want to comply with the pope's request, which they had refused many times before."[104]

The protections that Giannetti had enjoyed for years in Venice could no longer hold against the determination of the new pope. Through the Inquisition, Pius V had transformed the balance of power between Rome and the Italian states. In the months preceding Giannetti's arrest, a clear indication of the new relationship between the pope and the Italian princes came in the form of the arrest on June 22, 1566 of Giannetti's friend Pietro Carnesecchi, brought to trial before the Inquisition, and eventually executed in October of the following year, despite the protection that he had always enjoyed from Cosimo de'Medici. After a long history of tensions with the papacy, Cosimo now saw fit to come to terms with Rome.[105] Shortly after that, on July 6, 1566, Pius V invoked the case of Carnesecchi with the Venetian ambassador to invite the Serenissima to follow the example of Cosimo and hand over Giannetti: "The duke of Florence should be highly praised . . . having turned over to him [the pope] his close friend Carnesecchi."[106] Sent to Rome on August 19, Giannetti was incarcerated by the Inquisition, tried and condemned to life imprisonment.[107] Only in June 1575 did the Inquisition grant him "permission to freely leave the city and to travel to Fano," Giannetti's hometown.[108] As the Venetian ambassador Michele Suriano wrote to the senate in May 1569, Giannetti's life was spared partly because he had not been tried before for heresy, and partly because of the sensitive information that the Inquisition was able to gain from him: Giannetti, "who had been immersed in heresies for perhaps twenty years and had played a part in all sects, was sentenced to life in prison, but his life was saved, partly because they say through him they received information about many important things, and partly because he never recanted and therefore he cannot be regarded as a *relapsus.*"[109]

The case of Giannetti provides crucial insight into the diplomatic activity of the Italian Protestant refugees. First, Giannetti's letters to the Elizabethan court shed light on the role of the Italian refugees as "professionals of intelligence."[110] Thanks to their capacity to gather and circulate information across confessional borders, the Italian refugees were able not only to profit from the early modern market for news but also to strengthen their relations with their Protestant patrons and thus to navigate the perils of exile. More specifically, Giannetti's letters reveal that the Tudors were not misinformed about or uninterested in the Council of Trent, and that they pondered attentively its influence on religious and political affairs, well aware of the divisions within the Catholic front between the papacy and the European states, as well as within the college of cardinals between reformers and intransigents. As the following chapters show, assessing the legacy of Trent remained a critical matter for the English court up to the publication of Paolo Sarpi's *Istoria del Concilio Tridentino* in 1619.

Moreover, Giannetti's letters also highlight how the Italian philo-Protestants interpreted the council and what expectations they had from Trent. The widespread belief among Giannetti's associates in Venice that Trent would solve the religious strife and reunite not only Christianity but the whole world under one angelic pope should not be dismissed as a vain utopia. It was a conviction grounded in the uncertain outcome of Trent, which still in its third and last phase gave new strength to apocalyptic prophecies about "the restitution of all things" and about a forthcoming global religious renewal.[111] Thus, Giannetti's letters not only reveal the underground information that existed around the council but also document the complicated relationship between Trent and the many "myths and misunderstandings" that accompanied its long history and reception.[112]

Chapter 4

THE MERCHANT, THE QUEEN, AND THE REFUGEES

Chapters 2 and 3 have reconstructed the first encounter between Tudor diplomacy and Italian philo-Protestants and paid special attention to the ways in which the latter served the English court as secretaries, diplomatic agents, and intelligencers. After the suspension of diplomatic relations between Venice and England in 1559 the Italian philo-Protestants became even more influential, acting as Elizabeth's "eyes and ears" in Italy and enabling the information flow between the two states to continue. In Venice, one of the most important centers of news in early modern Europe, they were able to gather information on both continental and Mediterranean affairs, also keeping their English patrons up-to-date on the proceedings of the Council of Trent and on its religious and political consequences. The material hitherto examined has, however, left some crucial questions unanswered: On what channels of communication did the Italian philo-Protestants rely on to send their dispatches to England? Who delivered them to the English court? What protections did they enjoy in Venice in the absence of an English embassy?

To answer these questions, this chapter explores the relationship between Italian philo-Protestants and Venetian merchants, many of whom looked with sympathy at the Reformation.[1] It was this relationship that in many cases allowed the Italian philo-Protestants to circulate their dispatches and to circumvent the Inquisition. As is well-known, merchants occupied a prominent place among the Italian Protestant refugees. Scholars have extensively researched the Calvinist network of Lucchese refugees, which included prominent merchant families, such as the Calandrini, Burlamachi, and Diodati.[2] Several of these families became influential figures not only in the world of commerce but also in the Republic of Letters, among them Elia Diodati, who assisted Galileo Galilei in the publication of the *Dialogue Concerning the Two Chief World Systems*, and also sponsored the Latin translation of the work.[3] Through their connections with Protestant Europe some Italian merchants even reached the high ranks of Tudor diplomacy, such as the Genoese Orazio Pallavicino, who not only served Francis Walsingham, Elizabeth's principal secretary, as a secret agent, but on more than one occasion represented the English queen to the German Protestant princes.[4]

In the history of sixteenth-century Anglo-Venetian exchanges, however, the most important example is constituted by the Venetian merchants Giacomo and Placido Ragazzoni. Despite the fact that they never converted to Protestantism and always maintained a strong relationship with the Catholic Church, the Ragazzoni developed a special form of religious chameleonism that allowed them to traverse religious boundaries and to serve different patrons with little concern for their confessional affiliation. During the 1560s they played a central role in Anglo-Venetian relations, protecting the Italian philo-Protestants from the Inquisition and ensuring that their dispatches reached London. In this respect, the case study examined in the following pages also offers fresh evidence concerning the crucial role of merchants in early modern diplomacy.[5] On the one hand, the central position merchants occupied in the flow of economic and political information led governments to employ them as intelligencers and go-betweens; on the other, their familiarity with cross-cultural trade and their capacity to conduct commercial exchanges across religious and geographical boundaries enabled them to facilitate interfaith diplomatic contact with a higher degree of confessional mobility than states and their bureaucracies.[6]

"The Perfect Merchant"

The name of the Venetian merchant Giacomo Ragazzoni (1528–1610) is familiar to scholars of early modern diplomacy primarily because of his embassy to Constantinople in April 1571 during the war of Cyprus, when he assisted the *bailo* Marco Antonio Barbaro, the Venetian commercial representative to the Sublime Porte, in negotiations with the Ottomans.[7] Along with several written accounts, the embassy was recorded in a fresco executed in the 1580s by the Veronese painter Francesco Montemezzano, a student of Paolo Veronese, who portrayed the meeting between Ragazzoni and the grand vizier Sokollu Mehmed Pasha.[8]

While publicly Ragazzoni went to the Sublime Porte to ask for the release of a group of Venetian merchants arrested by the Ottomans, secretly his goal was to negotiate a separate peace treaty between Venice and Constantinople and to safeguard the republic's independence from the Holy League in the months that preceded the Battle of Lepanto. As Francesco Sansovino and other Venetian historians later pointed out, "passing through Constantinople, Giacomo Ragazzoni was sent by the Republic apparently to deal with the restitution of goods to the merchants, but in truth to handle other secret and more important tasks."[9]

Included and discussed in the influential early modern diplomatic treatise by Abraham de Wicquefort, *L'ambassadeur et ses fonctions*, Ragazzoni's embassy to the Sublime Porte became an example of the role played in international relations by the "ministers of the second order" (*ministres du second ordre*), "more proper to carry on an Intrigue with Safety, where the Secret is more necessary than Pomp" (*plus propre à conduire seurement une intrigue où le secret est plus necessaire que la pompe*)."[10] According to Wicquefort, the "ministers of the second order" have "no need to be so choice in their Steps, the Irregularity whereof does no Injury to the Dignity of their Master . . . and being less incommodious and less formal than the Embassador," they find "a more easy access," and their "Business dispatch'd with much more Expedition."[11] It was for this reason that in the early modern period the Republic of Venice made frequent use of ambassadors of citizen status, such as Ragazzoni, despite the fact that diplomatic appointments were a privilege of the nobility. The diplomacy of the *cittadini* offered important advantages

Figure 4. Francesco Montemezzano, *Giacomo Ragazzoni Meeting Sokollu Mehmed Pasha in Constantinople*, 1583 (Palazzo Ragazzoni, Sacile).

indeed, enabling nonpatricians to negotiate with more flexibility while leaving the republic out of direct diplomatic involvement.[12]

The official account of Ragazzoni's embassy to Constantinople is contained in the report delivered to the senate on August 16, 1571. The Venetian merchant admitted that the negotiations were not successful, but stated that he was satisfied nonetheless for having had the opportunity to visit the Sublime Porte and "to see the greatest prince in the world, and to meet and negotiate with the wisest, most just, most prudent, and bravest ruler of an empire alive on earth today."[13] Further information on the embassy, until now neglected by scholars, can be found in the autobiographical narrative included by Ragazzoni in his will, drafted on May 7, 1609:[14]

> Before it was time to marry my daughters, this exalted Republic faced the grievous challenge of the Turkish war, which left it deeply troubled, and especially dubious of what might happen with the league that it had negotiated with other Princes. And because the most illustrious Marco Antonio Barbaro, who was then the bailo in Constantinople, was confined to his home like a prison whence it was doubtful that he could deal with public affairs, it was decided through a public decree that the most excellent senate and the exalted Council of Ten would avail themselves of my service, on that occasion sending me immediately as they did to Constantinople . . . And having boarded a galley ship on March 5, 1571, in a few days I arrived in Ragusa and from there on to Constantinople with every urgency. And in the first meeting that I had with the most illustrious grand vizier Lord Mehmed Pasha, a man of the highest authority and prudence, I managed, though with great difficulty, to obtain a meeting and to stay with the most illustrious aforementioned Lord bailo.

As Ragazzoni explained, the peace negotiations ultimately never came to pass, and on June 18, he received new orders, as Venice had joined the Holy League in response to pressures from Pius V's envoy Marco Antonio Colonna.[15] Despite the failure of the mission, the diplomatic appointment to the Sublime Porte significantly enhanced Ragazzoni's prestige in Venice. When Benedetto Cotrugli's *Libro dell'arte di mercatura*, the famous treatise on double-entry bookkeeping and mercantile virtues, was published in Venice in 1573, the editor, Francesco Patrizi, dedicated it to Ragazzoni, labeling him "a true example of the most perfect and most noble merchant," while pointing out that he was sent to Constantinople "not only to retrieve mercantile goods (in itself a most important business) but for political matters concerning very prominent princes."[16] With these words, Patrizi was framing Ragazzoni's embassy to Constantinople in the light of Renaissance literature on the perfect merchant, echoing authors such as Cotrugli and Leon Battista Alberti, who advised merchants to acquaint themselves with the culture of Renaissance courts in order to win the favor of both secular and ecclesiastical rulers.[17] As Alberti explained in *I libri della famiglia* (Books on the Family), friendship with the powerful was the only defense from the power of fortune (*fortuna*) and an indispensable asset to safeguard the reputation (*fama*) of the family: "The friendship of princes is especially worth acquiring and employing in order to increase and expand the name, the reputation, the well-earned authority, and the fame of our kin and family."[18]

In truth, the embassy to the Ottoman Empire was only the most famous episode of a long-term strategy that Giacomo Ragazzoni and his brothers employed to move up the social hierarchy. They networked their way into the Venetian patriciate by serving as diplomatic agents not only for the republic but also for several Italian and European rulers, from the Counter-Reformation papacy to the Tudors, without much concern for their religious affiliation. The Ragazzoni operated within European diplomacy as a family consortium, using diplomacy as a tool of social mobility and taking advantage of their appointments to break with their mercantile past.[19] Having received the title of count of San Odorico from the doge in February 1577, Giacomo Ragazzoni commissioned Francesco Montemezzano to complete a cycle of frescos for his palace in Sacile to celebrate his family's connections with the European society of princes.[20] Along with the meetings with Sokollu Mehmed Pasha, Montemezzano portrayed Ragazzoni and his brothers next to the doge Sebastiano Venier, the French king Henry III, and the English queen Mary Tudor. Another fresco commemorated the visit of Charles V's daughter Maria of Austria to the Palazzo Ragazzoni.

This painting includes Ragazzoni's wife Picabella and their seven daughters, one of whom, Claudia, depicted wearing two strands of pearls, had just married the patrician Marcantonio Foscarini in 1583.[21] The other six daughters also later married members of the aristocracy, allowing the family to anchor itself in the world of the Venetian patriciate. In this respect, the case of the Ragazzoni could also be seen as part of the general social trend of the early modern Mediterranean—famously labeled by Fernand Braudel "the defection of the bourgeoisie"—that led several mer-

Figure 5. Francesco Montemezzano, *Giacomo Ragazzoni and His Family Meeting Maria of Austria,* 1583 (Staatliche Kunstsammlungen Dresden).

chants to move into the aristocracy by investing in feudal property and agri-culture and by marrying their richly dowered daughters into aristocratic circles.[22]

The same fresco also portrays Ragazzoni's brother Girolamo, bishop of Bergamo, who did not enter the family business but made his career in the Catholic Church, participating in the last phase of the Council of Trent along-side his patrons, Cardinals Giovanni Morone and Carlo Borromeo.[23] In

1583, when the fresco was executed, Girolamo had just been appointed papal nunzio to Paris, with the difficult task of conducting negotiations between the papacy and Henry III for the introduction of the Tridentine decrees into France.[24] In using diplomacy as a tool of social mobility the Ragazzoni were always careful in maintaining close connections not only with the Venetian patriciate but also with Counter-Reformation Rome. And yet, as the rest of the chapter will show, this did not prohibit them from doing business with Protestant Europe and from moving across confessional barriers whenever necessary.

Elizabeth I's Agent in Venice

While Ragazzoni's embassy to Constantinople is well-documented, less is known about his contact with Tudor England. A clear understanding of Ragazzoni's long relationship with the English court is nonetheless an essential foundation for reconstructing how diplomacy between Venice and England continued in the absence of resident ambassadors. In fact, the letters that Ragazzoni exchanged with the Elizabethan Privy Council during the 1560s, unstudied until now, reveal that his involvement was not limited to economic affairs but extended to the political and religious controversies that marked the relationship between Counter-Reformation Italy and Tudor England. While Ragazzoni's will conveyed a public image of the "perfect merchant," loyal to the Venetian Republic and to the Counter-Reformation papacy, his private correspondence provides insight into his role as a diplomatic broker and his ability to move freely across confessional divisions.

Ragazzoni's ties with the English court ran deep. Between 1542 and 1558, during the years of his apprenticeship in London, in addition to forming a trading company with the powerful patrician Giacomo Foscarini, Ragazzoni also succeeded in introducing himself to the English court.[25] During his sixteen years in London, Ragazzoni witnessed the several changes of regime that followed the death of Henry VIII and established a close relationship with Mary Tudor. According to his will, Ragazzoni participated in the celebrations for Mary's coronation and served as intermediary between her and the papacy.[26] Taking advantage of his brother Vettor's position as *cameriere* of Julius III, he ensured that Mary's letters expressing her intention to bring England back to Catholicism reached the pope in Rome:[27]

While I was in the kingdom of England not only did I see to the traffic of
goods and mercantile affairs with the highest diligence, and practicality, but
I furthermore managed to render myself as pleasing as possible to the most
majestic kings and queens of my time, by whom I was truly favored and esteemed beyond my merit, and principally so by Her Highness Queen Mary.
She, having been so swiftly raised to the supreme dignity of that crown, con-
fided in me that I should find a way to make His Holiness, Our Lord Julius
III, High Pontiff, understand that Her Majesty had no greater desire in this
world than to bring her realm under the obedience of the Holy Church, and
that to this end she would do every possible thing, but with time, as there was
a great number of heretics to be found in her reign. . . . I carried out this order quickly through my brother Monsignor Vettor Ragazzoni, who at that
time was in Rome as *cameriere di honore* of that pontiff.

Ragazzoni continued to profit from his English contacts even after his return to Venice in April 1558, playing a decisive role in Anglo-Venetian relations when the exchange of resident ambassadors between the two states had
ceased. On April 26, 1561, Ragazzoni wrote to the Privy Council underlining "my most devoted affection, and long-standing service to Her Majesty"
and stressing "the fervent desire that I have to serve that Crown, under which
I lived for several years, and messer Guido, for whom I did some favors simply because of his kindness and because of the close friendship that was established between us in England some time ago."[28] Ragazzoni was referring
to Guido Giannetti, discussed in the preceding chapter, who had just been
arrested in Venice. Imprisoned by the Inquisition the previous February, Giannetti's case was particularly complicated because of his strong Protestant
beliefs. These had previously led him not only to work as an informant
for the English government but also to participate in the anti-imperial
conspiracy—organized in the 1540s by the secretary of the English embassy
in Venice Baldassarre Altieri—that intended to pressure the Republic of Venice to join the League of Schmalkalden, hoping to bring Italy back to its
"ancient freedom."[29] Giannetti's role as intelligencer was well-known in
Rome and his name appeared frequently in inquisitorial records.[30] Aware of
these complications and the tensions between Venice and the papacy, Ragazzoni informed the Privy Council that the Inquisition was pushing to extra-
dite Giannetti to Rome: "I hope that, having such warm recommendations
from such a great Queen in support of my cause, I will not tire myself in vain,
despite knowing how complicated this affair is, because of the concerns in

Rome where Messer Guido is being summoned with the greatest insistence. I will keep Your Excellencies informed of what occurs with regard to this affair and it will be discussed in person with my brother Placido, who will present this letter."[31]

On May 10, Ragazzoni wrote a new letter to update the Privy Council on the case. Though he had presented Elizabeth's letters to the senate, Giannetti's fate was still uncertain because of pressure from Rome: "I presented Your Majesty's letter to these illustrious lords in an appropriate moment . . . they revealed themselves to be very dubious regarding this request, having had strong intentions, before receiving that letter, of sending Messer Guido Giannetti to Rome where he was being summoned with greatest insistence. However, until now nothing has been done with regard to this affair and I hope that what will be done hereafter will be more helpful than harmful to the aforementioned Messer Guido."[32]

Concluding his letter, Ragazzoni reassured the Privy Council that he would not cease to use every means he had, as well as those of his friends, to liberate Giannetti.[33] His intervention was successful, as twenty days later the Council of Ten accepted Elizabeth I's request and, through the Venetian ambassador to the papal court, declared "that respect must be shown to this man [Giannetti] and that he should be tried here, and not sent to Rome."[34] The republic clarified that its decision had been made strictly for economic reasons and did not have anything to do with religious affairs, explaining that for the English queen Venice ought to "have great respect, as our merchants do a lot of business on that island . . . and serious prejudice could be held against our merchants if Giannetti is sent to Rome."[35] Having finally been released on September 19, 1561, Giannetti wrote to Elizabeth, thanking her for the assistance that he received from the "very studious . . . Jacomo Ragazzoni," and rebuking the Venetians for "the high regard that they have for the Roman pontiff."[36] The protection of the English government allowed Giannetti to work in Venice as an informant for five more years, during which time he provided Elizabeth and her secretary of state William Cecil, 1st Baron Burghley, with fresh intelligence on Italian and continental politics, following with special attention the last phase of the Council of Trent.[37] Only in the summer of 1566, as the previous chapter has shown, did the determination of the new pope Pius V succeed in extraditing Giannetti and having him sent to Rome.

What the letters disclose, along with details of Giannetti's arrest, is the role played by Ragazzoni and his brothers as diplomatic intermediaries. In the first decades of Elizabeth's reign, when official contact between Venice and London was suspended, the Ragazzoni acted as unofficial ambassadors and became influential through their ability to facilitate cross-confessional exchanges. In an age in which permanent embassies were only slowly becoming the norm, information was still a mercantile asset, and the Ragazzoni profited from it, taking advantage of their personal connections to circulate intelligence in exchange for political and economic favors. As they learned in the Renaissance treatises by Alberti and and Cotrugli, if the merchant wished to protect his wealth and enhance the status of his family, securing a relationship with princes and governments was essential.

A Family of Go-Betweens

In Venice Giacomo Ragazzoni not only protected Elizabethan spies such as Giannetti; he also profited from his extensive mercantile and familial network and ensured that the letters sent by the Italian philo-Protestants from Venice reached the Elizabethan court. In this task he was assisted from London by his brother Placido Ragazzoni. Like Giacomo, Placido never converted to Protestantism and publicly always voiced his adherence to Catholic orthodoxy. Nonetheless he also carefully maintained his family's ties with Elizabethan England, taking care of the Ragazzoni's economic interests in London and also facilitating communications between the English court and the Italian philo-Protestants.

Already in 1561, in his exchanges with the Privy Council after the arrest of Giannetti, Giacomo Ragazzoni relied on Placido, whose diplomatic role was no less significant.[38] Indeed, when Giacomo left England in 1558, Placido remained there not only to take care of the family business but also to serve as an intermediary between the English government and the Venetians in London. With the difficulty in trade created by the suspension of diplomatic contact between the two states, the Venetian merchant community in London could not wait for an official decision from its government, and in December 1560 elected Placido as vice-consul to deal with the English authorities. Despite the fact that the Venetian senate never sanctioned the election, declaring that in the future "it shall be prohibited to elect consuls or vice-consuls without the direct license of our *Collegio*," Placido held his office until March 1563, when the republic elected a new consul, Giovanni da Cà da Pesaro.[39] In the following years, Placido continued to use his political connections to influence Venetian politics and protect his economic activities in England. In fact, on April 22, 1564, the doge Girolamo Priuli wrote to Elizabeth recommending Placido and asking that he be allowed to discharge his ships and continue "his mercantile affairs." Priuli reminded Elizabeth that the Venetian merchant and his brother Giacomo had both "spent the better part of their lives in these parts in the practice of commerce."[40] In 1569, Placido's close ties with Venetian diplomacy also allowed him to pressure the Venetian ambassador in Paris, Alvise Contarini, to obtain the release of three of his ships seized by Huguenot pirates.[41] To be sure, the appointment as vice-consul in London was only the first accomplishment of Placido's diplomatic career. In 1571, after his brother Giacomo had returned from Constantinople, Placido was sent to Sicily to represent Venice to Don John of Austria, the commander of the Holy League during the war of Cyprus.[42]

The diplomatic significance of Placido's years in London is confirmed by the diplomatic report that he completed in 1572, in which he gave an account of the recent history of England and Scotland, starting with the Wars of the Roses and concluding with the Elizabethan settlement and the Ridolfi plot.[43] It is important to note that, like Giacomo's will, Placido's report is not a transparent account but in fact a literary document and act of self-fashioning intended to convey an image of the author as a "perfect merchant" and a loyal servant of both the Venetian Republic and Counter-Reformation Rome. As is well-known, the reports of the Venetian ambassadors "are highly filtered, deeply pondered texts [that were] elaborated and rewritten with caution and attention," which "say only what the Senate permit[ted] be said."[44] Moreover, as has been observed, if Venetian ambassadorial reports contained only scarce references to sixteenth-century theological controversies, this was not due to lack of interest but rather to censorship and self-censorship.[45] This aspect is also apparent in Placido's *relazione*, which is perhaps more significant for what is omitted than for what is included. Indeed, Placido does not say a single word about his exchanges with the Elizabethan Privy Council or the Italian philo-Protestants. On the contrary, he makes every effort to underline his Catholic orthodoxy. In his report Placido stresses his close familiarity with

Mary Tudor and remembers having attended the mass celebrated by the bishop of Winchester, Stephen Gardiner, for the Queen's coronation: "Having found the entire kingdom contaminated by heresy and not only the sacrifice at the altar but all images removed from the Church of God, and wishing with pious zeal to see to all these disturbances the very day she entered the Tower of London, Royal Seat of that Kingdom, she had a solemn mass sung by the Most Reverend Bishop of Winchester, who had remained in prison from the time Henry VIII walked away from his obedience to the Roman Church: And I, Placido Ragazzoni, was present to hear this most holy mass."[46]

In representing Mary Tudor as the ideal Counter-Reformation Queen, Placido closely follows sixteenth-century Venetian historiography, which often represented the English ruler through the eyes of Catholic hagiography.[47] Placido's adherence to contemporary Venetian sources is also evident in his portrait of Elizabeth I as a staunch Calvinist who did not hesitate to persecute her own Catholic subjects: "Elizabeth, having thus taken the crown, and having spent all of her life with heretic tutors, had only just been crowned queen when she abolished Catholic rituals completely and reinstated the previously introduced heresy following the directives of Calvin. And to this she always held fast, burning at the stake many who chose to save their lives following the example of the great virtue of the holy Martyrs, who maintained until death their Catholic faith, rather than rejecting it and becoming heretics."[48]

These polemical tones became common in late sixteenth-century Venice, where Jesuit writings, including Nicholas Sanders's *De origine ac progressu schismatis Anglicani* (On the Origin and Growth of the Anglican Schism), circulated widely and influenced local historiography.[49] This was the case for the historian Cesare Campana, for example, who in his *Vita del Catholico et Invittissimo don Filippo secondo* (Life of the Catholic and Most Indomitable Philip II) drew on Sanders to praise Mary while blaming Elizabeth for her Calvinism and the persecutions suffered by English Catholics.[50] Though groups of patricians had a more positive view of the English Queen, as noted in the first chapter, very few of them were ready to endorse the imperial myth of Elizabeth as "Virgin Astraea" that Giordano Bruno would help to propagate in Venice at the end of the century.[51] Thus, in his report, subscribing to the judgments of Counter-Reformation historians, Placido also condemned Elizabeth and situated himself in the party that, by giving support to the

English Catholics, hoped to bring England back to the Roman Church. In creating an image of himself as the "perfect merchant," loyal to Counter-Reformation Rome, Placido carefully selected the information he presented, omitting his frequent contacts with the Elizabethan court due not simply to his mercantile activity but also to his role as diplomatic go-between.

Nonetheless, Placido's name comes up on more than one occasion in the dispatches sent from Venice by the Italian philo-Protestant Pietro Bizzarri, who like Giannetti also worked from Venice as an intelligencer for the English government. Though Bizzarri, unlike Giannetti, was never tried by the Inquisition, his Protestant sympathies had also led him to leave Italy. In 1545, at the age of twenty, Bizzarri moved to Wittenberg, "prompted," as he explained, "by the reputation of Philip Melanchthon, a most unique man in our time."[52] Bizzarri made a positive impression on Melanchthon. On November 10, 1546, the German reformer wrote in his favor, recommending "this honest man and visitor born in Italy, Pietro of Perugia," affirming that "he lived honestly among us, and diligently applied himself to the study of holy doctrine, and that he departed on his peregrinations not to cause harm to anyone but to see the churches of Germany."[53] Still, Bizzarri did not stay long in Germany and by July 1549, he was already in England, where he was named a fellow of St. John's College at the University of Cambridge. The Catholic restoration of Mary Tudor forced him to recommence his travels and move to Venice, probably following his patron Francis Russell, the second earl of Bedford, also in exile for religious reasons.[54] In the lagoon, after the succession of Elizabeth, Bizzarri began serving the English government as an informant and soon entered into contact with the Ragazzoni.

A first insight on the relationship between the Ragazzoni and Bizzarri is provided by the latter's *Historia della guerra fatta in Ungheria dall'invittissimo Imperatore de Christiani, contra quello de Turchi* (History of the War Fought in Hungary by the Indomitable Emperor of the Christians against the Emperor of the Turks, 1568), a historical account focused on the recent war between the empire and the Ottomans. Though it was written in Italian, the *Historia* was targeted at an English audience, as is suggested by the dedication to Francis Russell and by the eulogy of Elizabeth, whom Bizzarri praised for her political as well as linguistic skills.[55] In the *Historia,* Bizzarri also recalled the discussions that he had in Venice with Giacomo Ragazzoni on the consequences of the Dutch revolt against Spanish rule for European trade: "Finding myself in Venice, and being a friend of the Magnificent Lords

Giovanni Pesaro and Giacopo Ragazzoni, I came to discuss these differences with them, and I understood from them—as they were gentlemen no less praiseworthy for their very kind, frank, and liberal nature, than for their seriousness and prudence, and were well-versed in the affairs of both nations—that the damage that had resulted was truly inestimable."[56] The attention that the *Historia* paid to the Dutch revolt might indicate that the work expanded upon the exchanges that Bizzarri had with Ragazzoni.[57] As the news relevant to merchants and diplomats often overlapped, it is possible that through Ragazzoni, Bizzarri was able to gather the information that he then sent to his English patrons.[58]

The most important piece of evidence regarding their relationship emerges, however, from the dispatches that Bizzarri wrote regularly, almost on a weekly basis, between March 1565 and May 1568 to the English secretary of state William Cecil, 1st Baron Burghley, providing him with fresh intelligence on international affairs. His letters are for the most part collections of avvisi, the handwritten newsletters widely available in Venice. Taking advantage of the city's many commercial and diplomatic ties with Europe and the Mediterranean, Bizzarri was able to cast a wide net for information from major centers of news production, such as Rome, Constantinople, and Vienna, to smaller cities such as Milan, Genoa, or Messina, which could nonetheless offer useful perspectives on the affairs of the Spanish Empire.[59] As the most important European center of information on the Eastern Mediterranean, Venice also enabled Bizzarri to follow Ottoman affairs from an advantageous position.[60] Indeed, in the years following the siege of Malta, Bizzarri paid close attention to the Ottoman expansion in the Mediterranean, keeping his patrons up-to-date on the Sublime Porte, where England did not have a diplomatic representative until 1578.[61] To strengthen the relationship with his English patrons, he often boasted in his letters of his knowledge of Muslim empires. In 1578 Bizzarri reminded Burghley of his histories of the wars between the Ottomans, the Holy Roman Empire, and Venice, and in 1583 he sent to England copies of his Persian history, recently published in Antwerp by Cristophe Plantin.[62]

Bizzarri's letters offer important insight into the activity of a professional news-gatherer, but also bring to light the channels of communication through which the letters themselves traveled from Venice to London. On April 8, 1565, Bizzarri concluded his message saying that he was sending Cecil his letter "through Giacomo Ragazzoni, so that he would place it among the other letters that he sent to his brother Placido Ragazzoni, the Venetian merchant who is currently staying there."[63] This was not an isolated occurrence: in the following weeks, Bizzarri again entrusted his letters for Cecil to the "Magnifico messer Placido Ragazzoni."[64] Thus, the information collected in Venice by Bizzarri reached London through the familial network of the Ragazzoni, passing through Giacomo and then through his brother Placido, who in London delivered the avvisi to the English court. At other times, Bizzarri even mentioned Ragazzoni to Cecil, presenting him as a trusted courier through whom the Privy Council could easily send his instructions. On June 12, 1565, requesting that his patron confirm the reception of his letters, Bizzarri told Cecil that their exchange "could be very easily carried out by the Venetian merchant Placido Ragazzoni."[65] As the letters reveal, Bizzarri used the Ragazzoni's network to send to the English court not only his dispatches but also the texts that in the same years he printed in Venice, such as *De optimo principe*, a revised version of the manuscript he had presented to Elizabeth I in 1561.[66]

The Network in Crisis

The example of Giacomo and Placido Ragazzoni demonstrates that, in the vacuum left by the suspension of diplomatic contact in 1559 and the lack of resident ambassadors, a network of merchants and religious refugees allowed the negotiations and the flow of information to continue. Taking advantage of their ties with the Venetian patriciate, the Ragazzoni were able to grant the Italian reformers a certain degree of protection from the Inquisition. Through their mercantile and familial web, they also ensured that their dispatches reached London. And yet, while it enabled diplomacy to carry on with a higher degree of flexibility, an informal network was also more vulnerable than a permanent embassy, and its members were more exposed as they did not enjoy full diplomatic immunity. Indeed, in the late 1560s the growing confessional tensions between Rome and England, culminating in the excommunication of Elizabeth I in 1570, undermined the Anglo-Venetian network established by Ragazzoni and the Italian Protestant refugees.

The election of Cardinal Michele Ghislieri as Pope Pius V in January 1566 was in this respect a decisive turning point. Having made his career in the

Roman Inquisition, of which he became the head in 1558, Pius V made the fight against heresy the distinctive trait of his papacy.[67] His pontificate was the last chapter of "the Roman Inquisition's grip on power:" in the years of the Council of Trent, the Inquisition imposed itself at the top of the Catholic Church, fashioning itself as the supreme guarantor of orthodoxy against heretics and infidels.[68] Pius V's commitment to fighting heresy also had important consequences for papal diplomacy both in Italy and Europe. As has been noted, Ghislieri brought into European international relations principles and values drawn from the theology of the mendicant orders, shaped by a long commitment to the fight against heresy.[69] Among the first casualties of this shift was the Venetian ambassador and future doge Nicolò da Ponte, whom Pius V accused of heresy and excluded from the embassy sent by the republic to Rome to congratulate him after his election.[70] The strained relationship between Rome and England continued to grow until the excommunication of Elizabeth I on February 25, 1570.[71] While the excommunication raised strong objections from several Catholic princes, including Philip II, it deeply colored papal diplomacy. On October 28, 1570, the papal nunzio in France was instructed to monitor Anglo-French exchanges and harness the support of the Valois in order to isolate the excommunicated queen. The papacy intended to undermine the proposed marriage between Elizabeth I and Henry Duke of Anjou and to convince Charles IX to break his commercial relationship with England, in order to "raise up all those peoples against that evil woman" and to force "that tyrant to . . . return Religion to such a state, that she could lift herself out of excommunication."[72]

Yet Pius V's battle against heresy was not simply born from theological intransigence but also from a keen awareness of the power of information in confessional Europe. Long experience in the Roman Inquisition had convinced Ghislieri that a new politics of information was necessary to defeat heresy. To wit, his pontificate took several steps in this direction, starting with the reordering of the archive of the Holy Office, which had been sacked in 1559 by a Roman mob celebrating the death of Paul IV.[73] Pius V also reorganized ecclesiastical censorship, creating the Congregation of the Index of Prohibited Books in 1571.[74] The following year he promulgated the first regulations on the production of newsletters, striking at slanderous writings as well as prognostications and predictions.[75] Already in 1570 the execution in Rome of Niccolò Franco, the *poligrafo* and author of numerous defamatory broadsheets, emphasized the pope's determination to regulate the news in-dustry.[76] Ghislieri's continued attention to the handling and circulation of information had a lasting influence on the Catholic Church, and the re-strictions against avvisi continued under his successors. In 1609, commenting on Pius V's 1572 bull, the Roman lawyer Prospero Farinacci argued that the revelations of state secrets by the writers of newsletters should be punished no less seriously than the crime of high treason.[77] Still in 1712, the year of Pius V's canonization, which would make him the only papal saint of the early modern period, the eighteenth-century biographer Paolo Ales-sandro Maffei did not forget to highlight Ghislieri's determination in perse-cuting the authors of "pasquinades and secret avvisi," especially when they "spoke against the government, revealing its mysteries and criticizing its decisions."[78]

Along with the offensive launched by Pius V against England in order to isolate Elizabeth, the Anglo-Venetian network set up by the Ragazzoni en-countered trouble after new measures were taken by the Venetian govern-ment in the late 1560s to establish heavier controls on the news industry, with the intention that the "news of the affairs of the world and especially con-cerning the Turks" should not "circulate and be debated publicly."[79] These regulations became stricter in the following years, when the threat posed by the war of Cyprus led Venice to enact new laws against "the many in this city who make a public profession of writing the news."[80] Like papal Rome, the Republic of Venice also believed that the control of information and the use of secrecy were essential for government. As has been observed, "far from being opposed, secrecy and republican liberty converged in the patricians' minds."[81]

The hardening of confessional boundaries under the pontificate of Pius V and the increasing regulation of the news industry ultimately dis-mantled the information network set up in Venice by the Elizabethan Privy Council and the Ragazzoni. On July 6, 1566, only a few months after the election of the new pope, Giannetti was arrested in Padua. After being sent to Rome in August of that year, Giannetti was incarcerated by the Inquisi-tion, tried and condemned to life imprisonment.[82] The weakening of Anglo-Venetian protections also finally forced Bizzarri to leave Venice in May 1568. His last dispatches, sent in the winter and spring of that year, contain more and more information on inquisitorial trials and the repres-sion of religious dissent.[83] After his departure from Venice, Bizzarri's relationship with the English court was interrupted for several years, beginning again with a certain regularity only in 1573. Having fled to Germany and then to the Low Countries, Bizzarri continued to send his *avvisi* to England until 1586, but he never moved back to Italy.[84]

While the Italian refugees were left a choice of either exile or facing the Inquisition, the Ragazzoni succeeded in preserving their image as loyal Catholic subjects. Preventing accusations of heresy was especially important for a family of Venetian merchants with ambitions of social promotion. Thus, it was no coincidence that when in 1583 the Venetian *poligrafo* Francesco Sansovino dedicated to Giacomo Ragazzoni *Del governo et amministratione di diversi regni, et republiche, così antiche, come moderne* (On the Government and Administration of Different Kingdoms and Republics, Both Ancient and Modern), he omitted any reference to his patron's ties with Elizabethan England and with the Italian philo-Protestants. Carefully removing any compromising biographical detail, Sansovino celebrated Ragazzoni as the example of the "perfect merchant" who had always conducted his profession in line with Counter-Reformation orthodoxy, fighting heresy from his time in England, when he had offered aid to Mary Tudor "in the revolutions of that State," to "purge that kingdom from the evil seeds of heresy," and "to return that Province to the true cult of the Holy Church."[85]

This opposition between words and actions suggests that the Ragazzonis' public declarations of orthodoxy were also intended to quell suspicions about their continuous contact with Protestant Europe.[86] Such attention became necessary after the arrival in Venice in 1547 of the Holy Office, which in the following decades prosecuted for heresy dozens of merchants among whom "Evangelism," the tendency to reduce Christianity to its moral precepts and dismiss the dogmatic apparatus as indifferent, had planted deep roots.[87] For some time after, Venice's commercial ties with Protestant Europe continued to cause alarm in Rome. In 1581 the papal *nunzio* still lamented the "great freedom" (*tanta libertà*) granted by the republic to the Fondaco dei Tedeschi, where visitors "kept heretical books, ate meat and other foods of every kind as they liked on fasting days, and discussed religious matters as they pleased," gathering in the church of San Bartolomeo where "heretical doctrines were publicly preached . . . in German."[88]

The question of how to reconcile cross-confessional trade with the new Tridentine orthodoxy remained an unresolved problem in early modern Italy, and not only in Venice. While in 1598 the powerful Florentine family of the Torrigiani risked being excommunicated if they did not close their firm in the "heretical city" of Nuremberg, in seventeenth-century Lucca a widespread opinion argued that "although it is prohibited by sacred and canonical laws to trade and deal with heretics and schismatics, when it involves commerce . . . there is an exception to these laws, and it is permitted to do business with them."[89]

As this chapter has established, for Giacomo and Placido Ragazzoni diplomacy was first and foremost a tool of social mobility that they used to break away from their mercantile origins and to establish close ties with the Venetian patriciate and European aristocracy more generally. This plan that the Ragazzoni pursued for most of their lives led them to serve different patrons with little concern for their religious affiliation, acting as diplomatic intermediaries between Catholic and Protestant Europe as well as between the Republic of Venice and the Ottoman Empire. During the 1560s the Ragazzoni played a crucial role in Anglo-Venetian exchanges. After Elizabeth's succession to the English throne suspended the exchange of resident ambassadors with Venice, the Ragazzoni facilitated the exchanges between the two states serving the Elizabethan Privy Council on multiple occasions. Taking advantage of their ties with the Venetian patriciate they protected the Italian Protestant refugees in the service of Elizabeth from the Inquisition, and through their extensive mercantile and familial network ensured that their dispatches reached London.

In the end, the Anglo-Venetian network constructed in Venice by the Ragazzoni and the Italian philo-Protestants illustrates the complexity of diplomatic interaction in the early modern period, shifting the focus from resident ambassadors, on whom diplomatic historians have traditionally concentrated, to the multifaceted world of agents, intermediaries, and go-betweens who facilitated exchanges between states that could not officially communicate. The specific case study examined here also brings into focus the challenges that go-betweens faced, and their limits. While an unofficial network was more flexible than official diplomatic channels and more capable of crossing religious boundaries, it was also more exposed and did not enjoy full diplomatic immunity. Indeed, the hardening of confessional boundaries under the pontificate of Pius V caused the demise of the network set up in Venice by the Elizabethan Privy Council. At the same time, the reinforcement of the Roman Inquisition badly weakened the image of Venice as a free and tolerant city. While in the 1540s the *Serenissima* still appeared to be "the gateway of the Reformation in Italy" and an "Italian Geneva," twenty years later the distance between Venice and Protestant Europe had grown, forcing the Italian reformers to choose between leaving and conforming.[90] By the end of the 1560s, while a new wave of Protestant refugees fled to northern lands, a new phase in Anglo-Venetian relations had begun.

Chapter 5

Reading Tasso

The influence the Italian Protestant refugees gained over early modern diplomacy was not exclusively a product of their skills as intelligencers and propagandists, as discussed in the previous chapters, but also due to their role as cultural brokers. Disseminating into Protestant Europe the language and culture of their homeland, they put their cultural capital into practice and won the favor of powerful patrons.[1] In addition to publishing and translating Renaissance authors—many of them on the Index of Prohibited Books, such as Dante Alighieri, Niccolò Machiavelli, and Pietro Aretino—the Italian Protestant refugees capitalized on their reading skills, and by annotating Renaissance texts provided their patrons with useful knowledge for conducting diplomatic affairs. In this respect, they offer a new perspective on the early modern figure of the "facilitator," a scholar-secretary with one foot in the university and the other in the world of diplomacy, who was employed in aristocratic households to read and annotate texts not as a contemplative practice but as a goal-oriented activity, pursued with a political end in mind.[2] At the same time, the specific religious agenda of the Italian Protestant refugees marks a difference from other early modern "facilitators" and underlines how their experience as a persecuted minority shaped the ways in which they appropriated Renaissance texts. Indeed, their annotations bring to light not only their humanist training but also their concern for the intolerance that flared in confessional Europe and their desire to single out the diplomatic strategies available to contain religious violence.

This chapter focuses on two Italian Protestant refugees, the brothers Alberico (1552–1608) and Scipione Gentili (1563–1616), who, despite their exile, had successful academic careers in England and Germany. Specifically, it examines their annotations on the works of the Italian Renaissance poet Torquato Tasso (1544–95). The influence Tasso had on early modern diplomatic culture has recently been recovered by scholars, who have rightly considered the *Gerusalemme liberata* (Jerusalem Delivered, 1581) "the centerpiece for any discussion of the relationship between literature and diplomacy" during the early modern period, expressing "a diplomatic message of reconciliation in the form of an epic."[3] And yet, while scholars have carefully demonstrated the degree to which diplomacy was on the minds of many early modern playwrights and poets, including Tasso, far less attention has been devoted to exploring the ways in which literary texts were read in diplomatic circles.[4] Using insights from the history of books and reading, this chapter intends to pose new questions regarding the role of Tasso and literature in early modern diplomacy. How did diplomatic culture appropriate literary texts and shape their reception? To what extent did the reading of literary texts help to imagine new diplomatic practices? In what way did embassies contribute to the circulation and translation of literary texts across linguistic and confessional borders? The annotations by Alberico and Scipione Gentili offer answers to these questions. Examining both the literary and judicial implications of Tasso's *Liberata*, the Gentili introduced the Italian poet into a broader international context and appropriated his works within late sixteenth-century debates on just war, the law of nations, and diplomatic immunity.

Italian Refugees and French Ambassadors

On June 22, 1584, the Italian Protestant refugee Giacomo Castelvetro, native of Modena but exiled in England for religious reasons, wrote to Ludovico

Tassoni, secretary to Alfonso II d'Este, asking if Torquato Tasso had composed any new works and highlighting the positive reception that the *Gerusalemme liberata* had met with at the English court.[5] As Castelvetro noted, Queen Elizabeth was so fond of Tasso's poetry that she had already memorized several stanzas of the *Liberata*:[6]

> There remains only for me to warmly beseech you to do me the favor of writing to me regarding whether or not poor Tasso is still composing anything: you ought to know that an illustrious knight has asked me about it, saying that Her Majesty ordered him to inquire; and, if he is producing anything of value, you would be doing me a most significant service by sending me an example, so I beg of you as much as I am able, assuring you that this Queen does not believe His Highness our Duke any less fortunate for having had his praises sung by this great poet than Alexander the Great believed Achilles fortunate to have had the great Homer to praise him; and I'm told that she already knows many stanzas by heart.

Just a few years later Tasso's reputation also reached the court of James VI/I in Scotland. In 1592, having been appointed Italian tutor to James, Castelvetro reminded the Scottish king of Elizabeth's admiration for the author of the *Liberata*. As the English queen was accustomed to saying, Italian was worthy of being learned not only by every courtier but also by everyone who wished "to read the noble works . . . of the great poet Torquato Tasso, of whose talent the poet du Bartas says, Last in age, but first in honor."[7]

Too rarely scholars have noted the contribution that the Italian religious refugees played in the circulation of Tasso in the British Isles, precisely when the Italian poet began to be read and imitated by Philip Sidney and Edmund Spenser. Most important, Tasso became available to the Elizabethan audience during a specific diplomatic moment, when the crisis between England and Catholic Europe heightened in the years leading up to the episode of the Spanish Armada. The excommunication launched by Pope Pius V in 1570 and the growing tension with Philip II had hindered Elizabeth's diplomatic system, which for most of the 1570s and 1580s had its sole functioning permanent embassy in Paris. As the following pages show, the Italian Protestant refugees read Tasso in view of this international context and interpreted his works paying special attention to its diplomatic echoes.

To be sure, Italian was not the only language in which early modern English readers encountered Tasso. To offer a means of entry for readers unfamiliar with the Italian vernacular, the Italian reformers translated Tasso into Latin.[8] In 1584, long before the first English translations appeared in print, a partial Latin translation of Tasso's poem *Liberata* was published in London.[9] The Latin version of canto 1 was dedicated to Queen Elizabeth while the partial translation of canto 4—containing the description of the infernal council that strongly influenced John Milton—was dedicated to Philip Sidney.[10] The translator of the *Liberata* was the Italian refugee Scipione Gentili, who had left Italy in 1579 with his father Matteo and his brother Alberico. On June 21 of the same year Gentili matriculated into the University of Tübingen, though he soon moved to Wittenberg, and then in 1582 to Leiden, where he studied philology and law under the guidance of Justus Lipsius and Hugues Doneau.[11] Having been appointed professor of law at Altdorf in 1590, Gentili also looked, albeit unsuccessfully, for an academic appointment in England to join his father and his brother Alberico, who was nominated regius professor of civil law at Oxford in June 1587. For this reason Scipione's first works were all published in London, including his Latin translations of Tasso's epic poem and his *Annotationi sopra la Gierusalemme liberata* (Annotations on the *Jerusalem Delivered*), printed two years later in 1586. Both were printed, not coincidentally, at the London press of John Wolfe, the most active Elizabethan printer in the publication of Italian texts, well-known for his editions of Machiavelli, Aretino, and Castiglione.[12] In 1591 Wolfe also published Tasso's pastoral drama *Aminta*.[13]

In translating and commenting on the *Liberata*, Gentili was aware of the growing interest in Tasso in England, as his dedications to Elizabeth and Sidney clearly indicate. Nonetheless, despite his attempts to find patronage there, Gentili did not intend to address an exclusively English audience. The verses inserted at the beginning of *Solymeidos* are directed in fact "to the Italian poets," asking forgiveness for having translated at such a young age—in 1584 Gentili was only twenty-one—a poet whom even Virgil and "Latin ears" would have appreciated.[14] With these words Gentili was also underlining the classicist inspiration of his translation, namely his intention to rewrite Tasso's vernacular octaves closely imitating Virgil's Latin hexameters. From its first verses the *Solymeidos* made clear the close relationship between the *Aeneid* and the *Liberata* and translated its incipit, "*Canto l'arme pietose e 'l capitano / che 'l gran sepolcro liberò di Cristo*" (I sing of war, of holy war and him, Captain who freed the Sepulchre of Christ) with an unequivocally Virgilian intonation: *"Arma ducemque cano, Solymae qui primus in oris / Aeterni tumulum regis monimentaque fecit / Libera."*[15] Attentively read in Italy in the midst of the debate between Tassisti and Ariostisti, Gentili's *Solymedios* was republished in 1585 in Venice with a new preface by Aldo Manuzio the younger. In 1587 Tasso himself praised Gentili's verses, defining them as "truly elegant and refined."[16] The *Annotationi* also circulated widely and were reprinted repeatedly in editions of the *Liberata* during the seventeenth and eighteenth centuries, becoming one of the standard commentaries on the poem.

While in the *Solymeidos* Gentili was addressing an Anglo-Italian readership, with the *Annotationi* he intended to reach a French audience, specifically the French ambassador in England, Guillaume de l'Aubépine, baron de Châteauneuf, to whom the work was dedicated. In the dedication, Gentili points out the intimate relationship between epic and diplomacy that had existed since Homer recounted the embassy of Menelaus and Ulysses to the Trojans in the third book of the *Iliad*.[17] Gentili's choice of Châteauneuf could have been in part motivated by the growing French interest in the *Liberata*. At the French court Tasso's reputation had been publicized by the Italian poet Bartolomeo Delbene, friend of Pierre de Ronsard and Philippe Desportes, and Michel de Montaigne in his *Essais* had described the madness of the poet, whom he met at the hospital of Sant'Anna in Ferrara during his Italian journey.[18] Although the first French translations of the *Liberata* by Blaise de Vigenère and Jean du Vignau appeared only in 1595, Tasso's poem was already circulating in France and had been published in Italian in Lyon in 1581.[19]

The decision to dedicate a commentary on the *Liberata*, an epic poem about the first crusade, to Châteauneuf, a French ambassador close to the Catholic League, was hardly casual. The Ligueurs knew Tasso well, as he had visited Paris in 1570 with Cardinal Luigi d'Este who was sent there on a mission intended to oppose the influence of the Huguenots at court.[20] On that occasion Tasso composed the *Lettera del signor Torquato Tasso, nella quale paragona l'Italia alla Francia*, a text that compared Italian and French customs by drawing on Renaissance diplomatic reports as well as on ancient medical literature, starting with Hippocrates's climate theory to distinguish between northern and southern peoples.[21] Years later, French religious conflicts were the focus of Tasso's most relevant political work, the *Discorso in-*

torno alla sedizione nata nel regno di Francia l'anno 1585 (Discourse surrounding the Sedition Born in the Kingdom of France in the Year 1585), which blamed Henry III for the political upheaval, lamenting the "lack of religious zeal that he has shown, making peace with the Huguenots" and "making a close friendship and alliance with the Turk."[22] Tasso had no sympathy for the French king and at his death composed a madrigal that circulated in manuscript form in Rome celebrating his assassin, the Dominican Jacques Clément, whom Tasso praised as the "new Goliath" who "brought down the new Holofernes."[23]

An additional reason for dedicating the *Annotationi* to Châteauneuf was the theme of the *Liberata* itself. Scholars have underlined that Tasso's poem was deeply influenced by the Counter-Reformation controversies, which regarded Protestantism as an internal threat to Christianity parallel to the external threat constituted by Islam.[24] This was clear from the fact that in the poem Goffredo, the leader of the crusaders, fights both internal and external opponents and must first restore the unity of his Christian army before defeating the pagans and reconquering Jerusalem. The rebellion of the Christian soldier Argillano against his leader Goffredo in canto 8 thus linked the first crusade to the Counter-Reformation effort to fight heresy and reunify the Church, reducing the Reformation to a political problem born from disobedience to papal authority.[25]

Since in his *Annotationi* Gentili omitted explicit references to the contemporary religious wars, it is difficult to establish with certainty whether he also read the rebellion of Argillano in canto 8 as a political allegory inspired by anti-Protestant polemic. Nonetheless, it is remarkable that in examining the episode Gentili does not condemn but rather praises Argillano and his native town, "the most noble and ancient city of Ascoli" (*la nobilissima e antichissima città d'Ascoli*), "which took up arms for the freedom of Italy against the Roman empire at the height of its strength and forced the Roman people to accept the Italians into their citizenship."[26] If Gentili also identified Argillano with Protestantism he clearly did not condemn his rebellion, as in the text Gentili presents Argillano as the hero who stood up to Rome and defended Italy's freedom. It is not difficult to see how, beneath the reference to the ancient conflicts between Rome and Ascoli, the Roman past could be transposed onto the present of sixteenth-century religious conflicts, allowing Gentili to praise those who rebelled against the papacy in the attempt to preserve the balance of power in Italy. As the first chapter of this book has shown, the idea that religious reform was inextricably connected to the defense of "Italy's ancient freedom" was widespread among the Italian philo-Protestants.[27]

To better understand the reasoning behind Gentili's dedication to Châteauneuf, it is important to remember that in the 1580s the French embassy in London had already opened its doors to Italian refugees. Châteauneuf's predecessor, Michel de Castelnau, seigneur de Mauvissière, ambassador to Queen Elizabeth between 1575 and 1585, had admitted several Italian religious exiles to his residence in Salisbury Court. Among them were the lexicographer John Florio, language tutor of Castelnau's daughter, and the philosopher Giordano Bruno, who dedicated three of his Italian dialogues on the infinite universe to the French ambassador.[28] A close friend of Scipione's brother Alberico, Bruno was also a reader of Tasso, whose *Aminta* he quoted in his dialogues, though his preference was for Ludovico Ariosto.[29] In the 1580s the French embassy was at the center of a wide literary and espionage network, and could count among its guests several foreign scholars, including the Scottish poet William Fowler, translator of Petrarch and Machiavelli, who double-crossed Castelnau by acting as an informant for Francis Walsingham.[30]

Thus, in dedicating the *Annotationi* to Châteauneuf, Gentili was looking for the same patronage that had enabled Florio and Bruno to live at Salisbury Court. Presumably, however, Gentili was not entirely aware that the arrival of Châteauneuf in autumn 1585 had marked a sharp break with the embassy of Castelnau, a moderate Catholic with tendencies toward irenicism. Instead, Châteauneuf and his wife, Marie de la Chastre, also named by Gentili in the dedication of *Annotationi*, were closely connected to the Catholic League and would hardly have been favorable toward Italian Protestant refugees. It was likely because of Châteauneuf's religious beliefs that Gentili's dedication did not achieve the desired result and led him to spend the rest of his life in Germany and Switzerland following his mentor Daneau at the universities of Heidelberg, Basel, and finally Altdorf.[31]

Epic, diplomacy and the law of nations

With the dedication of the *Annotationi,* Gentili hoped to obtain the patronage of Châteauneuf, a French ambassador close to the league, by pleasing him

with a poem that, though superficially recounting the story of the first crusade, in fact celebrated the Counter-Reformation fight against Protestant heresy. And yet, the *Annotationi* contains a much more sophisticated reading of
the *Liberata*, developed in light of Gentili's own convictions, which elaborated a new secular idea of the law of nations and advanced new judicial
principles to contain the violence of confessional strife.

As is well-known, Tasso dedicated the *Liberata* to his patron Alfonso II
d'Este, celebrating him in canto 17 as an example of a "crusader prince" de-
scending from the poem's central hero, Rinaldo.[32] In linking Alfonso II
with Rinaldo, who, like Achilles in the *Iliad*, returns to fight with the Christian army only after a long absence, Tasso was probably referring to the contemporary controversies between the Este and Rome, which ended in 1598
with the devolution of Ferrara to the Papal States in the absence of a natural
heir.[33] In addition, in sixteenth-century Ferrara the myth of the crusader
prince also served to erase a thorny past, thereby hiding the Este's intimate
relationship with Protestantism. Alfonso II was the eldest son of a Calvinist
princess, Renée of France, who had welcomed to Ferrara Calvin and several
Italian reformers, from Bernardino Ochino to Celio Secondo Curione.[34] In
the first half of the sixteenth century Ferrara had been a center of various
forms of religious dissent, from the Calvinism of Renée's court to the radicalism of the Benedictine monk Giorgio Siculo, whose sect opposed both old
and new orthodoxies.[35] Thus, underlining Rinaldo's return to the Christian
army led by Goffredo was also a means of emphasizing the loyalty of the Este
to the papacy and Alfonso II's commitment to fighting heresy.

And yet, as scholars have noted, the official crusade ideology in the *Liberata*
is continually challenged by the poem's porous boundary between "Christian uniformity" and "pagan multiplicity," and by Tasso's recurrent attention
for the losers' motives, as in Satan's famous speech in canto 4. As Sergio Zatti
has argued, "the poetry of the *Gerusalemme liberata* is probably the first clear
example in Italian literature of a conscious identification with the forces of
evil, though it is nevertheless rejected at the level of ideology. It is the first
great example of solidarity with the 'pagan enemy.'"[36] The *Liberata*'s attempt
to find a common ground between pagans and Christians did not escape
Tasso's first Protestant readers. Indeed, examining the incipit of the *Liberata*,
Scipione Gentili argued that according to the law of nations "pious arms" are
not only "Christian arms" but also "the arms of those who opposed themselves to the Christians in that undertaking."[37] Thus, in fighting the Christians,

the pagans simply exercised their natural right of self-defense: "Despite the fact that the poet, in saying 'pious,' meant only Christian arms, and not at all those of the enemies . . . nonetheless, if this matter is examined applying the law of nations, as one should, it is possible to consider pious and just also the arms of those who opposed themselves to the Christians in that undertaking. Which is to say that Nature itself as a most pious mother teaches us to defend our life and our abilities from force and injury from enemies."[38] According to Gentili, the *Liberata* gave the lie to the doctrine of just war formulated by the Scholastics, which held that it was possible to distinguish clearly in a conflict between who was right and who was wrong. On this point the *Annotationi* referred the reader to the Italian lawyer Andrea Alciato, who had already refuted the opinion of those "who believed that war was just only for one side of the warring factions."[39]

This argument on the bilateral justice of war was echoed and more fully developed years later by Scipione's brother, Alberico, in his most famous work, the *De iure belli* (On the Law of War), published for the first time in London in 1589 and in a second, expanded edition in Hanau in 1598. In the *De iure belli* Gentili focused in detail on the doctrine of just war, arguing for the necessity of reformulating it beyond the scholastic doctrine, revived in sixteenth-century Spain by the School of Salamanca. Freed from the theological disputes on *iusta causa*, war proved to be always just "on both sides" (*ab utraque parte*) as it was nothing but "a just and public contest of arms" (*publicorum armorum iusta contentio*) conducted between sovereign states on the same juridical plane.[40] In the absence of a higher authority, the relationship between sovereign subjects was necessarily regulated by war, which Gentili considered a form of trial. Just as in court the rights of both sides were guaranteed until the moment of sentencing, so both opponents were in a condition of equality (*aequalitas*) until war had ended, distinguishing between the victor and the loser.[41] This was a principle to which Alciato, Gentili concludes in an echo of Scipione's *Annotationi*, had brought new light, noting that the rights of war always respected both contenders.[42]

Like Scipione, Alberico also esteemed Tasso highly. His opinion can be found in the tract that he wrote in defense of poetry and acting, published in Oxford in 1593 but written in the late 1580s in opposition to the Puritan scholar John Rainolds.[43] While defending poetry for its civic value, Gentili states that the author of the *Liberata* was "the supreme master of the poetic art," "a poet whom you would easily count the equal of Homer and Virgil."[44]

Tasso's ambivalent representation of the first crusade provided a wide range of examples through which to examine issues related to the concepts of just war and the law of nations.[45] According to the Gentili, the purpose of epic was not to celebrate the victory of one side over the other but rather to purge readers' passions by representing the brutal violence of war. Thus, the *Liberata* became a decisive source in formulating the notion of international law of war (*ius gentium bellicum*), the laws that, according to the *De iure belli*, we "have in common with our enemies and with foreigners."[46]

In reading Tasso's poem, Scipione and Alberico Gentili paid special attention not only to issues of Renaissance poetics but also to the rise of new diplomatic practices. From the ancient setting of the *Liberata* they believed that it was possible to extract juridical norms that could regulate the violence of sixteenth-century religious conflicts. As Scipione Gentili argues in the *Annotationi*, even in a war men were obliged to respect precise rules, and for this reason Tasso made reference to "the most ancient law of nations" (*antichissima legge delle genti*) in canto 6, when introducing the heralds and interrupting the duel between Tancredi and Argante at dawn.[47] In analyzing the final verses of canto 1 of the *Liberata*,[48] Gentili asks "if it is permissible to use poisoned weapons" (*se è lecito lo usare le arme venenate*), and rejects that possibility without hesitation.[49] In his opinion, it was a method of combat typical of the barbarians, practiced in the past by the Romans and the Gauls.[50] The practice, though common to all nations, was rigorously prohibited by natural law. Not even in war was it permissible to infringe upon the laws common to all mankind, which emphatically forbade the use of poisoned weapons "because to use fraud in war means to declare war on Nature, that is, the natural society, that man has with man, which should not be broken by anyone for any conflict."[51] Scipione Gentili's condemnation of poisoned weapons as always illegitimate, even in confrontation with the enemy, would later be recalled by Alberico in the *De iure belli*.[52]

Along with poisoning, Alberico Gentili furthermore considered any use of magical practices entirely illicit, recalling Tasso's condemnation of the "dark art" (*arti ignote*) of the magician Ismeno, introduced in canto 2 of the *Liberata*.[53] The distinction between white and black magic, between "spiritual" and "demonic" enchantments, was particularly important for Tasso, who had also focused on the topic in his dialogues.[54] Therefore, aligning himself with both Girolamo Cardano and Jean Bodin, Gentili saw enchantments and witchcraft as incompatible with the law of nations, thus contributing to the progressive "decline of magic" in early modern England: "Why need I say more? It is clear from this that such arts are unlawful in war, because a war, a contest between men, through these arts is made a struggle of demons; hence the famous Tasso for that reason, somewhere in the early part of his admirable Jerusalem, condemns such conduct of war."[55]

With reference to Tasso's poem, Gentili's *De iure belli* furthermore thoroughly affirms the wartime duty of honoring the fallen soldiers of both sides. Tasso had condemned the brutalities committed against the dead in war, as the bodies were often treated as nothing more than "cruelty to the earth, which is without feeling" (*saevitiam in terram, quae nihil sentit*).[56] In the margins of *De iure belli* Gentili recalls canto 10 of the *Liberata*, where the defeated Solimano, while escaping with Ismeno, contemplates the victorious Franks who honor their own dead while trampling and ravaging their enemies:

> The bustling Franks, exultant, trampling down
> the breasts and faces of his closest friends,
> spoiling each still-unburied corpse of gown
> and luckless armour with proud insolence.
> While in long files some sing of the renown
> Of their own cherished dead with last laments,
> he sees that others burn his rank and file,
> Turks, Arabs, pell-mell in one smouldering pile.[57]

Despite the marginal note indicating canto 10 of the *Liberata*, Gentili's observations against the practice of inflicting violence on the dead seem to allude more to canto 9. Indeed, the words of the *De iure belli* translate into Latin the verses in which Solimano, to vindicate the death of Lesbino, kills Argillano and then acts mercilessly toward the cadaver of his enemy, "on the dead corpse he wages war, dismounted from his courser . . . Oh boundless woe, that vainly thus assuages / with war on senseless clay the grief it bore!" (*al corpo morto / smontato del destriero anco fa guerra . . . Oh d'immenso dolor vano conforto / incrudelir ne l'insensibil terra!*).[58]

On the same page, Gentili further recalls several octaves from canto 19 of the *Orlando furioso*, where Ariosto had described the madness of Creon while Medoro begs Zerbino to let go of his fury and allow him to bury the body of his king.[59] The right of burial should be guaranteed to all human

beings, Gentili confirms, and it should not be denied even to criminals condemned to death or to heretics.[60] Thus, no one should dishonor the fallen
victims of battle. According to Gentili's interpretation, the law of nations established furthermore that cadavers had no part in the spoils of war and
should be returned to the enemy without expectation of any remuneration.
It was for this reason that in the *Republic* Plato had condemned the fury
of Achilles, who returned the body of Hector to Priam only after having
obtained a ransom, and for the same reason Tasso, in his dialogue *Della
nobiltà*, could not approve of the violence inflicted by the Homeric hero on
the dead body of his enemy: "Plato also censures Achilles, or rather Homer,
who represented Achilles, the son of a goddess and Peleus, a most self-
controlled hero, and brought up by the wise Charon, as enflamed with such
passion that he would not give up the corpse of Hector until it had been paid
a ransom."[61]

For Gentili, the representation of violence and war in the *Liberata* had a
precise poetic and ethical purpose. Recalling the sixteenth-century discussion on Aristotle's *Poetics* and drawing especially on Julius Caesar Scaliger,
Gentili quoted a famous passage of Lucretius's *De rerum natura*—cited also
in canto 1 of the *Liberata*—to argue that poets were like doctors (*poetae
medici sunt*), whose purpose was to instruct people and to reinforce the foundation of civil life.[62] Thus, in representing battles and killings, the *Liberata*
offered its readers not an apologetic image of the crusade against the infidels
but a lamentation of the ruthless violence of contemporary religious conflicts,
urging that limits be set on war through diplomacy and the law of nations.
This conception of the moral value of Tasso's *Liberata* is also advanced in
the first pages of *Annotationi*, which draw upon the famous opinion held by
Plato and Aristotle that "the true and exact end of the poet is nothing more
than to reinforce virtues and eliminate vices from the souls of his fellow
citizens."[63]

The Perfect Ambassador

In addition to the *Liberata,* Scipione and Alberico Gentili included in their
works several references to Tasso's dialogues, starting with the *Messaggiero*
(The Messenger), a highly influential text within the Renaissance literature
on the perfect ambassador.[64] The Gentili were familiar with the work in its

first printed edition, published in Venice in 1582 without the consent of Tasso, who at the time was still in the hospital of Sant'Anna.[65] Tasso would himself later revise the dialogue, modifying or erasing several passages of the *editio princeps* in which he had discussed in far greater detail the relationship between the ambassador and his prince, the notion of diplomatic immunity, and the legitimacy of simulation and dissimulation.[66] These topics are all taken up by Scipione in the *Annotationi* and by Alberico in his *De legationibus* (On Embassies), a treatise on the perfect ambassador published in London in 1585.

In the *Annotationi*, Gentili refers to the *Messaggiero* while examining canto 2 of the *Liberata*, in which the pagan army sends an embassy to the leader of the crusaders, Goffredo, to convince him to give up on the conquest of Jerusalem. Modeled on Illioneus's embassy to Latinus in book 7 of the *Aeneid*, this is an episode brimming with literary allusions, where Tasso, while representing a diplomatic encounter between Christians and Saracens, also sketched out the contours of his relationship to the epic tradition and to its rival narrative forms, such as chivalric romance and classical historiography.[67] In examining the behavior of the two pagan ambassadors, Alete and Argante, Gentili first focuses on diplomatic rituals, arguing that the ambassadors' "unknown clothes" (*veste ignota*) and "strange appearance" (*portamento estrano*) are nothing but "the clothing the Egyptians often wear during embassies" (*l'habito che solevano usare gli Egitti nell'ambascerie*), who also used to carry a wand when begging and supplicating someone.[68] Commenting on Alete's speech, "master of calumnies, who found new ways / to slander in the act of giving praise" (*gran fabro di calunnie adorne in modi / novi, che sono accuse e paion lodi*), Gentili also recalls the close relationship between diplomacy and dissimulation, a theme that underlies the entire *Liberata*.[69] Diplomatic messages therefore should not be read literally but in code, between the lines, and often when a prince is praised by an ambassador he should in fact suspect an evil intention.[70]

According to Gentili, this is exactly what happens between Goffredo and the two Egyptian ambassadors. The Christian prince had received them "kindly and pleasant then, at leave-taking / he honored them with gifts of choicest style" (*in dolci e grate / maniere, e gli onorò di doni eletti*),[71] while Argante disgraces his office by disrespecting diplomatic code and "thus from ambassador he turns to foe" (*di messaggier fatto è nemico*) because he does not observe "the law of nations and old custom" (*la ragion de le genti e l'uso an-*

tico).[72] For this reason, diplomatic immunity should be given only under precise conditions. While it is a right sanctioned by the law of nations, diplomatic immunity also requires that the ambassador not cause harm to the prince to whom he is sent: "The law of nations requires that just as the ambassador is given safe passage to return, so in return he must not harm the prince to whom he is ambassador."[73]

By examining Tasso's representation of diplomatic immunity, Gentili was addressing a topic that was particularly controversial in 1580s England, when foreign ambassadors were not only "honest spies" but actively participated in plots to overthrow Elizabeth I. The *Annotationi* invited readers to further examine the issue by consulting, in addition to the *Liberata*, Tasso's *Messaggiero* alongside Alberico Gentili's *De legationibus*.[74] Like the *Annotationi*, Alberico Gentili's treatise on embassies provides important evidence for the understanding of the early modern relationship between literature and diplomacy. In reality, the focus of Gentili's work is not diplomacy as a specific sector of statecraft, a meaning that began to emerge only in the eighteenth century, but rather the ambassador's moral profile and duties according to the literary tradition of the good ambassador.[75]

Dedicated to Philip Sidney, praised as the living image of the perfect ambassador, the *De legationibus* was published following the controversy that exploded surrounding the Spanish ambassador Bernardino de Mendoza, who was deeply implicated in the conspiracy to overthrow Elizabeth known as the Throckmorton Plot.[76] In January 1584 Mendoza was obliged to leave London and reestablish himself in Paris. On that occasion, along with the French Huguenot lawyer Jean Hotman, Gentili strongly defended the immunity guaranteed to diplomats by the law of nations. With an evident reference to the Mendoza controversy, the Italian lawyer argued that "in dealing with an ambassador who is a spy, I do not believe that severity can be carried beyond the point of refusing to admit him, or if he has been admitted, of expelling him."[77] According to Gentili the inviolability of the ambassador was a very old principle, one that was very clear to the ancients, who had developed complex ceremonies that reserved highest honors for diplomats. The ambassador was always to be considered immune not only in the territory of allies but also in the territory of enemies: "The ambassador is neither killed nor outraged."[78] Violating this principle meant opening the door to armed conflict. As Gentili would reassert years later in the *De iure belli*, the only response to violence against the ambassador was war.[79]

The publication of the *De legationibus* was a turning point in Gentili's career. The success enjoyed by the work, together with the support of his patron Robert Dudley, the earl of Leicester, led him to his appointment in June 1587 as regius professor of civil law at Oxford. After its publication, Gentili's treatise on embassies was well-received both in England and on the continent. Republished in Hanau in 1594 and 1607, the *De legationibus* soon became mandatory reading for anyone interested in the relationship between domestic and foreign policy. In 1588 the English scholar John Case praised the *De legationibus* in his *Sphaera civitatis*, suggesting that his readers consult the work attentively, and arguing that "without embassy . . . no state, no republic, no dominion can exist."[80]

Gentili's treatise has often been examined by scholars interested in the history of Machiavellianism and early modern republicanism. In fact, the third book of the work contains a remarkable republican defense of Machiavelli, as he is significantly labeled "a eulogist of democracy, and its most spirited champion."[81] Rarely, however, have scholars paid attention to the entirety of Gentili's *De legationibus* and to its dialogue with the Renaissance literature on the perfect ambassador, beginning with Tasso's *Messaggiero*.[82] As the Italian lawyer argued in the conclusion of his work, his treatise aimed at providing readers with a broader examination of the themes the *Messaggiero* had already offered.[83]

And yet, despite his great admiration for Tasso, Gentili did not hesitate to depart from the Italian poet on several issues, starting with the very definition of the ambassador. Leaving aside the philosophical framework of the *Messaggiero*, presented by Tasso himself as "the work of a man who writes as a philosopher and believes as a Christian,"[84] Gentili focuses on the final part of the dialogue, where the "contemplation of natural things" (*contemplazione delle cose naturali*) gives way to the examination of the "human messenger" (*messaggiero umano*).[85] The latter had been defined by Tasso as "a man who represents to a prince the person of another prince in order to establish public peace and friendship."[86] Peace was the only real end of the ambassador, while war was nothing but a means to obtain it. Thus, according to the Roman conception of just war later accepted also by Augustine and the Scholastics, the ambassador could never consider war as an end in itself but only as a means to arrive at a final pacification, as "if one were to wage war for the sake of war . . . it would be similar to an archer shooting an arrow without a target."[87] While Tasso argued that the ambassador always aims at peace, Gentili refutes this conviction, accusing the Italian poet of having confused the means with the end, instead of calling things by their proper name.[88] Furthermore, ambassadors of war had always existed, as book 12 of the *Aeneid* demonstrated in describing Idmon sent by Turnus to challenge Aeneas to a duel.[89] The ambassador must therefore complete his duty even when that duty entails informing a foreign prince of a declaration of war: "Nor do I agree with the reverend Torquato Tasso, who, opposing the view that some ambassadors are concerned with peace and some with war, maintains that every ambassador is a man of peace. . . . Unquestionably, in the case of instructions which are definite and order the ambassador to declare war, the view of Tasso is not tenable."[90]

Along with the embassy of war, the most important point of disagreement between Gentili and Tasso was related to the freedom of the ambassador in the face of orders from his prince. In a remarkable passage of the *Messaggiero,* Tasso admitted that, in the case that "the prince's wishes were unjust" (*le voglie del prencipe fossero ingiuste*), the ambassador was allowed to lie to the prince. As one could lie in two ways, "either by telling [the prince] something false or by omitting the truth" (*o dicendoli il falso o tacendoli il vero*), the *Messaggiero* explains that the first way of lying is reserved to princes only, who are often forced to act against "that which is just according to nature" (*quel ch'è giusto per natura*) but must "keep up the appearance of justice and the reputation of goodness" (*salvar l'apparenza della giustizia e la riputazione della bontà*).[91] The ambassador, however, is allowed to lie to the prince in the second way, "by omitting the truth," and for this reason is not strictly bound to the orders he received:[92]

> The ambassador, presenting and representing the proposals of one prince and the responses of another, should not always report them with the same words with which they were written or told to him because, in doing that, at times he would easily offend their spirit, producing hate and dissatisfaction, though his goal is to generate friendship. Keeping the truth of his commissions pure and intact in its essence, he can change their appearance and their likeness with words and with reasoning. If anything harsh or bitter were ever to happen between the princes, for whom he is a go-between, he can sweeten and smooth it out with agreeable and pleasant words and with a skillful and courteous way of negotiating, so that no dissatisfaction remains in the princes' hearts.

Thus, for Tasso the ambassador should not repeat literally the orders that he received but rather he should adapt them to his audience. Using his rhetorical skills he should change "their appearance and their likeness" while keeping the "essence" in order to promote peace and to avoid creating hostility between princes. Tasso considered perfect the ambassador who, aware of the gulf that separated morality and politics, "would prefer to act with absolutely honesty, but in his actions adapts himself to the orders of the prince and to the laws of the city" (*amerebbe cose assolutamente oneste, ma nell'operazioni s'accommoda a' commandamenti de' prencipi o alle leggi della città*), avoiding "rigid and strict honesty, stripped of any usefulness" (*l'onestà rigida e severa, spogliata d'ogni utilità*). In other words, he was not to behave like Cato, who "living in the city of Romulus as though he had been born in the Republic of Plato became the cause of many tumults in that city."[93] According to Tasso, because there was no room for ethics in Renaissance politics, the ambassador who intended to be a "uomo da bene" (good man) should retire in solitude outside of the human commonwealth.[94] This passage of the *Messaggiero* is full of literary references, starting with Lucretius, who in a famous passage of the *De rerum natura*, which Tasso translated in canto 1 of the *Liberata,* presented poetry as a sweet vehicle of bitter truth.[95] In justifying the recourse to dissimulation, the *Messaggiero* also echoes the *Cortegiano* by Baldassare Castiglione, who similarly cited Lucretius to argue that in giving to his prince "bitter-tasting medicine" (*medicina di sapore amaro*) the courtier should cover "the edge of the cup with a sweet cordial" (*l'orificio del vaso di qualche dolce liquore*).[96]

Gentili picked this passage of the *Messaggiero,* however, in order to thoroughly refute Tasso's ideas on the ambassador's autonomy. In the *De legationibus,* he argues that the ambassador should stick to the letter of his orders: "For my own part, no matter what distinction the excellent Tasso may make, I am of the opinion that such a thing should never be done by ambassadors. . . . Nor do I doubt that in cases where definite instructions have been given, ambassadors should not be allowed to diverge even a finger's breadth from them."[97] And yet Gentili also stated that the perfect ambassador should obey his prince's orders only if they did not go against his conscience. Taking this position, the Italian lawyer was in fact distancing himself not only from Tasso but from the whole literary tradition on the perfect ambassador, in which the diplomat was often reduced to a simple functionary, an obedient servant of the sovereign. Having received his orders, the diplomat was to complete the assigned mission without giving any weight to doubts or hesitations of moral character. He should direct all of his actions, as the Venetian humanist Ermolao Barbaro had clarified in the *De officio legati*, exclusively to the defense and growth of the state's power.[98] This was the position destined to become a common definition by the seventeenth century, as suggested by the maxim attributed to Henry Wotton, the English ambassador to Venice during the years of the Interdict and Gentili's former student: "The ambassador is a good man sent abroad to lie for the sake of his country" (*Legatus est vir bonus preregre missus ad mentiendum reipublicae causa*).[99]

Contrary to Tasso and to the Renaissance literature on the perfect ambassador, Gentili was convinced that passive obedience to the prince's will was far from a virtue. The ambassador should never be reduced to a mere functionary, subjecting himself entirely to his prince's orders. Certainly, the diplomatic profession constantly faced the perpetual antithesis between ethics and politics, between *lex Dei* and *lex principis*. Nonetheless, for Gentili there existed a clear hierarchy between these two laws that forced the ambassador to follow his own conscience, and to obey divine law first and foremost: "The ambassador's character is mixed, not double; and since in this mixture the right of God is the stronger, the other element should certainly be controlled by it."[100] Disobeying the prince naturally constituted an extreme course of action, as Gentili understood it. The sovereign placed all his trust in the ambassador and fidelity (*fides*) was considered one of the most important virtues in the diplomatic profession.[101] Resisting an unjust order to safeguard one's own conscience would not, however, represent an offense as great as passively obeying, and thereby contradicting one's own religious convictions. In this case the ambassador would stain himself with a grave sin, violating the *lex Dei*, and should be considered, without any pretext, entirely responsible for his actions: "Not even a resident ambassador should obey, if his sovereign wants him to do something which detracts even in the smallest degree from his obligations to God . . . no ambassador should be so mad as to prefer to sin against his religion rather than offend his king; nevertheless one, whoever he may be, who undertakes a clearly defined embassy which the law of his God hinders his accomplishing, acts very badly."[102]

Gentili knew very well that the ambassador that he was describing was far removed from the realities of European politics. Yet his intent was not to describe diplomatic practices so much as to delineate a normative model in opposition to the usual conduct of ambassadors: "I know very well how much these principles differ from the current code of morals. But I am depicting the ambassador, not as he generally is, but as he ought to be."[103] Gentili also knew that defending the ambassador's right to disobey unjust orders was a radical position, one that could easily be associated with political radicalism. For this reason, anticipating possible controversies, in *De legationibus* he carefully distinguished his position from the dangerous contemporary doctrines on tyrannicide, recently advanced in England by the Scottish humanist George Buchanan, also in close contact with Sidney and his circle.[104] According to Gentili, republicanism did not coincide with antimonarchism, but rather with the idea that the powers of the sovereign needed to be limited by a council of virtuous advisers who should attempt to control the monarch's actions within the limit of the law.[105] Only the magistrate has the right to resist the tyrant, while the subject must always obey the orders of his superiors. Gentili had no sympathy for the doctrine of popular resistance, as he clarified by arguing that in a political vacuum even tyranny could be legitimate to prevent anarchy and political disorder. Under extreme circumstances, a sovereign could legitimately govern against the will of his subjects, like the doctor of Plato's *Politicus*, sanctioned to cure diseases against the will of his patients.[106]

Hotly debated in late Elizabethan England, distinguishing between legitimate resistance to unjust orders and unlawful sedition against the ruler was a problem that also interested Scipione Gentili, who, like his brother, was convinced of the inadmissibility of tyrannicide. In the *Annotationi*, commenting on canto 4 of the *Liberata*, he similarly argues that while pagans praised the killing of tyrants, Christians must respect governors and remember that their power is ultimately sanctioned by God. Precisely for this reason, Gentili concludes, Dante had placed Brutus and Cassius in the last level of Hell directly in the mouths of Lucifer, the archetype of all rebels.[107]

By annotating, translating, and editing Torquato Tasso, Scipione and Alberico Gentili not only circulated his works outside of Italy, they also appropriated them in the context of their own concerns, in the effort to find a diplomatic solution to the religious strife that surrounded them. Looking carefully at both the literary and judicial implications of the *Liberata*, the Gentili interpreted Tasso's epic in light of contemporary discussions on just war and the law of nations. Similarly, they read Tasso's *Messaggiero* while considering the notion of diplomatic immunity and the ambassador's right to resist unjust orders.

Moreover, the dedication of Scipione Gentili's *Annotationi* to the French ambassador Guillaume de l'Aubépine, baron de Châteauneuf, sheds light on Tasso's circulation in sixteenth-century diplomatic circles and on the ways in which the *Liberata* was appropriated by its early readers. Indeed, in dedicating the *Annotationi* to Châteauneuf, Scipione Gentili subverted the official crusade ideology of the poem and pointed out its relevance for contemporary diplomacy. More specifically, for Gentili the *Liberata* prompted a reappraisal of the scholastic doctrine of just war and an examination of the notion of bilateral justice, which during armed conflicts respected both parties as equals, regardless of their faith. As Alberico Gentili argued in the *De legationibus,* presumably alluding to the conflicts between the Tudors and the papacy, it was permissible to exchange ambassadors even with excommunicated sovereigns, since diplomacy should never cease for religious reasons.[108] In the *Liberata* and in the *Messaggiero,* the Italian Protestant refugees found a crucial lens through which to comment on the problems posed by cross-confessional diplomacy in Reformation Europe. Far from celebrating the Counter-Reformation fight against heresy, Tasso's ambivalent representation of the first crusade prompted readers to imagine new diplomatic practices necessary in a Europe marked by a plurality of orthodoxies and religious truths.

Chapter 6

READING VENETIAN *Relazioni*

After Leopold von Ranke recovered them in the nineteenth century, the *relazioni* of the Venetian ambassadors shaped the rise of diplomatic history, coming to be regarded as "the essential expression of diplomatic activity" or even as "artworks of political culture."[1] While Ranke and his followers considered the relazioni neutral archival sources that allowed the historian to reconstruct the past *"wie es eigentlich gewesen"* (as it really happened), more recently scholars have demonstrated that the reports of the Venetian ambassadors were in fact "highly filtered, deeply pondered texts . . . elaborated and rewritten with caution and attention," which said only what the senate permitted to be said, often censoring contemporary events and distorting the image of other cultures.[2] As scholars of early modern Orientalism have pointed out, the relazioni on the Ottoman Empire—because of their prejudices and Veneto-centric views—have more to say about the observer, and his practice of representation, than the observed.[3] Though there have been numerous studies on the relazioni, little consideration has been given to their significant early modern circulation and to the ways they contributed to the spread of knowledge of international affairs beyond courts and governments. Indeed, despite the fact that they were originally made for the exclusive use of the Venetian Senate, relazioni were frequently copied, forged, and sold by individuals who profited from the expanding market for political information.[4]

Focusing on the manuscript miscellanies of Giacomo Castelvetro (1546–1616), a religious refugee in Elizabethan England closely associated with Alberico and Scipione Gentili (two figures discussed in the previous chapter), the following pages explore the ways in which Italian Protestant refugees accessed and appropriated Venetian relazioni. Drawing on the methods of book history and the history of reading, this chapter examines the material form in which Castelvetro encountered the reports of the Venetian ambassadors as well as the copious reading notes that he added in the margins. In this way, the chapter demonstrates first that Castelvetro did not simply copy diplomatic reports but instead carefully edited and manipulated them, opting for the manuscript medium over print because of its greater flexibility. Second, it shows that he appropriated the relazioni according to his own religious beliefs, using them as historical sources—long before Ranke's archival turn—to reconstruct the "secret history" of the Council of Trent. Finally, the marginal notes also offer insight into the political ideas of the Italian Protestant refugees who, combining Niccolò Machiavelli's republicanism with an Erastian conception of the relationship between church and state, argued that the only way to put an end to the European religious strife and to promote religious toleration was to strengthen the authority of civil powers over ecclesiastical matters. It was for this very reason that in his annotations Castelvetro saw the Ottoman Empire in a positive light—a place where, unlike confessional Europe, different faiths were tolerated and religion remained strictly under the control of the state.

From Modena to Edinburgh

Having fled his native city of Modena at the age of eighteen on June 4, 1564, Castelvetro headed first toward Lyon and then to Geneva, where he reached his "most learned" (*letteratissimo*) uncle Ludovico, the famous Renaissance philologist, translator of Aristotle as well as of Melanchthon, who was already in exile as a result of his religious ideas: "At the age of eighteen my brother Lelio and I departed on June 4 [1564] from the aforementioned city on a mule, hidden in two baskets, and in this way we went to Lyon on the Rhône to the house of the illustrious and very prosperous merchants Messer Nicolò and Messer Girolamo Pellicciari. . . . From there we continued on to Geneva, where I encountered the most learned Lord Ludovico Castelvetro, my paternal uncle."[5]

Castelvetro's religious beliefs and his resulting decision to flee Italy matured within a family that was profoundly affected by the Reformation. In particular, the influence of Ludovico on Giacomo can hardly be overestimated. In the rich library of his uncle, which included a wide selection of Protestant authors, the young Giacomo first encountered the texts that convinced him to break off from the Catholic Church.[6] Among these were the works of Erasmus of Rotterdam, whom Castelvetro regarded not only as the champion of European humanism, "a man of very deep learning" (*huomo di saver molto profondo*), but also as a religious reformer, who in the *Colloquies* "with the purity of his Latin tongue" (*con la purità della sua latina lingua*) taught his readers "the purity of the true religion of God" (*la purità della vera religione di Dio*).[7] Following Ludovico in the wanderings of exile, Castelvetro arrived in Basel, where in 1568 he matriculated at the university. Years later in the same city he would begin his career as editor of vernacular texts working in the printshop of Pietro Perna, for whom he edited *Le rime del Petrarca brevemente sposte per Lodovico Castelvetro* (The Poems of Petrarch Briefly Interpreted by Lodovico Castelvetro), an edition of Petrarch's *Canzoniere* and *Trionfi* with a commentary by his uncle Ludovico.[8]

In 1573 Castelvetro arrived in England, where his ambiguous confessional identity alarmed the authorities, who suspected he might be an "'Arriane' and hold strange opinions," disputing the divinity of Christ, or, in fact, a "Jesuit," and therefore possibly involved in one of the Catholic conspiracies to overthrow Elizabeth I.[9] Yet despite his nonconformist religious views, Castelvetro was able to make a successful career as translator, editor, and language teacher. Along with John Florio, the lexicographer famous for his dictionaries and for his translation of Montaigne's *Essais*, Castelvetro played a fundamental role in the diffusion of the Italian Renaissance in England and Scotland. Collaborating with the London publisher John Wolfe, Castelvetro edited works by Niccolò Machiavelli, Pietro Aretino, Giovan Battista della Porta, Torquato Tasso, and Giovanni Battista Guarini.[10] In 1589 he also edited *De iure belli*, the influential treatise on the law of nations composed by his fellow reformer Alberico Gentili, regius professor of civil law at Oxford, whose ideas about sixteenth-century diplomacy have been discussed in the previous chapter.[11]

Castelvetro shared with Gentili not only the experience of the religious refugee but also a conception of the relationship between church and state directly inspired by the work of the Swiss scholar Thomas Lüber, better known as Erastus. Both Castelvetro and Gentili believed that the civil magistrate was the ultimate authority on both secular and religious affairs and that the only legitimate change of religion must be decided by the prince and implemented progressively, as had happened in Germany with Luther and in England with Henry VIII.[12] This conviction put them in direct conflict with the Calvinist church and with English Puritans. Indeed, in 1589, Castelvetro published for John Wolfe the *editio princeps* of Erastus's treatise against excommunication, *Explicatio gravissimae quaestionis utrum Excommunicatio . . . mandato nitatur Divino, an excogitata sit ab hominibus* (Explanation of the Most Serious Matter of Whether Excommunication . . . Is Based Upon Divine Mandate or Has Been Devised by Men).[13] As the *Explicatio* also included the material relating to the dispute between Erastus and the Calvinist theologian Theodore Beza, Castelvetro's edition aroused intense controversy within Protestant Europe, making clear that the attack against excommunication was directed not only at the Catholic doctrine of papal power, but first and foremost at the Calvinist Presbyterian model of church organization.[14]

As a teacher of Italian Castelvetro had many illustrious students, including the Scottish king James VI/I, the future defender of the divine right of kings, who must have sympathized with the Erastian ideas of his preceptor. Dedicating to the Scottish king in 1592 his translation of Charles V's instructions to his son Philip II, Castelvetro flaunted his several intellectual talents, from his linguistic expertise to his knowledge of European affairs.[15] Castelvetro's keen ability to provide his patrons with intelligence and learning allowed him to establish strong connections with the courts in both Edinburgh and London, starting with the secretary of state Robert Cecil, who in 1598 listed Castelvetro among his informants.[16]

The Scribe as Author

Castelvetro's role as "professional of intelligence" can be reconstructed through the examination of his many manuscript miscellanies, today dispersed among different libraries in Britain, Europe, and North America and only partially examined by scholars.[17] They provide substantial insights into the reading and writing habits of a Renaissance intelligencer who copied and sold texts for profit, exploiting the expanding market for political information. The collection includes copies of works by numerous early modern political writers, from Francesco Guicciardini to Tommaso Campanella, Alfonso de Valdés to Antonio Pérez, and Edwin Sandys to James VI/I. Among them are also ten miscellaneous volumes, consisting mostly of Venetian relazioni—the final reports presented by Venetian ambassadors to the senate at the end of their mission.[18] They were copied between 1594 and 1595, when Castelvetro moved to Denmark and later to Sweden. In Copenhagen he benefited from the extensive library of the Danish ambassador Christian Barnekow, whom he had met in Scotland at the celebration of the baptism of James VI/I's son Henry. Having studied in Siena and Padua, Barnekow owned a large collection of Italian political manuscripts that Castelvetro copied and then rearranged in his miscellanies.[19] This section looks at Castelvetro's miscellanies specifically to show how, rather than simply copying Venetian relazioni, he instead edited them attentively, rearranging the texts by taking advantage of the flexibility of the manuscript medium.

By the end of the sixteenth century, relazioni had already begun to appear in print collections, such as the *Thesoro politico* (The Political Treasure), published in Paris in 1589.[20] That Castelvetro clearly had the *Thesoro politico* in mind while editing his anthology is evident from the frequent overlaps in the contents of the two collections. Both include several of the same ambassadorial reports on Italy and the Ottoman Empire as well as texts on reason of state and on papal conclaves, beginning with Scipione di Castro's *Avvertimenti a Marco Antonio Colonna* (Advice for Marco Antonio Colonna, 1589) and Francesco Lottini's *Discorso sopra le attioni del conclave* (Discourse on the Actions of the Conclave, 1589). Yet, despite the similarities with the *Thesoro politico*, Castelvetro followed a different editorial strategy, well aware of the advantages of circulating texts through the manuscript medium. As Harold Love famously demonstrated, manuscripts continued to play a crucial role after the spread of printing, because of their greater speed and confidentiality, and the possibility to offer readers privileged access to a text.[21] Written for the most part in a clean hand and containing title pages, tables of contents, headings, colophons, and marginalia, Castelvetro's miscellanies were intended to appeal to readers in their form as well as in their content.

Given the extensive experience he had acquired as editor of vernacular and Latin books between England and the continent, Castelvetro knew very well how to manipulate texts. Using these talents, in his miscellanies he did not just copy the relazioni but instead fragmented and reconstituted them, often selecting only what he found relevant and adding a new paratextual apparatus—including extensive and systematic marginal annotations—that altered their original meaning considerably. As historians of the book have demonstrated, for humanistically trained individuals reading was a "goal oriented activity," always an active rather than a passive pursuit, marked by a creative interaction between texts and their readers.[22] For example, in copying Bernardo Navagero's *relazione* on Rome (1558), Castelvetro did not reproduce the complete report but deliberately extracted only the sections regarding the procedure of papal conclaves and the double nature of the "papal prince," who was both the temporal prince of a state and the universal pastor of Christianity.[23] In so doing he detached the *relazione* from its original context and transformed it into a pamphlet against Paul IV, whose pontificate, marked by the promulgation of the first Roman Index and the reinforcement of the Holy Office, Castelvetro viewed as evidence of the transformation of the Roman Church into a papal monarchy. Again, transcribing Paolo Tiepolo's report on Spain (1563), Castelvetro abridged the text and focused on the section on the New World that described "those Indies . . . which, while navigating through the ocean toward the West, were found just a few years later, and where there was found much silver and gold and many other new things, that filled Europe with riches and marvels."[24] Castelvetro was thus manipulating, more than transcribing, ambassadorial records, often turning the content of the relazioni against the Roman Church and the Spanish monarchy.

In this respect Castelvetro's diplomatic miscellanies constitute a remarkable example of the role of the "scribe as co-author of the text" enabled by the malleability of handwritten texts.[25] Several scholars have noted that scribal publication allowed texts to be rearranged and newly combined to such an extent that the roles of the reader and the producer were often intertwined.[26] This is already visible in Castelvetro's title pages, where he inserted not only place and date but also added an inscription with his own name and a verse from the first book of the *Aeneid*, "*forsan et haec olim meminisse iuvabit*" (maybe the day will come when even this will be joy to remember).[27]

In juxtaposing the *Aeneid* and the relazioni of the Venetian ambassadors Castelvetro was probably aware of the role that Virgil played in the ideology of "the myth of Venice," that claimed a Trojan origin for the Italian Republic and presented Venice as the new Rome.[28] The reference to

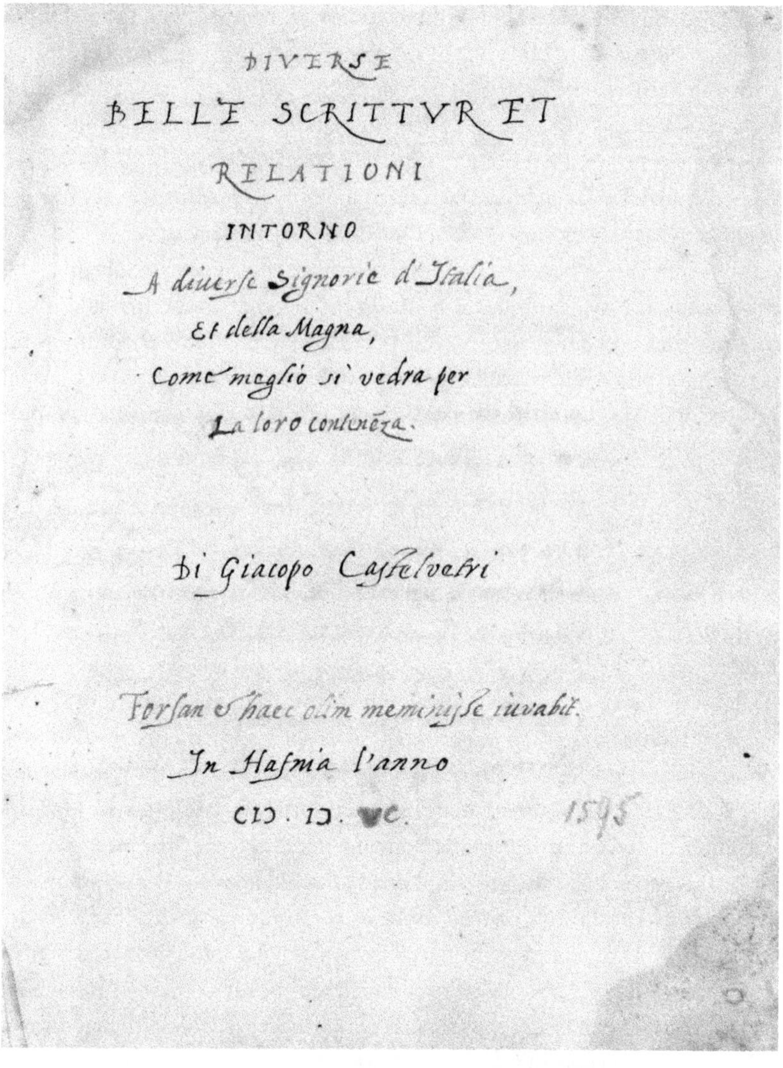

DIVERSE

BELLE SCRITTVR ET

RELATIONI

INTORNO

A diuerse Signorie d'Italia,

Et della Magna,

Come meglio si vedra per

La loro contenéza.

Di Giacopo Castelvetri

Forsan & haec olim meminisse iuvabit.

In Hafnia l'anno

CIƆ. IƆ. VC.

1595

Figure 6. Giacomo Castelvetro, *Diverse belle scritture et relationi intorno a diverse signorie d'Italia e della Magna*, Copenhagen 1585 (Newberry Library, Chicago: MS Vault Case 5086, vol. 116/2).

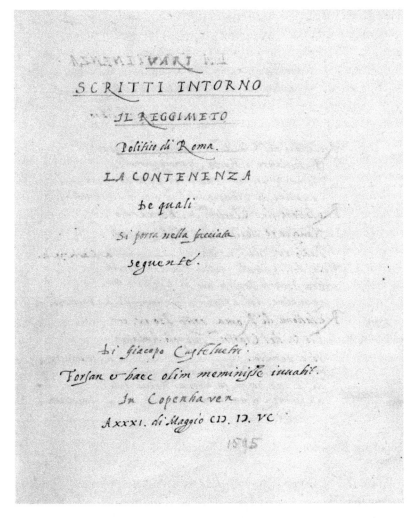

Figure 7. Giacomo Castelvetro, *Vari scritti intorno il reggimento politico di Roma*, Copenhagen, May 1595 (Newberry Library, Chicago: MS Vault Case 5086, vol. 59/2).

the *Aeneid* might have also pointed more broadly to the relevance of ancient epic for Renaissance diplomacy. Virgil of course furnished Renaissance readers with many episodes rich in diplomatic themes, among them Illioneus's embassy to Latinus requesting hospitality for the wandering Trojans, recounted in the seventh book of the poem and appropriated also by

Tasso in the *Messaggiero*.[29] On the other hand, the citation likely had a personal meaning for Castelvetro. Taken from Aeneas's speech aimed at encouraging the Trojans by reminding them that Troy was destined to rise again in Italy, it would have resonated deeply with a religious refugee who had been forced to leave his homeland and reestablish himself in a foreign country.

Regardless of the specific meaning Castelvetro assigned to Virgil's line, it seems clear that by inscribing each title page with his name and his Latin motto, he intended first and foremost to personalize his anthology, underlining his ownership over the texts there included and thus claiming for himself a semi-authorial status greater than that of a simple scribe. As he clarified in a miscellaneous volume of the anthology entitled *Selva di varie nobili scritture* (Forest of Many Noble Writings), he was not interested in producing a faithful copy of the reports of the Venetian ambassadors; instead he read them selectively, extracting only what was "worth remembering" in order to prepare a "pleasant apparatus that serves on the matters of state" and to shed light on the new Renaissance diplomatic practices.[30]

Moreover, the extent to which Castelvetro manipulated the texts of the *relazioni* and the copiousness of his marginal notes constitute further evidence of the fact that his miscellanies were not conceived for private use but were rather at the center of a "knowledge transaction," a working relationship established between a professional reader and his patrons through the exchange of learning and intelligence.[31]

Reading *Relazioni* through Machiavelli

While a few of Castelvetro's miscellanies have received critical attention, the copious reading notes he added in the margins have been almost entirely ignored by scholars.[32] Yet what makes the miscellanies remarkable is precisely the presence of Castelvetro's marginalia, which offer a rare view of the diplomatic culture of the Italian religious refugees and the ways in which they appropriated the reports of the Venetian ambassadors. This and the following sections examine Castelvetro's marginal notes to shed light on his use of the relazioni to unmask the "secret history" of the Council of Trent.

Along with corrections and editorial interventions, Castelvetro added in the margins personal observations on contemporary events and cross-reference notes to the texts that he consulted while reading the diplomatic

Dell'Apparotto.

Entrata, Spesa, Pace, Guerra, Guar=
die, Vittoriaglie, e Leggi.

Entrata.

Come non hauendone, ne habbia ⎧ Come non hauendone
a trovare. ⎨ a sufficienza, se ne
⎩ possa trovare.

STESA

Che veglia. non enim solum ⎧ S'habbia fatte spe=
ions amplificando, sed etiã, ⎨ se grandi, ouero
sumptus parum necessarios de- ⎨ picciole.
trahere, ait Artes. lib VI. Reth. ⎩

DELLA GVERRA.

⎧ Le forze ch'egli puo met=
⎪ tere insieme, e'l modo
⎪ tenuto in metterle sia
⎪ simigliante al nostro.
Le forze, che si ritrouaua in essere ⎨ Le guerre, che per l'adie-
la guerre, che prima s'hab- ⎨ tro habbia fatte, e la
bia fatte. Le forze de ⎨ riuscita loro, qual simi-
Nimici. ⎪ glianza habbiano co le nr̃a.
⎩

Della

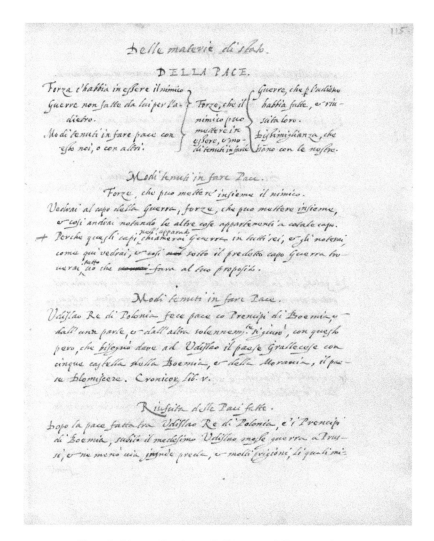

Figure 9. Giacomo Castelvetro, *Dell'Apparato delle materie di stato*
(Butler Library, New York: MS Western 32, 115r).

reports. These contain references to both ancient and Renaissance authors, from Aristotle to Polybius, and Lorenzo Valla to Francesco Guicciardini. The most frequently cited name in the reading notes is, however, that of Niccolò Machiavelli. It was through the author of *The Prince,* one of the harshest critics of the myth of Venice, that Castelvetro appropriated the reports of the

Venetian ambassadors. Castelvetro had a deep familiarity with Machiavelli. During the 1580s he had assisted the English printer John Wolfe in publishing Machiavelli's works in London. As his annotations made clear, Castelvetro shared the republican reading of Machiavelli held by Alberico Gentili and other Italian philo-Protestants for whom *The Prince* intended only on the surface to advise the tyrant while in fact enabling his readers to unmask the secrets of early modern politics.[33]

In Castelvetro's diplomatic anthology, references to Machiavelli at times clarify the meaning of the relazioni. Copying and reading Marco Foscari's famous report on the Florentine Republic (1527), for example, Castelvetro drew a family tree of the Medici on the back of the page and wrote, "You should check Machiavelli to understand why this tree is drawn."[34] Annotating Marino Cavalli's *relazione* on France (1547), he advised consulting the twelfth chapter of *The Prince* to find a gloss on the Venetian ambassador's remark that instead of using mercenaries it was preferable to "make one's own subjects into a good and disciplined army."[35] On other occasions Castelvetro's more detailed comments reveal the facets of his own reading of Machiavelli. While annotating Tommaso Sassetti's account of the Saint Bartholomew's Day massacre, he defended Machiavelli from the accusation of being ideologically responsible for the slaughter of the Huguenots by arguing that Gaspard de Coligny could have escaped from his murderers if he had read "the wise Machiavelli, who says that one should never trust the tyrant who has been offended even once."[36] Castelvetro further added in the margin that it was wrong to attribute to Machiavelli the idea that princes should be absolved from keeping their promises, for his portrait of the prince was meant only to open the eyes of his fellow citizens to the dangers of tyranny:[37]

> They attribute this wickedness to the honest Machiavelli, who does not say that this behavior is appropriate to the natural and good prince, but rather to the new prince who aims to tyrannize the free man, mortal enemy of every tyrannical government, like those that he saw rise as tyrants in his free city of Florence. He wrote this so that the Florentine people would know how different it is to live free rather than being subjected to the rule of a tyrant, and so that with magnificent virtue and bravery, the city might defend its ancient and beloved freedom.

This was not the only time that Castelvetro formulated a staunch republican defense of Machiavelli. While annotating the *Monarchia di Spagna*

(Monarchy of Spain) by the Italian philosopher Tommaso Campanella, Castelvetro accused the author of not having properly understood Machiavelli, who was not the preceptor of tyrants but on the contrary a republican thinker, who had described the prince to attack the Medici's despotic rule:[38]

> It is clear that this good monk did not understand Machiavelli, who would not be called impious, as he had an excellent and holy doctrine, which he used to bring awareness to his free citizens, among whom he saw born the usurper of their precious freedom. Rather, to make every tyrant odious to them he chose Borgia, as the most impious and cruel, who had already risen up as the new Prince of the land, so that the blind Florentines would open their eyes wider and hate all the more the arriving or rising usurper of their beloved liberty. And one sees that this is the case here, as when he speaks of the natural and good prince, he says that he must follow and observe his own just laws.

In the wake of Machiavelli Castelvetro also paid special attention to the political use of religion. According to the Italian Protestant refugees Machiavelli offered crucial insight into the religious crisis of Renaissance Italy and the responsibilities of the papacy in the Italian wars. As Machiavelli's *Discourses on Livy* state, while in Germany there were still the ancient "goodness" and "religion," which "make many republics there live free,"[39] in Italy the Roman Church had dissolved any true religious faith, "for as where there is religion one presupposes every good, so where it is missing one presupposes the contrary. Thus we Italians have this first obligation to the Church and to the priests that we have become without religion and wicked."[40] As is well-known, Machiavelli also considered the Church responsible for the political fragmentation of Renaissance Italy and for having kept the country divided, as "truly no province has ever been united or happy unless it has all come under obedience to one republic or to one prince, as happened to France and to Spain."[41] It is this famous chapter of the *Discourses* that Castelvetro was thinking of while annotating Paolo Tiepolo's *relazione* on Rome: "Rarely has it happened that barbarian soldiers have come to disturb the peace of Italy without being invited or called, or even forced to come, by the Popes, and then they dare to call themselves the Vicars of Christ, or the successors of Peter, being the Devil, the father of all conflict, discord, and war."[42]

Moving beyond Machiavelli, Castelvetro used Venetian relazioni to examine ecclesiastical principalities, a form of government *The Prince* famously refused to address, arguing that it would be presumptuous to discuss them since they are maintained by God.[43] As the following pages show, Castelvetro read the reports of the Venetian ambassadors in the effort to understand the double nature of the "papal prince," secular ruler of a state and at the same time universal pastor of Christianity.

The Council and the "Papal Prince"

One of the most annotated volumes among Castelvetro's miscellanies is entitled *Vari scritti intorno il reggimento politico di Roma* (Various Writings on the Political Government of Rome), dated May 31, 1595. In addition to several Venetian relazioni, the volume also contains other political texts, including Cosimo de' Medici's *Parere sulla corte di Roma* (Report on the Court of Rome).[44] The tension between the text and the reading notes is striking here, as in the marginalia Castelvetro turns Cosimo's praise of the papal court into a violent attack against the Roman papacy. Near the beginning, where Cosimo had argued that the Roman court was "the holiest, the most noble and the most illustrious," governed by the "true vicar of God, and legitimate successor of Saint Peter, and universal Patriarch, and omnipotent Lord of the world, to whom all we lords and Princes, of every state, are subjects," Castelvetro rebutted in the margin that "according to this Prince and all the papists, the Pope is the Omnipotent Lord of the world. In which case it follows that he is the great Devil, the true mouth of Christ having said more than once that the Prince of this world is the Devil."[45] Again, in the same volume Castelvetro's notes point out that the Reformation had revealed the true nature of the papacy, identifying the bishop of Rome as the Antichrist: "There have been some truly impudent flatterers, who have dared to say that all states, and all governments, are subject to the Pope, but one should not be surprised if true reformed Catholic Christians, without any fear of His wrath, nor his tyrannical strength, have said to him openly that he was the true son of the great Devil, who when tempting Christ said that all the governments of the world were his and that he could give them to whoever adored him, or who pleased him."[46]

With these words, Castelvetro was echoing the identification of the Roman Church with the Antichrist that had spread among the Italian reformers in the wake of Luther as well as through the writings of Bernardino

Ochino and Celio Secondo Curione.[47] In 1566, the Italian Calvinist Giovanni Battista Trento gave this conviction a remarkable visual representation in the *Mappe-monde nouvelle papistique*, whose allegorical map situates Rome in the devil's mouth and depicts Charon crossing the Acheron with an additional boat to fit the crowd of popes and cardinals destined for Hell.[48]

As the examination of the other annotations makes clear, however, Castelvetro was not interested in repeating a trite commonplace of Protestant propaganda. In his marginalia, the corruption of the papacy is presented as the historical outcome of a lengthy process that culminated in the Council of Trent. Throughout his copy of Antonio Soriano's report on Rome (1535) Castelvetro underlined the passages describing the fearful reactions that Luther's call for a general council produced in the papal curia, pointing out that "the fear of seeing with the council change *in capite et in membris*" was "the reason for which Leo X and later Clement VII avoided permitting a free council": "It is well-known to everyone that the idea of a council began to be debated many years ago, in the time of Leo X . . . but the fear of seeing with the council change in capite as in membris was the reason that, to escape the affair of the council, the most reverend Cardinal of San Sisto, legate to Germany, was easily persuaded to become the right instrument in seeing this need, the results of which the world can bear good witness to."[49]

As a result, the religious crisis was initially handled by the cardinal legate Tommaso De Vio, but according to Castelvetro, despite the fact that he was highly learned, he was so unskilled at politics that he did more damage than good for papal interests.[50] Nothing changed with Clement VII, who, harboring the same fears, held off opening the council for as long as he could.[51] Paul III stood out as remarkably different, as one who "with regard to the council, proceeded differently from Clement, because Clement was afraid, and he neither could nor knew how to hide it. On the contrary, Paul proceeded more astutely, because he never revealed his fear of the council."[52] As Castelvetro indicated in the margin, Paul III "pretended publicly that he wanted the council, but secretly detested it."[53] By dissimulating his real intentions Paul III succeeded in taking control of the council and subordinating it to what had been previously decided in Rome:

> [Paul III] holds that, with regard to the future council, it is appropriate to discuss but not to act; believing that, if any council should take place, it would only be in that manner and form which I described, having settled first every

matter in Rome and <u>decided according to the will of the pope</u> (*This is a fine council*) and the cardinals, and then presented it to the council to be approved, without further discussion . . . It is clear to those who rightly judge, that the council does not <u>suit His Holiness</u> nor perhaps the See. (*Please note that Soriano has a long nose with which he can sniff deeply*).[54]

The same view was formulated by the famous Venetian scholar Paolo Sarpi in the *History of the Council of Trent,* where he argued that Paul III "of all his virtues . . . esteemed most highly dissimulation."[55] Castelvetro shared with Sarpi, whom he met in Venice during the Interdict, not only his convictions on Paul III and the council specifically but also a general interpretation of history as the reign of hypocrisy and dissimulation, in which the protagonists always masked their intentions and the real causes were never transparent.[56] The history of the council was a perfect example of this theory, since in Trent, as Castelvetro saw it, religion was only a pretext to veil the political will of the popes. In addition, the examination of the conclaves revealed that the history of the Church was entirely secular and that the Holy Spirit, as Castelvetro often added in the margins, had no role in papal elections. As has been pointed out with regard to Sarpi, this conception of history was a reaction against the humanist tradition and was grounded in the belief that only by privileging official documents over speeches and orations was it possible to penetrate the hidden causes of past events.[57] In this respect, Castelvetro's marginalia can be considered an attempt to use the reports of the Venetian ambassadors to write a "secret history" of the council, contributing to the rise of a new historical genre that was destined to become highly popular in the age of *arcana imperii* and reason of state.[58] Long before the nineteenth-century "archival turn", Castelvetro already used relazioni as historical sources, judging them to be indispensable tools in exposing the real nature of the Counter-Reformation papacy.[59]

By annotating the texts included in his anthology, Castelvetro intended to shed light on what happened in Trent behind the scenes and to understand how the papacy was able to modify the balance of power and impose itself on the other Italian states. For this reason, in the Venetian relazioni he attentively annotated the passages describing the "two souls" of the papal prince, a temporal sovereign who was at the same time universal pastor of all Christendom.[60] As the Venetian ambassador Bernardo Navagero explained, the pope was not like the other princes and must "be regarded in two ways: as prince of the temporal state, which he holds, and as pope because of his spiritual authority."[61] Again, while annotating the report by Paolo Tiepolo, Castelvetro carefully underlined the passages on the double nature of the papal prince: "[The popes] are in no way like other common princes; since through the Person, whom they represent on earth, it seems that they exceed the human condition, and therefore they are not just like other princes who have jurisdiction over lives and properties of men, but they claim authority over the whole world, even in the states belonging to other rulers, at least in spiritual matters."[62]

This is, perhaps unsurprisingly, one of the most copiously annotated passages in Castelvetro's anthology. In the margin, after referring to Lorenzo Valla's famous rebuttal of the Donation of Constantine ("if you would like to see the truth of that see L. Valla on the Falsely [Believed and Forged] Donation"), Castelvetro contrasted the poverty of the primitive Church with the corruption of his present time, accusing the popes of being nothing but secular rulers who fought with other princes for the possession of Italy:[63]

> Note how the early Church until 300 years after the death of Christ always lived on charity, without ever possessing any estate or property. During that entire time, then, the Church was good and true, but then after it began to own goods, it immediately became corrupt.
>
> . . .
>
> The bishops of Rome, the poorest and meekest of the world, have become powerful and fight with the Emperors for dominance over Italy.

Castelvetro's effort to deconstruct the figure of the papal prince was not just the expression of an anti-Roman polemic. Tracing the growing strength of the papacy in the years of the Council of Trent was in fact essential for understanding sixteenth-century politics and the new balance of power between Rome and the European states. As the following chapter clarifies, this was a problem destined to remain at the height of Castelvetro's concerns also later in his life, when the oath of allegiance imposed over English subjects by his patron James I in January 1606 and the implementation of the Venetian Interdict in April of the same year reopened the controversy over the pope's authority in deposing secular rulers.

Along with several Venetian relazioni on the Roman court, Castelvetro also included in the same volume the *Discorso sopra la corte di Roma* (Discourse on the Court of Rome) by the papal nunzio and Cardinal Giovanni Francesco Commendone, well-known to Castelvetro's family and a correspondent of Ludovico and his brother Giovanni Maria even after their escape from Italy.[64] His *Discorso* was never printed but nonetheless benefited from a wide scribal circulation in the early modern period.[65] Once again Castelvetro fragmented and rearranged the text, dividing it into sections and adding new titles and marginalia. The notes indicate that turning Commendone's *Discorso* into an antipapal pamphlet was not his only goal, but that he was in fact returning his focus to the figure of the papal prince to further demonstrate in what respect the head of the Roman court was different from other sovereigns.[66]

Indeed, Castelvetro showed particular interest for the sections of the text dealing with the elective nature of the papal monarchy. As scholars have pointed out, this policy had important consequences for the Roman court, where the patronage system was continually dismantled and reorganized and posts were redistributed more frequently and with a higher degree of social mobility than in secular monarchies.[67] According to Commendone, as no hereditary succession existed in Rome, each election marked a sharp change with the past and this explained the peculiarity of the "papal prince," who, unlike secular rulers, had two souls but only one body. Having highlighted the passage explaining that "upon the death of the Pope everything <u>is immediately sent into tumult</u>, and the tumults lead to schisms," Castelvetro reiterated in the margin: "Upon the death of the pope everything is sent into tumult until schisms arise."[68] On a following page he annotated Commendone's comments about the alterations that marked the life of the papal state, in which the new sovereign is often radically different from his predecessor as in all elective monarchies: "As happens in republics, which all sooner or later change and pass from one form of state to another because of the natural shift of practices that occurs in cities, it likewise for the same reason happens in principalities and even more abruptly in those elective, because with admirable effort the successors are created of different nature than their predecessors."[69]

Commendone's description of the variability of the Roman court became a commonplace in early modern political literature, and its echo can be found again in the other texts included in Castelvetro's anthology. While repeating that in Rome "it seems that nothing can last at length in a state, because just as the air is inconstant, so Rome seems more prone to change than any other place," Tiepolo's *relazione* had pointed out that the popes "think that the further they distance themselves from the habits of their Predecessor, the more success they will have," and as a result the new pope often repealed the decision of the previous one.[70] Castelvetro annotated in the margin that this was the reason for the execution of "the gentle Carnesecchi," who after being absolved by Pius IV was sentenced to death by his successor Pius V.[71] In Castelvetro's opinion, the fate of Pietro Carnesecchi illustrated perfectly the outcome of Trent, highlighting the victory of the Inquisition over the council, and the waning of the expectations of religious reform.[72]

Learning from the Sublime Porte

Despite the special attention given to the Council of Trent, Castlvetro's anthology was not limited to confessional Europe and a whole volume collected relazioni on the Ottoman Empire. Like the Venetian ambassadors he regarded the Ottoman state as a major player in international politics, as its spatial extension spanning from the Mediterranean to the Indian Ocean made it the heir of the ancient Roman Empire.[73] This section examines the marginalia that Castelvetro added to the Venetian reports on Constantinople and argues that in attacking the Tridentine Church Castelvetro ultimately came to perceive Islam positively, as an example of a civic religion that allowed different faiths to coexist. This conviction was largely the result of Castelvetro's reading of the Quran, which he owned in the Italian translation published in Venice in 1547.[74]

Like other late sixteenth-century Italian political treatises directly influenced by relazioni, from the *Thesoro politico* to Giovanni Botero's *Relazioni universali* (Universal Relations, 1591), Castelvetro's diplomatic anthology used the reports of the Venetian ambassadors to study politics in a comparative perspective.[75] By collecting relazioni not solely on Rome and the Italian states, but also on the Holy Roman Empire, Spain, Portugal, France, England, and the Ottoman Empire, Castelvetro's diplomatic miscellanies compared different governments within and outside of Europe. As Castelvetro stressed in the volume on the Ottoman Empire, a comprehensive knowledge of geography was indispensable for understanding the complex politics of the Mediterranean. Only with the help of a cartographic apparatus, namely with a recent edition of Ptolemy's *Geography* updated with modern maps, was it

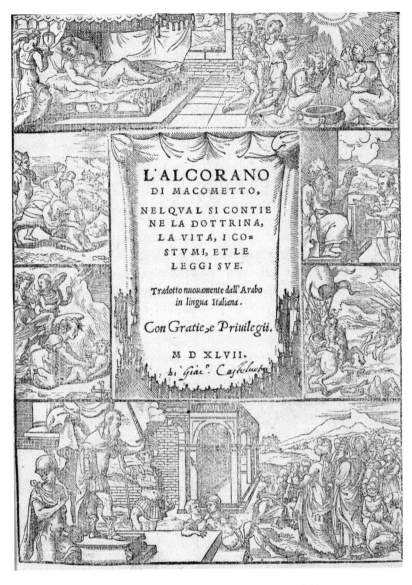

L'ALCORANO
DI MACOMETTO,

NELQVAL SI CONTIE
NE LA DOTTRINA,
LA VITA, I CO=
STVMI, ET LE
LEGGI SVE.

Tradotto nuouamente dall' Arabo
in lingua Italiana.

Con Gratie, e Priuilegii.

M D XLVII.

Figure 10. Giacomo Castelvetro's copy of *The Alcorano di Macometto*
(Copenhagen, Det Kongelige Bibliotek: 28, 270).

possible to profit from reading the copious Renaissance literature on the Turks: "The important thing is to read them in order, beginning with the most ancient, and following epoch by epoch, place by place, paying diligent attention to the maps of Ptolemy and the moderns, because without this designation and distinction there is no profit."[76]

Most of the relazioni copied by Castelvetro in this volume date from the years around the Battle of Lepanto (1571) and include reports already available in print, such as Marco Antonio Barbaro's *Relatione di Costantinopoli* (Report on Constantinople) and Matteo Venieri's *Relatione dello stato presente del gran Turco* (Report on the Present State of the Great Turk), both published in the *Thesoro politico* (1589).[77] The majority of the marginalia present in the volume are summary notes that often repeat the observations of the relazioni on the moral and political corruption that affected the Sublime Porte. As Lucette Valensi has demonstrated, at the end of the century the reports of the Venetian ambassadors progressively shifted from the initial curiosity and admiration for the Ottomans to repugnance and hostility against an empire that came to represent the recently recovered notion of Oriental despotism.[78] More interesting, however, is the fact that at times Castelvetro added personal observations and commented on the relazioni in light of his own readings. From the examination of his notes it becomes clear that he was not interested in celebrating Lepanto as the Christians' victory over the infidels. On the contrary, he presented Rome's appeal against the Turks as a political move aimed more at establishing papal authority over the Christian states than at launching a new crusade to reconquer Constantinople. The very order in which he arranged the Venetian reports on Constantinople suggests a polemical attitude toward the papacy and a keen attention to the Ottomans. Indeed, the volume opens with the *relazione* by Marco Antonio Barbaro describing the secret negotiations between Venice and the Ottomans over a separate peace treaty against the Holy League. It continues with an analogous discourse by Mehmed Pasha to Sultan Murad III, which is summarized in the margin as an extract of Machiavellian wisdom: "With prudence states are maintained, and with astuteness and stratagems they are secured."[79] Castelvetro also praises the historical awareness of the Ottoman ruling class, who studied the past to gather useful advice for their present, observing that "following past examples is an excellent thing for the preservation of the state."[80]

Remarkably, among the texts that Castelvetro used in annotating the Venetian reports on the Ottomans was the *Alcorano di Macometto*, the Italian translation of the Quran published in Venice in 1547 with a dedication to the French ambassador to Constantinople, Gabriel d'Aramon. The Quran circulated widely among the Italian reformers, and Castelvetro might have first encountered the text in the Latin version by Theodor Bibliander, a copy of which was owned by his uncle Ludovico.[81] It has been observed that the *Alcorano di Macometto* is not a straightforward translation but a sophisticated rewriting, and that in abridging the text of the Quran it presents Muhammad as the "armed prophet" described by Machiavelli, a new prince who wielded religion as a tool of government.[82] The debt to Machiavelli is clear from the beginning of the text, which opens with an oration urging Muhammad to follow the example of the "great lords who, from humble beginnings with the favor of simulated religion, came to the highest office," reinforcing his power as "all the ancient hero-kings and rulers from the beginning of the world did, not having a more secure way of governing than the fear and awe of their feigned religion."[83]

The reading of the *Alcorano* led Castelvetro to consider carefully the political implications of Islam. In fact, its Machiavellian analysis of Islam in purely secular terms is echoed in several of Castelvetro's marginalia that pay particular attention to the relationship between the strong faith of the Ottomans and their military virtue. In his annotations on the *relazione* by Giacomo Soranzo, for whom the Turks "are very observant of their religion, very careful not to transgress, violate, or challenge it" and "speak of their prophet with the highest respect," to the point that "not only do they not blaspheme but neither does their language have words for blasphemy," Castelvetro remarks "this is indeed worthy of praise and it ought to cause we Christians to flush from perpetual shame."[84] A note on a following passage praises the Ottomans for their obedience to their superiors, which, being grounded in their sincere religiosity, highlighted the political strength of Islam: "They are extremely obedient to their lords, being convinced that disobeying them is to go against God's will (*And this is praiseworthy*)."[85] Looking at the Sublime Porte through Machiavelli and the *Alcorano*, Castelvetro moves beyond the prudent and allusive language of the Venetian ambassadors to comment explicitly on the religious foundation of the Ottoman Empire. While, as Machiavelli had pointed out, the corruption of the Roman Church had left the Italians without religion and politically divided, the Ottoman Empire appeared solid and powerful precisely because it was founded on an inclusive civic religion. In exchange for external obedience to the laws, the Sultan allowed everyone to profess his own faith: "He allows the peoples reduced to servitude to profess the religion of their choosing, fearing that they will become desperate <u>if forced into a new religion, and hoping</u> even to make them over time into Muslims (*In this the Sultan shows more goodness and wisdom than any Christian prince, or republic, with the exception of the Polish or the Transylvanian one*)."[86]

The example of the Ottoman Empire indicated that religious tolerance was not harmful but in fact favorable to the state, preventing civil strife and promoting conquest and expansion. According to Castelvetro, confessional Europe could take a lesson from the Turks, who allowed several religious minorities to exist and who refused to use violence against those subjects who professed a different faith. Such remarks on the virtues of the Ottomans were hardly accepted in Counter-Reformation Italy, where the humanist Turcophilia had been replaced by the military rhetoric of the "Christian soldier."[87] And yet, in early modern Venice, where Castelvetro would arrive in 1599—as discussed in the next chapter—such ideas on the Ottomans found favorable reception at times. The violent "war of words" that accompanied the Venetian Interdict of 1606–7, when Paul V excommunicated the doge and the senate, led several Venetian patricians, including Leonardo Donà and Niccolò Contarini, to esteem the Sublime Porte as a model to imitate in order to repel Rome's intrusion into the affairs of state.[88] In contrast to the Tridentine papacy and its attempt to use spiritual power for political purposes, the Ottoman Sultan came to represent not only the Machiavellian *"principe nuovo"* but also a powerful example of how to bring religion back under the control of the state.

Ultimately, Castelvetro's manuscript miscellanies prompt a reconsideration of Venetian relazioni, that historians have traditionally regarded as neutral archival sources able to reconstruct the past *"wie es eigentligh gewesen."* The profound impact that Ranke's "discovery" of the relazioni had on diplomatic history led scholars to neglect the ways in which diplomatic reports circulated and were appropriated by their previous readers, but Castelvetro's miscellanies offer new means for recovering the early modern uses of Venetian relazioni.[89]

Through Castelvetro's miscellanies it becomes apparent that diplomatic documents meant to be accessed only by government circles in fact enjoyed a wide circulation even outside the inner circles of power, reaching readers excluded from high politics, including religious refugees. The dissemination of relazioni was facilitated by the practice of scribal publication, through which readers became producers of new copies and scribes acted as coauthors, freely adapting and rearranging relazioni to serve different ideological agendas with little concern for preserving the original reports. Moreover, Castelvetro's ability to take advantage of the malleability of the manuscript medium to fragment and reconstitute the texts of the Venetian ambassadors shows that relazioni did not have a stable or fixed meaning but were instead highly flexible texts that circulated in multiple copies and material forms, from print to manuscript. Thus, the miscellanies call attention to the complex and creative interaction between diplomatic texts and their readers, who did not passively receive but rather actively appropriated them regardless of the intentions of the authors. To use the words of Michel de Certeau and Roger Chartier, it might be argued that, like other texts, diplomatic reports do not exist but for the readers who give them meaning.[90]

Castelvetro's miscellanies also reveal that long before Ranke's archival turn, relazioni were already used as historical sources, and that in the Renaissance their extensive circulation beyond government circles had a significant influence on the writing and reading of history. While the transformation of information into a commodity aroused skepticism about the very possibility of understanding the past, it also contributed to the emergence of new methods of reading history critically.[91] Collecting and annotating relazioni led Castelvetro to question the humanist tradition and to reconceive history not as a branch of rhetoric and a source of moral examples, but as a form of "unmasking" able to penetrate the secrets of early modern politics.[92] Finally, reading and appropriating the reports of the Venetian ambassadors enabled the Italian Protestant refugees not only to reconstruct the "secret history" of the Council of Trent but also to further elaborate their republican and Erastian convictions, for which only the strengthening of civil powers over religious affairs would put an end to the confessional strife and promote religious toleration.

Chapter 7

GREAT EXPECTATIONS

To the Brescian nobleman Giovanni Andrea Ugoni, a sympathizer of the Reformation, Venice appeared to be an "Italian Geneva." In his *Della dignità et eccellenza della gran città di Venetia* (On the Dignity and Excellence of the Great City of Venice), published in 1562, Ugoni appropriated expressions commonly used for Geneva to label Venice as a "city of God" (*città d'Iddio*), "holy city" (*città santa*), "that seems to be more a temple of God than a theater of the world" (*che pare più tosto uno tempio d'Iddio che uno teatro del mondo*).[1] Ugoni was echoing what had until shortly before then been a pervasive belief among the Italian philo-Protestants. In the 1540s Bernardino Ochino regarded Venice as "the gateway" of the Reformation in Italy, while Pier Paolo Vergerio and Baldassarre Altieri were convinced that it would be the Venetian ruling class to start the religious reform that they hoped for.[2] By the time Ugoni was writing, however, the distance between Venice and Protestant Europe had grown. The closure of the Council of Trent (1563) and the reorganization of the Inquisition under Pius V (1566–72) provided the Catholic Church with new tools for the repression of heresy and brought Italian Protestantism close to extinction. While during the 1540s and 1550s heresy had spread in Venice through the streets and squares, and theological matters could be discussed in the public arena, by the 1560s religious dissent had been forced into private spaces and had therefore progressively become an individual phenomenon. As the records of the Venetian Inquisition suggest, in the last decade of the century the Holy Office shifted its focus from heresy to other concerns, such as witchcraft, magic, and superstition.[3]

And yet the myth of Venice as the "Italian Geneva" did not suddenly disappear with the hardening of confessional boundaries. In fact, the myth survived well into the seventeenth century, when—perhaps for the last time—groups of Italian Protestant refugees still believed that the Reformation could be introduced into Italy through Venice. These were not just utopian dreams that arose within marginal groups removed from the centers of politics. On the contrary, upon closer examination they reveal themselves to be expectations grown out of the shifting diplomatic context in Europe and, specifically, of the reopening of formal diplomatic ties between England and Venice in 1603. After forty-four years, England reestablished the exchange of resident ambassadors with the Italian Republic, ending the suspension of diplomatic contact that had lasted through the entire reign of Elizabeth. James I's clash with Rome over the oath of allegiance (1606) and the support he gave to Venice during the Interdict (1606–7) convinced the Italian refugees that the Protestant cause in Italy could still count on England's support.[4] Not even the renowned prudence of James I—whom Sarpi considered "more resolute with his words than with his actions" (*ad scribendum quam ad agendum promptior*)—undermined these expectations, which found their political point of reference at the English court in Prince Henry, the leader of the more bellicose Protestant faction.[5] Only later did the death of Prince Henry in 1612 and the progressive movement of James toward Spain make it clear that the myth of Venice as an "Italian Geneva" was no longer supported by the reality of confessional Europe.

This chapter reexamines the reopening of Anglo-Venetian diplomacy in the early seventeenth century in two main ways. First, it discusses the attempt made by the English ambassador Henry Wotton to open his private chapel to local religious dissidents and to transform his embassy into a clandestine Protestant church. Second, the chapter reconstructs the role that Italian refugees played as English agents and propagandists in Venice. Less closely observed than resident ambassadors, they were able to operate with a higher degree of freedom, acting as intermediaries between the English embassy and the Venetian intelligentsia without directly involving official representatives. They proved especially effective as smugglers of prohibited books, which were intended to radicalize the widespread antipapal sentiments that emerged during the Interdict and to convince the republic to break with Rome.

The Embassy Reopens

On December 15, 1603, the Venetian ambassador to England, Niccolò Molin, informed the senate that James I had appointed as his representative to the republic Henry Wotton, whom he described as "an individual of the best quality, who has spent a long time in many courts in Italy."[6] Indeed, before he arrived in Venice in the summer of 1604, Wotton already had extensive experience with Italian affairs. After studying at Oxford in the 1580s, attending the lectures of Alberico Gentili, Wotton spent several years on the continent, traveling throughout the Holy Roman Empire and Italy. Between 1591 and 1593, Wotton visited Venice, Padua, Rome, and Naples, as well as Siena and Florence, the latter a city that he regarded as a "paradise inhabited with devils," and in this respect opposed to Venice, which "hath scarce heard of those vices which are here practised."[7] From Italy Wotton worked as informant for his English patrons, providing them with intelligence on international affairs in addition to rare publications. Writing to Edward, Lord Zouche in June 1592, Wotton declared that he had found in Florence "Machiavil's Tales, and certain other works of his, not commonly seen," while in November of the same year he informed his patron of the recent publications by the Jesuit scholar Antonio Possevino.[8] Wotton's work as intelligencer was soon noted in England and in 1594 he was appointed secretary of Robert Devereux, the second earl of Essex, the powerful and ambitious aristocrat, who in February 1601 tried unsuccessfully to overthrow Elizabeth I.[9] After the execution of Essex Wotton moved back to Italy, and while searching for new patrons, offered his service to the grand duke Ferdinando I de' Medici:[10]

> Although you do not lack sufficient servants or means, perhaps nonetheless occasions could arise in which you might avail yourself of a foreigner who would be less suspect in certain cases. For which reason I most humbly offer

myself if it might be useful to you to send me to any part of the world. And if I can be helpful in no other way to Your Highness . . . at least in those things which relate to the Kingdom of England and Scotland, and to the Princes in confederation with them, I will act as an interpreter of the truth through the practice and experience that I have had of them.

The offer was warmly accepted and Wotton served Ferdinando as diplomatic agent until 1603. Through Wotton the Medici court attentively followed the transition between the Tudors and the Stuarts, receiving information on the execution of Essex and the demise of his faction, as well as particulars on the character of James VI/I.[11] In the spring of 1601, Wotton also acted as intermediary in the epistolary exchanges between Ferdinando and Sir Anthony Sherley, the English nobleman who claimed to be the Persian ambassador sent to Europe by Shah Abbas.[12] Having been nominated English ambassador to Venice in 1603, Wotton did not interrupt his exchanges with the Medici, but continued to correspond with Ferdinando to keep an eye on the English community in Tuscany. As the only English resident ambassador in Italy he was responsible for the English subjects in all the ports of the peninsula, including Livorno.[13] Moreover, Florence was a particular cause of concern because of the English Catholic community that resided in the city. As he wrote to Robert Cecil in 1608, many English travelers were drawn to Florence because of the "beauty and security of the place, and purity of the language" but there risked encountering "a certain knot of bastard Catholics," led by Toby Matthew, the son of the archbishop of York, whose recent conversion to Catholicism had created controversy in England.[14]

Wotton's arrival in Venice in the summer of 1604 marked the return of the exchange of resident ambassadors between England and Venice that had ceased in 1559. On October 1, 1604, in his first audience with the Venetian Collegio, Wotton declared that he had been sent to Venice by James I, "because of the long-standing affection he holds for this most Serene Republic" (*per l'antica affettione che porta a questa Serenissima Repubblica*) as well as for "the desire to enjoy peace and friendship with all the Princes of Christendom" (*per il desiderio di haver pace, et amicitia con tutti i Principi della Christianità*).[15] The English ambassador, however, also clarified that, being a Protestant, he was bound to his conscience and could not live in Venice if he was not allowed to profess his own faith, at least privately, behind the walls of the embassy, located in the sestiere of Cannaregio next to the church of

San Girolamo and close to the Venetian ghetto.[16] Wotton explained that "he could not claim to live without practicing his religion but he truly promised that he would keep this practice to himself and to his entourage, without ever admitting into his house either the Flemish or the Germans, nor even the English who were not under his employ," adding that "the sermons would always be delivered in the English language, which is not understood by anyone who is not of that nation."[17]

Wotton's request did not come unexpectedly to the Venetian government. On August 27, 1603, the Venetian secretary Scaramelli had already informed the senate of his conversation with the English secretary of state Robert Cecil, who requested freedom of worship for the English ambassador in Venice.[18] According to Cecil, however, the English embassy and its chapel should also have been open to the many English in Venice and not only to Wotton's entourage. If the Venetian ambassador in London was allowed to celebrate the Catholic Mass in his residence for the other Italians in the city, the same right should have been granted to the English ambassador in Venice. Scaramelli replied that the republic would have certainly granted the English ambassador the right to profess his faith within his own residence, but if the embassy's chapel was potentially open to the large number of English and other Northern Protestant communities in Venice it risked troubling the diplomatic contact between the two states that had just been reestablished:[19]

> Though I might even have agreed that his Lordship the English Ambassador could do whatever he wished in his private home, I had to nonetheless tell his Lordship that it is not proportionate, because at this time in London there are no Venetians, with the exception of the two Federici brothers who are of very humble conditions, and six or seven other houses of Italians, who, if they could not hold their mass in the house of the Venetian ambassador would have held it instead in that of the French ambassador as they did until now, and on the other hand there are thousands of Englishmen in Venice, and if they were joined by the Flemish who are also of a different religion than us, his Lordship the ambassador could in this way gather such a multitude that it would necessarily provoke a scandal and cause reciprocal difficulty.

As the Venetian reaction to Wotton's arrival suggests, by the early seventeenth century the debate over the ambassador's freedom of worship and on the semipublic nature of embassy chapels had become a very serious matter in European diplomacy. Establishing whether an ambassador was allowed to celebrate religious rites at his residence could compromise and suspend the relationship between states. The problem was constituted by the special status enjoyed by early modern embassies, fluid spaces that functioned as both residence and business and for this reason undermined conventional distinctions between the public and private spheres.[20] Ambassadors' private chapels often functioned not simply as places of domestic worship but also as clandestine churches open to local religious dissidents. As has been noted, it was through this "fiction of privacy" that early modern European states were able to accommodate religious dissent and to unofficially allow a certain degree of religious tolerance while officially maintaining their commitment to confessional uniformity.[21] Only later, during the seventeenth and the eighteenth centuries, would embassy chapels find a legal justification in the principle of extraterritoriality, for which they did not violate the laws of their host country because they did not stand on the territory of that country. In this way native dissidents who attended chapel services did not violate local law because they were temporarily outside of its jurisdiction.[22]

To be sure, the fact that in early seventeenth-century Venice the English embassy served as a meeting place for local groups of Protestants and dissidents was not a secret. The English traveler Thomas Coryat, who visited Venice in the summer of 1608, noted that Wotton "hath service and sermons in his house after the Protestant manner," adding that his goal was "to winne many soules to Jesus Christ, and to draw divers of the famous Papists of the city to the true reformed religion, and profession of the Gospell."[23] While the Venetian government turned a blind eye to the fact that the English ambassador did not limit the use of his chapel to his entourage, the matter aroused concern in Rome. In December 1604, Wotton was contacted by Antonio Possevino, the famous Jesuit scholar, author of the *Bibliotheca selecta* and the leader of the Society of Jesus in the Veneto.[24] To approach Wotton, Possevino relied first on intermediaries, such as English Catholics in the city or the French ambassador in Venice, Philippe Canaye de Fresnes, who had recently converted to Catholicism abandoning his Calvinist faith.[25] Finally Possevino was able to meet Wotton at the church of Santi Giovanni e Paolo.[26] As indicated by the report that he wrote after the meeting, Possevino intended both to verify James I's disposition toward Rome and the Jesuits and to determine whether the Protestant services hosted at the English embassy also included religious dissidents in Venice. Possevino feared that through his ambassadors James I intended to use the same evangelizing strategies employed by the Jesuits in England to opposite ends, in order to "gain, that is, convert Catholics and reduce them to the false light of their false gospel" (*guadagnare, cioè convertire i catolici et ridurgli alla falsa luce del loro falso evangelo*).[27] Possevino thus regarded the English embassy in Venice not just as a site of diplomatic exchange but rather as a space of conversion, through which heresy could also propagate in the other cities of the republic, starting with Padua and its university.[28]

Possevino and Wotton continued to exchange letters throughout 1605.[29] The following year, however, the pronouncement of the Venetian Interdict and the expulsion of the Jesuits from the republic left no space for mediation. In 1606, in a pamphlet published under a pseudonym, Possevino attacked Wotton directly, singling out the English embassy in Venice as one of the main instigators of the clash between Venice and Rome. The Jesuit scholar denounced the Calvinism practiced at the English embassy, lamenting that its influence had even reached the Venetian government and pointing a finger at Wotton's close relationship with the Venetian scholar Paolo Sarpi, the legal and theological adviser of the republic. According to Possevino, Venice's rebellion against Rome had been instigated "by the English ambassador with whom Friar Paolo has such frequent contact, as has been seen, despite the fact that said ambassador is plainly Calvinist and allows the preaching of heresy to go on in his home completely freely."[30] Possevino's accusations had a resounding echo and contributed to keeping Rome's suspicions about the English embassy in Venice raised well after the Interdict. Still in 1625, a report from the Venetian Inquisition pointed a finger at the English and Dutch embassies, arguing that through them heresy spread throughout Italy, reaching even women and children: "In Venice and in other cities under his dominion live heretics for different causes and under different pretexts. Some of them stay there as members of the English and Dutch ambassadors' *familia* or as their servants . . . in their homes they practice the rites of their sect . . . and lately they have even rung bells, leaving the doors open, allowing every kind of person to come in in great numbers, even women and children."[31]

In 1606, the immediate result of Possevino's pamphlet was to compromise the position of Wotton in the lagoon and to force him to issue an official reply before the Venetian government. On December 13, 1606, the English ambassador went to the Collegio and rebutted the Jesuit scholar, who had accused him of "publicly preaching Calvinism in his residence" (*l'Ambasciator d'Inghilterra nel suo palazzo fa pubblicamente predicar il Calvinismo*), and of welcoming there "many Venetian gentlemen."[32] Wotton denied that Protestant rites were celebrated in his household and, playing on the blurred distinction between public and private that characterized early modern embassies, replied that the accusation was in itself contradictory "because if it is in the ambassador's palace it is not a public matter, and if it is a public matter it is not in the palace of the ambassador."[33] Moreover, mocking Possevino's mistaken information, Wotton reassured the Venetian authorities, explaining that at the time he did not even have a chaplain residing with him at the embassy. It was true that for several months, between the fall of 1606 and the summer of 1607, the English embassy in Venice lacked a chaplain. Nathaniel Fletcher, brother of the more famous playwright John, who accompanied Wotton to Venice as the embassy's chaplain, left in September 1606 and was replaced by William Bedell only in the summer of 1607.[34] Wotton also dismissed Possevino's suggestion that the Interdict was caused by Venice's decision to reestablish diplomatic contact with heretics. Echoing the ideas of his former teacher Alberico Gentili, the English ambassador explained that difference of faith did not hinder diplomatic contact, and for this reason a Catholic state like the Republic of Venice had the full right to exchange ambassadors with Protestant England without being excommunicated: "How can it be true that sermons are preached in my house when it is three months that I am without a chaplain? This is gross ignorance on the part of the author, and I must say that if the Jesuits are thus badly informed when they are only as far off as Perugia, how are we to believe what they report on Japan, Germany, Poland, Muscovy, and other distant parts? Nor need I point out that the pope has not excommunicated either the King of Spain nor the Archdukes for receiving ambassadors from my master."[35]

Despite Wotton's effort to clear himself from Possevino's accusations, Rome continued to keep a close eye on the English embassy in the years that followed the Venetian Interdict. In February 1608 the papal nuncio Berlinghiero Gessi expressed his concern to the Venetian authorities about the attempts made to spread heresy throughout the lagoon and complained that Wotton imported prohibited books into the city.[36] Gessi's alarm was not well-received, however, by the doge Leonardo Donà, who answered him briskly that "the Republic lived just as Catholically as Rome did, or even more" (*la Republica viveva tanto cattolicamente quanto si faceva in Roma, e più*).[37] With regard to Wotton's books, Donà responded that the library of an ambassador could not be searched as it was protected by the law of nations: "If among his things he had hidden a few books it was not appropriate that they searched for them or prohibited them, as it would mean violating the law of nations, in that it would not respect the ministers of the princes."[38]

Indeed, despite the fact that the Inquisition had confiscated the books shipped to him, Wotton succeeded in having them returned, explaining to the Venetian authorities that these were "books that had come for the personal use of a public man" (*libri venuti per uso proprio di un huomo publico*).[39] With these words Wotton was playing once again on the "mixed" nature of the ambassador, a private individual who also represented a public authority to another government—an issue that his teacher Gentili had discussed at length in the *De legationibus*.[40] To be sure, Wotton did not keep his library to himself but in fact circulated in Venice a wide range of prohibited books. These included the vernacular translation of the Bible by the Italian Calvinist Giovanni Diodati published in Geneva in 1607 and the *Book of Common Prayer*, translated into Italian by his chaplain William Bedell.[41] The harshest controversy took place when Wotton tried to bring to Italy James I's *Apology* of the oath of allegiance, which will be discussed later in this chapter.[42]

Spreading prohibited books was part of a larger plan that the English ambassador had conceived during his first Venetian embassy. Together with Sarpi, Wotton's effort to spread religious dissent in Venice intended ultimately to put pressure on the Venetian patriciate and to bring the republic into an international Protestant alliance able to oppose the papacy and the Habsburgs. In January 1609 Wotton outlined this very plan to James I, sending to London Giovan Francesco Biondi, the former secretary of the Venetian ambassador Pietro Priuli and a recent convert to Protestantism.[43] Biondi presented James with a letter that invited the English king to install himself as the head of Protestant Europe and to challenge the papacy in his own territory by introducing "the Religion into Italy" (*la Religione in Italia*). Venice, where the controversy of the Interdict allowed hostility against Rome to grow, was ideally suited to this goal:[44]

> There is no more appropriate place for such a great undertaking than Venice, as the better part of Venetian minds have perceived the papal tyranny because of past scandals and political interest; because the Inquisition is there only by name; because they speak against the pope with every freedom and

without any fear; because many books have been disseminated there, which will have positive effects in their time and because there is already an infinite number of them that shine the true light; because there they regard the pope as the Antichrist, his cult as mere idolatry, and among them some of the principle citizens, upon finding the opportunity, will be inclined to increase their disposition. In sum, Venice is the best place because it is already largely well-disposed to receive the faith.

The letter urged James I to act rapidly before the memory of the Interdict lost steam, leading the Venetians to either forget about the recent clash with Rome or to lose any religious faith and become atheists. To put the plan into effect, it was necessary to employ three instruments. The first of these was to send ministers to Venice who could guide the Protestant community. As the letter pointed out, more ministers could have easily come from Geneva together with Wotton's chaplain William Bedell.[45] Beginning in the spring of 1606 Wotton had been in touch with Giovanni Diodati, the prominent Genevan theologian and translator of the Bible, who in September 1608 visited Venice and became convinced that the widespread antipapal sentiments raised by the Interdict created a favorable atmosphere for bringing the Reformation into Italy through that city.[46] Wotton had a close relationship with the Italian Calvinist network, to a great extent composed of exiles from Lucca, to which Diodati belonged. During his time as ambassador in Venice he relied on the banking firm of the prominent Lucchese merchants Burlamachi and Calandrini as financial intermediaries in his transactions with the secretary of state in London.[47]

The second element the letter mentioned as necessary to executing the plan of bringing the Reformation to Italy was a *fondaco* of the English merchants, the creation of which would have allowed Protestantism to spread under the pretext of commerce.[48] It was also with this goal in mind that, shortly after his arrival in Venice, Wotton presented to the Venetian collegio the request of the English merchants, who asked to be treated like their German colleagues and demanded their own fondaco.[49] The fact that the reopening of the English embassy in Venice could have led to the creation of a second Protestant fondaco in addition to that of the German merchants was of deep concern to Rome. In December 1603 the Venetian ambassador Francesco Vendramin faced the harsh criticism of Pope Clement VIII, who protested that in dealings with England and other Protestant states Venice exclusively followed the "reason of state without any other concern" (*ogni cosa a ragion di stato senza alcun altro riguardo*).[50]

Finally, the letter argued that it was necessary to have agents in the city who could circulate small-format books (*libretti*), recruit sympathizers of the Reformation, and act as intermediaries between them and the ministers. On the one hand, by spreading Protestant books, agents would assist converts in their spiritual rebirth, "performing the same task with souls that the obstetrician performs with the bodies of newly born babies." On the other hand, the use of agents was indispensable for the protection of the ambassador, who could plausibly deny being directly involved:[51]

> The third way to set forth in the service of God is that it will be necessary to have in that city the assistance of a person secretly maintained by Your Majesty, one who will see to the dissemination of small-format books, who will open minds, and once they are open, will bring them under the instruction of the ministers, thus performing the same task with souls that the obstetrician performs with the bodies of newly born babies. He will also eliminate the need for the ambassador to involve himself in this business, and he will give him means to affirm and to be believed (in case any incident arises) that he had had no part, leaving all responsibility to that specific person and erasing any shadow of suspicion that either Your Majesty or the ambassador could have had any part in the plan.

As the letter suggests, in order to reconstruct the activities of the English embassy and its role in the smuggling of prohibited books in Venice during and after the Interdict, it is necessary to expand the focus beyond Wotton to his agents recruited from among the ranks of the Italian philo-Protestants. Permitting Wotton to keep a safe distance from the public eye and to avoid direct diplomatic involvement, the Italian philo-Protestants played a pivotal role in the production and circulation of books, facilitating the exchanges between the English ambassador and the Venetian intelligentsia.

Scribal Communities

Traditionally regarded as the clash between the medieval church and the modern state, or between the opposed values of the Renaissance and the Counter-Reformation, the Venetian Interdict is today studied as an exceptional event in the history of communication and information.[52] Well aware that the Interdict was first and foremost a battle for the control of political communication, Paolo Sarpi explained to the Venetian ruling class that such a battle was necessarily fought not through armies but through words and pamphlets: "The substance of the books appears unimportant as it is only words, but from those words arise the opinions of the world, giving rise to factions, seditions and, finally, to war. They are just words, but with them they bring armies."[53] This section focuses on the Italian Protestant refugees employed by Wotton and brings to light the many ways in which they manufactured and circulated prohibited books in Venice. A well-documented case is the one of the Italian Protestant refugee Giacomo Castelvetro, whose diplomatic miscellanies were examined in the previous chapter. Despite the fact that his name does not appear often in the historiography on the Interdict, Castelvetro played a crucial role as Protestant propagandist, which recalls closely the "person" in charge of disseminating "small-format books" described in Wotton's plan to bring "the Religion into Italy." His rich collection of papers, only partially examined by scholars, contains new evidence not only of the prohibited books that circulated in Venice but also of the different channels of communication employed by English diplomacy to spread religious dissent in Italy. Print was by no means the only medium through which the war of words was fought. The circulation of texts in manuscript form was no less decisive and, at times, also interacted with orality, reaching a wide audience.[54] The circulation of handwritten texts permitted the avoidance of censorship and also, most importantly, formed a bond among the Venetian circles dissatisfied with Rome, providing them with a shared set of readings and values.

Having spent most of his life in exile in Switzerland, England, Scotland, and Scandinavia, Castelvetro moved back to Italy in 1599 and reestablished himself in Venice. In the lagoon he entered the circle of Paolo Sarpi, who in his letters considered him "a good man, through and through" (*un uomo da bene compitamente*).[55] After the English embassy in Venice reopened in 1604, Castelvetro was recruited once again as a diplomatic agent by his patron Robert Cecil and became closely associated with Wotton's chaplain William Bedell.[56] Despite his close relationship with English diplomacy, Castelvetro did not live at the embassy but frequented it regularly, officially in his role of language teacher. Castelvetro included Wotton among the characters in his

Anglo-Italian language textbook and still in 1611 he was considered an employee of the English embassy who "had the job of teaching Italian language" (*haveva il carico d'insegnar la lingua Italiana*).[57] Though Castelvetro never officially figured in Wotton's entourage, the following pages show that in Venice he was employed by English diplomacy in several capacities, working as language teacher, translator, intelligencer, and propagandist, fully participating in the polyglot culture of "vernacular humanism," in which the teaching of foreign vernaculars was directly related to the conduct of political and diplomatic negotiations.[58]

While in Venice Castelvetro lived in the house of the printer Giovanni Battista Ciotti, for whom he worked as editor.[59] Castelvetro edited many texts for Ciotti, including the poems by Giovanni Battista Marino and Angelo Grillo.[60] Moving between the world of diplomacy and that of the printing industry, Castelvetro facilitated contact between Wotton's embassy and the Venetian intelligentsia. Ciotti's print shop was an important meeting place not only for bibliophiles but also for scholars and members of the political arena. Among them were also illustrious foreign visitors, such as the Italian philosopher Giordano Bruno and the German scholar Gaspar Schoppe.[61] Ciotti could count on a wide international network and in his print shop it was possible to access prohibited books, including the *Historiae sui temporis* by the French historian Auguste de Thou and the writings of the Italian philosopher Tommaso Campanella.[62] Despite the fact that the Council of Ten confiscated Campanella's writings because of their anti-Venetian views, Ciotti held manuscript copies in his print shop, where Castelvetro copied and annotated them (fig. 11).[63]

While working in Ciotti's print shop, Castelvetro built an impressive collection of prohibited books that included Protestant tracts, pasquinades, diplomatic reports, accounts of papal conclaves, and several anti-Roman lampoons. Castelvetro's papers are relevant not only for their content but also for their material form. In fact, most of the texts that Castelvetro collected in Venice are handwritten copies of prohibited books. A bibliographic examination of these copies gives rise to some hypotheses on their circulation and on their social uses. Their clean hand, their paratextual apparatus with indexes, title pages, page numbers, and marginal notes, and the fact that the same text was often copied more than once, all indicate that Castelvetro did not copy prohibited books just for his personal use. Castelvetro was, in fact, a professional scribe who made his career by copying and selling handwrit-

Figure 11. Giacomo Castelvetro's annotations to Tommaso Campanella's *Compendio della Monarchia del Messia* (Wren Library, Trinity College, Cambridge: MS R.4.5, cc. 44v–45r).

ten texts. While in Venice, he employed the manuscript medium as part of a precise communication strategy pursued in agreement with the English embassy on one side and Sarpi's circle on the other. Through the exchange of handwritten texts, Castelvetro intended to bring together communities of like-minded individuals, by reinforcing among Venice's intelligentsia the anti-Roman views that had emerged during the Interdict and by strengthening its sympathy toward England. As scholars have pointed out, an essential quality of manuscript circulation was the fostering of a close solidarity among those with similar beliefs and values.[64] Just as scribal circulation excluded the many, it was more strongly inclusive of the few who had access to the text, with the result of bonding groups of like-minded individuals into a community, sect, or political faction.

Among those readers whom Castelvetro provided with prohibited books was the Franciscan preacher Fulgenzio Manfredi, who sided with Venice in the Interdict controversy of 1606–7, attacking Rome from the pulpit of Santa Maria dell'Umiltà, which had remained vacant after the expulsion of the Jesuits.[65] From Castelvetro, Manfredi received John Calvin's *Cathechism* and the Italian translation of the *Diálogo de Mercurio y Carón* (Dialogue between Mercury and Charon) by the Spanish humanist Alfonso de Valdés, composed originally in 1529 to justify the Sack of Rome.[66] The effects of Manfredi's sermons were gauged carefully by Wotton, who informed James I that the "concourse unto him on the feast days is great in number, and great in quality, consisting of the principal senators and gentlemen."[67] Castelvetro also had a keen understanding of the power of preaching and of the large audience that oral communication could reach. This is confirmed by his observations on the Lenten sermons delivered in 1609 by Sarpi's right hand Fulgenzio Micanzio. On March 31, 1609, having heard Micanzio's sermons, Castelvetro wrote to Christopher von Dohna, the German scholar who acted in Venice as the envoy of Christian I, prince of Anhalt, that "if I hadn't heard them—not having missed a single one—I would never have believed that he had such audacity, nor that he had such a powerful love of truth in his heart."[68] Despite the efforts of the nunzio to stop him, Micanzio's sermons had a powerful impact on the Venetians and, according to Castelvetro, freed them from the fear of openly discussing the Scriptures: "Today the men who listen have no fear of wishing to read the Gospel and to reflect on it!"[69]

Thus, the texts copied by Castelvetro circulated through different channels of communication, from manuscript to orality, and became weapons in the war of words that erupted with the Interdict. This is further confirmed by the fact that Castelvetro often did not copy the texts in their entirety but carefully selected specific passages that could serve his anti-Roman polemic. This was the case of Francesco Guicciardini's *Storia d'Italia*, of which Castelvetro copied only the censored passages on the temporal power of the papacy.[70] Similarly, in transcribing *Del senso delle cose* (On the Meaning of Things) by the Italian philosopher Tommaso Campanella—in whom Wotton also had an interest—Castelvetro copied only the fourth book, which dealt with false miracles and demonic magic as practiced by those who "through the art of the demon do marvelous things to those who don't understand, and without this demon often they sing in the street in the presence of fools, but this is a trick and not wisdom."[71]

Distinguishing between true and false miracles, Campanella had labeled as false magicians infidels and pagans such as Muhammad, Numa Pompilius, Romulus, Pythagoras, and Minos, and recalled that Cato "was amazed that two priests in meeting did not laugh at the jokes that they made for the people, while preaching on the gods."[72] In the margin Castelvetro appropriated Campanella's argument and added an anti-Roman note, writing that "the wise man would be all the more amazed if he had lived to see what priests and friars make their populace believe in our time, and he would have esteemed rightly that among them they laugh at the people."[73] Campanella's criticism of demonic magic was therefore turned by Castelvetro into an attack against the political use of religion employed by the Roman Church to exploit the credulity of believers. While Campanella attentively distinguished between the pope and the cunning lawgivers, such as Muhammad and Numa Pompilius, who only pretended to be sent by God, Castelvetro erased this distinction, considering the papal prince nothing but another impostor, a false magician who deceived his followers for political purposes.

While Castelvetro often accessed the texts in Ciotti's print shop, as in the case of Campanella's writings, at times he also copied and disseminated books that came directly from the English embassy. This was the case with Edwin Sandys's *Relation of the State of Religion*, "a unique attempt to produce an overview of religious practices and beliefs throughout western Europe," originally published in London in 1605 and based on the author's travels throughout Italy and the continent.[74] A student of Richard Hooker and a figure destined to have an important career as a politician and colonial entrepreneur, Sandys pondered in the *Relation* whether a possibility for reconciliation among the Christian churches still existed, and argued in favor of a pragmatic coexistence among the different confessions. In a famous passage, often cited by scholars of Renaissance irenicism, the *Relation* pointed out that "a kind of men there is whom a man shall meet withal in all Countries, not many in number, but sundry of them of singular Learning and Piety . . . [who] have entred into a meditation whether it were not possible, that by the travel and mediation of some calmer minds, than at this day do usually write or deal on either side, these flames of controversies might be extinguished or asslaked, and some godly or tolerable peace re-established in the Church again."[75]

In his copy, however, Castelvetro followed the Italian translation of the *Relation*, a detail that further confirms his close relationship with Wotton's embassy. Indeed, the translation was the result of the collaboration between Wotton's chaplain, William Bedell, and Sarpi, who expanded the texts with additional notes.[76] The additions were already attributed to Sarpi by Hugo Grotius, who in 1637 argued that the "book published in English by Knight Edwin Sandys was translated into Italian with additions by friar Paolo, without indicating his name."[77] While in its original English version the *Relation* expressed an irenic hope of a reunification of Christianity, the Italian translation altered the meaning radically, turning the text into an anti-Roman pamphlet highlighting the temporal aims of the Counter-Reformation papacy. In his copy Castelvetro did not omit Sarpi's additions. At the end of the second chapter, having labeled the Catholic veneration of the saints and Mary a "horrible blasphemy" (*bestemmia horribile*), Castelvetro emphasized the importance of Sarpi's comment, which held that the "beginning and origin of the corruption of the Church" (*principio, et origine della corrotione della Chiesa*) took place when "the Roman Pontiffs assumed temporal power over the kingdoms and principalities," with the result of creating "a Hierarchy that, excluding the faithful from having access to the common goods of the Church, turned the Roman Pontiff into an absolute Emperor above every other power."[78] Interestingly, while the Italian translation of Sandys's *Relation* was printed in Geneva only in 1625 and revised by Giovanni Diodati, Castelvetro's copy indicates that the text had at least a limited circulation long before its appearance in print.[79]

The most remarkable piece of evidence pertaining to Castelvetro's activity as propagandist is constituted, however, by the presence among his papers of pamphlets in support of James I's *Apology for the Oath of Allegiance.* The *Apology* defended the oath that the English king imposed upon his subjects in 1606 in response to the Gunpowder Plot. Limiting the papal power to depose kings and expanding the princes' sovereignty over spiritual affairs, James I opened a major debate in Europe that ran parallel to the Venetian Interdict.[80] In July 1609 Wotton presented a copy of James I's *Apology* to the doge and, in order to underline the relevance of the work, explained to the Venetian authorities that "as the pope . . . had appointed a special congregation of cardinals to deliberate about the means how to stop the inundations of the Tiber . . . so was it now grown as necessary for other princes to consult together how to stop the inundations of popes themselves, and to contain them within their spiritual pretences."[81] The *Apology* enjoyed a limited circulation in Venice and the circle of Sarpi closely monitored the dispute between James I and cardinal Robert Bellarmine on the oath of allegiance and the reactions that it sparked in Italy.[82]

Nonetheless, Wotton's attempt to circulate James's *Apology* in Italy met with a swift reaction from Rome, which placed the work on the Index. In August 1609 Wotton informed London about the censure, and demanded more copies, arguing that the "prohibition will do nothing in this place but increase the desire and price of the thing prohibited."[83] In his letters Wotton also mentioned that Ciotti assured him that more copies would be arriving from Switzerland soon. The copies obtained by Ciotti might have been the same used by Castelvetro to compose his summaries of James's *Apology*. What is certain is that Castelvetro's papers shed new light on the Italian reception of James's work and show that summaries of the text enjoyed a manuscript circulation in spite of Catholic censorship. In a short pamphlet entitled "De papi," Castelvetro presented the *Apology* as the work of a clement king who preferred to persuade his subjects with the pen rather than the sword, to use reason over violence, and summed up its content in a nutshell:[84]

> Because who is that Prince who can tolerate that in his realm some subjects do not recognize him as king? Or that to be loyal to the pope they consider themselves forced to be unloyal to their king? And none less than the King of England found himself in this situation, and he did not wish to see his mercy exploited by their wickedness. Finally it happened that he preferred to draw his pen rather than his sword, and he focused on subduing them, though he could have destroyed them. Thus he chose to convince them with reason rather than conquer them with violence *Maluit sanguinem suffundere quam effundere* [He preferred to bring the blood to one's cheek rather than to let it out of one's body]. . . . This king then, to rebut these papal letters, and to justify his actions, composed a book entitled *The Oath of Allegiance*, without putting his name to it, however. Because he did not care under what title the truth appeared, as long as his enemies recognized what they had done.

Several contemporary marginal annotations confirm that Castelvetro gave particular attention to the controversy over the oath of allegiance. In annotating Campanella's *Discorsi ai Principi d'Italia*, for example, Castelvetro questioned the author's belief that the pope is at the same time prince and pastor and that "by discharging the subjects from the oath, he has the power to dethrone any mighty prince on earth."[85] In contrast to Campanella, Castelvetro claimed that the pope could do nothing against "Elizabeth, of blessed memory [*di felicissima memoria*], the Kings of Denmark, Sweden and today our king James."[86] In another passage, while Campanella argued that the pope "creates and overthrows kings and gives law to the universe," Castelvetro replied sarcastically in the margin by asking, "Why didn't the pope depose the kings of England, Denmark, Sweden and all the princes of Germany?"[87]

Circulating pamphlets in support of James's oath of allegiance was only one of many occasions on which Castelvetro brought the views of the English king to Italian readers. In 1615 Castelvetro translated James's *Remonstrance for the right of kings, and the independence of their crowns*, written against the French Cardinal Jacques Davy du Perron.[88] In the dedication Castelvetro pointed out that his translation intended to present James "before the Princes and the Lords of Italy, because they are ignorant of any other language that is not their own" and to show them "how unreasonably the popes usurped the power to deprive princes of their reigns and kings of their crowns (at their will)."[89] These examples suggest that while attending the English embassy in Venice, Castelvetro was employed as a translator and language teacher but he in fact performed a precise diplomatic function. Participating alongside Wotton and Sarpi in the war of words stirred by the Venetian Interdict and James I's oath of allegiance, Castelvetro acted as a cultural go-between, introducing the ideas of his former student James I into Italy.

Great Expectations

Because he was not officially part of Wotton's entourage, Castelvetro did not enjoy full diplomatic immunity and in September 1611 he was arrested by the Inquisition. The prompt intervention of English diplomacy succeeded in having Castelvetro liberated and kindled great expectations in Sarpi's circle, giving the impression that England and Venice had resisted Rome's pressures. And yet these expectations were destined to be short-lived and to be replaced by disillusionment, after Prince Henry's death in November 1612 made progressively clear James I's unwillingness to intervene on the continent to defend the Protestant cause. As the following pages point out, the fate of Castelvetro coincided with a more general shift in European diplomacy and can be regarded as a turning point that marked the demise of the alliance be-

tween the Italian Protestant refugees and English diplomacy that had begun after Henry VIII's break with Rome.

While circulating prohibited books in Venice, Castelvetro had been
tracked diligently by papal diplomacy. On January 3, 1609, Gessi sent a brief
report on him to Rome:[90]

> Castelvetro, of whom I already wrote to Your Most Illustrious Lordship, is
> not a man of letters, and although according to the information that I have
> he is of the poorest mind and hardly Catholic, and thus not very capable of
> subverting others with his reason, there is nevertheless a danger that he might
> distribute evil books which it is said he has, either because he inherited them
> from his uncle or because he was a bookseller in the past, or because he pro-
> cured them in some other way. I'm now told that he is expecting to teach Ital-
> ian language to certain foreigners.

Castelvetro's associates in Venice warned him about Rome's intention to
arrest him. Even Sarpi reproached him for his lack of prudence, being preoccupied about Castelvetro's fate as there was no other man in Venice more
watched by Rome than he.[91] In February 1611, having been recalled to
England with Wotton, William Bedell also suggested to Castelvetro that it
was more prudent for him to leave Venice.[92] Indeed, only a few months later,
on September 4 of that year, Castelvetro was arrested by the Inquisition. His
situation was complicated not only because he had already been tried by the
Inquisition, and was therefore considered a relapsed heretic, but also because
of his family's ties with the Reformation. His uncle Ludovico, the famous
humanist scholar, had died in exile in Switzerland in 1571, and his brother
Lelio had been burned at the stake in December 1609.

Nonetheless the new English ambassador Dudley Carleton, who had replaced Wotton in November 1610, defended Castelvetro in front of the doge
and succeeded in having him liberated.[93] On September 10 the senate decided that "Giacomo Castelvetro, man and servant of the House of the Lord
Ambassador of England" (*Giacomo Castelvetro huomo, et servitor di Casa del
signor Ambasciator de Inghilterra*) would be freed and brought to the house
of Carleton under the condition that he immediately leave the republic.[94]
Having left Venice for England, Castelvetro brought with him his rich collection of anti-Roman papers, leaving them at his death to Adam Newton,
Prince Henry's tutor and the translator of Sarpi's *Historia del Concilio*.

According to Carleton, the liberation of Castelvetro had been possible precisely because his papers had been sequestered by English agents before the inquisitors could get to them.[95]

Castelvetro's arrest and subsequent release had a significant echo in both England and Venice. On October 9, 1611, James wrote personally to the republic to thank the Venetian government for the liberation of his former Italian tutor. According to James, on this occasion Venice succeeded in defending its sovereignty against Rome, without yielding to those "who under the shadow of religion, intrude in those matters that have very little to do with religion" (*qui sub religionis umbra in id quod minime est religionis invadunt*).[96] In Venice, the freeing of Castelvetro and the victory of English diplomacy over the Inquisition further inflamed hopes in Sarpi's circle. Sarpi himself wrote to Groslot de l'Isle, arguing that Castelvetro's freeing was "a truly great thing" (*cosa grandissima*) and had led the republic to reassert its jurisdiction in religious affairs against Rome:[97]

> Eight days ago now, Castelvetro was put in prison by the Inquisition. The English ambassador asked that he be freed, and the Republic agreed, and had him freed from prison, without saying anything to the Inquisition, or to the nunzio or any other ecclesiastic, which is the biggest step that has ever been taken, because the Holy Office up until now has been dependent upon Rome, despite the fact that by having representatives in it the Republic impeded its tyranny. Having released him from imprisonment without further comment is a truly great thing, but whoever did it did not understand the consequences. If the pope remains silent, he is lost; if he speaks of it, either he will lose even more, or he will be ruined.

The following October, the same opinion was reiterated by Giovan Francesco Biondi in a letter to Carleton. Having underlined that Castelvetro's liberation was not a "simple moment" (*semplice momento*) but that it contained "great mysteries, and consequences of tremendous significance" (*misteri alti, et conseguenze di sommo rilievo*), Biondi explained that the controversy had changed the power dynamic between Venice and Rome, weakening the authority of the Inquisition: "As a result the pope is forced to fall into one of two difficult situations. Either, by remaining silent, he allows the Venetians to enjoy that authority and sovereignty that they have achieved over the Inquisition with the liberation of Castelvetro, or, making noise about it, and clamoring, he will make plain those things that were before hidden, by giving these Lords the opportunity to open their eyes in their own interest."[98]

The aspirations Sarpi's group maintained—that through its ambassadors in Italy, England could reopen the Interdict and convince Venice to break with Rome—were attached less to the figure of James I and more to his son Prince Henry, who at court was the leader of the more intransigent Protestant faction.[99] Though his interest was piqued by James I's clash with the papacy and though he shared his defense of the power of the princes against Robert Bellarmine, Sarpi considered the English king too concentrated on his writings and rather indecisive in his foreign policy, "more doctor than king" (*più dottor che re*), "more resolute with his words than with his actions" (*ad scribendum quam ad agendum promptior*).[100] Sarpi had already distanced himself from James during the controversy over the oath of allegiance, saying that despite their common opponent, Venice and London had responded differently to the papacy's intervention in international affairs. Sarpi noted that it would have been better if James "had treated only regal matters, and had abstained from theological issues," pointing out that it was not appropriate "to mix heaven and earth, human and divine affairs."[101]

For Sarpi's circle, in opposition to James stood Prince Henry, who was already well-known in Italy despite his young age, especially after his marriage negotiations with Tuscany and Savoy.[102] For his part, Henry took special interest in Italy. Through his tutors, who included Italian refugees such as Theodore Diodati and John Florio, he developed a particular taste for Italian art and culture.[103] His interest in Italy also led him to follow the Venetian Interdict with attention. Wotton's embassy had provided Henry with detailed reports on the controversies between Venice and Rome.[104] During the Interdict Henry had also received Sarpi's writings in defense of the republic from the Venetian ambassador in England.[105] Venetian diplomacy held Henry in high esteem. In the *relazione* he delivered to the senate in 1607 the Venetian ambassador Niccolò Molin praised Henry, noting that he was "of most noble wit and greatest promise" (*di nobilissimo ingegno e di grandissima aspettazione*), and he aimed at being a soldier rather than a scholar, making him in this respect the opposite of James, who appeared to hate "all the trouble and anxiety of Government" (*li travagli e li pensieri che porta il governo delle cose di Stato*), preferring "to retire himself with eight or ten of his men, than to live openly, as is the habit of the country and the desire of the people."[106] Henry's commitment to the Protestant cause led Sarpi to believe

that England could regain the international role it had played under Elizabeth and counterbalance the Habsburgs: "All over one hears about the great
virtue of the prince, son to the King of England, but the world will have long
to wait to bear fruit from him: because the King of England, though he is
accomplished in the Protestant religion, does not seem to be worth much to
the rest; he would like to do everything with words."[107]

On November 6, 1612, however, the death of Prince Henry dashed
Sarpi's hopes and echoed throughout Venice. As the Venetian ambassador
to England Antonio Foscarini remarked, Prince Henry's death would cause
"a substantial change in world affairs."[108] While Henry had served as
spokesman for the militant Protestant faction in the royal family, with his
disappearance the power dynamics in the English court shifted in favor of the
Hispanophile faction. James moved progressively closer to Spain and the
Spanish match became the focus of his foreign policy.[109] Sarpi's circle grew
increasingly dissatisfied with the English king and looked with concern
at his refusal to intervene in the Palatinate in support of his son-in-law
Frederick V.[110] In February 1622, commenting on the rumors of James's
possible conversion to Catholicism, Sarpi's right-hand man Fulgenzio Micanzio argued that the English king was "in government of State the most
instable and irresolute, in Religion the most contemner of it, in freindshipps
and Confederacions the farthest from Love, to his owne blood the most
voyd of Charitye, the most lost in Pleasures, and in a word, the cause of all
evill."[111]

Sarpi's circle continued to maintain close relationships with English diplomacy, and Dudley Carleton was a key participant in the plan that led to
the publication of Sarpi's *Historia del Concilio Tridentino* in London in 1619.[112]
In the meantime, Carleton continued to rely on the Protestant diaspora in
Lucca to handle his financial transactions with England, as Wotton did before him. And yet, James's Hispanophile turn would mark an irreversible crisis in the relationship between Italian Protestant refugees and English diplomacy. The alliance created by Cromwell after Henry VIII's break with
Rome lost its reason for being in light of James's plan to reconcile Christianity. Moving away from the militant Protestantism that colored the last decades of Elizabeth's reign, James sought a pacification with Spain and Catholic Europe, convinced that his role was to promote the reconciliation of
Christendom and begin a new age of religious ecumenism.[113]

The shift in the balance of power in Europe was felt profoundly in Venice. The publication in London of Sarpi's *Historia*, which James intended to use in his ecumenical plan, made clear that the margins of freedom the Sarpian circle had at home were limited. If in Protestant Europe Sarpi was transformed into a hero of freedom of speech, becoming, in Milton's words, "the great unmasker of the Trentine Councel," in Venice his legacy was not well-received. There is no better evidence of this than the publishing history of Sarpi's works: of the 172 editions of Sarpi's writings published in Europe between the seventeenth and eighteenth centuries, only three appeared in Venice.[114] While Sarpi's *Historia* was published in London, the outbreak of the Thirty Years' War brought the myth of Venice as the "Italian Geneva" to its end. The hopes of introducing the Reformation into Italy rapidly waned from the public arena and new heterodoxies took center stage. As Wotton had feared, the crisis of the Interdict had led groups of the Venetian intelligentsia not toward the Protestant Reformation but rather toward atheism and unbelief, the new focus of early modern "culture wars."[115]

As this chapter has demonstrated, during the years of the Venetian Interdict and for some time thereafter, the Italian Protestant refugees continued to play a crucial role as English diplomatic agents, smuggling prohibited books and spreading religious dissent. They relied especially on the scribal medium, not only because of its capacity to circulate ideologically charged texts with more discretion and far from the eyes of censors, but also as a tool of community formation. By exchanging manuscript texts they intended to bond together into a scribal community those groups of like-minded individuals who in seventeenth-century Venice shared the same anti-Roman sentiments that emerged during the Interdict. In this way, the Italian refugees also served as go-betweens, facilitating the transactions between the English embassy and the Venetian intelligentsia, despite the fact that Venetian laws prohibited patricians from having contact with foreign ambassadors.

Finally, this chapter has suggested that the reopening of the English embassy in Venice in October 1604 initiated the last phase in the alliance between Italian Protestant refugees and English diplomacy that had begun under Henry VIII. The support that James I gave to Venice during the Interdict and his clash with Rome over the oath of allegiance convinced the Italian Protestant refugees that Venice could experience a religious schism and break away from the papacy. Yet in the second decade of the seventeenth-century, the shift within the English court, marked by Prince Henry's death and by James I's turn to Spain, made clear that the time of the Interdict had passed and that the new balance of power in confessional Europe left no room for the myth of Venice as the "Italian Geneva."

Conclusion

Since its nineteenth-century beginnings and throughout the twentieth century, diplomatic history has largely been dominated by its Whiggish perspective, which regarded the establishment of permanent embassies in Renaissance Italy as a crucial step in the teleological history of the "modern state," an institution marked by the "monopoly of legitimate physical force," and by the concentration of "all the material resources of organization in the hands of its leaders."[1] Traces of this state-centered paradigm can still be found in Garrett Mattingly's *Renaissance Diplomacy*, the classic work that remains the most influential study of premodern diplomacy, at least in the Anglophone world.[2] Mattingly traced the origins of Western diplomacy back to fifteenth-century Italy, when resident embassies were established among the Italian states. The central character in *Renaissance Diplomacy* is the resident ambassador, a figure Mattingly examined primarily on the basis of early modern prescriptive diplomatic literature and considered "an agent for the preservation and aggrandizement of the state," an obedient servant of "the new omnicompetent, egotistic states."[3]

In recent years Mattingly's work has been repeatedly reappraised and many scholars have criticized him for reproposing a Burckhardtian notion of the Renaissance and for reducing premodern diplomacy to "an Italian invention that spreads beyond the Alps and creates modernity." They have also noted that his work neglects the "many forms of non-ambassadorial mediation" that do not fit neatly into his "model of a secular and increasingly professionalized Renaissance diplomatic corps."[4] To measure the distance that separates current diplomatic history from Mattingly it is also useful to consider the specific historical moment in which the work was published in 1955. As Robert Kingdon pointed out, *Renaissance Diplomacy* appeared when "the cold-war diplomatic conflicts between the Communist world and the West were at their height," and it was marked by "a pronounced moral concern" for the rise of twentieth-century totalitarian regimes. Indeed, Mattingly's work grew out of his "reactions to the events of his day, from his horror at the moral evil contained in the growth of fascism"—which he witnessed directly while in Florence during the 1920s—"and from his dismay at the failure of isolationists in America and elsewhere to recognize the dimension of that evil."[5] The meaning of Renaissance humanism in light of twentieth-century totalitarianism was a topic hotly debated by many of Mattingly's interlocutors, such as Felix Gilbert, Hans Baron, and Paul Oskar Kristeller, all of whom are mentioned in the foreword of *Renaissance Diplomacy*. Mattingly's "moral concern" led him to see a close relationship between past and present, between Renaissance diplomacy and the contemporary "myth of the state." Following this line of thought he argued that after spreading from Italy to Europe, the institution of permanent diplomacy "continued to develop . . . throughout the period which ended in 1914," during which it "was drawn into service of the rising nation-states," serving "at once to nourish their growth and to foster their idolatry. It still serves them and must go on doing so as long as nation-states survive."[6]

The state-centered paradigm that has long dominated diplomatic history and that is still visible in Mattingly's *Renaissance Diplomacy* has been the first polemical target of this book. The history of Anglo-Venetian diplomacy that has been examined in the previous chapters offers a perfect counterexample for rethinking early modern diplomacy beyond the myth of the "modern state." This is first of all because Tudor England hardly fits the model of the modern state founded on the monopoly of legitimate physical force. As scholars have observed, in the case of Henry VIII and Elizabeth I it is hard even to speak of a "foreign policy," since Tudor sovereigns rarely engaged in long-term strategic thinking about international affairs and more often developed their diplomacy as day-to-day responses to specific events and circumstances.[7] Moreover, the history of Anglo-Venetian diplomacy under the Tudors challenges the centrality of resident ambassadors and brings to light an alternative history of early modern diplomacy, centered on informal exchanges and on lower-level go-betweens who conducted diplomacy on the ground. As the first chapter has shown, the crisis triggered by Henry VIII's break with Rome and later by Elizabeth's ascension to the throne suspended the exchange of resident ambassadors for forty-four years. The absence of formal representatives did not mean, however, that there were no other channels of communication. Thus, moving beyond the paradigm set by Mattingly in *Renaissance Diplomacy*, which focused on the rise of permanent embassies, this book has attempted to reconstruct how early modern diplomacy worked outside of formal diplomatic channels, even between states that could not officially communicate through their embassies.

In this respect, Elizabeth I's contact with Venice is a case in point. After the exchange of resident ambassadors was suspended, Elizabeth not only continued to exchange letters with the Venetian government but exploited her personal relationship with the Italian Protestant refugees to recruit them as diplomatic agents. In the second half of the sixteenth century, Elizabeth and her ministers grouped the Italian refugees into a "patronage network," using them to supplement formal diplomacy and to form interstitial, supplementary, and parallel structures.[8] This occasional diplomacy was not simply a way to cope with the lack of formal representatives. Entrusting diplomatic duties to individuals not formally recognized as ambassadors in reality presented many advantages, offering early modern rulers a higher degree of confidentiality and flexibility. To be sure, Elizabeth was not the only sovereign to employ such a strategy. In Renaissance Italy the ascent to power of figures such as Francesco Sforza and Lorenzo de' Medici was based precisely on their capacity to weaken the local elites by creating a parallel diplomatic corps formed of clients and secretaries, many of them "new men," who depended entirely on their patrons for protection and support.[9] In sixteenth-century France, during the wars of religion, the Guises developed their own diplomatic service—alternative to but not always in conflict with that of the Valois—through which they were able to maintain a wide web of alliances, even with Lutheran Germany, despite the confessional divide.[10]

Along with challenging the traditional state-centered paradigm of diplomatic history and bringing to light the complex and constant interplay between formality and informality, the main purpose of this book has been to recover the agency of religious refugees in early modern diplomacy. Focusing on the Italian philo-Protestants who fled to Northern Europe during the sixteenth century, the book has brought to light the many different diplomatic roles performed by religious refugees. First and foremost, they acted as intelligencers and cultural brokers, who provided their patrons with news of international affairs as well as with rare publications from the continental book market. In this respect, they performed a role similar to other early modern "facilitators," "pragmatic readers," "secretaries," and "professionals of intelligence," who gathered information and annotated books to provide useful political knowledge to their employers.[11] Yet, the Italian Protestant refugees were not just carriers of information and books for their patrons. Taking advantage of their cultural capital and of their extensive web of contacts in Italy and Europe, they were able to exercise a certain degree of agency in early modern diplomacy, circulating news and information to influence the "public sphere" and to pressure elites and governments to bring forth their own religious and political agenda. In this respect, the book has proposed that early modern religious refugees be regarded as a "transnational advocacy network" that used information and ideas to leverage more powerful actors and to influence state diplomacy indirectly.[12] Thus, the goal of *The Refugee-Diplomat* has been not simply to recover another group of diplomatic go-betweens but to reconsider the tension between state and nonstate agents as a central phenomenon of early modern diplomacy.[13]

In addition, this book has shown the role of the Italian Protestant refugees in the transformation of early modern diplomatic culture. The examination of their publications, letters, and reading notes has revealed their position at the center of some of the most important intellectual debates of the period regarding the law of war, the rights of non-Christians, cross-confessional diplomacy, and the relationship between secular and religious powers. Along with the prominent Italian Protestant lawyer Alberico Gentili, well-known for defending the ambassador's right to resist unjust orders and for his secular approach to international law, the book has brought to light other significant and nonetheless still little-known figures, such as Baldassarre Altieri, Guido Giannetti, Pietro Bizzarri, Gentili's brother Scipione, and Giacomo Castelvetro. The many case studies examined reveal the Italian refugees' complex and sophisticated diplomatic culture, based not only on the reading of prescriptive treatises and ambassadorial records, from Torquato Tasso to the Venetian *relazioni*, but also on the direct knowledge of international affairs matured in close contact with Renaissance embassies and with the political arena of early modern Venice. Despite the differences among the many figures discussed in the book, a common element in their diplomatic culture could be identified in their reading of Niccolò Machiavelli, whom they regarded as a republican thinker who had written *The Prince* not to advise the tyrant but to unmask the very logic of politics. Through Machiavelli the Italian Protestant refugees considered the role of the Catholic Church in the crisis of sixteenth-century Italy and its transformation after the Council of Trent, but they also pondered the shifting balance of power in Europe outside of strict confessional parameters, arguing that only the strengthening of secular authorities over religious affairs could have brought the age of confessional strife to an end. In this respect, figures such as Gentili and Castelvetro also belong to the history of Erastianism, and their ideas and activities allow a more precise understanding of the "Anglo-Venetian seventeenth century," that ties together Paolo Sarpi and Thomas Hobbes.[14]

Finally, by recovering the agency of religious refugees in early modern diplomacy, this book has attempted to reinsert history at the center of the growing field of refugee studies, questioning its dominant presentist approach and making a call for a closer dialogue among historians, political theorists, and scholars of international relations. Although today the history of early modern Europe seems much less relevant to contemporary affairs than it once did, phenomena such as asymmetrical warfare, terrorism, and "clashes of civilizations" were not unknown to an epoch marked by the explosion of religious violence at all levels of society. Indeed, "contemporary interest sections, protecting powers, and front missions, which allowed the actual business of diplomacy to continue when conventional bilateralism fails" found their prototypes in the strategies that rulers employed in Reformation Europe to overcome the religious divide and "to negotiate without the appearance of negotiating with heretics and infidels."[15] Despite the fact that historians should always be careful not to establish direct connections between past and present and avoid attempting to draw lessons from past events, it is also true that a better knowledge of diplomacy's past might be useful for understanding its current transformation in the age of globalization. In the end, in fact, diplomacy "is shaped not only by its present form but also by our awareness of its past and our expectations about its futures."[16]

Notes

Where not otherwise indicated, *more veneto* dates have been adapted to the modern style (beginning the year on January 1 rather than March 1). All translations are my own where not otherwise stated. The following abbreviations are used in the notes.

Archives and Libraries

ACDF   Archivio della Congregazione per la Dottrina della Fede, Rome.
ASF   Archivio di Stato, Florence.
ASV   Archivio di Stato, Venice.
ASVT   Archivio Segreto Vaticano.
BAV   Biblioteca Apostolica Vaticana, Rome.
BL   British Library, London.
BLB   Bancroft Library, University of California, Berkeley.
BLC   Butler Library, Columbia University, New York.
BMV   Biblioteca Nazionale Marciana, Venice.
BNF   Biblioteca Nazionale Centrale, Florence.
BUP   Biblioteca Universitaria, Padova.
DKB   Det Kongelige Bibliotek, Copenhagen.

FCM   Fondazione Cini, Microfilmoteca, Venice.
FS   Folger Shakespeare Library, Washington, DC.
MC   Museo Civico Correr, Venice.
NL   Newberry Library, Chicago.
SP   State Papers, National Archives, London.
SCS   Special Collections, Stanford University, Stanford, CA.
SNL   Scottish National Library, Edinburgh.
TCL   Trinity College Library, Cambridge.

Printed Publications

Alberi   *Relazioni degli ambasciatori veneti al Senato*, 15 vols., ed. Eugenio
             Alberi (Firenze: Società editrice fiorentina, 1839–1863).
Bell   Gary Bell (ed.), *A Handlist of British Diplomatic Representatives
             1509–1688* (London: The Royal Historical Society, 1990).
CRP   *The Correspondence of Reginald Pole*, ed. Thomas Meyer (Aldershot:
             Ashgate, 2002–2008).
CSP *Foreign*   *Calendar of State Papers, Foreign Series, of the Reign of Elizabeth*, 23
             vols., ed. Joseph Stevenson (London: Longman, Green, Longman,
             Roberts & Green, 1863–1950).
CSP *Venetian* *Calendar of State Papers and Manuscripts Relating to English Affairs
             Existing in the Archives and Collections of Venice, and in other Libraries
             in Northern Italy*, 38 vols., ed H.R. Brown and A.B. Hinds (London:
             1864–1940).
CT   *Concilium Tridentinum. Diariorum, actorum, epistularum, tractatuum
             nova collectio*; voll. 13, edidit Societas Goerresiana, Friburgi
             Brisgoviae, Herder, 1901–).
DBI   *Dizionario biografico degli italiani* (Rome: Istituto della Enciclopedia
             Italiana, 1960–).
HW   Logan Pearsall Smith, *The Life and Letters of Sir Henry Wotton*, II
             vols. (Oxford, Clarendon Press, 1907).
LP   *Letters and Papers, Foreign and Domestic of the Reign of Henry VIII*
             (London: 1862–1932), 29 vols.
NV   *Nunziature di Venezia* (Roma: Istituto storico italiano per l'età
             moderna e contemporanea, 1958–).
ODNB   *Oxford Dictionary of National Biography*, eds. H.C.G. Matthew and
             Brian Harrison (Oxford: Oxford University Press, 2004–).
OED   *Oxford English Dictionary* (Oxford: Oxford University Press, 2000–).
PC   Massimo Firpo, Dario Marcatto, *I processi inquisitoriali di Pietro
             Carnesecchi (1557–1567). Edizione critica, voll. 2*, Città del Vaticano,
             Archivio Segreto Vaticano, 1998–2000.
PCA   Sergio Pagano, *Il processo di Endimio Calandra e l'Inquisizione a
             Mantova nel 1567–1568* (Città del Vaticano: Archivio Segreto
             Vaticano, 1991).

PM   Massimo Firpo, Dario Marcatto, con la collaborazione di Luca
            Addante e Guido Mongini, *Il processo inquisitoriale di Giovanni
            Morone*, nuova edizione critica, 2 vols. Roma, Libreria Editrice
            Vaticana, 2013.
PS   Massimo Firpo, Sergio Pagano, *I processi inquisitoriali di Vittore
            Soranzo (1550–1558). Edizione critica,* 2 vols., Città del Vaticano,
            Archivio Segreto Vaticano, 2004.
SPP   *State Papers Published under the Authority of his Majesty's Commission:
            King Henry VIII* (London: 1830–52).
Tedeschi,   John Tedeschi, *The Italian Reformation of the Sixteenth Century and
   The Italian   the Diffusion of Renaissance Culture: A Bibliography of the Secondary
   Reformation   Literature (Ca. 1750–1997)* (Ferrara: Panini, 2000).

Other Abbreviations

b.   busta
f.   filza
fasc.   fascicolo
c.   leaf
n.   number
r.   register
vol.   volume

Introduction

1. Andreas Zimmermann, ed., *The 1951 Convention Relating to the Status of Refugees
and its 1967 Protocol: A Commentary* (Oxford: Oxford University Press, 2011), article 1A(2).

2. Michael Ignatieff, "The Refugees & the New War," *New York Review of Books*, December 17, 2015.

3. Hannah Arendt, *The Origins of Totalitarianism* (New York: Harcourt, 1951).

4. On refugees in contemporary political philosophy and international relations, see also Emma Haddad, *The Refugees in International Society: Between Sovereigns* (Cambridge: Cambridge University Press, 2008); Alexander Betts and Gil Loescher, eds., *Refugees in International Relations* (Oxford: Oxford University Press, 2011); Serena Parekh, *Refugees and the Ethics of Forced Displacement* (New York: Routledge, 2017).

5. Giorgio Agamben, *Homo Sacer: Sovereign Power and Bare Life* (Stanford, CA: Stanford University Press, 1998), 133–34. See also Giorgio Agamben, *Means without End: Notes on Politics* (Minneapolis: University of Minnesota Press, 2000), 15–26.

6. Seyla Benhabib, *The Rights of Others: Aliens, Residents and Citizens* (Cambridge: Cambridge University Press, 2004).

7. Philip Marfleet, "Refugees and History: Why We Must Address the Past," *Refugee Survey Quarterly* 3 (2007): 137; Olivier Forcade and Philippe Nivet, eds., *Les réfugiés en Europe du XVIe au XXe siècle* (Paris: Nouveau Monde, 2008); Jérôme Elie, "Histories

of Refugees and Forced Migration Studies," in *The Oxford Handbook of Refugee and Forced Migration Studies*, ed. Elena Fiddian Qasmiyeh, Gil Loescher, Katy Long, and Nando Sigona, 1–10 (Oxford: Oxford University Press, 2014).

8. On the "myth of Westphalia" and its reappraisal in recent scholarship, see Andreas Osiander, "Sovereignty, International Relations and the Westphalian Myth," *International Organization* 2 (2001): 251–87; David Armitage, *Foundations of Modern International Thought* (Cambridge: Cambridge University Press, 2013); Jane Newman, "'Mediating Amicably?' The Birth of the *Trauerspiel* out of the Letter of Westphalia," in *Early Modern Diplomacy, Theatre and Soft Power: The Making of Peace*, ed. Natalie Rivère de Carles, 69–78 (London: Palgrave Macmillan, 2016).

9. Marfleet, "Refugees and History,"137.

10. See the first uses of the word listed in the *Oxford English Dictionary*, including John Evelyn's *Diary* (1687): "The poore & religious Refugieès who escaped out of France in the cruel persecution." In Italian *rifugiato* appears only in the twentieth century, despite the fact that *rifuggito* was already included in 1611 by John Florio in the *New World of Words* ("runne away again, fled unto for helpe, eschewed or fled from") and in 1612 in the *Vocabolario degli Accademici della Crusca*.

11. Heinz Schilling, *Early Modern European Civilization and Its Political and Cultural Dynamism* (Hanover, NH: Brandeis University Press, 2008), 40.

12. Nicholas Terpstra, *Religious Refugees in the Early Modern World: An Alternative History of the Reformation* (Cambridge: Cambridge University Press, 2015), 4.

13. Terpstra, *Religious Refugees*, 7.

14. Terpstra, *Religious Refugees*, 2.

15. Alain Tallon, *L'Europe au XVIe siècle: États et relations internationales* (Paris: Presses Universitaires de France, 2010); Andrea Gamberini and Isabella Lazzarini, eds., *The Italian Renaissance State* (Cambridge: Cambridge University Press, 2012).

16. Jason Dittmer and Fiona McConnell, "Introduction: Reconceptualising Diplomatic Cultures," in *Diplomatic Cultures and International Politics: Translations, Spaces, Alternatives*, ed. Jason Dittmer and Fiona McConnell (New York: Routledge, 2016), 13–14.

17. Mercedes García-Arenal and Gerard Wiegers, *Entre el Islam y Occidente: Vida de Samuel Pallache, judío de Fez* (Madrid: Siglo XXI de España Editores, 1999), English translation in Mercedes García-Arenal and Gerard Wiegers, *A Man of Three Worlds: Samuel Pallache, a Moroccan Jew in Catholic and Protestant Europe*, trans. Martin Beagles (Baltimore: Johns Hopkins University Press, 2003); Simon Schaffer, Lissa Roberts, Kapil Raj, and James Delbourgo, eds., *The Brokered World: Go-Betweens and Global Intelligence, 1770–1820* (Sagamore Beach, MA: Science History Publications, 2009); Natalie Rothman, *Brokering Empire: Trans-Imperial Subjects between Venice and Istanbul* (Ithaca, NY: Cornell University Press, 2011); Sanjay Subrahmanyam, *Three Ways to be Alien: Travails and Encounters in the Early Modern World* (Waltham, MA: Brandeis University Press, 2011); Daniel Riches, *Protestant Cosmopolitanism and Diplomatic Culture: Brandenburg-Swedish Relations in the Seventeenth Century* (Boston: Brill-Leiden, 2013); Maartje van Gelder and Tijana Krstić, eds., *"Cross-Confessional Diplomacy and Diplomatic Intermediaries in the Early Modern Mediterranean,"* special issue of the *Journal of Early Modern History* 19 (2015). For an overview of the growing field of "new diplomatic history," see Daniela Frigo, ed., *Politics and Diplomacy in Early Modern Italy* (Cambridge: Cambridge Uni-

versity Press, 2000), 1–24; John Watkins, "Toward a New Diplomatic History of Medieval and Early Modern Europe," *Journal of Medieval and Early Modern Studies* 38, no. 1 (2008): 1–14; Catherine Fletcher and Jennifer Mara DeSilva, "Italian Ambassadorial Networks in Early Modern Europe: An Introduction," *Journal of Early Modern History* 14 (2010): 505–12; Renzo Sabbatini and Paola Volpini, eds., *Sulla diplomazia in età moderna: Politica, economia, religione* (Milan: Franco Angeli, 2011); Isabella Lazzarini, "Storia della diplomazia e International Relation studies fra pre- e post-moderno," *Storica* 65 (2016): 9–41; Tracey A. Sowerby and Jan Hennings, eds., *Practices of Diplomacy in the Early Modern World c. 1410–1800* (London: Routledge, 2017).

18. Isabella Lazzarini, *Communication and Conflict: Italian Diplomacy in the Early Renaissance, 1350–1520* (Oxford: Oxford University Press, 2015), 31.

19. Lucien Bély, *Espions et ambassadeurs au temps de Louis XIV* (Paris: Fayard, 1990); Paolo Preto, *I servizi segreti di Venezia: Spionaggio e controspionaggio ai tempi della Serenissima* (Milano: Il Saggiatore, 1994); Brendan Dooley, *The Social History of Skepticism: Experience and Doubt in Early Modern Culture* (Baltimore: Johns Hopkins University Press, 1999); Mario Infelise, *Prima dei giornali: Alle origini della pubblica informazione* (Rome: Laterza, 2002); Filippo De Vivo, *Information and Communication in Venice: Rethinking Early Modern Politics* (Oxford: Oxford University Press, 2007); John-Paul Ghobrial, *The Whispers of the Cities: Information Flows in Istanbul, London and Paris in the Age of William Trumbull* (Oxford: Oxford University Press, 2013); Catherine Fletcher, *Diplomacy in Renaissance Rome: The Rise of the Resident Ambassador* (Cambridge: Cambridge University Press, 2015), 105–21; Lazzarini, *Communication and Conflict*, 69–85. In general, on the early modern information overload, see Ann Blair, *Too Much to Know: Managing Scholarly Information before the Modern Age* (New Haven, CT: Yale University Press, 2010).

20. Francesco Senatore, *"Uno mundo de carta": Forme e strutture della diplomazia sforzesca* (Naples: Liguori, 1994).

21. Niccolò Machiavelli, "Memoriale a Raffaello Girolami quando ai 23 d'Ottobre partì per la Spagna all'Imperatore," in Niccolò Machiavelli, *Opere*, ed. Corrado Vivanti, 3 vols. (Torino: Einaudi, 1997), 1:731; English translation in Niccolò Machiavelli, *The Chief Works and Others*, trans. Allan Gilbert, 3 vols. (Durham, NC: Duke University Press, 1989), 1:118.

22. Christopher Bayly, *Empire and Information: Intelligence Gathering and Social Communication in India, 1780–1870* (Cambridge: Cambridge University Press, 1999), 5.

23. Bayly, *Empire and Information*, 5.

24. Michael J. Levin, *Agents of Empire: Spanish Ambassadors in Sixteenth-Century Italy* (Ithaca, NY: Cornell University Press, 2005), 183–99; Marika Keblusek and Badeloch Vera Noldus, eds., *Double Agents: Cultural and Political Brokerage in Early Modern Europe* (Leiden: Brill, 2011); Diana Carrió-Invernizzi, ed., *Embajadores culturales: Transferencias y lealtades de la diplomacia española de la Edad Moderna* (Madrid: Universidad Nacional de la Educación a Distancia, 2016).

25. Fletcher, *Diplomacy in Renaissance Rome*, 145–67; Sowerby and Hennings, *Practices of Diplomacy*, 185–253.

26. Christian Windler, "Diplomatic History as a Field for Cultural Analysis: Muslim-Christian Relations in Tunis," *Historical Journal* 1 (2001): 79–106; Rothman, *Brokering Empire*; Van Gelder and Krstić, *"Cross-Confessional Diplomacy."*

27. John Tedeschi, "The Cultural Contributions of Italian Protestant Reformers in the Late Renaissance," in *Libri, idee e sentimenti religiosi del Cinquecento italiano*, ed. Adriano Prosperi and Albano Biondi, 81–108 (Modena: Panini, 1987).

28. Carlo Cipolla, "The Diffusion of Innovations in Early Modern Europe," *Comparative Studies in Society and History* 14 (1976): 46–52 (48). On the problem of cultural translation in Renaissance Europe, see also Peter Burke and Ronnie Po-chia Hsia, eds., *Cultural Translation in Early Modern Europe* (Cambridge: Cambridge University Press, 2007) and Karen Newman and Jane Tylus, eds., *Early Modern Cultures of Translations* (Philadelphia: University of Pennsylvania Press, 2015).

29. Robert Darnton, "What Is the History of Books?" in *The Kiss of Lamourette: Reflections in Cultural History* (New York: Norton, 1990), 107–35.

30. Roger Chartier, *The Order of Books: Readers, Authors, and Libraries in Europe between the Fourteenth and the Eighteenth Centuries* (Stanford, CA: Stanford University Press, 1994), 8.

31. Lazzarini, *Communication and Conflict*, 105.

32. Lazzarini, *Communication and Conflict*, 104–19.

33. De Vivo, *Information and Communication in Venice*, 16.

34. Peter Lake and Steve Pincus, "Rethinking the Public Sphere in Early Modern England," *Journal of British Studies* 2 (2006): 270–92.

35. Margaret E. Keck and Kathryn Sikkink, *Activists beyond Borders: Advocacy Networks in International Politics* (Ithaca, NY: Cornell University Press, 1998); Riches, *Protestant Cosmopolitanism*.

36. First formulated by the German philosopher Jürgen Habermas in his classic work *Strukturwandel der Öffentlichkeit: Untersuchungen zu einer Kategorie der bürgerlichen Gesellschaft* (Neuwied, Berlin: Luchterhand, 1962) (English translation in *The Structural Transformation of the Public Sphere: An Inquiry into a Category of Bourgeois Society*, trans. Thomas Burger, with Frederick Lawrence [Cambridge, MA: MIT Press, 1991]), the notion of the "public sphere" has been extensively discussed and reappraised by historians of early modern Europe. See Roger Chartier, *The Cultural Origins of the French Revolution* (Durham, NC: Duke University Press, 1991), 20–37; De Vivo, *Information and Communication*; Peter Lake and Steven Pincus, *The Politics of the Public Sphere in Early Modern England* (Manchester: Manchester University Press, 2007); Lucien Bely, ed., *L'opinion publique en Europe (1600–1800)* (Paris: PUF, 2011); Sandro Landi, *Stampa, censura e opinione pubblica in età moderna* (Bologna: Il Mulino, 2011); Massimo Rospocher, *Beyond the Public Sphere: Opinions, Publics, Spaces in Early Modern Europe* (Bologna: Il Mulino, 2012).

37. Adriano Prosperi, "Una esperienza di ricerca al S. Uffizio," in *L'inquisizione romana: Letture e ricerche* (Rome: Storia e Letteratura, 2003), 221–261 (246); Paolo Rossi, *Un altro presente: Saggi sulla storia della filosofia* (Bologna: Il Mulino, 1999). On the meaning of Ranke's famous "wie es eigentlich gewesen," see Anthony Grafton, *The Footnote: A Curious History* (Cambridge, MA: Harvard University Press, 1999), 62–93.

38. Frances A. Yates, *The French Academies of the Sixteenth Century* (London: Warburg Institute, 1947), 199.

39. Giorgio Spini, "Riforma italiana e mediazioni ginevrine nella Nuova Inghilterra puritana," in *Ginevra e l'Italia: Raccolta di studi promossa dalla Facoltà Valdese di Teolo-*

gia di Roma, ed. Delia Cantimori, Luigi Firpo, Giorgio Spini, Franco Venturi, and Valdo Vinay, 451–89 (Florence: Sansoni, 1959), republished later in Giorgio Spini, *Barocco e puritani. Studi sulla storia del Seicento in Italia, Spagna e New England*, 239–69 (Florence: Vallecchi, 1991).

40. Alfred Claghorn Potter, *Catalogue of John Harvard's Library* (Cambridge, MA: John Wilson and Son, 1919), 205; Niccolò Balbani, *The Italian Convert: News from Italy of a Second Moses. Or the Life of Galeacius Caracciolus, the noble Marquis of Vico* (Boston: Thomas Fleet, 1751). The text was republished in Boston by S. Hall in 1794. See Emidio Campi, "The Italian Convert: Marquis Galeazzo Caracciolo and the English Puritans," in *Church and School in Early Modern Protestantism: Studies in Honor of Richard A. Muller on the Maturation of a Theological Tradition*, ed. 153–63 (Leiden: Brill, 2013).

41. Delio Cantimori, *Eretici italiani del Cinquecento*, ed. Adriano Prosperi (Turin: Einaudi, 1992).

42. Cantimori, "Avvertenza," in *Eretici italiani*, 5.

43. Eric Cochrane and John Tedeschi, "Delio Cantimori: Historian (1904–1966)," *Journal of Modern History* 4 (1967): 438–45; Anne Jacobson Schutte, "Periodization of Sixteenth-Century Italian Religious History: The Post-Cantimori Paradigm Shift," *Journal of Modern History* 61 (1989): 269–84; John Jeffries Martin, *Venice's Hidden Enemies: Italian Heretics in a Renaissance City* (Berkeley: University of California Press, 1993), 5–9; John Tedeschi, ed., *The Correspondence of Roland H. Bainton and Delio Cantimori: 1932–1966. An Enduring Transatlantic Friendship between Two Historians of Religious Toleration* (Florence: Olschki, 2002).

44. Carlo Ginzburg and Adriano Prosperi, *Giochi di pazienza: Un seminario sul Beneficio di Cristo* (Turin: Einaudi, 1975); Silvana Seidel Menchi, *Erasmo in Italia, 1520–1580* (Turin: Bollati Boringhieri, 1987); Adriano Prosperi, *L'eresia del Libro grande: Storia di Giorgio Siculo e della sua setta* (Milan: Feltrinelli, 2000); *Massimo Firpo, Juan de Valdés e la Riforma nell'Italia del Cinquecento* (Rome: Laterza, 2016).

45. John Jeffries Martin, *Myths of Renaissance Individualism* (New York: Palgrave, 2004), 43–44.

46. Cantimori, "A proposito di L. Febvre. Au coeur religieux du XVIème siécle," in *Eretici italiani*, 551–52.

47. Delio Cantimori, "Note sugli studi storici in Italia dal 1926 al 1951," in *Storici e storia: Metodo, caratteristiche e significato del lavoro storiografico*, 268–80 (Turin: Einaudi, 1971); Brunello Vigezzi, "La *nuova storiografia* e la storia delle relazioni internazionali," in *Federico Chabod e la 'nuova storiografia' italiana dal primo al secondo dopoguerra (1919–1950)*, ed. Brunello Vigezzi, 415–77 (Milan: Jaca Book, 1984); Brunello Vigezzi, *Politica estera e opinione pubblica in Italia dall'unità ai giorni nostri* (Milan: Jaca Book, 1991); Barbara Bracco, *Storici italiani e politica estera: Tra Salvemini e Volpe 1917–1925* (Milan: Franco Angeli, 1998).

48. Benedetto Croce, *La storia come pensiero e come azione* (Naples: Bibliopolis, 2002), 81–96.

49. Delio Cantimori, "Introduction to Leopold von Ranke, *Storia dei Papi*, trans. Claudio Cesa (Florence: Sansoni, 1965), ix–xxxviii (xii–xiii), republished in Cantimori, *Storici e storia*, 172–96.

50. Cantimori, *Eretici italiani*, 16. On Cantimori's notion of "mondo sotterraneo," see Luisa Mangoni, "Europa sotterranea," in *Politica e storia contemporanea: Scritti (1927–1942)*, ed. Delio Cantimori, xiii–xlii (Turin: Einaudi, 1991). On Cantimori's political writings, see Michele Ciliberto, *Intellettuali e fascismo: Saggio su Delio Cantimori* (Bari: De Donato, 1977).

51. Silvana Seidel Menchi, "The Age of Reformation and Counter-Reformation in Italian Historiography, 1939–2009," *Archiv für Reformationsgeschicthe* 100 (2009): 204–5.

52. Schutte, "Periodization." See also the special issue of *Studi storici* 4 (1993), dedicated to Cantimori, especially the articles by Massimo Firpo, Giovanni Miccoli, Adriano Prosperi, Antonio Rotondò, Silvana Seidel Menchi, and Corrado Vivanti. For a recent overview of the Italian scholarship on the Reformation, see Lucia Felici, ed., *Ripensare la Riforma protestante: nuove prospettive degli studi italiani* (Turin: Claudiana, 2015).

53. Benjamin J. Kaplan, "Diplomacy and Domestic Devotion: Embassy Chapels and the Toleration of Religious Dissent in Early Modern Europe," *Journal of Early Modern History* 4 (2000): 341–61, and Benjamin J. Kaplan, "Fictions of Privacy: House Chapels and the Spatial Accommodation of Religious Dissent in Early Modern Europe," *American Historical Review* 4 (2002): 1031–64.

54. Filippo De Vivo, "Coeur de l'Etat, lieu de tension: Le tournant archivistique vu de Venise (XVe–XVIe siècle)," *Annales: Histoire, Sciences Sociales* 68 (2013): 699–728. See also Ann Blair and Jennifer Mulligan, eds., *"Toward a Cultural History of the Archives,"* special issue of *Archival Science* 7 (2007); Ann Laura Stoler, *Along the Archival Grain: Epistemic Anxieties and Colonial Common Sense* (Princeton, NJ: Princeton University Press, 2009); Randolph Head, ed., "Archival Knowledge Culture in Europe, 1400–1900," *Archival Knowledge* 10 (2010); Filippo De Vivo, Andrea Guidi, and Alessandro Silvestri, eds., *Archivi e archivisti in Italia tra medioevo ed età moderna* (Rome: Viella, 2015).

55. Ralph A. Griffiths and John E. Law, eds., *Rawdon Brown and the Anglo-Venetian Relationship* (Stroud, Gloucestershire: Nonsuch, 2005).

56. William Sherman, *Used Books: Marking Readers in Renaissance England* (Philadelphia: University of Pennsylvania Press, 2008).

57. Infelise, *Prima dei giornali*; De Vivo, *Information and Communication in Venice*.

58. Stephen Orgel, *The Reader in the Book: A Study of Spaces and Traces* (Oxford: Oxford University Press, 2015), 24.

59. Massimo Firpo, "Politica imperiale e vita religiosa in Italia nell'età di Carlo V," *Studi storici* 42, no. 2 (2001): 245–61.

60. Sergio Pagano, *Il processo di Endimio Calandra e l'inquisizione di Mantova nel 1567–1568* (Vatican City: Biblioteca Apostolica Vaticana, 1991); Massimo Firpo and Dario Marcatto, eds., *I processi inquisitoriali di Pietro Carnesecchi, 1557–1567*, 2 vols. (Vatican City: Archivio Segreto Vaticano, 1998–2000); Massimo Firpo and Sergio Pagano, eds., *I processi inquisitoriali di Vittore Soranzo, 1550–1558*, 2 vols. (Vatican City: Archivio Segreto Vaticano, 2004).

61. Watkins, "Toward a New Diplomatic History"; Timothy Hampton, *Fictions of Embassy: Literature and Diplomacy in Early Modern Europe* (Ithaca, NY: Cornell University Press, 2009); John Watkins, *After Lavinia: A Literary History of Premodern Marriage Diplomacy* (Ithaca, NY: Cornell University Press, 2017).

62. Hampton, *Fictions of Embassy*; Carole Levin and John Watkins, *Shakespeare's Foreign Worlds: National and Transnational Identities in the Elizabethan Age* (Ithaca, NY: Cornell University Press, 2009). András Kiséry, *Hamlet's Moment: Drama and Political Knowledge in Early Modern England* (Oxford: Oxford University Press, 2016).

1. When Diplomacy Fails

1. William Thomas, *The History of Italy* (London: Thomas Berthelet 1549), 73r–74r.
2. Thomas, *The History of Italy*, 85r.
3. Luigi Firpo, ed., "Inghilterra," in *Relazioni di ambasciatori veneti al Senato*, 14 vols. (Turin: Einaudi, 1965–96), 1:XIV–XIX; Luigi Firpo, ed., *Ambasciatori veneti in Inghilterra* (Turin: Einaudi, 1978), XXXIII–XXXV; John Watkins, "Elizabeth through Venetian Eyes" *Explorations in Renaissance Culture* 30 (2004): 121–38; John M. Currin, "England's International Relations 1485–1509: Continuities amidst Change," in *Tudor England and Its Neighbours*, ed. Susan Doran and Glenn Richardson, 14–43 (Basingstoke: Palgrave, 2005); John M. Currin, "Henry VII, France and the Holy League of Venice: The Diplomacy of Balance," *Historical Research* 82 (2009): 526–46; Levin and Watkins, *Shakespeare's Foreign Worlds*, 111–40; Maria Fusaro, *Political Economies of Empire in the Early Modern Mediterranean: The Decline of Venice and the Rise of England 1450–1700* (Cambridge: Cambridge University Press, 2015), 110–38.
4. See Ludovico Falier, *Relazione d'Inghilterra*, in Albèri 1:3, p. 25: "mostra di continuare nell'amicizia, dalla quale facilmente si scosterebbe per non avere voluto assentire all'inchiesta del divorzio." On the *cittadini originari* and their role in Venetian bureaucracy, see Andrea Zannini, *Burocrazia e burocrati a Venezia in età moderna: i cittadini originari (sec. XVI–XVIII)*, (Venice: Istituto veneto di scienze, lettere ed arti, 1993). On the diplomatic role of the *cittadini originari*, see Andrea Zannini, "Economic and Social Aspects of the Crisis of Venetian Diplomacy in the Seventeenth and Eighteenth Centuries," in Frigo, *Politics and Diplomacy*, 109–46, esp. 132–35.
5. ASV, Senato, Deliberazioni, Secreti, r. 71, May 30, 1559.
6. Massimo Firpo, *La presa di potere dell'Inquisizione romana (1550–1553)* (Rome: Laterza, 2014).
7. See ASV, Senato, Dispacci Inghilterra, II, n.10, 79r–80r: Giovan Carlo Scaramelli to the Venetian Senate (March 20, 1603): "che Inglesi rapaci, et crudeli sono divenuti odiosi a tutte le nationi . . . con aspetto simulato di vasselli mercantili vanno indifferentemente depredando nelle viscere degli altri Dominij tutte le navi, et tutti gli huomini."
8. See ASV, Senato, Dispacci Inghilterra, II, n. 50, 253r: Giovan Carlo Scaramelli to the Venetian Senate (October 22, 1603).
9. Fernand Braudel, *The Mediterranean and the Mediterranean World in the Age of Philip II*, 2 vols. (Berkeley: University of California Press, 1996), 1:606–29. See, more recently, Maria Fusaro, "After Braudel: A Rassessment of Mediterranean History between the Northern Invasion and the Caravane Maritime," in *Trade and Cultural Exchange in the Early Modern Mediterranean: Braudel's Maritime Legacy*, ed. Maria Fusaro, Colin Heywood, and Mohamed-Salah Omri, 1–22 (London: Tauris, 2010); Colin

Heywood, "The English in the Mediterranean, 1600–1630: A Post-Braudelian Perspective on the 'Northern Invasion,'" in Fusaro, Heywood, and Omri, *Trade and Cultural Exchange*, 23–44; as well as Maria Fusaro, *Uva passa. Una guerra commerciale tra Venezia e l'Inghilterra (1540–1640)* (Venice: Il Cardo, 1996) and Maria Fusaro, *Political Economies of Empire in the Early Modern Mediterranean: The Decline of Venice and the Rise of England 1450–1700* (Cambridge: Cambridge University Press, 2015).

10. Fusaro, *Political Economies*, 351.

11. Paolo Piccolomini, "Due lettere inedite di Bernardino Ochino," *Archivio della Società romana di storia patria* 28 (1907): 201–7.

12. Marin Sanudo, *Diarii*, ed. Rinaldo Fulin, Federico Stefani, Nicolò Barozzi, Guglielmo Berchet, Marco Allegri, 59 vols. (Venice: Visentini, 1879–1903), XXX, colonne 216–17: Gasparo Contarini to Niccolò Tiepolo (Worms, April 1521). On Sanudo's knowledge of the Reformation see Ottavia Niccoli, "Il mostro di Sassonia: Conoscenza e non conoscenza di Lutero in Italia nel Cinquecento," in *Lutero in Italia*, ed. Lorenzo Perrone, 5–25 (Casale Monferrato: Marietti, 1983). On the reception of Luther in sixteenth-century Italy, see in the same volume the articles by Albano Biondi, Salvatore Caponetto, Adriano Prosperi and Silvana Seidel Menchi.

13. *Il Principe*, XII, in Niccolò Machiavelli, *Opere*, I, ed. Corrado Vivanti (Turin: Einaudi: 1997), 152–53.

14. On Contarini, see Hubert Jedin, "Contarini und Camaldoli," *Archivio italiano per la storia della pietà* 2 (1959): 51–117; Gigliola Fragnito, *Gasparo Contarini: Un magistrato veneziano al servizio della Cristianità* (Florence: Olschki, 1988); Elizabeth Gleason, *Gasparo Contarini: Venice, Rome, and Reform* (Berkeley: University of California Press, 1993); Stephen D. Bowd, *Reform before the Reformation: Vincenzo Querini and the Religious Renaissance in Italy* (Leiden: Brill, 2002); Constance M. Furey, *Erasmus, Contarini, and the Religious Republic of Letters* (Cambridge: Cambridge University Press, 2006); Adriano Prosperi, *Lutero: gli anni della fede e della libertà* (Milan: Mondadori, 2017), 107–19.

15. Guido Ruggiero, "Constructing Civic Morality, Deconstructing the Body: Civic Rituals of Punishment in Renaissance Venice," in *Riti e rituali nelle società medievali*, ed. Jacques Chiffoleau, Lauro Martines, and Agostino Paravicini Bagliani (Spoleto: Centro italiano di studi sull'Alto Medioevo, 1994), 175–90 (184).

16. Edward Muir, *Civic Ritual in Renaissance Venice* (Princeton, NJ: Princeton University Press, 1981), 103–19.

17. Gaetano Cozzi, *Venezia barocca: Conflitti di uomini e idee nella crisi del Seicento veneziano* (Venice: Il Cardo, 1995), 34–35: "Il cattolicesimo, oltre ad essere il complesso di dogmi e di tradizioni che essi, magari con qualche riserva e qualche insofferenza, accettavano . . . costitutiva un elemento fondamentale per la loro società. Garantiva il rispetto per la gerarchia, per l'autorità, ispirava ai popoli le norme morali indispensabili per una buona convivenza nell'ambito statuale."

18. Federica Ambrosini, "Tendenze filoprotestanti nel patriziato veneziano," in *La Chiesa di Venezia tra Riforma protestante e Riforma cattolica*, ed. Giuseppe Gullino, 155–81 (Venice: Edizioni Studium Cattolico Veneziano, 1990); Federica Ambrosini, *Storie di patrizi e di eresia nella Venezia del '500* (Milan: Franco Angeli, 1999); John Martin, *Venice's Hidden Enemies: Italian Heretics in a Renaissance City* (Berkeley: University of California Press, 1993).

19. Fabrizio Biferali and Massimo Firpo, *Immagini ed eresie nell'Italia del Cinquecento* (Rome: Laterza, 2016), 414, xvi.

20. On the Venetian Inquisition, see Paul F. Grendler "The Tre Savii sopra eresia 1547–1605: A Prosopographical Study," *Studi veneziani* 3 (special issue, 1979): 233–40; Andrea Del Col, "Organizzazione, composizione e giurisdizione dei tribunali dell'Inquisizione romana nella repubblica di Venezia (1500–1550)," *Critica storica* 25 (1988): 155–67; Andrea Del Col, "L'Inquisizione romana e il potere politico nella repubblica di Venezia (1540–1560)," *Critica storica* 28 (1991): 189–250; Martin, *Venice's Hidden Enemies*, 51–70; Andrea Del Col, *L'Inquisizione in Italia: dal XII al XXI secolo* (Milan: Mondadori, 2006), 342–94.

21. Silvana Seidel Menchi, "Protestantesimo a Venezia," in Gullino, *La Chiesa di Venezia tra Riforma protestante e Riforma cattolica*, 131–54.

22. On the Reformation in the Venetian *relazioni*, see Franco Gaeta, "La Riforma in Germania nelle *relazioni* degli ambasciatori veneti al Senato," in *Venezia centro di mediazione tra oriente e occidente (secoli XV-XVI): aspetti e problemi*, eds. Hans Georg Beck, Manoussos Manoussacas and Agostino Pertusi, 2 vols. (Florence: Olschki, 1977), 2:571–97.

23. Niccolò Tiepolo, *Relazione ritornato ambasciatore da Carlo V* (1532), in Albèri 1:1, pp. 127, 133: "li nobili o li cittadini antichi governatori del dominio, ed in esso posto sartori, calzolari ed altri artefici."

24. Giacomo Soranzo, *Relazione d'Inghilterra* (1554), in Albèri 1:3, p. 70: "con tante variazioni e mutazioni sono stati costretti gli uomini quasi a non sapere che credere, né sopra che fondarsi." On how England was regarded by Venetian ambassadors, see Michael Wyatt, *The Italian Encounter with Tudor England: A Cultural Politics of Translation* (Cambridge: Cambridge University Press, 2005), 19–28.

25. Daniele Barbaro, *Relazione d'Inghilterra* (1551), in Albèri 1:2, pp. 249–50: "nessuna cosa è più incostante dei decreti loro circa la religione, perché oggi fanno una cosa e dimani un'altra."

26. Daniele Barbaro, *Relazione d'Inghilterra* (1551), in Albèri 1:2, pp. 249–50: "sì intorno la Santissima Trinità e gli Angeli, come intorno la creazione del mondo, e l'umanità di Cristo, e la virtù dei sacramenti."

27. Michele Suriano, *Relazione di Filippo II re di Spagna* (1559), in Albèri 1:3, p. 359: "la mutazione della fede ... è la maggiore alterazione che possa nascere in un regno, perché oltre l'offesa che si fa a N.S. Iddio, ne segue la mutazione de' costumi, delle leggi, dell'obbedienza e finalmente dello stato."

28. Gino Benzoni, "Ranke's Favorite Source: The Relazioni of the Venetian Ambassadors," *Courier* 22, 1 (1987): 11–26.

29. ASV, Senato, Dispacci ambasciatori, Inghilterra, f. 1, n. 4, cc. 10r–11v (11v): Giovanni Michiel to the Venetian Senate (London, March 19, 1555); ASV, Senato, Dispacci ambasciatori, Inghilterra, f. 1, n. 12, cc. 29r-v: Giovanni Michiel to the Venetian Senate (May 13, 1555), deciphered by Luigi Pasini in ASV, Senato, Dispacci ambasciatori, Inghilterra, decifrazioni, f. 1, n. 73, pp. 12–13; ASV, Senato, Dispacci ambasciatori, Inghilterra, f. 1, n. 21, cc. 52r-v: Giovanni Michiel to the Venetian Senate (London, June 26, 1555). I wish to thank Dr. Michela Dal Borgo for her kind help and for pointing me toward Luigi Pasini's *decifrazioni*.

30. ASV, Senato, Dispacci ambasciatori, Inghilterra, f. 1, n. 58, cc. 138r–139r: Giovanni Michel to the Venetian Senate (London, March 24, 1556).

31. ASV, Senato, Dispacci ambasciatori, Inghilterra, f. 1, n. 8, cc 21r-v: Giovanni Michiel to the Venetian Senate (London, April 15, 1555).

32. ASV, Senato, Dispacci ambasciatori, Inghilterra, f. 1, n. 45, cc11r–112v: Giovanni Michel to the Venetian Senate (November 18, 1555), deciphered by Luigi Pasini in ASV, Senato, Dispacci ambasciatori, Inghilterra, decifrazioni, f. 1, n. 73, pp. 56–59: "tutta piena di cavallieri et gente nobile suspetta per la maggior parte nella religione, et per ciò più ardita e licentiosa."

33. ASV, Senato, Dispacci ambasciatori, Inghilterra, f. 1, n. 7, cc. 19r–20r: Giovanni Michiel to the Venetian Senate (London, April 8, 1555), deciphered by Luigi Pasini in ASV, Senato, Dispacci ambasciatori, Inghilterra, decifrazioni, f. 1, n. 73, p. 9; ASV, Senato, Dispacci ambasciatori, Inghilterra, f. 1, n. 5, cc. 12r–13r (11v): Giovanni Michiel to the Venetian Senate (London, March 26, 1555), deciphered by Luigi Pasini in ASV, Senato, Dispacci ambasciatori, Inghilterra, decifrazioni, f. 1, n. 73, pp. 4–6 (p. 4). See also ASV, Senato, Dispacci ambasciatori, Inghilterra, f. 1, n. 6, cc. 15r-v: Giovanni Michiel to the Venetian Senate (London, April 1, 1555), deciphered by Luigi Pasini in ASV, Senato, Dispacci ambasciatori, Inghilterra, decifrazioni, f. 1, n. 73, p. 7: "non solo per coniurar contra li fedeli cattolici, chiamati da loro i papisti, . . . metter quella maggior perturbatione et confusione nel Regno che havessero potuto con danno et forse total pericolo delle ditte Maestà come autori della renovatione di essa religione."

34. Adriano Prosperi, *Tribunali della coscienza: Inquisitori, confessori, missionari* (Turin: Einaudi, 1996), 117–34; Firpo, *La presa di potere*.

35. Elena Bonora, "*Ubique in omnibus circumspecti*: Diplomazia pontificia e intransigenza religiosa," in Sabbatini and Volpini, *Sulla diplomazia in età moderna*, 61–76.

36. Elena Bonora, "Il sospetto di eresia e i 'frati diplomatici' tra Cinque e Seicento," in *Hétérodoxies croisées: Catholicismes pluriels entre France et Italie, XVIe-XVIIe siècles*, ed. Gigliola Fragnito and Alain Tallon (Rome: Publications de l'École française de Rome, 2015), *http://books.openedition.org/efr/2823*.

37. Pio Paschini, *Un amico del card. Polo: Alvise Priuli* (Rome: Lateranum, 1921); Firpo and Pagano, *I processi inquisitoriali*; Massimo Firpo, *Vittore Soranzo vescovo ed eretico* (Rome: Laterza, 2006); Massimo Firpo, *Storie di immagini, immagini di storia: Studi di iconografia cinquecentesca* (Rome: Edizioni di Storia e Letteratura, 2010),119–71.

38. ASV, Capi del Consiglio di dieci, Dispacci degli ambasciatori, b. 24, n. 14: Domenico Morosini to the Capi del Consiglio di Dieci, Rome (August 31, 1555).

39. On Pole's English legation, see Carlo De Frede, *La restaurazione cattolica in Inghilterra sotto Maria Tudor nel carteggio di Girolamo Seripando* (Naples: Libreria Scientifica Editrice, 1971), 43–82; Thomas F. Mayer, *Reginald Pole: Prince & Prophet* (Cambridge: Cambridge University Press, 2000), 252–301.

40. Massimo Firpo, *Juan de Valdés and the Italian Reformation* (Farnham: Ashgate, 2015), 111. On Valdés, Pole, and the spirituali, see also Massimo Firpo, *Inquisizione romana e Controriforma: Studi sul cardinal Morone (1509–1580) e il suo processo d'eresia* (Bologna: Il Mulino, 1992) (later republished in a new expanded edition by Morcelliana [Brescia, 2005]), and *Juan de Valdés e la Riforma*.

41. PC, II, 2, 492. On the accusations against Pole by both Catholic and Protestant authors, see Paolo Simoncelli, *Il caso Reginald Pole: Eresia e santità nelle polemiche religiose del Cinquecento* (Rome: Edizioni di Storia e Letteratura, 1977); Mayer, *Reginald Pole*, 356–99; Anne Overell, *Italian Reform and English Reformations, c. 1535–1585* (Aldershot: Ashgate, 2008), 145–66.

42. BMV, MS It. VII.176 (8619): Niccolò Contarini, *Delle Historie Venetiane, et altre a loro annesse: cominciando dall'anno 1597, e successivamente*, 545v. On Contarini's view of Elizabeth, see Cozzi, *Venezia barocca*, 167–68. An anthology of Contarini's *Historie* is available in Gino Benzoni and Tiziano Zanato, eds., *Storici e politici veneti del Cinquecento e del Seicento* (Milan: Ricciardi, 1982), 151–442. On the *Historie*, see also Tiziano Zanato, "Per l'edizione critica delle 'Istorie veneziane' di Niccolò Contarini," *Studi veneziani* 4 (1980): 129–98. On Bruno's views of Elizabeth, see also for further bibliography, Diego Pirillo, *Filosofia ed eresia nel tardo Cinquecento: Bruno, Sidney e i dissidenti religiosi italiani* (Rome: Edizioni di Storia e Letteratura, 2010), 87–141.

43. Federica Ambrosini, "'Mestier da donne?' Opinioni su Elisabetta d'Inghilterra e sul governo femminile nella Venezia della Controriforma," *Archivio Veneto* 5, 123 (1984): 27–75. On Sanders, see also for further bibliography, Stefania Tutino, *Law and Conscience: Catholicism in Early Modern England, 1570–1625* (Farnham: Ashgate, 2007), 21–31, 147–59.

44. BNM, 14.D.170: Nicholas Sanders, *De origine ac progressu Schismatis Anglicani* (Rome: Bartolomeo Bonfadini, 1586). The inscription on the title page (*Illustrissimo Domino Oratori Veneto*) indicates that the copy was donated by William Allen to a Venetian ambassador. The date and the name of the dedicatee, presumably Giovanni Gritti, can be gathered from ASV, Senato, Dispacci degli ambasciatori e residenti, Roma, f. 21, cc. 278r–279r: Giovanni Gritti to the Venetian Senate (Rome, August 8, 1587); ASV, Senato, Dispacci degli ambasciatori e residenti, Roma, f. 21, cc. 284r–285v: Giovanni Gritti to the Venetian Senate (Rome, August 15, 1587); ASV, Senato, Dispacci degli ambasciatori e residenti, Roma, f. 21, cc. 299r–301r: Giovanni Gritti to the Venetian Senate (Rome, August 29, 1587). For the circulation of Sanders's work in Venice see Ambrosini, "Mestier da donne?" 40n42.

45. CSP, Ven, VII, p. 467, n. 506: Alvise Contarini to the Senate (Paris, April 11, 1571). I cite from the CSPVen as the original dispatch in ASV, Senato, Dispacci ambasciatori, Francia, f. 7. is *Deperita inconsultabile* (unavailable for consultation due to deterioration). On the importance of the English embassy in Paris for Elizabethan diplomacy, see John Bossy, *Giordano Bruno and the Embassy Affair* (New Haven, CT: Yale University Press, 1991); David Potter, *Foreign Intelligence and Information in Elizabethan England: Two Treatises on the State of France, 1580–1584* (Cambridge: Cambridge University Press, 2004); Watkins, "Elizabeth through Venetian Eyes."

46. ASV, Collegio, Esposizioni principi, reg. 4, cc 55r-v, November 21, 1578.

47. Lisa Jardine, "Gloriana Rules the Waves: Or, the Advantage of Being Excommunicated (and a Woman)," *Transactions of the Royal Historical Society* 14 (2004): 209–22.

48. Fusaro, *Political Economies of Empire*, 70–83.

49. ASV, Collegio, Lettere principi, 33: Elizabeth I to Niccolò da Ponte (Greenwich, March 15, 1582); ASV, Collegio, Lettere principi, 33: Elizabeth to Niccolò da Ponte (Windsor, December 24, 1582); ASV, Collegio, Lettere principi, 33: Elizabeth to Niccolò

da Ponte (Westminster, April 20, 1584); ASV, Collegio, Lettere principi, 33: Elizabeth to Pasquale Cicogna (Greenwich, March 22, 1585). On the currant trade between England and the Ionian Islands, see Fusaro, *Uva passa*, and Fusaro, *Political Economies of Empire*, 43–57.

50. ASV, Collegio, Lettere principi, 33: Elizabeth I to Niccolò da Ponte (Greenwich, March 15, 1582): "l'antica, e stretta amicitia tra i Nostri Regni"; "affetione, che portiamo generalmente a tutti quelli della natione Italiana, et si particolarmente alla vostra Inclita Repubblica."

51. ASV, Senato, Dispacci Inghilterra, II, n. 3, 58r–59v: Giovan Carlo Scaramelli to the Venetian Senate (London, February 19, 1603).

52. Prosperi, *Tribunali della coscienza*; Firpo, *La presa di potere*; Bonora, *"Ubique in omnibus circumspecti."*

53. Carlo Ginzburg, *Nessun isola è un'isola: Quattro sguardi sulla letteratura inglese* (Milan: Feltrinelli, 2000).

54. Sharon Kettering, *Patrons, Brokers, and Clients in Seventeenth-Century France* (Oxford: Oxford University Press, 1986).

2. Tudor Diplomacy and Italian Heterodoxy

1. Vittorio Gabrieli, "Bernardino Ochino: *Sermo de Christo*: un inedito di Elisabetta Tudor," *La Cultura* 21 (1983): 151–74, English translation in Elizabeth I, *Translations, 1544–1589*, ed. Janel M. Mueller and Joshua Scodel (Chicago: Chicago University Press, 2009), 302–3: "Et si nihil aliud commendaret opus, authoritas scriptoris ornaret satis, qui propter religionem et Christum, patria expulsus cogitur in locis peregrinis, et inter ignotos homines vitam traducere."

2. Diarmaid MacCulloch, *Thomas Cranmer: A Life* (New Haven, CT: Yale University Press, 1996), 394–96.

3. Bernardino Ochino, *Prediche nomate Laberinti del libero arbitrio o ver servo arbitrio, Prescienza, Predestinatione e libertà divina, e del modo per uscirne* (Basel: [Pietro Perna] 1561).

4. On the Italian Protestant church of London, see Luigi Firpo, "La Chiesa italiana di Londra nel Cinquecento e i suoi rapporti con Ginevra," in Delio Cantimori, Giorgio Spini, Franco Venturi, Valdo Vinay, eds., *Ginevra e l'Italia* (Florence: Sansoni 1959), later republished in Luigi Firpo, *Scritti sulla Riforma in Italia* (Naples: Prismi, 1996), 117–94; Stefano Villani, "The Italian Protestant Church of London in the Seventeenth Century," in *Exiles, Emigrés and Intermediaries*, ed. Barbara Schaff, 217–36 (Amsterdam: Rodopi, 2010).

5. On the Italian reformers in early modern England, see Wyatt, *Italian Encounter*, 98–101, Overell, *Italian Reform*.

6. SP 1/142, c. 111v: Thomas Cromwell to Edmund Harvel (January 21, 1539).

7. SP 1/142, cc. 117v: Thomas Cromwell to Edmund Harvel (January 21, 1539).

8. SP 1/142, cc. 116r–117v: Thomas Cromwell to Edmund Harvel (January 21, 1539).

9. In August 1533 Henry VIII ordered Gregorio Casali, his last resident ambassador to the papal court, to leave Rome. On Casali, see Adriano Prosperi, "Casali, Gregorio" in *DBI* 21:92–97, and Catherine Fletcher, *Our Man in Rome: Henry VIII and His Italian Ambassador* (London: Bodley Head, 2012).

10. SP 1/142, c. 112r: Thomas Cromwell to Edmund Harvel (January 21, 1539).

11. SP 1/91 c.75: Harvel to Thomas Cromwell (Venice, March 11, 1535); BL, Cotton Nero B/VII f.121: Harvel to Starkey (Venice, April 21, 1535).

12. The only article dedicated to Harvel is by Robert Barrington, "Two Houses Alike in Dignity: Reginald Pole and Edmund Harvell," *Historical Journal* 4 (1996): 895–913. For essential biographical information, see Horatio Brown, "The Marriage Contract, Inventory and Funeral Expenses of Edmund Harvel," *English Historical Review* 77 (1905): 70–77, and especially Jonathan Woolfson, "Harvel, Edmund" in ODNB (http://www.oxforddnb.com/view/article/39717, accessed October 7, 2017).

13. ASV, Proprio Vadimoni 7 (33), 51v (February 3, 1549). On Harvel's marriage, see Brown, "Marriage Contract"; ASV, Consiglio dei Dieci, Deliberazioni Comuni r. 13 (May 11, 1540). The permission to carry arms was renewed in 1542, when Harvel's servants numbered thirteen. See ASV, Consiglio dei Dieci, Deliberazioni Comuni, r. 15 (March 15, 1542).

14. ASV, Senato, Deliberazioni, Terra, registro 34 (August 29, 1545): "Il magnifico Domino Sigismondo Aroel oratore del Serenissimo Re de'Inghilterra è stato longo tempo in questa città, parte del qual tempo ha negociato come homo privato, et dapoi ha havuto carico de persona publica . . . fino che continuerà in tal officio ello non sia astretto a pagar tassa alcuna, et sia depenato ogni suo debito."

15. CSP *Venetian*, 5:291–92n615.

16. BAV, MS Rossiano 997, cc. 46v–47r: Leonico Tomeo to Harvel (Padua, August 31, 1524), BAV, MS Rossiano 997, cc 47r–47v: Leonico Tomeo to Harvel (Padua, August 7, 1524). On Leonico and his circle of English students, see Daniela De Bellis, "La vita e l'ambiente di Niccolò Leonico Tomeo," *Quaderni per la storia dell'università di Padova* 12 (1979): 37–73; Jonathan Woolfson, *Padua and the Tudors: English Students in Italy* (Toronto: University of Toronto Press, 1988), 103–18.

17. LP, 4, no. 6192: Richard Croke to Girolamo Ghinucci (Venice? February 2, 1530); LP, 4, no. 6235: Richard Croke to Edward Fox (Venice, January 21, 1530); LP, 4, no. 6491: Richard Croke to Henry VIII (Venice, July 1, 1530), LP, 4, no. 6540: Richard Croke to Henry VIII (Venice? 1530); LP, 4, no. 6595: Richard Croke to Henry VIII (Venice, August 31, 1530); LP, 4, no. 6607: Richard Croke to Henry VIII (Bologna, September 7, 1530); LP, 4, no. 6670: Richard Croke to John Stokesley (Venice, 1530); LP, 4, no. 6694: Richard Croke to Henry VIII (Venice, October 19, 1530); LP, 4, no. 6695: Richard Croke to Henry VIII (Venice, October 19, 1530); LP, 4, no. 6696: Richard Croke to Thomas Cranmer (Venice, 1530); LP, 4, 6712: Richard Crooke to Henry VIII (Venice, November 3, 1530); LP, 4, no. 6727: Richard Croke to Henry VIII (Venice? November 1530); LP, 4, no. 6786: Richard Croke's expenses (1530). On Henry VIII's contacts with Padua to obtain the annulment of the marriage with Catherine of Aragon, see Cesare Vasoli, *Profezia e ragione: Studi sulla cultura del Cinquecento e del Seicento* (Naples: Morano, 1974), 182–212; De Bellis, "La vita e l'ambiente," 59–61; and Woolfson, *Padua and the Tudors*, 42–44.

18. BAV, MS Rossiano 997, cc. 30v–31v: Leonico to Pole (Padua May 31, 1524); BAV, MS Rossiano 997, 27r–29v: Leonico to Pole (Pauda March 15, 1529); BAV, MS Rossiano 997, 54r–56r: Leonico to Pole (Padua February 8, 1531).

19. BL Add. 28590, cc 5r–6v: Pole to Charles V (Venice, June 17, 1535); BL, Add. 28590 c. 7r: Charles V to Pole (Palermo, October 14, 1535).

20. Reginald Pole, *Pro ecclesiasticae unitatis defensione* (Rome: Antonio Blado, 1538). The text was sent to the English court in manuscript form in 1536: see SP 1/104, cc.1–280. On the *De unitate*, see Mayer, *Reginald Pole*, 13–61; Ethan H. Shagan, *Popular Politics and the English Reformation* (Cambridge: Cambridge University Press, 2003), 36–44; John Edwards, *Archibishop Pole* (Ashgate: Farnham, 2014), 39–83.

21. BL, Cotton Nero B/VII f.114: Harvel to Starkey (Venice, January 18, 1536).

22. Among the many studies on the circulation of Protestant ideas in sixteenth-century Venice, see Karl Benrath, *Geschichte der Reformation in Venedig* (Halle: Niemeyer, 1886); Pio Paschini, *Venezia e l'Inquisizione romana da Giulio III a Paolo IV* (Padua: Antenore, 1959); Aldo Stella, "Utopie e velleità insurrezionali dei filoprotestanti italiani (1545–1547)," *Bibliothèque d'Humanisime et Renaissance* 27, 1 (1965): 133–61; Paul Grendler, *The Roman Inquisition and the Venetian Press, 1540–1605* (Princeton, NJ: Princeton University Press, 1977); Manfredo Tafuri, *Venezia e il Rinascimento: religione, scienza, architettura* (Turin: Einaudi, 1985), 79–122; Seidel Menchi, "Protestantesimo a Venezia"; Salvatore Caponnetto, *La Riforma protestante nell'Italia del Cinquecento* (Turin: Claudiana, 1992), 129–34; Massimo Firpo, *Riforma protestante ed eresie nell'Italia del Cinquecento* (Rome: Laterza, 1993), 11–28; Martin, *Venice's Hidden Enemies*; Ambrosini, *Storie di patrizi*; Adriano Prosperi, "Ortodossia, diversità, dissenso. Venezia e il governo della religione intorno alla metà del Cinquecento," in *L'Inquisizione romana. Letture e ricerche* (Rome: Edizioni di Storia e Letteratura, 2003), 141–51. For further bibliography, see Tedeschi, *The Italian Reformation*, 713–34.

23. Among the many studies on the *spirituali*, see Adriano Prosperi, *Tra Evangelismo e Controriforma: G.M. Giberti (1495–1543)* (Rome: Storia e Letteratura, 1969); Dermot Fenlon, *Heresy and Obedience in Tridentine Italy: Cardinal Pole and the Counter-Reformation* (Cambridge: Cambridge University Press, 1972); Simoncelli, *Il caso Reginald Pole*; Paolo Simoncelli, *Evangelismo italiano del Cinquecento. Questione religiosa e nicodemismo politico* (Rome: Storia e Letteratura, 1979); Gigliola Fragnito, "Gli *spirituali* e la fuga di Bernardino Ochino" in *Gasparo Contarini*, 251–306; Gigliola Fragnito, "Evangelismo e intransigenti nei difficili equilibri del pontificato farnesiano," *Rivista di storia e letteratura religiosa* 25 (1989): 20–47; Gleason, *Gasparo Contarini*; Martin, *Venice's Hidden Enemies*, 71–96; and the many studies by Massimo Firpo, including *Tra alumbrados e "spirituali": Studi su Juan de Valdés e il valdesianesimo nella crisi religiosa del '500 italiano* (Florence: Olschki, 1990) and *Valdesiani e spirituali. Studi sul Cinquecento religioso italiano* (Rome: Edizioni di Storia e Letteratura, 2013). For further bibliography, see Tedeschi, 822–30.

24. On Harvel's role in Pole's household, see BAV, Vat lat. 5967 514v–515r (CRP, I, pp. 84–85, n. 79): Pole to Priuli (Treville, Summer 1535); BAV, Vat lat. 5967, 507v–508v (CRP, I, pp. 94–95, n. 93): Pole to Priuli (Venice, April 5, 1536); BAV, Vat lat. 5967 513 r-v (CRP, I, pp. 104–5, n. 109): Pole to Priuli (Rovolon, July 22 and 23, 1536). Along with Alvise Priuli and Donato Rullo, Harvel knew also Pole's "butler" Bernardino Sandro: see LP, 9:659: Bernardino Sandro to Thomas Starkey (Venice, April 13, 1535).

25. LP, 19, I, n. 395: the Privy Council to Harvel (London, April 25, 1544).

26. ASV, Senato, Deliberazioni, Secreti, registro 65, f. 77v: (December 28, 1546). On December 19, the Collegio already approved Harvel's request: see ASV, Collegio, Lettere, Secreta, f. n. 18 (December 19, 1546).

27. ASV, Collegio, Esposizioni principi, filza 1, cc. 540–541 (March 2, 1547). See Barbaro's diplomatic report in Albèri 1:2, pp. 225–71.

28. LP, 12, II, 484: Harvel to Richard Morison (Venice, August 8, 1537).

29. LP, 12, II, 1127: Harvel to Thomas Cromwell (Venice, November 25, 1537).

30. LP, 14, I, 884: Harvel to Thomas Cromwell (Venice, April 28, 1539); LP, 14, I, 884: Harvel to Thomas Cromwell (Venice, April 20, 1539).

31. LP, 9, 1029: Harvel to Thomas Starkey (Venice, December 28, 1535).

32. LP, 17, 321: Harvel to Henry VIII (Venice, May 12, 1542).

33. LP, 17, 1009: Harvel to Henry VIII (Venice, October 31, 1542); LP, 17, 1103: Harvel to Henry VIII (Venice, November 19, 1542); LP 18, 601: Harvel to Henry VIII (Venice, May 26, 1543); LP 19, 773: Harvel to Henry VIII (Venice, December 22, 1544);

34. LP, 20, 292: Harvel to Henry VIII (Venice, March 1, 1545).

35. LP, 17, 767: Harvel to Henry VIII (Venice, September 10, 1542).

36. Tallon, *L'Europe au XVIe siècle,* 158. On the influence that Renaissance diplomacy had on the early modern market of information, see Bely, *Espions et ambassadeurs*; Senatore, *"Uno mundo de carta"*; Infelise, *Prima dei giornali*; Levin, *Agents of Empire,* 154–82; De Vivo, *Information and Communication in Venice;* Ghobrial, *Whispers of Cities;* Lazzerini, *Communication and Conflict*; Elena Bonora, *Aspettando l'imperatore: Principi italiani tra il papa e Carlo V* (Turin: Einaudi, 2015), 217–45; Fletcher, *Diplomacy in Renaissance Rome,* 105–21.

37. On diplomacy and social mobility in early modern Europe, see Fletcher and DeSilva, *"Italian Ambassadorial Networks."*

38. *Memoriale a Raffaello Girolami quando ai 23 d'Ottobre partì per la Spagna all'Imperatore,* in Niccolò Machiavelli, *Opere,* ed. Corrado Vivanti, 3 vols. (Turin: Einaudi, 1997), 1:731; English translation in Niccolò Machiavelli, *The Chief Works and Others,* trans. Allan Gilbert, 3 vols. (Durham, NC: Duke University Press, 1989), 1:118.

39. Thomas Hoby, *A Booke of the Travaile and Life of Me Thomas Hoby,* ed. Edgar Powell (London: Royal Historical Society, 1902), 8, 61.

40. On Brucioli, see Giorgio Spini, *Tra Rinascimento e Riforma: Antonio Brucioli* (Florence: La Nuova Italia, 1940), and Andrea Del Col, "Il controllo della stampa a Venezia e i processi di Antonio Brucioli (1548–1559)," *Critica storica* 17 (1980): 457–510.

41. LP, 14, II, n. 280: Harvel to Thomas Cromwell (Venice, October 4, 1539). Published for the first time in 1532 by Lucantonio Giunti, Brucioli republished his translation in August 1539, just before Harvel approached him: *La Biblia quale contiene i sacri libri del Vecchio Testamento, tradotti da la hebraica verità in lingua toscana per Antonio Brucioli* (Venice: Bartolomeo Zannetti, 1539).

42. Antonio Pellegrini, *I segni de la natura de l'huomo* (Venice: Giovanni de Farri et fratelli, 1545). On Pellegrini, see Leandro Perini, "Spigolature erasmiane," in Achille Olivieri, ed., *Erasmo e la cultura padana nel '500* (Rovigo: Minelliana: 1995), 67–74.

43. Pellegrini, *I segni de la natura,* 2r.

44. Pellegrini, *I segni de la natura,* 4r-v.

45. Paul F. Grendler, *Critics of the Italian World, 1530–1560: Anton Francesco Doni, Niccolò Franco and Ortensio Lando* (Madison: University of Wisconsin Press, 1969), 104–35.

46. On Lando, see Grendler, *Critics of the Italian World*, 21–38, 111–27, and especially the many studies by Silvana Seidel Menchi, among them "Spiritualismo radicale nelle opere di Ortensio Lando attorno al 1550," *Archiv für Reformationsgeschichte* 65 (1974): 212–79 and "Chi fu Ortensio Lando?" *Rivista storica italiana* 3 (1994): 501–64. On Lando's translation of More's *Utopia*, see Silvana Seidel Menchi, "Ortensio Lando cittadino di Utopia: un esercizio di lettura" in *La fortuna dell'Utopia di Thomas More nel dibattito politico europeo del '500* (Florence: Olschki, 1996), 95–118.

47. Ortensio Lando, *Lettere di molto valorose donne, nelle quali chiaramente appare non essere né di eloquentia né di dottrina alli huomini inferiori* (Venice: Gabriel Giolito de Ferrari, 1548), Aiiv: "ne hò saputo per hora, dove meglio ricorrere che à voi, il quale, di cortesia, e di lealtà potete fronteggiare con il più honorato Cavalliere che il sol vegga, ò che la terra calchi." On the *Lettere di molto valorose donne*, see Francine Daenens, "Donne valorose, eretiche, finte sante. Note sull'antologia giolitina del 1548," in *La scrittura epistolare femminile tra archivio e tipografia secoli XV–XVII*, ed. Gabriella Zarri, 181–207 (Rome: Viella, 1999); Serena Pezzini, "Dissimulazione e paradosso nelle *Lettere di molto valorose donne* (1548) a cura di Ortensio Lando," *Rivista di letteratura italiana* 1 (2002): 67–83; Meredith K. Ray, *Writing Gender in Women's Letter Collections of the Italian Renaissance* (Toronto: University of Toronto Press, 2009), 45–80.

48. Lando, *Lettere di molto valorose donne*, A2r-v.

49. Lando, *Lettere di molto valorose donne*, 25v–26r. Lando included Apollonia Huttinger also in his *Oracoli de moderni ingegni si d'huomini come di donne* (Venice: Gabriel Giolito, 1550), 86rv. On Harvel's wife, see ASV, Proprio Vadimoni 7 (33), 51v (February 3, 1549); and Brown, "Marriage Contract."

50. Daenens, "Donne valorose."

51. SP, 1/82, c. 88r: Aretino to Henry VIII (Venice, January 16, 1534). See Aretino's defense of Henry VIII in *Pronostico dello anno MDXXXIIII* in Pietro Aretino, *Operette politiche e satiriche*, II, ed. Marco Faini (Rome: Salerno, 2012), 181–82. The *Pronostico* earned Aretino "trecento scudi": see *Lettere scritte a Pietro Aretino*, ed. Paolo Procaccioli, 2 vols. (Rome: Salerno, 2003–4), 1: 207: Thomas Cromwell to Aretino (London, July 20, 1534). Aretino's contacts with Henry VIII's court have not been systematically studied by scholars. For some observations, see Angelo Romano, *Periegesi aretiniane: Testi, schede e note biografiche intorno a Pietro Aretino* (Rome: Salerno, 1991), 50–55; Juan Carlos D'Amico, "Aretino tra Inghilterra e Impero: una dedica costata cara e una lettera non pubblicata," *Filologia e critica* 1 (2005): 72–94; Wyatt, *Italian Encounter*, 67–70.

52. See Pietro Aretino, *Lettere*, ed. Paolo Procaccioli, 6 vols. (Rome: Salerno, 1997–2002), 2:42: Aretino to Edmund Harvel (Venice, June 12, 1538); 3:514–15: Aretino to Ludovico Dall'Armi (Venice, February 1546).

53. Aretino, *Lettere*, 4: 15: "imperoche egli liberò da la tirannia de i Romani i corpi de le nationi Inglesi; et voi gli havete liberate da quella de i Pontefici l'anime. onde regnate dentro al core de le conscientie de i vostri popoli, con preminenza superna." The citation is taken from the first version of Aretino's dedication to Henry VIII. See Francesco Erspamer, Introduzione to Pietro Aretino, *Lettere: Libro secondo* (Milan-Parma: Guanda, 1998), xxxvi–xxxviii; Fabio Massimo Bertolo, *Aretino e la stampa: Strategie di autopromozione a Venezia nel Cinquecento* (Rome: Salerno Editrice, 2003), 84–94.

54. On the relationship between literature and diplomacy in the early modern period, see Hampton, *Fictions of Embassy.*

55. On Italian humanism in Henry VIII's England, see Denis Hay, *Polydore Vergil: Renaissance Historian and Man of Letters* (Oxford: Clarendon Press, 1952); Sergio Rossi, *Ricerche sull'Umanesimo e sul Rinascimento in Inghilterra* (Milan: Vita e Pensiero, 1969); Cecil Clough, *The Duchy of Urbino in the Renaissance* (London: Variorum Reprints, 1981); Jonathan Woolfson, ed., *Reassessing Tudor Humanism* (New York: Palgrave, 2002); Wyatt, *Italian Encounter,* 28–43.

56. SPP: 9, p. 188: Harvel to Henry VIII (Venice, September 27, 1542).

57. See Aretino, *Lettere,* 4:169: Aretino to Benedetto Agnelli (Venice, November 1547); Aretino, Lettere, 4:293–94: Aretino to Tiziano Vecellio (Venice, April 1548); Aretino, *Lettere,* 4:402–3: Aretino to Ercole Gonzaga? (Venice, June 1548); Aretino, *Lettere,* 5:52–53: Aretino to Philip Hoby (Venice, July 1548); Aretino, *Lettere,* 5:139: Aretino to Philip Hoby (Venice, January 1549); Aretino, Lettere, 6:187: Aretino to Lo (Venice, January 1553). See also Aretino, *Lettere scritte a Pietro Aretino,* 2:251: Anthony Denny to Aretino (London, December 19, 1547); Aretino, *Lettere scritte a Pietro Aretino,* 2:256: Philip Hoby to Aretino (Augsburg, June 23, 1548); Aretino, *Lettere scritte a Pietro Aretino,* 2:256–57: Philip Hoby to Pietro Aretino (Augsburg, July 23, 1548); Aretino, *Lettere scritte a Pietro Aretino,* 2:257: Philip Hoby to Aretino (Brussels, October 4, 1548). On the affair, see d'Amico, "Aretino tra Inghilterra."

58. On March 15, 1542, Altieri was listed by the Council of Ten as Harvel's secretary together with another thirteen servants living at the English embassy: see Consiglio dei Dieci, Deliberazioni Comuni, r. 15: March 15, 1542. There is no thorough study dedicated to Altieri. An essential biographical sketch is provided by Emilio Comba, *I nostri protestanti* (Florence: Claudiana, 1897), 2:185–218; Gottfried von Buschbell, *Reformation und Inquisition in Italien: um die Mitte des XVI Jahrunderts* (Padeborn: Schöningh, 1910), 24–25, 242–45, and Delio Cantimori, "Altieri, Baldassarre," DBI 2:559, and with more detailed information by Massimo Firpo and Dario Marcatto in PM, 1069–70, n. 70. For some observations on his diplomatic role, see Stella, "Utopie e velleità insurrezionali" and Paolo Simoncelli, "Inquisizione romana e Riforma in Italia," *Rivista storica italiana* 1 (1988): 50–57. On the relationship between Altieri and Aretino, see *Lettere scritte a Pietro Aretino,* 1:280–81: Baldassarre Alteri to Aretino (April 10, 1536); *Lettere scritte a Pietro Aretino,* 1:281–82: Baldassarre Alteri to Aretino (Modena, April 28, 1536); Aretino, *Lettere,* 5:139: Aretino to Philip Hoby (Venice, January 1549), where Aretino declared that "di XX anni e più, è a me M. Baldessari fratello."

59. Aretino, *Lettere,* 2:438–39: Aretino to Baldassarre Altieri (Venice, August 22, 1542): "Ecco che Iddio, doppo tanti vostri aggiramenti, vi ha pur collocato dove e le virtù e i costumi di voi sono onorate e laudati. Certo che il vedervi fermo a i servigi del Signor Gismondo Hervelo, grave e saputo Imbasciatore del clemente e del severo Re di Inghilterra, mi tien tutto l'animo in riposo. . . . Exercitatevi dunque ne lo scrivere i secreti de i suoi alti negozii, attendendo a interpretar la mente di lui con l'acuratezza de la solita prudenza. Intanto non mancate di participare parte de l'ore che vi avanzano, a quegli studi da cui traete la fama del nome."

60. Salvatore Silvano Nigro, "Il segretario," in *L'uomo barocco,* ed. Rosario Villari (Rome: Laterza, 1991), 96. On Renaissance secretaries, see also Douglas Biow, *Doctors,*

Ambassadors, Secretaries: Humanism and Professions in Renaissance Italy (Chicago: University of Chicago Press, 2002), 155–96, and Marcello Simonetta, *Rinascimento segreto: il mondo del segretario da Petrarca a Machiavelli* (Milan: Franco Angeli, 2004).

61. Biow, *Doctors, Ambassadors, Secretaries*, 157–58. See also Fletcher, *Diplomacy in Renaissance Rome*, 2–3.

62. ASV, Capi del Consiglio di dieci, Dispacci degli ambasciatori, 14, n. 69–70 (deciphered): Giacomo Zambon to the Capi del consiglio di dieci (London, September 20, 1545). On Harvel's difficult relationship with Altieri's associates see ASV, Capi del Consiglio di dieci, Dispacci degli ambasciatori, 14, n. 66 (deciphered): Giacomo Zambon to the Capi del consiglio di dieci (London, September 3, 1545).

63. Horatio Brown, *The Venetian Printing Press 1469–1800* (Amsterdam: Gérard Th. van Heusden, 1969), 210–12. On the history of censorship in sixteenth-century Venice, see Grendler, *Roman Inquisition*, and Del Col, "Il controllo della stampa."

64. ASV, Sant'Uffizio, b. 39, c. 47v–48r (trial against Girolamo Donzellini): the texts mentioned are Francesco Negri's *Tragedia del libero arbitrio* and Celio Secondo Curione's *Pasquino in estasi*. On Curione and his relationship with Altieri, see Lucio Biasiori, *L'eresia di un umanista: Celio Secondo Curione nell'Europa del Cinquecento* (Carocci: Rome, 2015), 36–39.

65. Ugo Rozzo and Silvana Seidel Menchi, "Livre et Réforme en Italie," in *La Réforme et le livre. L'Europe de l'imprimé (1517–v. 1570)*, ed. Jean-François Gilmont, 327–74 (dossier conçu et rassemblé par) (Paris, CERF, 1990); Seidel Menchi, "*Protestantesimo a Venezia*," 137–39.

66. Roger Chartier, "Leisure and Sociability: Reading Aloud in Early Modern Europe," in *Urban Life in the Renaissance*, ed. Susan Zimmerman and Ronald F.E. Weissman, 103–20 (Newark: Delaware Press, 1989), 104.

67. Michel de Certeau, *The Mystic Fable*, 2 vols. (Chicago: University of Chicago Press, 2015), 2:120–34; quote from 122–23; Chartier, *Order of Books*, 4–5.

68. Martin Luther, *Werke: Briefwechsel* (Weimar: Hermann Böhlaus, 1947), 10:201–6: The brothers of the church of Venice, Vicenza and Treviso to Luther (Venice, November 26, 1542).

69. Luther, *Werke*, 10:203: The brothers of the church of Venice, Vicenza and Treviso to Luther (Venice, November 26, 1542).

70. Luther, *Werke*, 10:206: The Brothers of the church of Venice, Vicenza and Treviso to Luther (Venice, November 26, 1542): "Memor itaque tu nostri sis, benignissime Luthere, non tam apud Deum precibus tuis ardentissimus, ut ipsius cognitione foeliciter impleamur per spiritum Christi, quam erudita, iucunda et frugi scriptorum ac literarum tuarum frequentia, ut ii, quos verbo veritatis genuisti, citius formentur et adolescant in virum perfectum aetatis Christi, quandoquidem hic famem atque penuriam verbi Dei acerbissimam patimur, non tam Antichristianorum feritate et inclementia, quam librariorum summa improbitate et avaritia paene incredibili, qui vestra scripta huc afferunt et ea sic fraudulenter opprimunt, donec carius illa venditaverint, non sine magno totius Ecclesiae detrimento."

71. Luther, *Werke*, 10:382–83: The Brothers of the church of Venice, Vicenza and Treviso to Luther (Venice, August 30, 1543).

72. Bucer's influence on the Italian reformers deserves further attention. See J. V. Pollet, *Martin Bucer: Études sur la correspondence,* 2 vols. (Paris: Presses Universitaires de France, 1958); Simoncelli, "Inquisizione romana"; and Silvana Seidel Menchi, "Les relations de Martin Bucer avec l'Italie," in *Martin Bucer and Sixteenth-Century Europe,* ed. Christian Krieger and Marc Lienhard, eds., 557–69 (Leiden: Brill, 1993).

73. *Opera Calvini,* XIII, c. 327. In 1550 the text was published in Florence in an Italian translation by Ludovico Domenichi: see Enrico Garavelli, *Lodovico Domenichi e i "Nicodemiana" di Calvino,* intro. Jean-François Gilmont (Rome: Vecchiarelli, 2004).

74. PC, II, 3: 1096, 1101; II, 1: 151.

75. On Soranzo, see Pio Paschini, *Tre ricerche sulla storia della chiesa nel Cinquecento* (Rome: Edizioni Liturgiche, 1945), 91–151; Simoncelli, "Inquisizione romana"; and Firpo, *Vittore Soranzo.*

76. PS, I, 365, 410 (see also 243–44): "Tenni sua amicitia ma secretta, perché sendo infamissimo non voleva infamasse me anchora, et la tenni per curiosità, per haver dei libri, ché 'l ne faceva mercantia et li vendeva carissimi." On Soranzo's involvement in the clandestine book trade, see also PS, I, 242.

77. PS, I, 400, 402. PS, II, 569–582. Cfr. BAV, Vat. Lat. 10755, cc. 89v–93v: Martin Luther to Altieri (Wittenberg, November 12, 1544), printed in Luther, *Werke,* 10 n. 4012, pp. 679–82, and republished in PS, II, 512–518; BAV, Vat. Lat. 10755, cc. 97v–110r: Martin Bucer to the brothers in Venice, Ferrara, Modena, and Bologna (Strasbourg, December 23, 1541); BAV, Vat. Lat. 10755, cc. 114v–116v: Martin Bucer to the brothers in Italy and Sicily (Spira, April 1, 1544), reprinted in PS, II, 512–18 and PS, II, 518–27.

78. On Donzellini, see Leandro Perini, "Ancora sul libraio-tipografo Pietro Perna e su alcune figure di eretici italiani in rapporto con lui negli anni 1549–1555," *Nuova Rivista storica* 3–4 (1967): 363–400, and Anne Jacobson Schutte, "Donzellini Girolamo," in DBI 41, 238–43.

79. ASV, Sant'Uffizio, b. 39, cc. 46v–47r (trial against Girolamo Donzellini): "fui per mezzo di amici introdotto nella casa del Signor Sighismondo Arovello, all'hora qui Ambasciatore per la corona di Inghilterra. dove pratticando, hebbi a conversar col suo secretario: che si chiamava Baldasar Altieri: homo letterato: ma quanto poi conobbi, molto avaro et ambitioso, et in nove opinioni di religione molto intricato: et che non solo leggeva libri prohibiti dalle leggi, ma ancho procurava che altri li leggessero. Intendendo costui da me che io haveva letto la logica, la filosofia naturale e morale di Filippo Melantone, li quali libri per esser profani, né trattar cose di religione et si vendevano publicamente per tutta Italia et si leggevano anco da catolici: mi persuadeva che io dovesse legger anchor libri del medesimo autore in materia di religione: dicendomi lui esser in la sua dottrina moderatissimo, et in poche cose discordante dalla chiesa Romana: et mi diede un libro chiamato Loci communes theologici, composto da esso Melantone, il quale io lessi et benché in quello trovai molte cose che non si accordavano colla mia fede: nondimeno le sue ragioni non hebbero alcuna forza presso di me, si che ponto mi mutassi dal mio credere: et restai quello istesso che era innanzi che tal libro leggessi. Et questa fu la prima tentatione che a me fu fatta." Donzellini's relationship with Harvel is confirmed by the inventory of his goods made after the latter's death. See ASV, Proprio Mobili, 8, c.155r (Venice, February 3, 1550).

80. On Carpan, see Massimo Firpo, *Artisti, gioiellieri, eretici: Il mondo di Lorenzo Lotto tra Riforma e Controriforma* (Rome: Laterza, 2001), 149–65. On Lotto's portrait of Carpan, see Martin, *Myths of Renaissance Individualism*, 21–23.

81. ASV, Sant'Uffizio, b. 29, fasc. 17, c. [12r] (trial against Bartolomeo Carpan): "perché l'imbasciator de Inghilterra preditto me disse che erano libri santi."

82. ASV, Sant'Uffizio, b. 29, fasc. 17, c. 5r., (trial against Bartolomeo Carpan).

83. ASV, Sant'Uffizio, b. 17, fasc. 3 (trial against Cinzio Polo); ASV, Sant'Uffizio, b. 11, fasc. 2 (trial against Andrea Ugoni); PS, I: 242, 400, 402.

84. ASV, Sant'Uffizio, b. 7, fasc. 20 (trial against Francesco Stella), partially published by Andrea Del Col, "Eterodossia e cultura fra gli artigiani di Porcia nel secolo XVI," *Il Noncello* 46 (1978): 53–54: "poveri contadini et persone idiote, a' quali predicavano et s'hanno ingegnato persuadere che l'imagini di santi sono cose vilissime et ch'un cane è più degno d'esser riverito che non è una imagine di nostra Donna o d'alcun santo." On Stella, see also Brown, *Venetian Printing Press*, 112–21, and Perini, "Ancora sul libraio-tipogtafo."

85. Luther, *Werke*, 10: 204: The brothers of the church of Venice, Vicenza and Treviso to Luther (Venice, November 26, 1542).

86. ASV, Sant'Uffizio. b. 156, fasc. Libri proibiti, Massime, Cataloghi, 1545–71: Altieri to the Protestant community in Bologna (Venice, June 18, 1545): "è venuto di qua per vedere se col mezzo di vendere libri si può guadagnare il pane' On Perna and his relationship with the English embassy in Venice, see Leandro Perini, *La vita e i tempi di Pietro Perna* (Rome: Edizioni di Storia e Letteratura, 2002), 64–68. On religious heterodoxy in sixteenth-century Bologna, see Guido Dall'Olio, *Eretici e inquisitori nella Bologna del Cinquecento* (Bologna: Istituto per la storia di Bologna, 1999).

87. ASV, Sant'Uffizio. b. 156, fasc. Libri proibiti, Massime, Cataloghi, 1545–71: Altieri to the Protestant community in Bologna (Venice, June 18, 1545): "state dunque saldi et non vi rimoviate da quella speranza ch'havete appresa nel santo evangelio che vi è stato predicato et annonciato . . . s'haverete al quanto di patientia vi prometto ch'in pochi giorni vedrete tutta la vostra città christiana, pensate fuorse ch'habbia sparso il suo seme costi senza speranza di raccoglierne il frutto nel suo tempo, dico che ci vuol piantare una chiesa et tale che pubblicamente gli possa senza impedimento riferirgli le debite gratie gli honori et culto che gli conviene in congregatione iustorum et lo farrà certamente."

88. Salvatore Caponetto, *Melantone e l'Italia* (Turin: Claudiana, 2000), 86–87: Matthias Guttich to Melanchton (Venice, February 15, 1544): "in tanta difficultate, ubi ecclesiam non licet in unum aliquem congregare locum propter legatum pontificis . . . colligit et largitur miseris. In summa quicquid fit in hac misera ecclesia, istius magno labore fit, ipse excitat, reliqui post sequuntur."

89. Caponetto, *Melantone e l'Italia*, 86–87: Matthias Guttich to Melanchton (Venice, February 15, 1544).

90. Luther, *Werke*, 10:204–5: The brothers of the church of Venice, Vicenza and Treviso to Luther (Venice, November 26, 1542): "Nam si in Germania, ubi tot sunt Ecclesiae recte institutae, totque viri sanctissimi, spiritu ferventissimi, atque omni eruditione praestantes, huiusmodi venenum tantum invaluit . . . quanto magis apud nos ea pestis evagata est, ut indies fiat insolentior! ubi nullas publice habemus, sed quilibet sibi ipsi est

ecclesia. . . . . Omnes videri sibi malunt magistri, quam discipuli, cum parum habeant eruditionis; omnes prophetae, cum nihil sciant, neque spiritu Dei agantur."

91. ASV, Sant'Uffizio, b. 11, fasc. 2 (trial against Andrea Ugoni, Brescia, July 1552), c. 228.

92. On Henry VIII and the League of Schmalkalden, see Rory McEntegart, *Henry VIII, the League of Schmalkalden, and the English Reformation* (London: The Royal Historical Society, 2002).

93. ASV, Capi del Consiglio di dieci, Dispacci degli ambasciatori, 14, n. 69–70 (deciphered): Giacomo Zambon to the Capi del consiglio di dieci (London, September 20, 1545).

94. On Vergerio, see Anne Jacobson Schutte, *Pier Paolo Vergerio: The Making of an Italian Reformer* (Geneva: Droz, 1977), and more recently Silvano Cavazza, "Pier Paolo Vergerio nei Grigioni e in Valtellina (1549–1553): attività editoriale e polemica religiosa," in *Riforma e società nei Grigioni, Valtelllina e Valchiavenna tra '500 e '600*, ed. Alessandro Pastore, 33–62 (Milan: Franco Angeli, 1991); Ugo Rozzo, ed., *Pier Paolo Vergerio il giovane, un polemista attraverso l'Europa del Cinquecento* (Udine: Forum, 2000); Robert A. Pierce, *Pier Paolo Vergerio the Propagandist* (Rome: Edizioni di Storia e Letteratura, 2003).

95. BUP, MS 1656, cc. 81r–93v: *Oratione al doge Francesco Donado per il suo ingresso, esortatione alla Riforma della Chiesa*. Altieri's handwriting has been recognized by Ugo Rozzo, "La lettera al doge Francesco Donà del 1545 e il problema politico della Riforma in Italia," *Acta Histriae* 8 (1999): 29–48. The manuscript has been published by Aldo Stella, "L'orazione di Pier Paolo Vergerio al doge Francesco Donà sulla riforma della Chiesa (1545)," *Atti dell'Istituto Veneto di Scienze, Lettere ed Arti: Classe di scienze morali, lettere e arti* 128 (1969–70): 1–39. On Vergerio's letter to Donà, see also Salvatore Caponetto, Review of A. Stella, "L'orazione di Pier Paolo Vergerio al doge Francesco Donà sulla riforma della Chiesa (1545)," *Rivista storica italiana* 2 (1971): 466–68; Schutte, *Pier Paolo Vergerio*, 201–5. The letter was printed in 1547, and made to conform to the Tuscan vernacular in *Orationi diverse et nuove di eccellentissimi auttori* (Florence: Anton Francesco Doni, 1547), 7r–12v.

96. BUP, MS 1656, c. 89v: "Ci sono di libri stampati nelle materie di religione, si vendono in publico, i buoni popoli se li comprano, et leggono."

97. BUP, MS 1656, c. 89v: "far vedere questi libri da persone fideli et veraci, et che non habbino interessi, et se saranno buoni in tutte le parti, si harranno lasciar liberamente leggere et con severe pene prohibire, che non si scriva contra di loro." On Politi, see Giorgio Caravale, *Sulle tracce dell'eresia: Ambrogio Catarino Politi (1484–1553)* (Florence: Olschki, 2007).

98. BUP, MS 1656, c. 91r-v.

99. BUP, MS 1656, c. 92r: "vedono i popoli, vedono che in questa chiesa vi sono delle cose, le quali in somma bisogna emendare, Hanno aspettato et aspettano anchora, che un legitimo concilio faccia lo effetto, et quando harranno aspettato et aspettato, et che vedano per il concilio non se ne faccia altro, vorran far da per loro, et tutto non starà bene ciò, che farà un popolo, et una moltitudine, La potrebe far delle cose, lequali sarebbono in dishonor di Dio, et in qualche gran alterazione delle cose publice, Anchora è tempo di potervi occorrer, et rimediar; Adunque non si dorma, Principe eccellentissimo. Questa è materia tale, per la quale vostra Serenità medesima doverebbe per mia fe' in

persona propria, non solo per i suoi oratori, andare d'intorno, andar dai Pontefici, da i Imperatori, dai Re, andar nel concilio medesimo, et ivi esshortar, pregar, supplicar, ogn'uno, che per l'amor di Dio si spogli d'ogni passione, et d'ogni interesse, et attenda alla Emendatione et instauratione della chiesa, alla salute et securezza di popoli, alla gloria di Dio."

100. BUP, MS 1656, c. 92v–93r: "voi siete padre di tanti gran gentilhuomeni, tanti cittadini, tanti popoli, che sono sotto il dominio vostro, per figliuoli li havete tutti, et non per subditi, così fu sempre l'usanza della vostra santa Republica. Or se i padri debbono haver cura di nutrir i figliuoli, di vestir i figliuoli, di custodirli dai pericoli delle vite, di acquistar loro della robba, vogliam dire, che non ne debbono haver di quella parte, che importa più, che è l'anima, anzi la debbono haver precipuamente di questa, et sarebbe un empio padre, un scempio padre colui, che al figliuolo dicesse: vedi, figliolo, io ti darò da vivere, et da vestire, io ti difendarò la vita corporale, ma quanto aspetta all'anima tua io non me ne voglio impacciare, né poco né molto." On the Venetian osmosis between the political and the spiritual spheres, see Paolo Prodi, "Structure and Organization of the Church in Renaissance Venice: Suggestions for Research," in *Renaissance Venice*, ed. John R. Hale, 409–30 (London: Faber and Faber, 1973).

101. Silvana Seidel Menchi, "Characteristics of Italian Anticlericalism," in *Anticlericalism in Late Medieval and Early Modern Europe*, ed. 271–81 (Leiden: Brill, 1993), 273. On anticlericalism in early modern Italy, see also Ottavia Niccoli, *Rinascimento anticlericale. Infamia, propaganda e satira in Italia tra Quattrocento e Cinquecento* (Rome: Laterza, 2005).

102. Stella, "Utopie e velleità insurrezionali."

103. Watkins, "Toward a New Diplomatic History"; Prosperi, "Una esperienza di ricerca al S. Uffizio," 246; Rossi, *Un altro presente.*

104. Stella, *"Utopie e velleità insurrezionali,"* 168: Baldassarre Altieri to Philip, Landgrave of Hesse (Venice, June 20, 1546): "Cuperem ad hoc solemnes litteras, quibus pateret dominos protestantes me constituere suum agentem, ut appellant, non solum hic Venetiis, verum per universam Italiam meque commendarent omnibus principibus, rebuspublicis, civitatibus ac ditionibius ipsius Italiae."

105. ASV, Consiglio dei Dieci, Deliberazioni, Secrete, r. 65 (June 4, 1546); ASV, Senato, Deliberazioni, Secrete, f. 21 (July 24, 1546).

106. BMV: MS Italiani, Classe VII, 808 (7296): "Annali di 1545–1546" (June 8) (without pagination).

107. MC MS Cicogna 2552, "Annali delle cose della Repubblica di Venezia dall'anno 1541–1548" (June 8) (without pagination): "non si trattava de fede ma de stato. Che questi Principi sono Signori grandi, et sono quasi tutta l'Alemagna, che hanno la mira ad opporsi alla grandezza dell'Imperatore"; "che se voleano haver rispetto alla fede bisogneria far altro, non bisognaria dar fomento a quelli che fanno simonie accennando ai preti." See the same account, with some variations, in BMV MS Italiani, Classe VII, 808 (7296): "Annali di 1545–1546."

108. Lorenzo Campana, "Monsignor Giovanni della Casa e i suoi tempi," *Studi storici* 1 (1907): 367: Alessandro Farnese to Giovanni della Casa (Rome, June 5, 1546): "ha procurato et mendicato, per diversi mezzi, lettere de' protestanti credentiali, non a fine di negotiar per loro, ma solo per potere, sotto cotal colore, viver libero et scrivere delle cose tanto di quel dominio come d'altri a suo arbitrio, et far capo alla setta con cautela."

109. Buschbell, *Reformation und Inquisition*, 244–45: Ottavio Raverta to Marcello Cervini (Venice, January 4, 1547): "ha fatto venire molti di quei libbri di Luthero adversum Papatum Rome a Sathana inventum et insieme quella opera del Bucero contro il Concilio di Trento."

110. Buschbell, *Reformation und Inquisition*, 94n5: Dionigi Zannettini to Marcello Cervini (Bologna, December 12, 1547).

111. ASV, Archivi propri ambasciatori, Germania, 1, 141v: Alvise Mocenigo to the Senate (Marxheim, October 1–2, 1546).

112. Stella, "Utopie e velleità insurrezionali," 169, Guido Giannetti to Giovanni Federico di Sassonia (Marburg, June 24, 1546). On Giannetti, see chapter 3.

113. Stella, "Utopie e velleità insurrezionali," 169–70, Guido Giannetti to Giovanni Federico di Sassonia (Marburg, June 24, 1546): "Nemlich do sich die Sachenn . . . dermassenn zutragenn soltten das mit zuthuenn etzlicher Hernn und Fürstenn durch das Trientisch Concilium ein Zug wieder die Fürstenn und Stennde der deutzschenn Nationn beschlossenn wurde. Der Meinung Inen das reine ware Evangelium und Bekentnis des gotlichen Worts widerumb zu. . . . So konte man vorauff verdacht sein wie mann den Babst als desselbenn Conciliumbs Obersthaupt in seinen eigenenn Lanndnen angreiffen mochte."

114. Stella, "Utopie e velleità insurrezionali," 170, Guido Giannetti to Giovanni Federico di Sassonia (Marburg, June 24, 1546).

115. ASV, Consiglio dei Dieci, Deliberazioni secrete, filza 6 (October 13, 1546); ASV, Senato, Deliberazioni, Secreti, r. 65, ff. 60r-v (October 18, 1546). On Dall'Armi, see Stella, "Utopie e velleità insurrezionali," 147–50.

116. ASV, Capi del Consiglio di dieci, Dispacci degli ambasciatori, 14, n. 69–70 (deciphered): Giacomo Zambon to the Capi del consiglio di dieci (London, September 20, 1545).

117. ASV, Capi del Consiglio di dieci, Dispacci degli ambasciatori, 14, n. 64–65 (deciphered): Giacomo Zambon to the Capi del consiglio di dieci (London, September 2, 1545): "questi signori trattano al presente di promuover a Vostra Serenità certi partiti o di lega secreta insieme o simil cosa."

118. ASV, Capi del Consiglio di dieci, Dispacci degli ambasciatori, 14, n. 69–70 (contemporary chancery deciphering): Giacomo Zambon to the Capi del consiglio di dieci (London, September 20, 1545): "si dechiari protestante come loro."

119. ASV, Capi del Consiglio di dieci, Dispacci degli ambasciatori, 14, n. 69–70 (contemporary chancery deciphering): Giacomo Zambon to the Capi del consiglio di dieci (London, September 20, 1545).

120. ASV, Capi del Consiglio di dieci, Dispacci degli ambasciatori, 14, n. 73–74 (contemporary chancery deciphering): Giacomo Zambon to the Capi del consiglio di dieci (London, October 29, 1546).

121. ASV, Capi del Consiglio di dieci, Dispacci degli ambasciatori, 14, n. 78–79 (contemporary chancery deciphering): Giacomo Zambon to the Capi del consiglio di dieci (London, February 3, 1547), informing the Venetian government that William Paget had terminated Dall'Armi's commission.

122. On Dall'Armi's death see Stella, "Utopie e velleità insurrezionali," 158.

123. Carlo Ginzburg, ed., *I costituti di don Pietro Manelfi* (DeKalb: Northern Illinois University Press, 1970).

124. See Altieri's letter to Francisco de Enzinas (Venice, June 22, 1547) in Pollet, *Martin Bucer*, II, 481–82, no. 5.

125. Aretino, *Lettere,* V, 179, p. 139: Aretino to Philip Hoby (Venice, January 1549).

126. ASV, Sant'Uffizio, b. 7, fasc. 20: trial against Francesco Stella (Venice, April 1, 1549): "Ha piaciuto al Signor Iddio d'accelerare la mia partita, la quale ho da fare tra 8 giorni alla più lunga, et in questo mezzo ho da mettermi all'ordine, et subito poi montare a cavallo, n'ho tempo da fermarmi in nessun luogo per il rispetto importante che voi sapete. Et perché questa mia levata non voglio che sia intesa da nessuno se non da voi solo, però volendo venire mettetevi in ordine fra 5 o 6 giorni et po venetevene qui che ci levaremo di conpagnia."

127. Camillo Renato, *Opere, documenti e testimonianze*, ed. Antonio Rotondò (Florence: Sansoni: 1968), 232–35.

128. Altieri's death was mentioned to the Venetian inquisitors by Girolamo Allegretti on September 11, 1550. See ASV, Sant'Uffizio b. 8, f. 10 (trial against Girolamo Allegretti).

129. ASV, Collegio, Esposizioni principi, filza 1, cc. 540r–541v (March 2, 1547).

130. Harvel's last letters to the English court concern the Dall'Armi affair: see LP, 21, II, 269: Harvel to Lord William Paget (Venice, October 15, 1546); LP, 21, III, 603: Harvel to Henry VIII (Venice, December 23, 1546).

131. CSP *Venetian*, V, 291–92, n. 615.

132. ASV, Collegio, Lettere secrete, f. 18: August 9, 1555 (not numbered).

133. ASV, Sant'Uffizio, b. 39, c. 47v (trial against Girolamo Donzellini), PC, II, 3, pp. 1096–97. On Vanni's relationship with the Italian reformers, see Overell, *Italian Reform*, 95–96.

134. ASV, Consiglio di Dieci, Deliberazioni secrete, f. 8: January 30, 1555 (not numbered).

135. See David Potter, "Mid-Tudor Foreign Policy and Diplomacy: 1547–63," in *Tudor England and Its Neighbours*, ed. Susan Doran and Glen Richardson, 106–38 (Basingstoke: Palgrave, 2005).

136. ASV, Senato, Dispacci degli ambasciatori, Inghilterra, f. 1, n. 47, cc. 115r–116r: Giovanni Michiel to the Senate (London, December 3, 1555).

137. ASV, Senato, Dispacci degli ambasciatori, Inghilterra, f. 1, n. 82, cc. 188r-v: Giovanni Michiel to the Senate (London, September 22, 1556).

138. ASV, Senato, Dispacci ambasciatori, Inghilterra, f. 1,n. 97, cc. 222r-v: Giovanni Michiel to the Senate (January 4, 1557).

3. Spying on the Council of Trent

1. Adriano Prosperi, *Il Concilio di Trento: una introduzione storica* (Turin: Einaudi, 2001), 165–68: "la custodia dei documenti nell'Archivio segreto vaticano si impose come garanzia del controllo e della gestione delle informazioni."

2. Paolo Sarpi, *The historie of the Councel of Trent* (London: Robert Baker and John Bill, 1620), 1. See the original text in Paolo Sarpi, *Istoria del Concilio Tridentino*, ed. Corrado Vivanti (Einaudi: Turin, 2011), 5: "Io subito ch'ebbi gusto delle cose umane, fui preso

da gran curiosità di saperne l'intiero, e dopo l'aver letto con diligenza quello che trovai scritto e li publici documenti usciti in stampa o divulgati a penna, mi diedi a ricercar nelle reliquie de'scritti de prelati et altri nel concilio intervenuti, le memorie da loro lasciate e li voti o pareri detti in publico, conservati dagli autori proprii o da altri, e le lettere d'avisi da quella città scritte, non tralasciando fatica o diligenza, onde ho avuto grazia di vedere sino qualche registro intiero di note e lettere di persone ch'ebbero gran parte in quei maneggi." It was probably through his friendship with Roberto Bellarmino that Sarpi was able to access the correspondence of Marcello Cervini, legate to the council and later pope Marcellus II. See Corrado Vivanti, *Quattro lezioni su Paolo Sarpi* (Naples: Bibliopolis, 2005), 121–57.

3. Hubert Jedin, *Storia del Concilio di Trento*, 4 vols. (Brescia: Morcelliana, 1973–81), 4:2, pp. 302–6. On Trent, see also more recently Paolo Prodi, "Controriforma e/o riforma cattolica: superamento di vecchi dilemmi nei nuovi panorami storiografici," in *Crisi e rinnovamenti nell'autunno del Rinascimento a Venezia*, ed. Vittore Branca and Carlo Ossola, 11–21 (Florence: Olschki, 1991); Paolo Prodi and Wolfgang Reinhard, eds., *Il concilio di Trento e il moderno* (Bologna: Il Mulino, 1996); Prosperi, *Tribunali della coscienza*; Alain Tallon, *Le France et le concile de Trente (1518–1563)* (Rome: École française de Rome, 1997); Ronnie Po-Chia Hsia, *The World of Catholic Renewal* (Cambridge: Cambridge University Press, 1998); John O'Malley, *Trent and All That: Renaming Catholicism in the Early Modern Era* (Cambridge, MA: Harvard University Press, 2000); Prosperi, *Il Concilio di Trento*; Firpo, *Inquisizione romana*; Simon Ditchfield, "In Sarpi's Shadow: Coping with Trent the Italian Way," in *Studi in memoria di Cesare Mozzarelli*, 2 vols. (Milan: Vita e Pensiero, 2008), 1:585–606; Massimo Firpo and Ottavia Niccoli, *Il cardinale Giovanni Morone e l'ultima fase del concilio di Trento* (Bologna: Il Mulino, 2010); Paolo Prodi and Wolfgang Reinhard, eds., *Il paradigma tridentino: Un'epoca di storia della chiesa* (Brescia: Morcelliana, 2010); John O'Malley, *Trent: What Happened at the Council* (Cambridge, MA: Belknap Press of Harvard University Press, 2013); Michela Catto and Adriano Prosperi, eds., *Trent and Beyond: The Council, Other Powers, Other Cultures* (Turnhout: Brepols, 2017).

4. On other Protestant reactions to Trent, see Robert M. Kingdon, "Some French Reactions to the Council of Trent," *Church History* 2 (1964): 149–56; Robert E. McNally, "The Council of Trent and the German Protestants," *Theological Studies* 25 (1964): 1–22; Theodore W. Casteel, "Calvin and Trent: Calvin's Reactions to the Council of Trent in the Context of His Conciliar Thought," *Harvard Theological Review* 1 (1970): 91–117; Catto and Prosperi, eds., *Trent and Beyond*.

5. Prosperi, *Il Concilio di Trento*, 44–50.

6. Firpo and Niccoli, *Il cardinale Giovanni Morone*; Gigliola Fragnito and Alain Tallon, eds., *Hétérodoxies croisées: Catholicismes pluriels entre France et Italie, XVIe–XVIIe siècles* (Rome: Publications de l'École française de Rome, 2015) (http://books.openedition.org/efr/2823).

7. PC, II, 2, 509: "un poco di più … di quello che harrei fatto ordinariamente per curiosità d'intendere delle cose d'Inghilterra et poterne avvisare il cardinale d'Inghilterra ch'era allhora in Italia." On the trial against Carnesecchi, see PC, I, pp. III-XCIX, and PC, II, 1, pp. V-CLI.

8. PC, II, 2, 512.

9. PC, II, 2, 571: "gentilhuomini parte venetiani parte forastieri . . . si sogliono raggunare la matina . . . sotto la loggia di San Marco et quivi ragionare e discorrere ciascuno secondo il suo senso sopra li avvisi che si hanno delle cose del mondo."

10. PC, II, 2, 512: "Io l'ho detto mille volte et lo replico di nuovo che a Venetia s'intendeno le nove di tutto il mondo et per ognuno et senza difficultà niuna, perché quelli Signori hanno ambasciadori per tutto et le lettere che essi scrivono—massime non concernenti l'interesse del loro Stato—si leggano publicamente in Pregai donde poi si divulgano per tutta la città. Et qualche volta havevo qualche avviso da messer Guido Giannetti, il quale era avvisato dalli amici suoi di là." On Giannetti's knowledge of English affairs, see also PC, II, 1, 252; II, 2, 401; II, 2, 473; II, 2, 571; II, 2, 598.

11. PC, I, 142 (see also PC II, 3: 1196 and 1088); ASV, Capi del Consiglio di Dieci, Dispacci degli ambasciatori, f. 25, n.5–6: Paolo Tiepolo to the Capi del Consiglio di Dieci (Rome, July 6, 1566).

12. The only studies dedicated to Giannetti are Aldo Stella, "Guido da Fano eretico del secolo XVI al servizio del Re d'Inghilterra" *Rivista di storia della Chiesa in Italia* 13, no. 2 (1959): 196–238; and Guido Dall'Olio, "Giannetti, Guido" in DBI 54, 453–55. See also the detailed biographical sketch by Massimo Firpo in PM, I, p. 282, n. 82.

13. SP 70/9 f. 13: Giannetti to Cecil (Venice, December 2, 1559).

14. On Casali, see Adriano Prosperi, "Casali, Gregorio," in DBI, 21, 92–97; and Fletcher, *Our Man in Rome.*

15. PC, II, 1, 198–99.

16. SP 1/73 c.18 (Westminster, December 7, 1532).

17. SP 1/135 c.10r: Giannetti to Cromwell (London, August 2, 1538); SP 1/135 c.12r: Giannetti to Cromwell (London, August 2, 1538); BL: Cotton Vitellius B/XIV c.251r: Giannetti to Cromwell (Rome, April 1538); BL, Cotton Vitellius B/XIV cc.270r–271r: Giannetti to Cromwell (Rome, February 5, 1539).

18. Stella, "Utopie e velleità insurrezionali," 169–70.

19. *Calendars of State Papers, Foreign Series, of the Reign of Edward VI, 1547–1553* (London: Longman, 1861), 235n601: Bartolomeo Balbani to Francis Yaxley (Antwerp, January 3, 1553). For Giannetti's relationship with Balbani, see also PC, II, 2, 512, and PCA, 299.

20. PC, II, 3, 1116. On Pole's role in England during the reign of Mary Tudor, see De Frede, *La restaurazione cattolica*, 43–82. On the accusations moved against Pole by Italian Protestant refugees, especially by Vergerio, for his role in the Catholic restoration in England, see Simoncelli, *Il caso Reginald Pole*, Mayer, *Reginald Pole*, 302–99; Overell, *Italian Reform*, 145–66.

21. PC, II, 1, 198–99.

22. PC, II, 1, 198–99.

23. On *avvisi* in early modern Venice, see Infelise, *Prima dei giornali*; Mario Infelise, "From Merchants' Letters to Handwritten Political Avvisi: Notes on the Origins of Public Information," in *Correspondence and Cultural Exchange in Early Europe, 1400–1700,* ed. Francisco Bethencourt and Florike Egmond (Cambridge: Cambridge University Press, 2007), 33–52.

24. ASV, Capi del Consiglio dei Dieci, Lettere di rettori, Padova, b. 83, n. 73r (Padua, July 14, 1566).

25. Filippo De Vivo, "Public Sphere or Communication Triangle?" in *Beyond the Public Sphere: Opinions, Publics, Spaces in Early Modern Europe*, ed. Massimo Rospocher (Bologna: Il Mulino, 2012), 128.

26. Livio Sanuto, *Geografia distinta in XII libri* (Venice: Damiano Zenaro, 1588), 2.

27. On Venice as center of information on the East, see Hans J. Kissling, "Venezia come centro di informazioni sui Turchi," in *Venezia centro di mediazione tra oriente e occidente (secoli XV-XVI): aspetti e problemi*, eds. Hans Georg Beck, Manoussos Manoussacas, and Agostino Pertusi, 2 vols. (Florence: Olshcki, 1977), 1:97–109; Robert Mantran, "Venise, centre d'information sur les Turcs," in Beck, Manoussacas, and Pertusi, *Venezia centro di mediazione tra oriente e occidente*, 1:111–16; Eric Dursteler, "Power and Information: The Venetian Postal System in the Early Modern Eastern Mediterranean, 1573–1645," in *From Florence to the Mediterranean: Studies in Honor of Anthony Molho*, ed. Diogo Curto et al., 601–23 (Florence: Olschki, 2009), 601–23; Johann Petitjean, *L'intelligence des choses: Une histoire de l'information entre Italie et Méditerranée (XVIe–XVIIe siècles)* (Rome: École française de Rome, 2013).

28. SP 70/18, cc. 11r–12r: Giannetti to Elizabeth I (Venice, September 7, 1560): "in poter del Turco, accrescendogli potentia nel mar mediterraneo, e riputatione sopra tanta forza di si gran Principe christiano."

29. SP 1/111, cc. 189r-v: Giannetti to Richard Pate (Rome, November 21, 1536). On Richard Pate, see Kenneth Carleton, "Pates, Richard (1503/4–1565)," ODNB (http://www .oxforddnb.com/view/article/21522, accessed October 8, 2017), and Tracey Sowerby, "Richard Pate, the Royal Supremacy, and Reformation Diplomacy," *Historical Journal* 54, no. 2 (2011): 265–85.

30. On the third phase of the council, see Jedin, *Storia del Concilio di Trento*, 4:367–404; and more recently Firpo and Niccoli, *Il cardinale Giovanni Morone* and O'Malley, *Trent*, 168–247.

31. SP, 70/35, cc. 119r-v: Giannetti to Cecil (Venice, March 14, 1562).

32. SP 70/21 cc. 89r–90v: Giannetti to Elizabeth I (Venice, December 21, 1560): "In detta bolla il Concilio è convocato a la città di Trento, rimovendone la sospensione fatta da Iulio Terzo. Il giorno da cominciarlo è la prossima pasqua di resurrettione. Le cause di congregarlo son dette: il voler estirpar le heresie, rimuovere lo schisma, corregger li costumi." For the text of the *Ad ecclesiae regimen*, see CT, VIII, 104–107.

33. SP 70/40, cc. 7r–9v: Giannetti to Cecil (Venice, August 1, 1562). See CT, VIII, 698–704.

34. Schutte, *Pier Paolo Vergerio*, 80–104; Giorgio Caravale, "La polemica protestante contro il Tridentino," in *L'uomo del Concilio: il cardinale Giovanni Morone tra Roma e Trento nell'età di Michelangelo*, ed. Roberto Pancheri and Domenica Primerano, 47–61 (Trent: Temi, 2009). See the account of Vergerio's meeting with Luther and his memorandum on the bull in *Nuntiaturberichte aus Deutschland 1533–1559 nebst ergänzenden Actenstücken*, I: *Nuntiaturen des Vergerio 1533–1536*, ed. Walter Friedensburg (Gotha: Friedrich Andreas Perthes, 1892), 540–41, and 548–88.

35. On Vergerio's pamphlets, see Simoncelli, *Il caso Reginald Pole*, 76–145; Cavazza, "Pier Paolo Vergerio; Silvano Cavazza, "La censura ingannata: polemiche antiromane e usi della propaganda in Pier Paolo Vergerio," in *La censura libraria nell'Europa del secolo XVI*, ed. Ugo Rozzo, 273–95 (Udine: Forum, 1997); Pierce, *Pier Paolo Vergerio*; Giorgio

Caravale, *Predicazione e inquisizone nell'Italia del Cinquecento: Ippolito Chizzola tra eresia e controversia antiprotestante* (Bologna: Il Mulino, 2012), 167–80. Still useful on Vergerio's long bibliography is Friedrich Hubert, *Vergerios publizistische Thätigkeit, nebst einer bibliographischen Übersicht* (Göttingen: Vandenhoeck & Ruprecht, 1893).

36. Pier Paolo Vergerio, *Al serenissimo re d'Inghilterra Edoardo sesto de' portamenti di Papa Giulio III: Et quale habbia ad essere il concilio, che egli intende di fare* (Poschiavo: Dolfino Landolfi, 1550); Pier Paolo Vergerio, *Al Serenissimo Re d'Inghilterra Edoardo sesto: Della creatione del nuovo Papa, Giulio terzo, & ciò che di lui sperare si possa* (N. p.: n. p., 1550); Pier Paolo Vergerio, *Ad serenissimum Angliae regem, etc. Ecclesiae Christi defensorem, Eduardum VI: De creatione Iulii III pontificis romani, tum quid de eius papatu sperari possit* (Basel: Jean Oporin, 1550); Pier Paolo Vergerio, *Risposta ad un libro del Nausea vescouo di Vienna scritto in laude del concilio tridentino* (Poschiavo: Dolfino Landolfi, 1552); Pier Paolo Vergerio, *Alla serenissima regina d'Inghilterra del concilio di Trento* (Tübingen: [Morhard] 1562). On Vergerio and England, see Ann M. Overell, "Vergerio's Anti-Nicodemite Propaganda and England," *Journal of Ecclesiastical History* 5 (2000): 296–318.

37. Robert Scribner, *For the Sake of Simple Folk: Popular Propaganda for the German Reformation* (Oxford: Clarendon Press, 1994), xxii–xxiii.

38. Vergerio, *Al serenissimo re d'Inghilterra Edoardo sesto de' portamenti di Papa Giulio III*, p. 16r.

39. Cavazza, *Pier Paolo Vergerio*, 50.

40. Pier Paolo Vergerio, "A quegli venerabili padri domenicani, che difendono il Rosario per cosa buona," partially reproduced in Silvano Cavazza, "'Quei che vogliono Cristo senza croce': Vergerio e i prelati riformatori italiani (1549–1555)," in Ugo Rozzo, ed. *Pier Paolo Vergerio il giovane, un polemista attraverso l'Europa del Cinquecento*, ed. Ugo Rozzo, 136–41 (Udine: Forum, 2000), 138: "che i christiani debbono star patienti, et consentire agli errori et alle idolatrie, et non aprire bocca, né far parola in contrario, fin a tanto che non sia fatto il concilio." Pole was the focus of several attacks from Vergerio. See, for example, Francesco Negri, *Della tragedia intitolata Libero Arbitrio* (Basel: Johann Oporin, 1550). The preface to the second edition was drafted by Vergerio as noted by Cavazza, "Pier Paolo Vergerio," 52. On Vergerio and Pole, see Simoncelli, *Il caso Reginald Pole*, 76–145; and Overell, *Italian Reform*, 145–66.

41. Hubert Jedin and Paolo Prodi, eds., *Il concilio di Trento come crocevia della politica europea* (Bologna: Il Mulino, 1979); Prosperi, *Il Concilio di Trento*, 44–50.

42. SP 70/17, cc. 15r–16v: Giannetti to Elizabeth I (Venice, August 3, 1560): "Serenissima e Clementissima Regina. Havendo il Papa offerto Concilio generale all'Imperatore, al Re di Francia, al Re di Spagna, e ad altri Principi, il Re di Spagna accetta l'offerta. Del luogo dove si debbe tenere, essendogli proposta la città di Trento, si rimette a quello, che piacerà all'Imperatore, e al Re di Francia. Il Papa, o suo consiglio sopra ciò apena che ardisce darlo a Trento, temendo la presente potentia di Germania, e non si assecurando tanto sotto la protettione di Ferdinando, quanto già si assicuravano sotto quella di Carlo Quinto, il quale oltra l'Imperio Germanico haveva tanti altri reami, che rendevano la sua potentia formidabile." On Charles V's conciliar politics, see Jedin, *Storia del Concilio di Trento,* 1:251–302, and more recently Firpo, "Politica imperiale e vita religiosa."

43. SP 70/17, c. 15r: Giannetti to Elizabeth I (Venice, August 3, 1560): "Vedendo chiaro il Tridentino haver operato contrario effetto a la intentione, essendo per occasione di

quello divenuta maggiore e più gagliarda la parte protestante. E lo domanda, (non so quanto caldamente) in città libera di Germania."

44. SP 70/21, cc. 45r–47r: Giannetti to Elizabeth I (Venice, December 7, 1560): "superiore al Papa (e la Chiesa di Francia non l'ha mai inteso altramente) e libero, e securo si che gli Alamanni vi possino essere uditi: cosa che il Papa non concederebbe mai, se li Re di Christianità di propria autorità nol facessero."

45. SP 70/39, c. 25r: Giannetti to Elizabeth I (Venice, July 11, 1562). See CT, VIII, 618.

46. SP 70/32, cc. 40r–41r: Giannetti to Elizabeth (Venice, November 15, 1561): "Non è huomo che creda, che li Papali sieno per fare in Concilio cosa che voglino. Hanno pensato chiamando Concilio a Trento impedire il corso de la riformatione in Francia: e pare che più tosto l'habbino affrettato. Temono mandare avanti il Concilio, e parimente il rivocarlo. Rivocandolo, qualch'altra provintia senz'altro aspettare si commoverebbe da la sua posta a riformatione di chiesa. Onde le cose anderebbono per Roma di male in peggio. Mandandolo avanti, benché Protestanti non vi comparissino, li Vescovi Spagnuoli, Francesi, e Tedeschi per Imperadore facilmente al primo tratto verrebbono a questo punto, che tengono, che il Papa al Concilio non sia superiore, ma debba sottoporsi: dove si havrebbe a disputare de la potestà del Papa. Talché mentre fuggissino i pericoli, in quelli ricaderebbono tuttavia. In questo modo, Auribus Lupum tenent."

47. ASV, Capi del Consiglio dei Dieci, Lettere di rettori, Padova, b. 83, n. 73r (Padua, July 14, 1566).

48. Desiderius Erasmus, *Opera omnia* (Amsterdam: North Holland, 1969–2017), 2:1, pp. 498–99: "Dicitur in eos, qui eiusmodi negotio involvuntur, quod neque relinquere sit integrum neque tolerari possit . . . quod ut lepus auribus quippe praelongis commodissime tenetur, ita lupus quod aures habet pro corpore breviores, teneri iis non potest neque rursum citra summum periculum e manibus dimitti belua tam mordax." English translation by Margaret Mann Phillips, in Erasmus, *Adages*, 7 vols. (Toronto: University of Toronto Press, 1982–2006), vol. 5, pp. 404–5.

49. SP 70/41 c. 106r: Giannetti to Elizabeth I (Venice, September 12, 1562): "aborriscono quella predicatione: e sarebbono presti di fare ogni cosa per sbandirla del mondo"; "che questa dottrina tende a camino di non obedire a magistrati, di rivoltare e rinovare stato e signoria."

50. SP 70/40 cc. 244v: Giannetti to Elizabeth I (August 29, 1562); SP 70/41 c. 106r: "si scuopre ogni di più gagliarda la parte de professori de l'Evangelio"; Giannetti to Elizabeth I (Venice, September 12, 1562): "Ne le terre di Savoia sono popoli, che stanno su l'armi per non essere forzati ne la religione" [In the lands of Savoy there are communities, who take up arms to avoid being forced on religious matters].

51. SP 70/40 cc. 244r-v: Giannetti to Elizabeth I (Venice, August 29, 1562): "che per conto di Religione si vada a pericolo di mutatione di stato, cosa che non vorrebbono vedere, che avvenisse in Italia."

52. SP 70/36, c. 118r–119r: Giannetti to Elizabeth I (Venice, April 25, 1562): "Questi Illustrissimi Signori Venetiani a grande instantia del Papa finalmente vi hanno mandato doi ambasciadori huomini del lor Senato gravi e prudenti: I quali, se in Trento non si procederà d'altra maniera, dovranno essere solamente spettatori" [Those illustrious Venetian lords, at the pope's great insistence, finally sent two dignified and prudent

ambassadors from their Senate: if things do not proceed differently in Trent, these men will be only spectators].

53. See Guido Dall'Olio, "Gelido, Pietro," in DBI 53, 2–5. For the relationship between Giannetti and Gelido, see PCA, 293.

54. Hubert Jedin, "La politica conciliare di Cosimo I," *Rivista storica italiana*, 62 (1950): 345–74, 477–96; and Massimo Firpo, *Gli affreschi di Pontormo* (Turin: Einaudi, 1997), 327–39, 393–403.

55. SP 70/21, cc. 46r-v: Gianetti to Elizabeth I (Venice, December 7, 1560): "Per tanto ha grandemente sollecitato il Duca di Fiorenza di andar a Roma, volendo consigliarsi con lui sopra ciò, facendo grande stima de la sua amistà, e del suo consiglio. L'ha sommamente honorato e accarezzato, e allogiato a sue spese lui e la Duchessa nel suo palazzo papale. Si è consigliato seco sopra i suoi affari, spetialmente in questo più importante del Concilio nel quale ha detto haver il Duca in luogo di suo consigliero."

56. SP70/21 c. 90v. Giannetti to Elizabeth I (Venice, December 21, 1560): "Ma quello che importa più è che il Duca di Fiorenza vorrebbe dal Papa, e dal Imperatore, o almanco di consenso del Imperatore, esser criato Re di Toscana: e il Papa vorrebbe farlo. Ma l'Imperatore gagliardamente lo diniegò . . . con dire, che essendo esso Re di Romani, non deve interporre altro Re in Italia."

57. Prosperi, *Tribunali della coscienza*, 75–83.

58. PCA, 293: "in casa di monsignore Carnesecca . . . si leggeva qualche volte l'Historie dello Slidano. . . . Mi ricordo bene di messer Guido Giannetti, che lui ancora ci veniva et praticava domestichissimamente lì: et potria esser che anco lui l'havesse inteso a legger perché ci veniva alle volte a disinare, et doppo desinare si leggeva." Sleidanus's *Commentaries* circulated in Italy in translation: Giovanni Sleidano, *Commentarii overo historie nelle quali si tratta de lo stato de la Repub. e de la religione christiana* ([Geneva: Antoine Davodeau, Jacques Bourgeois, François Jaquy], 1557). On the Italian translation of Sleidanus, see Dennis E. Rhodes, "La traduzione italiana dei *Commentarii* di Giovanni Sleidano," *La Bibliofilia* 3 (1966): 283–87. Sarpi acknowledges his debt toward Sleidanus in Sarpi, *Istoria del Concilio Tridentino*, 5. On the influence of the work in Italy, see Adriano Prosperi, "Lo stato della religione tra l'Italia e il mondo: variazioni cinquecentesche sul tema," *Studi storici* 1 (2015): 29–48.

59. On Giulia Gonzaga's relationship with Carnesecchi, see Camilla Russell, *Giulia Gonzaga and the Religious Controversies of Sixteenth-Century Italy* (Turnhout: Brepols, 2006), 127–208; and Susanna Peyronel Rambaldi, *Una gentildonna irrequieta: Giulia Gonzaga fra reti familiari e relazioni eterodosse* (Rome: Viella, 2012), 232–56.

60. Carnesecchi, II, 2, 715: "quando piacerà a Dio di fare che tutto sia un ovile et un pastore. Di che pare che s'avvicini il tempo, intendendosi che anche molti giudei sono illuminati, ma che non si risolvono a pigliare il battesmo perché vogliono aspettare che siano terminate le controversie che veggono essere tra noi christiani circa le cose della fede. Hora staremo a vedere quel che Dio vorrà fare, attendendo a pregare Sua divina Maestà che ci conceda un pastore il qual sia atto a congregare et riunire insieme le povere pecorelle smarite, introducendo nelli buoni et salutiferi pascoli quelle che non vi sono ancor entrate et riducendovi quelle che ne fussino uscite."

61. On the myth of the angelic pope, see Marjorie Reeves, *The Influence of Prophecy in the Later Middle Ages: A Study in Joachimism* (Oxford: Clarendon Press, 1969), 393–

504; Cesare Vasoli, "L'immagine sognata: il 'papa angelico'," in *Storia d'Italia. Annali 16. Roma, la città del papa: Vita civile e religiosa dal giubileo di Bonifacio VIII al giubileo di papa Wojtyla*, ed. Luigi Fiorani and Adriano Prosperi, 75–109 (Turin: Einaudi, 2000); Adriano Prosperi, "Un papato 'spirituale': programmi e speranze nell'età del Concilio di Trento," in *Il Papato e l'Europa*, ed. Gabriele de Rosa and Giorgio Cracco, 239–54 (Soveria Mannelli: Rubbettino, 2001).

62. Delio Cantimori, "'Nicodemismo' e speranze conciliari nel Cinquecento italiano," in *Studi di storia* (Turin: Einaudi, 1959), 518–39, English translation in *The Late Italian Renaissance*, ed. Eric Cochrane, 244–65 (New York: Harper, 1970), 257. See also Delio Cantimori, *Prospettive di storia ereticale* (Rome: Laterza, 1960), republished in Cantimori, *Eretici italiani del Cinquecento*, 421–81.

63. Yates, *French Academies*, 199.

64. Cesare Cantù, "Spigolature negli archivi toscani," *Rivista contemporanea* 21 (1860): 387.

65. Cantù, "Spigolature negli archivi toscani," 387: "Et in ogni modo a questo si verrà contra la voglia et potentia sua et di tutti i principi, perché come disse Gamaliel, la cosa viene da Dio et non dissolvetur." Gelido is referring to *Acts* 5:39.

66. On Di Capua, see Andrea Gardi, "Pietro Antonio di Capua (1513–1578): Primi elementi per una biografia," *Rivista di storia e letteratura religiosa* 2 (1988): 262–309; and Dario Marcatto, *"Questo passo dell'heresia": Pietroantonio di Capua tra valdesiani, spirituali e inquisizione* (Naples: Bibliopolis, 2003).

67. Giannetti entered into the service of Di Capua through Vittore Soranzo: see PS, I, p. 411.

68. PC, II, 3, pp. 1090–1094. PM, I, 370, 384, 682.

69. PC, II, 3, p. 1230.

70. On Di Capua at the council, see Gardi, "Pietro Antonio di Capua," 285–98.

71. Édouard Frémy, *Un Ambassadeur libéral sous Charles IX et Henri III* (Paris: E. Leroux, 1880); Alain Tallon, "Diplomate et 'politique': Arnaud du Ferrier" in *De Michel de l'Hospital à l'édit de Nantes: politique et religion face aux églises*, ed. Thierry Wanegffelen, 305–33 (Clermont-Ferrand: Presses universitaires Blaise-Pascal, 2002); Anna Bettoni, "La dissidence discrète d'Arnaud du Ferrier (1577)," *Les Dossiers du Grihl*, (accessed December 20, 2015): https://journals.openedition.org/dossiersgrihl/5851.

72. CT, IX, 841–844. On Du Ferrier's participation in the council, see Tallon, *La France et le concile de Trente*, 394–408, 444–46.

73. NV, VIII, p. 76: Giovanni Antonio Fachinetti to Michele Bonelli (Venice, July 20, 1566).

74. Michel de Montaigne, *Journal de voyage*, ed. François Rigolot (Paris: Presses Universitaires de France, 1992), 68.

75. Tallon, "Diplomate et 'politique,'" 314–18.

76. NV, VIII, p. 76.

77. PCA, 299: "Io ho pratticato con messer Guido da Fano in casa degli ambasciatori di Francia, dove si ragionava di queste cose di religione alla ugonotta secondo gli avisi che venivano et secondo le persone che venivano di Francia. Et mi ricordo particolarmente che venne l'ambasciatore Ferrerio, qual era stato a Roma mandato dal regno di Francia, et ragionò molto lungamente del negocio che haveva trattato a Roma . . . et la

conclusione fu che a Roma non farebbono mai cosa buona se non per forza. Et a tutto questo fu presente Guido Giannetti. Mi sono anco ritrovato dell'altre volte dove secondo, come ho detto di sopra, gli avisi et le persone che venivano si parlava di queste cose di Francia circa alla religione, et tutti mi parevano d'una opinione, così italiani come francesi: et per il più delle volte vi era presente il detto messer Guido. Ho anco ragionato con lui particolarmente sotto le loggie di San Marco, secondo l'occasione d'avisi ch'egli haveva da un messer Bartholomeo Compagno, se ben mi ricordo, che gli scriveva d'Inghilterra, et discorrevamo sopra di quelli et alle volte ragionavamo in favore delle cose degli ugonotti."

78. Seidel Menchi, *Erasmo in Italia*, 240–69; Alain Tallon, "Le 'parti français' et la dissidence religieuse en France et en Italie," in *La Réforme en France et en Italie: contacts, comparaisons et contrastes*, ed. Philip Benedict, Silvana Seidel Menchi, and Alain Tallon, 381–99 (Rome: Ecole française de Rome, 2007).

79. SP 70/49 cc. 2r-v: Giannetti to Elizabeth I (Venice, January 16, 1563); SP 70/49 cc. 4r–6v: Giannetti to Cecil (Venice, January 16, 1563). On the articles presented by the French ambassadors, see Sarpi, *Istoria del concilio tridentino*, 2:1027–37, and Tallon, *Le France et le concile de Trente*, 705–15 and 842–67, for the text of the articles.

80. SP 70/69 cc. 108r–110v: Giannetti to Elizabeth I (Venice, March 25, 1564). On the French reactions to Trent, see Kingdon, "Some French Reactions"; Thomas I. Crimando, "Two French Views of the Council of Trent," *Sixteenth-Century Journal* 2 (1988): 169–86; Bernard Plongeron, "Unità tridentina e diversità francese: filoromani, giansenisti, gallicani e costituzionali" in *I tempi del concilio: Religione, cultura e società nell'Europa tridentina*, ed. Cesare Mozzarelli and Danilo Zardin, 145–69 (Rome: Bulzoni, 1997).

81. SP 70/69 c. 108v: Giannetti to Elizabeth I (Venice, March 25, 1564).

82. SP 70/69 c. 109v: Giannetti to Elizabeth (Venice, March 25, 1564): "si può nel regno di Francia, sbatter per nullo, con quattro ragioni: la prima che non è stato legitimamente congregato: la seconda che si doveria farlo di nuovo, e non seguitare il camino del precedente a farne tutto uno: la terza, che il Papa ha fatto che l'ambasciatore di Spagna vi sedesse in modo, che si era fatto pregiuditio a la Maestà del Re di Francia: la quarta che il Papa rimane sopra il Concilio: e non il Concilio sopra il Papa: e questo contra l'antica appellatione de l'Università di Theologia di Parigi."

83. On the conflicts between council and Inquisition, see Alain Tallon, "Le Concile de Trente et l'Inquisition Romaine," *Mélanges de l'Ecole Française de Rome* 106 (1994): 129–59; Prosperi, *Tribunali della coscienza*, 117–34; Firpo, *La presa di potere*.

84. Firpo, *Inquisizione romana*; Firpo and Niccoli, *Il cardinale Giovanni Morone*.

85. See Firpo, *Inquisizione romana* and the critical edition of the trial in PM.

86. SP 70/10, c. 63r: Giannetti to Cecil (Venice, January 20, 1560): "Il Papa haveva ne i suoi consigli per il primo il Cardinal Morone, quell'amico del Cardinal Polo, che il suo antecessore Paolo quarto teneva in prigione per heretico." On the conflict between Pius IV and the Inquisition, see Elena Bonora, "Inquisizione e papato tra Pio IV e Pio V," in *Pio V nella società del suo tempo*, ed. Maurilio Guasco and Angelo Torre, 49–83 (Bologna: Il Mulino, 2005).

87. SP 70/69, c. 110r: Giannetti to Elizabeth I (Venice, March 25, 1564).

88. Walter Friedensburg, "Giovanni Morone und der Brief Sadolets an Melanchthon vom 17. Juni 1537," *Archiv für Reformationsgeschichte* 1 (1903), 380: "molto meglio proce-

dere con questi moderni heretici con mansuetudine che volerli irritare con ingiurie." On the sixteenth-century attempts to find a diplomatic solution to the confessional strife, see Tallon, *L'Europe au XVIe siècle*, 208–10.

89. See Gigliola Fragnito, "La terza fase del concilio di Trento, Morone e gli 'spirituali,'" in Firpo and Niccoli, *Il cardinale Giovanni Morone*, 53–78.

90. SP 70/52 cc. 122v–123r: Giannetti to Elizabeth I (Venice, March 13, 1563): "li Prelati Italiani in Trento non vogliono attentare di riformar Papa, Cardinali, e corte Romana. . . . Così dove bisognerebbe medicare la testa, e i membri vitali, purgano l'unghie a pena."

91. SP 70/66, c. 100r: Giannetti to Elizabeth I (Venice, December 18, 1563): "dove potevano fare ciò che voluto havessino, mediante un concilio condotto da loro, non habbino voluto fare più che tanto."

92. On Vergerio in Trent, see Schutte, *Pier Paolo Vergerio*, 188–215. On Vergerio's exchange with Delfino, see ND, II, 1: p. 356 (Delfino to Carlo Borromeo, Schwarzach, May 13, 1561); Josef Šusta, ed., *Die römishce Kurie und das Konzil von Trient unter Pius IV. Actenstücke zur Geschichte des Konzils von Trient*, 4 vols. (Vienna: A. Hölder, 1904), 1:28: Carlo Borromeo to the Ercole Gonzaga (Rome, May 30, 1561); 1:32–33: Carlo Borromeo to Ercole Gonzaga (Rome, June 18, 1561); 1:42–43: the papal legates to Trent to Carlo Borromeo (Trent, July 7, 1561); 1:57–59: Carlo Borromeo to the papal legates to Trent (Rome, July 12, 1561); 1:95–96: Carlo Borromeo to Ercole Gonzaga (Rome, November 8, 1561); 1:97–99: Carlo Borromeo to Ercole Gonzaga (Rome, November 15, 1561); 1:119–20: Carlo Borromeo to Ercole Gonzaga (Rome, December 3, 1561).

93. Šusta, ed., *Die römishce Kurie*, 1:76–77: Carlo Borromeo to Ercole Gonzaga (Rome, September 20, 1561). On Ludovico Castelvetro and his nephew Giacomo, see chapters 6 and 7 of this book.

94. On Grimani and the Inquisition, see Pio Paschini, *Tre illustri prelati del Rinascimento: Ermolao Barbaro, Adriano Castellesi, Giovanni Grimani* (Rome: Lateranum, 1907); Peter J. Laven, "The 'causa' Grimani and Its Political Overtones," *Journal of Religious History* 4 (1967): 184–205; Tallon, "Le Concile de Trente"; Prosperi, *Tribunali della coscienza*, 129–32; and Massimo Firpo, "L'iconografia come problema storiografico: Le ambiguità della porpora e i 'diavoli del Sant'Ufficio. Identità e storia nei ritratti di Giovanni Grimani," *Rivista storica italiana* 3 (2005): 825–71.

95. Paschini, *Tre illustri prelati*.

96. CSP *Foreign*, V, n. 226, p. 109 (Venice, June 20, 1562).

97. On Pius V, see Ludwig von Pastor, *The History of the Popes, from the Close of the Middle Ages*, vol. 17, trans. and ed. Ralph Francis Kerr (London: Kegan Paul, Trench, Trubner & Co., 1929); Aniceto Fernandez, ed., *San Pio V e la problematica del suo tempo* (Alessandria: Cassa di Risparmio di Alessandria 1972); Nicole Lemaitre, *Saint Pie V* (Paris: Fayard, 1994); Guasco and Torre, *Pio V nella società*.

98. SP 70/82, cc. 41r–42r: Giannetti to Elizabeth I (Padua, January 25, 1566): "Serenissima e Clementissima Regina l'haver io cambiato stanza da Venetia a Padova, è cagione, che io non ho scritto a Vostra Maestà, già sono molti mesi et il non ritrovarmi a Venetia, dove s'intende più de le cose importanti, fa che le mie lettere non sieno come vorrei che fussino, degne di presentarsi a Vostra Real Altezza. Nondimeno . . . prendo la presente occasione di scrivere del nuovo Pontefice Romano. . . . Il mese prossimo di

Marzo farà nove anni, ch'egli da Paolo Quarto fu fatto Cardinale detto Alessandrino, prima essendo fra Michele Inquisitore de l'heresia in Roma, per altro, semplice e povero frate de l'ordine di San Domenico: ma Cardinale in tempo di quel Papa fu sommo Inquisitore: dipoi sotto Pio Quarto è stato uno de Cardinali Presidenti al'Inquisitione: et hora tanto in alto è salito, che i suoi Principi e Monarchi si gl'inchineranno per reverentia."

99. ASV, Capi del Consiglio dei Dieci, Dispacci degli ambasciatori, f. 25, n. 5–6: Paolo Tiepolo to the Capi del Consiglio dei Dieci (Rome, July 6, 1566): "homo tristissimo, et perniciosissimo, sopra il qual il Papa ha l'occhio addosso dal primo tempo."

100. ASV, Capi del Consiglio dei Dieci, Dispacci degli ambasciatori, f. 25, n. 7–8: Paolo Tiepolo to the Capi del Consiglio dei Dieci (Rome, July 13, 1566): "si può più cavar che da qual si voglia altro."

101. NV, VIII, p. 76: Giovanni Antonio Fachinetti to Michele Bonelli (Venice, July 20, 1566): "mandar Guido a Roma sarebbe un disautorizzare il tribunale della S. Inquisitione di Vinetia."

102. ASV, Capi del Consiglio dei Dieci, Dispacci degli ambasciatori, f. 25, n. 5–6: Paolo Tiepolo to the Capi del Consiglio dei Dieci (Rome, July 6, 1566): "non saria dignità di questo principal Tribunal dell'Inquisition far, che una causa sua fusse giudicata da un Inferior"; "desiderava che fosse ritenuto, et mandato qua un Guido Zanetti da Fano, et ha scolari a dozena in Padoa, homo di pessima dottrina, et di gran scandolo, si come nella inquisition è provato."

103. ASV, Consiglio dei Dieci, Deliberazioni, segrete, r. 8, f, 65r (August 7, 1566).

104. SP 70/93, c. 75r: Bizarri to Cecil (Venice, August 24, 1566): "Il povero messer Guido Giannetti da Fano è stato finalmente condotto a Roma ligato e per man di sbirri. . . . O Dio, che l'havesse mai creduto! Et pur è così. . . . So ancora quant'egli amava V.S. La prego dunque haverlo raccomandato appresso di Sua Maestà affin che s'ottenga qualche favor appresso questi Signori Venetiani de quali molti si sono maravigliati che volesser mai condiscender a la richiesta del Papa al quale tante volte per avanti l'avevano negato."

105. Firpo, *Gli affreschi di Pontormo a San Lorenzo*; PC, II, 1, pp. V-CLI.

106. ASV, Capi del Consiglio dei Dieci, Dispacci degli ambasciatori, f. 25, n.5–6: Paolo Tiepolo to the Capi del Consiglio dei Dieci (Rome, July 6, 1566): "haveva da lodarsi assai, del duca di Fiorenza . . . che le havesse dato il Carnesecchi suo amico intrinsico."

107. ACDF, *Decreta Sancti Officii*, 1565–1567, c. 78v (October 9, 1566).

108. ACDF, *Decreta Sancti Officii*, 1574–1576, c. 111v (June 30, 1575): "concessit sibi licentiam libere exeundi Urbem et eundi Fanum."

109. ASV, Senato, Dispacci degli ambasciatori e residenti, Roma, f. 4, cc. 169–171 (Michele Suriano, May 28, 1569): "il quale è stato forsi XX anni immerso nelle heresie et ha havuto parte in tutte le sette, è stato condennato in prigion perpetua, et li è stata salvata la vita, parte perché dicono che per lui si ha havuto notitia di molte cose importanti, parte perché non è mai stato abiurato et però non si può haver per relapso."

110. De Vivo, *Information and Communication in Venice*, 74–85.

111. Cantimori, "'Nicodemismo' e speranze conciliari"; Marion Leathers Kuntz, *Guillaume Postel, Prophet of the Restitution of All Things. His Life and Thought* (The Hague: Kluver Boston, 1981); Vasoli, "L'immagine sognata"; Prosperi, "Un papato 'spirituale.'"

112. Simon Ditchfield, "Tridentine Catholicism," in *The Ashgate Research Companion to the Counter-Reformation*, eds. Alexandra Bamji, Geert H. Janssen, and Mary Laven, 15–31 (Farnham, Surrey: Ashgate: 2013); John W. O'Malley, *The Council of Trent: Myths, Misunderstandings and Unintended Consequences* (Rome: Gregorian and Biblical Press, 2013).

4. The Merchant, the Queen, and the Refugees

1. Martin, *Venice's Hidden Enemies*, 73–96, 235–47.

2. Marino Berengo, *Nobili e mercanti nella Lucca del Cinquecento* (Turin: Einaudi, 1965), 357–454; Simonetta Adorni Braccesi, *Una città infetta: la Repubblica di Lucca nella crisi religiosa del Cinquecento* (Florence: Olschki, 1994); Simonetta Adorni Braccesi and Carla Sodini, eds., *L'emigrazione confessionale dei lucchesi in Europa* (Florence: Edifir, 1999); Ole Peter Grell, *Brethren in Christ: A Calvinist Network in Reformation Europe* (Cambridge: Cambridge University Press, 2011).

3. Stéphane Garcia, *Élie Diodati et Galilée: naissance d'un réseau scientifique dans l'Europe du XVII siècle* (Florence: Olschki, 2004),

4. Lawrence Stone, *An Elizabethan: Sir Horatio Palavicino* (Oxford: Clarendon Press, 1956); Stefano Villani, "Pallavicino, Orazio," in DBI, 80, 2014.

5. Rita Mazzei, *La trama nascosta: Storie di mercanti e altro (secoli XVI–XVII)* (Viterbo: Sette Città, 2011); Isabella Lazzarini, "I circuiti mercantili della diplomazia italiana nel Quattrocento,' in *Il governo dell'economia: Italia e Penisola Iberica nel basso Medioevo*, ed. Lorenzo Tanzini and Sergio Tognetti, 155–77 (Rome: Viella, 2014).

6. On cross-cultural trade, along with Philip D. Curtin, *Cross-Cultural Trade in World History* (Cambridge: Cambridge University Press, 1984), see Francesca Trivellato, *The Familiarity of Strangers: The Sephardic Diaspora, Livorno, and Cross-Cultural Trade in the Early Modern Period* (New Haven, CT: Yale University Press, 2009), and Francesca Trivellato, Leor Halevi, and Cátia Antunes, eds., *Religion and Trade: Cross-Cultural Exchanges in World History 1000–1900* (Oxford: Oxford University Press, 2014).

7. Braudel, *The Mediterranean*, 2:1088–92, and Benjamin Arbel, *Trading Nations: Jews and Venetians in the Early Modern Mediterranean* (Leiden: Brill, 1995), 72–74. For a biographical sketch of Ragazzoni, see Luciano Pezzolo, "Sistema di valori e attività economica a Venezia, 1530–1630," in *L'impresa: industria commercio banca secc. XIII–XVIII*, ed. Simonetta Cavaciocchi (Florence: Le Monnier, 1991), 986–88; Isabella Cecchini and Luciano Pezzolo, "Merchants and Institutions in Early Modern Venice," *Journal of European Economic History* 41 (2012): 104–7. The first biography of Ragazzoni was published in the year of his death by Giuseppe Gallucci, *La vita del clarissimo signor Jacomo Ragazzoni* (Venice: Giorgio Bizzardo, 1610).

8. Giorgio Tagliaferro, "Montemezzano, Francesco," in *DBI* 76, 132–36. The frescos made for Ragazzoni's palace in Sacile are reproduced and examined in Roberto de Feo, "Gli affreschi di Francesco Montemezzano in Palazzo Ragazzoni di Sacile ed un inedito," in *Francesco Montemezzano in Palazzo Ragazzoni - Flangini - Billia: Arte, storia e cultura nel Giardino della Serenissima*, ed. Francesco Amendolagine, Roberto De Feo, and Gilberto Ganzer, 35–52 (Sacile: Città di Sacile, 1993), and Elisabetta Borean, "Palazzo

Ragazzoni," in *Gli affreschi nelle ville venete: Il Cinquecento*, ed. Giuseppe Pavanello and Vincenzo Mancini (Venice: Marsilio, 2008), 434–35.

9. Francesco Sansovino, *Historia universale dell'origine, guerre, et imperio de' Turchi* (Venice, 1654), 15: "essendo passato a Constantinopoli Giacomo Ragazzoni, mandato dalla Republica, per trattare esteriormente la restitutione delle mercantie a lor mercanti, ma intrinsecamente con altre secreti e più importanti commissioni." Paolo Paruta, *Historia vinetiana* (Venice, 1645), 91–92; Gallucci, *La vita*, 63–64.

10. Abraham de Wicquefort, *The Rights, Privileges and Office of Embassadors and Publick Ministers* (London: Charles Davis, 1740), 34. Original text in Abraham de Wicquefort, *L'ambassadeur et ses fonctions* (Cologne: Pierre Marteau, 1715), 63.

11. Wicquefort, *Rights, Privileges and Office*, 34. Original text in Wicquefort, *L'ambassadeur et ses fonctions*, 63: "ils n'ont que faire de ménager leurs démarches, dont l'irrégularité ne fait point de tort a la dignité du Maistre . . . & estant moins incommode & moins façonnier que l'Ambassadeur, il trouve ses accés plus faciles & ses expeditions plus promtes."

12. Zannini, "Economic and Social Aspects," 133–34. See also Zannini, *Burocrazia e burocrati*.

13. Jacopo Ragazzoni, "Relazione dell'impero ottomano," in Albèri 3:2, p. 95: "avendo avuto occasione di vedere il maggior principe del mondo, e di conoscere e negoziar con il più savio, giusto, prudente e valoroso, governator di un imperio che oggidì viva in terra."

14. ASV, Notarile, Testamenti (notaio Pietro Partenio), 784, n. 244 (May 7, 1609): "Prima che fosse il tempo del maritar delle mie figliuole successe a questa eccelsa Repubblica il grave accidente della guerra Turchesca, che la pose in gravi pensieri, incerta massime di quello potesse riuscir della lega che trattava con gli altri Prencipi. Et perché l'illustrissimo Marco Antonio Barbaro che si ritrovava Bailo a Constantinopoli in quel tempo era stato serrato in casa come priggione, dove si dubbitava, che non potesse trattar le cose pubbliche, fu deliberato per decreto pubblico dall'Eccellentissimo Senato, et eccelso Consiglio dei Dieci di servirsi della persona mia, in tal occasione mandandomi, come fecero imediate a Costantinopoli . . . et montato sopra una galea sotto li cinque Marzo 1571 passai in brevi giorni a Ragusi, et di la a Costantinopoli con ogni possibile prestezza e nel primo abboccamento ch'io ebbi col Signor Illustrissimo Mahemet Bassa Primo Visir soggetto di grandissima autorità e prudenza ottenni se ben con molta difficoltà di potermi abboccare et stantiare con l'Illustrisimo Signor Bailo soprascritto."

15. ASV, Notarile, Testamenti (notaio Pietro Partenio), 784, n. 244 (May 7, 1609): "quando improvvisamente nella mattina dell'istesso giorno, che fu alli 18 giugno dell'istesso anno che eravamo per concluder il negocio ci capitorno lettere di Venetia con la revocatione de li primi ordini dati et questo perché intesosi a Roma della mia espeditione e partita per Costantinopoli fu mandato l'Illustrissimo Marc Antonio Colonna a Venetia per la conclusione della lega."

16. Francesco Patrizi, "Al molto mag.co et magnanimo M. Giacomo Ragazzoni," in Benedetto Cotrugli, *Della mercatura et del mercante perfetto* (Venice: Giovanni Franco, 1573): "non per restitution sola di robbe de mercanti (ancorche per se importantissimo negotio) ma per cose de stati di grandissimi prencipi."

17. On the Renaissance literature on the perfect merchant, see Christian Bec, *Les marchands écrivains, affaires et humanisme à Florence, 1375–1434* (Paris: Mouton, 1967); Vittore Branca, ed., *Mercanti scrittori: ricordi nella Firenze tra Medioevo e Rinascimento* (Milan: Rusconi, 1986); Ugo Tucci, *Mercanti, navi e monete nel Cinquecento veneziano* (Bologna: Mulino, 1981), 43–94; Ugo Tucci, "Introduzione" to Benedetto Cotrugli, *Il libro dell'arte di mercatura* (Venice: Arsenale, 1990), 3–128; Giacomo Todeschini, *Il prezzo della salvezza: Lessici medievali del pensiero economico* (Rome: Carocci, 1994), 90–92.

18. Leon Battista Alberti, *I libri della famiglia*, ed. Ruggiero Romano and Alberto Tenenti (Turin: Einaudi, 1994), 335: "E le amicizie de' principi massime si voglion acquistare e aoperare per accrescere e amplificare a' suoi e alla famiglia sua nome e buona fama e degna autorità e laude." On the notion of "friendship," see Christiane Klapisch-Zuber, "Parenti, amici, vicini. Il territorio urbano d'una famiglia mercantile nel XV secolo," *Quaderni storici* 33 (1976): 953–82; D.V. Kent, *Friendship, Love and Trust in Renaissance Florence* (Cambridge, MA: Harvard University Press, 2009); and Isabella Lazzarini, *Amicizia e potere: Reti politiche e sociali nell'Italia medievale* (Turin: Einaudi, 2010).

19. On diplomacy and social mobility in sixteenth-century Italy, see Catherine Fletcher, "War, Diplomacy and Social Mobility: The Casali Family in the Service of Henry VIII," *Journal of Early Modern History* 14 (2010): 559–78; Megan K. Williams, "'Dui Fratelli . . . Con Dui Principi': Family and Fidelity on a Failed Diplomatic Mission," *Journal of Early Modern History* 14 (2010): 579–611.

20. Tagliaferro, "Francesco Montemezzano," 132–36.

21. A genealogical tree of the Ragazzoni family is in MCV, MS Cicogna 3427.

22. Braudel, *Mediterranean*, 2:729–31.

23. Ragazzoni's speech at the Council of Trent is in CT 9/6, pp. 1098–103. He dedicated to Giovanni Morone his translation of Cicero's *Philippics*: *Le Filippiche di Marco T. Cicerone contra Marco Antonio fatte volgari per Girolamo Ragazzoni* (Venice, 1556). On Ragazzoni's role in the Tridentine church, see also Angelo Giorgio Ghezzi and Lisa Longhi, *La visita apostolica di Gerolamo Ragazzoni a Milano (1575–1576)*, 2 vols. (Rome: Bulzoni, 2010).

24. On Ragazzoni's nunciature in France, see Ivan Cloulas, "Les rapports de Jérôme Ragazzoni, évêque de Bergame, avec les ecclésiastiques pendant sa nonciature en France (1583–1586)," *Mélanges d'archéologie et d'histoire* 72 (1960): 509–50; Pierre Blet, ed., *Girolamo Ragazzoni évêque de Bergame nonce en France. Correspondence de sa Nonciature 1583–1586* (Rome-Paris: Editions E. de Boccard, 1962).

25. Roberto Zago, "Foscarini, Giacomo," DBI 49, 365–70. In his will Ragazzoni remembers his apprenticeship and his partnership with Foscarini: ASV, Notarile, Testamenti (notaio Pietro Partenio), 784, n. 244, dated May 7, 1609.

26. Gallucci, *La vita*, 14–15.

27. ASV, Notarile, Testamenti (notaio Pietro Partenio), 784, n. 244, dated May 7, 1609: "Né io attesi solamente mentre fui nel Regno d'Inghilterra alli traffichi, et negocij mercantili con somma diligenza, et realtà, ma procurai ancora di rendermi quanto più potei grato alli Serenissimi Re et Regine del mio tempo, da quali veramente fui favorito, et stimato oltre ad ogni mio merito et principalmente dalla Serenissima Regina Maria, la

quale essendo così presto assunta alla suprema dignità di quella Corona confidò in me che io dovessi trovar modo di far intendere alla Santità di Nostro Signore Giulio Terzo sommo Pontefice che la Maestà sua non haveva altro desiderio maggiore in questo mondo, che di ridurre il suo Regno all'obbedienza di santa Chiesa, et che a questo effetto farebbe ogni cosa possibile, ma con un poco di tempo stante la moltitudine grande di Heretici, che si ritrovava nel suo Regno . . . il quale ordine fu da me prontamente esseguito per il mezzo di Monsignor Vettor Ragazzoni mio fratello, che in quel tempo si ritrovava in Roma cameriere di honore di quel Pontefice." Presumably drawing on Ragazzoni's will, Gallucci also recounts this episode, *La vita*, 13–14.

28. SP 70/25, c. 107: Ragazzoni to the Privy Council (Venice, April 26, 1561): "il desiderio ch'io ho ardentissimo di far servitio á quella Corona sotto la quale sono vissuto tanti anni et á messer Guido innanzi che hora ho fatto qualche favore per cagione semplicemente della sua gentilezza et della stretta amicitia che un tempo fa si contrasse fra noi in Inghilterra."

29. Stella, "Utopie e velleità insurrezionali," 169; Stella, "Guido da Fano eretico"; Guido Dall'Olio, "Guido Giannetti," DBI 54, 453–55. For a detailed discussion of Giannetti's relationship with Tudor diplomacy, see chapter 3 of this book.

30. See, for example, PC, II, 2:512.

31. SP 70/25, c. 107r: Ragazzoni to the Privy Council (Venice, April 26, 1561): "Et spero che havendo così calde raccomandationi di tanto gran Reina in aiuto, non m'affaticarò in vano, con tutto ch'io conoschi quanta difficultà habbia questo negocio, Per rispetto delle cose di Roma, ove il detto messer Guido è dimandato con grandissima instantia. Di quello che andarà seguendo in questa materia tenirò avvisate l'Eccellentie vostre et vene parlerà anco a' bocca Messer Placido mio fratello presentator di questa lettera."

32. SP 70/27, c. 73r: Ragazzoni to the Privy Council (Venice, May 10, 1561): "Io presentai con buona occasione la lettera di sua Maestà a questi signori Illustrissimi . . . essi si mostrarono molto suspesi in questa dimanda, havendo dato molto innanzi che havessero la lettera grande Intentione di dover mandare messer Guido Giannetti a Roma d'onde era et è tutta via dimandato con grandissima instantia. Ma però infino ad hora non s'è fatto altro in questa materia et spero che quello si farà da qui in poi sara piu tosto á sollevatione che á danno del detto messer Guido."

33. SP 70/27, c. 73r: Ragazzoni to the Privy Council (Venice, May 10, 1561): "nella causa del quale non cesso di adoperare tutte le forze mie, et del amici miej."

34. ASV, Consiglio dei Dieci, Deliberazioni, Secrete, r. 7 (Venice, May 31, 1561): "che si dovesse haver rispetto a questo huomo [Giannetti], et che 'l si havesse a iudicare de qui, et non mandar a Roma."

35. ASV, Consiglio dei Dieci, Deliberazioni, Secrete, r. 7 (May 31, 1561): "haver molto rispetto, facendo i nostri mercadanti tante facende in quell'isola . . . potendo seguir grandissimo preiudicio alli Mercadanti nostri quando il Zanoti si mandasse a Roma."

36. SP 70/30, cc. 115r–115v: Guido Giannetti to Elizabeth I (Venice, September 27, 1561): "il gran rispetto, che hanno al Romano Pontefice."

37. See chapter 3.

38. SP 70/25, f. 107r: Ragazzoni to the Privy Council (Venice, April 26, 1561).

39. ASV, Senato terra, f. 38 (January 15, 1561); *CSPVenetian*, VII: 321 (March 6, 1563).

40. SP 70/70, f. 89: Girolamo Priuli to Elizabeth I (Venice, April 22, 1564): "hanno speso gran parte della età loro nel esercitio della mercantia in queste parti."

41. BMV, MS It. VII 2380 (9751), cc. 72r–73r: Ragazzoni to Alvise Contarini (Venice, February 17, 1569).

42. Placido Ragazzoni, "Relazione del regno di Sicilia," in Albèri 5:473–84. Gallucci, *La vita*, 75.

43. Placido Ragazzoni, *Relazione delle cose d'Inghilterra, et della Scotia*, in SCS, MSS Codex 93F, 24r–32v, where it is included in a seventeenth-century collection of political and geographical documents entitled *Memorie storiche di diversi luoghi et altro*. I have also consulted the *relazione* in MCV, MS Cicogna 973.7. On Ridolfi and his relationship with the Medici, see Anna Maria Crinò, "Un altro memoriale inedito di Roberto Ridolfi," in *Fatti e figure del Seicento anglo-toscano: Documenti inediti sui rapporti letterari, diplomatici, culturali fra Toscana e Inghilterra*, ed. Anna Maria Crinò, 67–78 (Florence: Olschki, 1957).

44. Benzoni, "Ranke's Favorite Source," 26.

45. Filippo De Vivo, "How to Read Venetian Relazioni," *Renaissance and Reformation* 34, nos. 1–2 (2011): 32–33.

46. SCS, MSS Codex 93F, 26r: "havendo trovato tutto il Regno contaminato d'Heresia et levato dalla Chiesa di Dio non solamente il sacrificio dello Altare, ma tutte l'Imagini, volendo con pietoso zelo provedere a tanti disordini il giorno medesimo che entrò nella torre di Londra Sedia Regale di quel Regno, fece cantare Messa solenne al Reverendissimo Vescovo di Vincestre, stato continuamente prigione dal tempo che Arrivo VIII si levò dall'obedienza della Chiesa Romana: Et io Placido Ragazzoni mi trovai presente ad udire questa santissima Messa."

47. Ambrosini, "'Mestier da donne?'" 27–75. In MCV, MS Cicogna 973.7, Ragazzoni comments on Mary Tudor's death. These comments are absent from SCS, MSS Codex 93F.

48. SCS, MSS Codex 93F, 26r-v: "Havendo adunque Elisabetta presa la Corona, et essendo nel tempo della sua Vita stata sempre con Maestri Heretici, non fu così presto Coronata Regina che levò in tutto il Viver Cattolico, et rimessa la già introdotta Heresia sotto li Documenti di Calvino, nel qual modo ha sempre perseverato, castigando co' supplicio di fuoco molti, che più tosto morendo hanno voluto mantenersi la santa fede Cattolica, che rifiutandola, et diventare Heretici campare la Vita con esempio di gran bontà ad imitazione de santi Martiri."

49. On Sanders, see also for further bibliography, Tutino, *Law and Conscience*, 21–31, 147–59.

50. Gino Benzoni, "Campana, Cesare," DBI 17, 331–34

51. Federica Ambrosini, *Paesi e mari ignoti: America e colonialismo europeo nella cultura veneziana (secoli XVI–XVII)* (Venice: Deputazione editrice, 1982), 199–200; Frances Yates, *Astraea: The Imperial Theme in the Sixteenth Century* (London: Penguin, 1975), 83–86, 108–10, 212–14; Pirillo, *Filosofia ed eresia*, 87–141.

52. SP 83/19, c. 75r: Bizzarri to Francis Walsingham (Antwerp, July 11, 1583): "mosso dalla fama di Filippo Melantone, uomo rarissimo a' tempi nostri." On Bizzarri, see

Massimo Firpo, *Pietro Bizzarri esule italiano del Cinquecento* (Turin: Einaudi, 1971); Silvana Seidel Menchi, "Bizzari, Pietro," DBI 10, 738–41.

53. Philipp Melanchthon, *Opera quae supersunt omnia*, 4 vols. (Halle: C.A. Schwetschke and Son, 1834–1860), 4:269–70 (Wittenberg, November 10, 1546): "hunc honestum virum et hospitem natum in Italia, Petrum Perusinum"; "Honeste apud nos vixit, et doctrinae coelestis studia diligenter coluit, et hanc peregrinationem suscepit, non ut cuiquam noceret, sed ut videat Ecclesias Germaniae."

54. See Wallace T. MacCaffrey, "Russel, Francis, second earl of Bedford" (1526/7–1585) in ODNB (http://www.oxforddnb.com/view/article/24306, accessed October 9, 2017).

55. Pietro Bizzarri, *Historia della guerra fatta in Ungheria dall'invittissimo imperatore de christiani, contra quello de Turchi* (Lyon: Rouillé, 1568), 206, where Bizzarri also mentions Elizabeth I's Italian tutor Giovanni Battista Castiglione, on which see Massimo Firpo, "Castiglione, Giovanni Battista," DBI 22, 82–84. On Castiglione, see also ASV, Senato, Dispacci ambasciatori, Inghilterra, f. 1, n. 12, cc. 29r-v: Giovanni Michiel to the Venetian Senate (May 13, 1555), and ASV, Senato, Dispacci ambasciatori, Inghilterra, f. 1, n 69, cc. 162r-v: Giovanni Michiel to the Venetian Senate (June 2, 1556)

56. Bizzarri, *Historia*, 134–35: "Io ritrovandomi in Venetia, e havendo ivi ammistà co i Magnifici Signori Giovanni Pesaro e Giacopo Ragazzoni, venni con essi a ragionamento sopra queste differenze, e intesi da loro come da gentil'huomini non meno lodevoli per la loro molto benigna, candida e liberal natura, che per gravità e prudenza, e come molto prattichi ne negotij dell'una e l'altra Natione, che 'l danno che da quelle succedeva, era veramente inestimabile."

57. Bizzarri, *Historia*, 135–60.

58. On the role of merchants' letters in the birth of political information, see Infelise, "From Merchants' Letters"; Francesca Trivellato, "Merchants' Letters across Geographical and Social Boundaries," in Francisco Bethencourt and Florike Egmond, eds., *Cultural Exchange in Early Modern Europe* (Cambridge: Cambridge University Press, 2007), 81–103.

59. On the geography of information in early modern Europe see Infelise, *Prima dei giornali*, 106–21.

60. On Venice as center of information on the East, see Kissling, "Venezia come centro di informazioni"; Mantran, "Venise, centre d'information"; Dursteler, "Power and Information"; Petitjean, *L'intelligence des choses*, 212–26.

61. Bell, 283.

62. SP, 83/9, cc. 35r–36r: Bizzarri to Burghley (Antwerp, September 23, 1578); SP, 83/19, cc. 155r-v: Bizzarri to Francis Walsingham (Antwerp, July 15, 1583). On Bizzarri's historical works, see Firpo, *Pietro Bizzarri*, 129–88.

63. SP, 70/77, c.107r: Bizzarri to William Cecil (Venice, April 8, 1565): "Mitto autem per Jacobum Ragazonum, ut ipse interserat unam cum litteris quas mittit suo fratri Placido Ragazono Mercatori Veneto isthic commoranti."

64. SP, 70/78, cc. 20r–21r: Bizzarri to William Cecil (Venice, May 5, 1565); SP, 70/78, cc. 50r–51r: Bizzarri to William Cecil (Venice, May 12, 1565); SP, 70/78, cc. 70r–71r: Bizzarri to William Cecil (Venice, May 19, 1565).

65. SP, 70/78, c. 126r: Bizzarri to William Cecil (Venice, June 2, 1565): "Id autem per Placidum Ragazzonum mercatorem Venetum facillime transigi poterit."

66. SP, 70/78, c. 126r: Bizzarri to William Cecil (Venice, June 2, 1565). The *De optimo principe* is the first text published in Pietro Bizzarri, *Varia opuscula* (Venice: Paolo Manuzio, 1565), 3–26. The previous manuscript draft of the text is preserved in BL Royal 12 A XLVIII, cc. 1r–24r.

67. On Pius V, see Pastor, *History of the Popes*, vol. 17; Fernandez, ed., *San Pio V*; Lemaitre, *Saint Pie V*; Guasco and Torre, *Pio V nella società*.

68. Firpo, *La presa di potere*.

69. Bonora, "*Ubique in omnibus circumspecti*," 67. On papal diplomacy under Pius V, see also Pierre Blet, "Pio V e la riforma Tridentina per mezzo dei nunzi apostolici," in Fernandez, *San Pio V*, 35–46; Lemaitre, *Saint Pie V*, 277–98; Marco Penzi, "La politica francese di Pio V: tra riforma cattolica e guerra contro l'eresia," in Guasco and Torre, *Pio V nella società*, 251–76; Bonora, "Il sospetto d'eresia."

70. See Giuseppe Gullino, "Da Ponte, Nicolò," DBI 32, 723–28.

71. On Elizabeth I's excommunication and its consequences, see Tutino, *Law and Conscience*, 11–31.

72. A. Lynn Martin, ed., *Correspondence du nonce en France Fabio Mirto Frangipani (1568–1572 et 1586–1587)* (Rome: École Française de Rome, 1984), 117: Frangipani to Rusticucci (Paris, October 28, 1570): "commover contra quella mala femina quei popoli tutti"; "quella tirana a . . . restituire la Religione in stato tale, che ella venisse a liberarsi dalla scomunica."

73. On the archive of the Roman Inquisition, see John Tedeschi, "The Dispersed Archives of the Roman Inquisition," in *The Inquisition in Early Modern Europe: Studies on Sources and Methods*, ed. Gustav Henningsen and John Tedeschi, 13–32 (Dekalb: Northern Illinois University Press, 1986); Adriano Prosperi, "Per l'apertura dell'archivio dl S. Uffizio," in *L'Inquisizione romana*, 297–310.

74. Gigliola Fragnito, "Pio V e la censura," in Guasco and Torre, *Pio V nella società*, 129–58.

75. Infelise, *Prima dei giornali*, 155–58; Mario Infelise, "Roman *Avvisi*: Information and Politics in the Seventeenth Century," in *Court and Politics in Papal Rome 1492–1700*, ed. Gianvittorio Signorotto and Maria Antonietta Visceglia, 212–28 (Cambridge: Cambridge University Press, 2002).

76. Angelo Mercati, *I costituti di Niccolò Franco (1568–1570) dinanzi all'Inquisizione di Roma esistenti nell'Archivio Segreto Vaticano* (Vatican City: Biblioteca Apostolica Vaticana, 1955); Niccoli, *Rinascimento anticlericale*, 158–73.

77. Dooley, *Social History of Skepticism*, 26–27.

78. Paolo Alessandro Maffei, *Vita di San Pio V* (Venice: Tommasini, 1712), 303: "parlassero contro il governo, rivelandone gli arcani e censurandone le risoluzioni." On Pius V's biographies see Miguel Gotor, "Le vite di San Pio V dal 1512 al 1712 tra censura e storia," in Guasco and Torre, *Pio V nella società*, 207–49.

79. ASV, Consiglio dei X, parti secrete, reg. 8, c. 82r (March 17, 1567). See Infelise, *Prima dei giornali*, 154.

80. Preto, *I servizi segreti*, 89: "i molti in questa città, che fanno publica professione di scriver nuove"; Infelise, *Prima dei giornali*, 154; Simone Lonardi, "Informazione, spionaggio e segreto di stato a Venezia nella prima età moderna," *Bollettino della Società Letteraria* (2012): 157–74.

81. De Vivo, *Information and Communication in Venice*, 42.

82. On Giannetti, see chapter 3.

83. SP 70/96 cc. 71r–72r: Bizzarri to Cecil (Venice, January 18, 1568); SP 70/98, cc. 79r–79v: Bizzarri to Cecil (Venice, May 23, 1568).

84. See the register of Bizzarri's letters in Firpo, *Pietro Bizzarri*, 293–308.

85. Francesco Sansovino, *Del governo et amministratione di diversi regni, et republiche, così antiche, come moderne* (Venice: Altobello Salicato, 1583), *2v: "nelle rivolutioni di quello Stato"; "purgar quel Regno dalle cattive semenze della heresia' e 'ritornare quella Provincia al vero culto di Santa Chiesa."

86. Giacomo Ragazzoni's conformity to Tridentine orthodoxy emerges from his will. On the uses of wills to study early modern religious dissent, see Silvana Seidel Menchi, "Se l'eretico fa testamento," in *La fede degli italiani: Per Adriano Prosperi*, ed. Guido dall'Olio, Adelisa Malena, Pierroberto Scaramella, 33–40 (Pisa: Scuola Normale Superiore, 2011).

87. On the diffusion of Evangelism among Venetian merchants, see Martin, *Venice's Hidden Enemies*, 73–96, 235–47. See the definition of Evangelism given by Delio Cantimori in the letter to Eva Maria Jung cited in Ginzburg and Prosperi, *Giochi di pazienza*, 20–21. On the long controversy over the term and on the different definitions of Evangelism suggested by scholars, see Elizabeth G. Gleason, "On the Nature of Sixteenth-Century Italian Evangelism: Scholarship, 1953–1978," *Sixteenth-Century Journal* 9, no. 3 (1978): 3–26, and Tedeschi, *The Italian Reformation*, , 822–30.

88. Alberto Bolognetti, "Relazione dello stato et forma delle cose ecclesiastiche nel dominio dei signori Venetiani," in Aldo Stella, *Chiesa stato nelle relazioni dei nunzi pontifici a Venezia. Ricerche sul giurisdizionalismo veneziano dal XVI al XVIII secolo* (Vatican City: Biblioteca Apostolica Vaticana, 1964), 279–80: "teneano libri heretici, mangiavano carne et altri cibi d'ogni sorte in giorni prohibiti a voglia loro, ragionavano come a loro piaceva delle cose della religione," "nella chiesa di San Bartolomeo, dove si predica in lingua tedesca, fosse stato solito di predicarsi publicamente dottrina heretica." On the Fondaco dei Tedeschi, see Karl-Ernst Lupprian, *Il Fondaco dei Tedeschi e la sua funzione di controllo del commercio tedesco a Venezia* (Venice: Centro Tedesco di Studi Veneziani, 1978); Gerhard Rösh, "Il Fondaco dei Tedeschi," in *Venezia e la Germania* (Milan: Electa, 1986), 51–72.

89. Rita Mazzei, "Convivenza religiosa e mercatura nell'Europa del Cinquecento," in *La formazione storica dell'alterità: studi di storia della tolleranza offerti a Antonio Rotondò*, ed. H. Méchoulan et al., 395–428 (Florence: Olschki, 2001), 402–3: "dove è proibito dalle leggi sacre e canoniche l'haver commercio e pratica con li eretici e scismatici, quando però si tratta della mercatura . . . si eccettua dalle medesime leggi, e si permette con questi il trattare." On cross-cultural trade in early modern Italy, see Rita Mazzei, *Itinera mercatorum: Circolazione di uomini e beni nell'Europa centro-orientale 1550–1650* (Lucca: Fazzi, 1999), 181–222; Eric Dursteler, *Venetians in Constantinople: Nation, Identity, and Coexistence in the Early Modern Mediterranean* (Baltimore: Johns Hopkins University Press, 2006); Trivellato, *Familiarity of Strangers*; Rothman, *Brokering Empire*; Ingrid Houssaye Michienzi, *Datini, Majorque et le Maghreb (14e–15e siècles): Réseaux, espaces méditerranées et stratégies marchandes* (Leiden: Brill, 2013); Germano Maifreda, ed., *"Mercanti, eresia e Inquisizione nell'Italia moderna,"* special issue of *Storia economica* 17 (2014): 1; Fusaro, *Political Economies of Empire*.

90. Seidel Menchi, *"Protestantesimo a Venezia,"* 141–49.

5. Reading Tasso

1. John Tedeschi, "The Cultural Contributions of Italian Protestant Reformers in the Late Renaissance," in *Libri, idee e sentimenti religiosi del Cinquecento italiano*, ed. Adriano Prosperi and Albano Biondi, 81–108 (Modena: Panini, 1987).

2. Jardine and Grafton, "*Studied for Action.*"

3. Hampton, *Fictions of Embassy*, 81.

4. Among the authors of the Western canon, special attention has been devoted to Shakespeare and diplomacy. See Hampton, *Fictions of Embassy*, 138–62; Levin and Watkins, *Shakespeare's Foreign Worlds*, 111–40; Joanna Craigwood, "Shakespeare's Kingmaking Ambassadors," in *Diplomacy and Authority from Dante to Shakespeare*, ed. Jason Powell and William T. Rossiter, 199–217 (Aldershot: Ashgate, 2013); Kiséry, *Hamlet's Moment*.

5. On Castelvetro see chapters 6 and 7 of this book.

6. Angelo Solerti, *La Vita di Torquato Tasso*, 3 vols. (Turin: Loescher, 1895), 2:204–5: "Nè mi resta altro che caldamente pregarla di favorirmi di scrivermi, se il povero Tasso vada tuttavia componendo cosa alcuna, o no: che Vostra Signoria sappia, che un illustre cavaliere me l'ha domandato, dicendo che Sua Maestà gli ha imposto d'informarsene; e componendo egli cosa che vaglia, mi farebbe un segnalatissimo favore a mandarmene un esempio, onde ne la prego quanto più posso e so, assicurandola che questa reina non stima meno avventuroso il Serenissimo nostro Duca per avere cotesto gran poeta cantate le sue loda, che sì facesse Alessandro Achille, per aver egli avuto il grande Omero; e mi dicono che ella ne sappia di già molte stanze a mente."

7. SNL, MS 23.1.6, *Ragionamento di Carlo V Imperatore tenuto al re Philippo suo figliuolo*; Castelvetro's dedication to James VI/I is dated August 16, 1592: "per potere intendere i nobili poemi . . . del gran poeta Torquato Tasso, di cui parlando il valente suo poeta du Bartas, dice Dernier en age, premier en honneur."

8. On early modern translations from vernacular into Latin, see Peter Burke, "Translations into Latin in Early modern Europe," in *Cultural Translation in Early Modern Europe*, ed. Peter Burke and R. Po-Chia Hsia, 65–80 (Cambridge: Cambridge University Press, 2007), and on early modern England, see John Binns, *Intellectual Culture in Elizabethan and Jacobean England: The Latin Writings of the Age* (Leeds: Francis Cairns, 1990).

9. Scipione Gentili, *Solymeidos libri duo priores de Torquati Tassi Italicis expressi* (London: John Wolfe, 1584). On the first English translations of the *Liberata*, see Charles P. Brand, *Torquato Tasso: A Study of the Poet and of His Contribution to English Literature* (Cambridge: Cambridge University Press, 1965), 238–46, where Gentili is, however, mentioned only briefly. A more detailed analysis can be found in Clifford C. Huffman, "The Earliest Reception of Tasso in Elizabethan England," *Rivista di Letterature Moderne e Comparate* 32 (1979): 245–61.

10. Scipione Gentili, *Plutonis concilium: ex initio quarti libri Solymeidos* (London: John Wolfe, 1584). On Tasso's influence on Sidney, see Barbara Brumbaugh, "*Jerusalem Delivered* and the Allegory of Sidney's Revised Arcadia," *Modern Philology* 101 (2004): 337–70.

11. On Gentili's biography, see Angela De Benedictis, "Gentili, Scipione," in DBI 53, 268–72.

12. On Wolfe, see Clifford C. Huffman, *Elizabethan Impressions: John Wolfe and His Press* (New York: AMS, 1988). In the same years Wolfe also published several works by Alberico Gentili: on the relationship between the Italian lawyer and the English printer, see in particular Ian Maclean, "Alberico Gentili, his Publishers, and the Vagaries of the Book Trade between England and Germany, 1580–1614" in *Learning and the Market Place: Essays in the History of the Early Modern Book* (Leiden: Brill, 2009), 291–337.

13. Torquato Tasso, *Aminta* (London: John Wolfe, 1591).

14. Gentili, *Solymeidos libri*, opening address *Poetis Italis.*

15. Gentili, *Solymeidos*, I.v.1–3, 1r, alluding to the incipit of Virgil's *Aeneid*. I am quoting Tasso from *Gerusalemme Liberata*, ed. Lanfranco Caretti (Milan: Mondadori, 1983), I.3 (English translation by M. Wickert, *The Liberation of Jerusalem*, with intro. and notes by M. Davie [Oxford: Oxford University Press, 2009], 3). Gentili's attempt to rewrite Tasso imitating Virgil is examined by Guido Baldassarri, "Poema eroico o 'romanzo'? Riscritture della Liberata dal Camilli al Gentili," in *Scritture di scritture: testi, generi, modelli nel Rinascimento*, ed. G. Mazzacurati and M. Plaisance (Rome: Bulzoni, 1987), esp. 453–59.

16. Scipione Gentili, *Solymeidos* (Venice: Altobello Salicato, 1585); Tasso, *Le lettere di Torquato Tasso*, ed. C. Guasti, 5 vols. (Florence, 1853), 3:165n785, Torquato Tasso to Alberto Parma (Mantua, March 29, 1587): "leggiadrissimi invero e politissimi."

17. Scipione Gentili, *Annotationi sopra la Gierusalemme liberata di Torquato Tasso* (Leida [London]: John Wolfe, 1586), dedication "All'illustrissimo signore, il signor Guglielmo del' Aubespine."

18. See Jean Balsamo, "L'Arioste et le Tasse: Des poètes italiens, leurs libraires et leurs lecteurs français," in *L'Arioste et le Tasse en France au XVIe siècle*, 11–26 (Paris: ENS, 2003), 19.

19. Torquato Tasso, *Gerusalemme Liberata* (Lyon: Alessandro Marsilij [Petro Roussin] 1581). On the sixteenth-century French translations of the *Liberata*, see Rosanna Gorris, "*Concilii celesti e infernali*: Blaise de Vigenère traduttore della *Gerusalemme Liberata*," *Studi di letteratura francese* 19 (1993): 385–409, and Françoise Graziani, "Sur le chemin du Tasse: la fidélité du traducteur selon Vigenère, Baudoin et Vion Dalibray," in Balsamo, *L'Arioste et le Tasse en France*, 203–16.

20. Solerti, *La Vita di Torquato Tasso*, 1:135–52.

21. Torquato Tasso, "Lettera del signor Torquato Tasso, nella quale paragona l'Italia alla Francia," in *Tre scritti politici*, ed. Luigi Firpo (Turin: Utet, 1980), 99–125. On the *Lettera* see also Antonio Corsaro, "La *Lettera dalla Francia* du Tasse" in *L'Arioste et le Tasse en France*, 233–44.

22. Torquato Tasso, "Discorso del signor Torquato Tasso intorno alla sedizione nata nel regno di Francia l'anno 1585," in *Tre scritti politici*, 163: "poco zelo che egli ha mostrato della religione, facendo pace con gli Ugonotti"; "tenendo amicizia stretta e confederazione co 'l Turco."

23. Luigi Firpo, "Un madrigale inedito del Tasso e una testimonianza di Campanella," *Giornale storico della letteratura italiana* 127 (1950): 375–77.

24. See David Quint, *Epic and Empire* (Princeton, NJ: Princeton University Press, 1993), 213–47.

25. Quint, *Epic and Empire,* 213–47. On the conflict between "uniformity" and "multiplicity" in the *Liberata*, see Sergio Zatti, *L'uniforme cristiano e il multiforme pagano:*

Saggio sulla Gerusalemme Liberata (Milan: Il Saggiatore, 1983), 30–31, which examines the rebellion of Argillano.

26. Gentili, *Annotationi*, 124: "nella somma grandezza dell'imperio Romano sollevò l'arme per la libertà d'Italia, e costrinse il popolo di Roma a ricevere gli Italiani nella loro cittadinanza" (examining *Liberata*, 8.58).

27. See chapter 2 of this book.

28. On Florio's and Bruno's connections with the French embassy in London, see Frances Yates, *John Florio: The Life of an Italian in Shakespeare's England* (Cambridge: Cambridge University Press, 1934), 61–86. Bruno's role within the French embassy has been reexamined by John Bossy in his controversial *Giordano Bruno*, later reappraised in John Bossy, *Under the Molehill: An Elizabethan Spy Story* (New Haven, CT: Yale University Press 2001). For a critical discussion of Bossy's reconstruction of Bruno's English years, see Jill Kraye, "John Bossy on Giordano Bruno," *Heythrop Journal* 33 (1992): 324–27.

29. Lina Bolzoni, "Osservazioni su Bruno e Ariosto," *Rinascimento* 40 (2000): 19–43.

30. On Fowler, especially on his role as translator of Machiavelli, see Alessandra Petrina, *Machiavelli in the British Isles: Two Early Modern Translations of* The Prince (Aldershot: Ashgate, 2009).

31. De Benedictis, "Gentili, Scipione."

32. *Liberata*, 17.90. On the myth of the crusader prince in Tasso's Ferrara, see Giovanni Ricci, *Ossessione turca: In una retrovia cristiana dell'Europa moderna* (Bologna: Il Mulino, 2002), 59–75.

33. Quint, *Epic and Empire*, 213–47.

34. On Renée of France in Ferrara, see Chiara Franceschini, "La corte di Renata di Francia (1528–1560)," in *Storia di Ferrara*, 7 vols., ed. Adriano Prosperi, 6:185–214 (Ferrara: Corbo Editore, 1987–2004). For further bibliography, see Tedeschi, "The Italian Reformation," 416–29.

35. Prosperi, *L'eresia del Libro Grande*.

36. Zatti, *L'uniforme cristiano*, 37, English translation in Sergio Zatti, *The Quest for Epic: From Ariosto to Tasso*, intro. Albert Ascoli, ed. Dennis Looney (Toronto: University of Toronto Press, 2006), 154.

37. Gentili, *Annotationi*, 1.

38. Gentili, *Annotationi*, 2: "Quantunque il poeta, dicendo pietose, intenda solo dell'arme Christiane, e non punto di quelle de' nemici . . . nientedimeno, se con la ragione delle genti, come si deve, si vorrà questa cosa essaminare, pietose etiandio, et giuste si potranno addimandare l'arme di coloro che alli Christiani in quella impresa si opposero. Conciò sia cosa, che la natura istessa come pijssima madre c'insegna a difender la vita e le facoltà nostre dalla forza & ingiuria de' nemici."

39. Gentili, *Annotationi*, 2: "Ed è già stata rifiutata da quel celebre Giureconsulto Andrea Alciato la opinione di quei Leggisti, i quali volevano, che la guerra fusse giusta solamente da una parte de' guerreggianti."

40. Alberico Gentili, *De iure belli libri tres* (Hanau: Heirs of Wilhelm Anton: 1612) 47, English trans. by John C. Rolfe in Alberico Gentili, *De iure belli libri tres*, (Oxford: The Clarendon Press, 1933), 31); Gentili, Gentili, *De iure belli libri tres* (Hanau: Heirs of Wilhelm Antonius, 1612), 17 (English trans., 12).

41. Gentili, *De iure belli*, 49–50.

42. Gentili, *De iure belli*, 51–52.

43. John W. Binns, "Alberico Gentili in Defense of Poetry and Acting," *Studies in the Renaissance* 19 (1972): 224–72.

44. Binns, "Alberico Gentili," 257 (Latin text, 236: "Torquatum Tassum, poetam, quem feceris Homero, et Virgilio facile parem, et rei poeticae summum hodie magistrum").

45. On the representation of war in Tasso and in Renaissance epic, see Michael Murrin, *History and Warfare in Renaissance Epic* (Chicago: University of Chicago Press, 1994), and Lina Bolzoni, "'O maledetto, o abominoso ordigno': la rappresentazione della guerra nel poema epico-cavalleresco," in *Storia d'Italia XVIII: Guerra e pace*, ed. Walter Barberis, 201–47 (Turin: Einaudi, 2002).

46. Gentili, *De iure belli*, 1–2: "iura, quae cum hostibus quae cum externis communia nobis sunt" (English trans., 3).

47. Gentili, *Annotationi*, 93, referring to *Liberata*, 6.51 (English trans., 107).

48. *Liberata*, 1.89.

49. Gentili, *Annotationi*, 19.

50. Gentili, *Annotationi*, 19.

51. Gentili, *Annotationi*, 19: "si perché usar simil fraude s'è un guerreggiare contra la Natura, overo la società naturale, che l'huomo ha con l'huomo, ne per alcun dissidio si può o si deve rompere da veruno."

52. Gentili, *De iure belli*, 256.

53. *Liberata*, 2.1–2 (English trans., 22).

54. Keith Thomas, *Religion and the Decline of Magic: Studies in Popular Belief in Sixteenth- and Seventeenth-Century England* (London: Weidenfeld and Nicolson, 1971). On Tasso's interest in magic and demonology, see Ezio Raimondi, *Rinascimento inquieto* (Palermo: Manfredi, 1965), 197–227; Patrizia Castelli, "'Ali bianche vestì' la demonologia nel manierismo tassiano," in *Tasso e l'università*, ed. Walter Moretti and Luigi Pepe, 389–410 (Florence: Olschki, 1997), and Walter Stephens, "La demonologia nella poetica del Tasso," in Moretti and Pepe, *Tasso e l'università*, 411–32.

55. Gentili, *De iure belli*, 261 (English trans., 161): "Quid plura dico? Hinc patet, has esse illicitas in bello artes, quod bellum contentio hominum, fit per eas contentio daemonum. Ut ita Tassus nobilis in bello id damnat per istam rationem alicubi prioris suae bonae Solymeidos."

56. Gentili, *De iure belli*, 457 (English trans., 279).

57. *Liberata*, 10.26: "E scorrer lieti i Franchi, e i petti e i volti / spesso calcar de' suoi più noti amici,/ e con fasto superbo a gli insepolti / l'arme spogliare e gli abiti infelici; / molti onorare in lunga pompa accolti / gli amati corpi de gli estremi uffici, / altri suppor le fiamme, e l' vulgo misto / d'Arabi e Turchi a un foco arder ha visto" (English trans. p. 188). Compare with Gentili, *De iure belli*, 457.

58. *Liberata*, 9.88 (English trans., 180).

59. *Orlando furioso*, 19.11–12. Compare Gentili, *De iure belli*, 457.

60. Gentili, *De iure belli*, 458.

61. Gentili, *De iure belli*, 460 (English trans., 280–81): "Contra Achillem et Plato est: aut verius contra Homerum: qui Achillem deae, et Pelei filium, viri moderatissimi, et a sapientissimo Chirone educatum, tanta perturbatione refertum induxerit: ut nec, nisi ac-

cepto pretio, Hectoris cadaver reddiderit." Compare with Plato, *Republic*, 3.391b–c; and Torquato Tasso, "Il forno overo de la nobiltà," in *Dialoghi*, ed. Ezio Raimondi, 3 vols. (Florence: Sansoni, 1958), 2.1:87–88.

62. Binns, "Alberico Gentili," 238. Gentili draws especially on Julius Caesar Scaliger, *Poetices libri septem* (Lyon: Antoine Vincent, 1561), but he is also well-acquainted with the works by Girolamo Fracastoro, Francesco Patrizi, Antonio Riccoboni, and Jacopo Zabarella. Compare Lucretius, *De rerum natura*, 1:936–8, famously quoted by Tasso in the *Liberata*, I.3. On the history of this literary topos, see Valentina Prosperi, *"Di soavi licor gli orli del vaso": La fortuna di Lucrezio dall'Umanesimo alla Controriforma* (Turin: Aragno, 2004). In *Annotationi* (p. 3) Scipione Gentili also grasped Tasso's Lucretian quotation.

63. Gentili, *Annotationi*, 3: "il vero e dritto fine del poeta non è altro, che di giovare inserendo le virtù, e sterpando gli vitij dagli animi de'cittadini."

64. On Tasso's relationship with Renaissance diplomatic culture, see Hampton, *Fictions of Embassy*, 54–62; Daniela Frigo, "Prudenza politica e conoscenza del mondo: un secolo di riflessione sulla figura dell'ambasciatore (1541–1663)," in *De l'ambassadeur: Les écrits relatifs à l'ambassadeur et à l'art de négocier du Moyen Âge au début du XIXe siècle*, ed. Stefano Andretta, Stéphane Péquignot and Jean-Claude Waquet (Rome: École française de Rome, 2015), http://books.openedition.org/efr/2909. On the influence of Tasso on Renaissance diplomatic literature, see also Daniel Ménager, *Diplomatie et théologie à la Renaissance* (Paris: Presses universitaires de France, 2001).

65. Torquato Tasso, *Il messaggiero* (Venice: Bernardo Giunti, 1582). On the editions of the *Messaggiero*, see Ezio Raimondi, "Introduzione" to Tasso, *Dialoghi*, 1:23–29 and 102–11.

66. See Luigi Firpo, "Introduzione" to Tasso, *Tre scritti politici*, 21–28.

67. Hampton, *Fictions of Embassy*, esp. 73–96.

68. Gentili, *Annotationi*, 34; *Liberata*, 2.57.

69. On Tasso and dissimulation, see Francesco Erspamer, "Il *pensiero debole* di Torquato Tasso" in *La menzogna*, ed. Franco Cardini, 120–36 (Florence: Ponte alle Grazie, 1989), and Sergio Zatti, "Il linguaggio della simulazione nella *Liberata*" in *Forma e parola: Studi in memoria di Fredi Chiappelli*, ed. Dennis J. Dutschke et al., 423–47 (Roma: Bulzoni, 1992), 423–47.

70. Gentili, *Annotationi*, 34–45; *Liberata*, II.58 (English trans., 33).

71. *Liberata*, 2.92.

72. *Liberata*, 2.95.

73. Gentili, *Annotationi*, 39: "La ragion delle genti vuole, che si come all'ambasciadore si presto securo ritorno così egli nel ritornare non ingiurij in alcun modo quel principe al quale ha fatta la sua ambasciata."

74. Gentili, *Annotationi*, 39.

75. Daniela Frigo, "Prudence and Experience: Ambassadors and Political Culture in Early Modern Italy," *Journal of Medieval and Early Modern Studies* 38, no. 1 (2008): 15–34.

76. Alberico Gentili, *De legationibus libri tres* (London: Thomas Vautrollier, 1585), 146; English trans. in Alberico Gentili, *De legationibus libri tres*, trans. G. J. Laing (New York: Oxford University Press, 1924), 201.

77. Gentili, *De legationibus*, 45: "cum legato speculatore non arbitror agi durius posse, quam ut non admittatur, vel expellatur admissus" (English trans., 65).

78. Gentili, *De legationibus*, 40: "Legatus neque caeditur, neque violatur" (English trans., 58).

79. Gentili, *De iure belli libri*, 220.

80. John Case, *Sphaera civitatis* (Oxford: Joseph Barnes, 1588), 621: "sine legatione . . . nulla omnino civitas, nulla respublica, nullum imperium constet." On Case, see above all C. B. Schmitt, *John Case and Aristotelianism in Renaissance England* (Kingston, Ontario: McGill-Queen's University Press, 1983).

81. Gentili, *De legationibus*, 109: "Machiavelli was a eulogist of democracy, and its most spirited champion" [Machiavellus Democratiae laudator, et assertor acerrimus] (English trans., 156). Gentili's Machiavellianism has been the subject of extensive study: see, for example, Diego Panizza, *Alberico Gentili giurista ideologo dell'Inghilterra elisabettiana* (Padua: La Garangola, 1981); Peter S. Donaldson, *Machiavelli and the Mystery of State* (Cambridge: Cambridge University Press, 1988); Victoria Kahn, *Machiavellian Rhetoric: From the Counter-Reformation to Milton* (Princeton, NJ: Princeton University Press, 1994); Giuliano Procacci, *Machiavelli nella cultura europea dell'età moderna* (Rome: Laterza, 1995); Sydney Anglo, *Machiavelli—The First Century: Studies in Enthusiasm, Hostility and Irrelevance* (Oxford: Oxford University Press, 2005). For further observations, see also Diego Pirillo, "Republicanism and Religious Dissent: Machiavelli and the Italian Protestant Reformers," in *Machiavellian Encounters in Tudor and Stuart England: Literary and Political Influences from the Reformation to the Restoration*, ed. Alessandro Arienzo and Alessandra Petrina, 121–40 (Aldershot: Ashgate, 2013).

82. With the exception of Hampton, *Fictions of Embassy*, esp. 52–54. For observations on Gentili and Tasso, see also Christopher R. Warren, "Gentili, the Poets and the Laws of War," in *The Roman Foundations of the Law of Nations: Alberico Gentili and the Justice of Empire*, eds. Benedict Kingsbury and Benjamin Straumann, 146–62 (Oxford: Oxford University Press, 2010), 156–59.

83. Gentili, *De legationibus*, 146.

84. Tasso, *Dialoghi*, 3:297–468, at 299: "opera d'uomo che scrive come filosofo e crede come cristiano." On the philosophical background of the *Messaggiero*, see Guido Baldassarri, "Fra 'dialogo' e 'nocturnales annotationes': Prolegomeni alla lettura del *Messaggiero*," *La rassegna della Letteratura Italiana* 76 (1972): 265–93; Gustavo Costa, "La dimensione magico-ermetica del sublime nel *Messaggiero* tassiano," in Dutschke et al., *Forma e parola*, 371–88; Castelli, "'Ali bianche vestì,'" and Stephens, "La demonologia." On philosophy and rhetoric in Tasso's *dialoghi*, see also Franceso Tateo, "I *Dialoghi* del Tasso fra dialettica e retorica," in Moretti and Pepe, *Tasso e l'università*, 199–211; Erminia Ardissino, *Tasso, Plotino, Ficino: in margine a un postillato* (Rome: Edizioni di Storia e Letteratura, 2003); and Massimo Rossi, *"Io come filosofo era stato dubbio": la retorica dei* Dialoghi *di Tasso* (Bologna: Il Mulino, 2007).

85. Tasso, *Dialoghi*, 3:425.

86. Tasso, *Dialoghi*, 3:440: "uomo che rappresenta appresso un principe la persona d'un altro principe affine d'amicizia e di pace."

87. Tasso, *Dialoghi*, 3:436: "s'uno guerreggiasse per guerreggiare . . . simile ad un arciero il qual saettasse senza aver mira ad alcun bersaglio." On the history of the doctrine of just war in the early modern period, see Roland H. Bainton, *Christian Attitudes toward War and Peace: A Historical Survey and a Critical Re-Evaluation* (Eugene, OR: Wipf and

Stock, 1960); Richard Tuck, *The Rights of War and Peace: Political Thought and the International Order from Grotius to Kant* (Oxford: Oxford University Press, 1999); Adriano Prosperi, "'Guerra giusta' e cristianità divisa tra Cinquecento e Seicento," in *Chiesa e guerra. Dalla "benedizione delle armi" alla "Pacem in terris*," ed. Mimmo Franzinelli and Riccardo Bottoni, 29–90 (Bologna: Il Mulino, 2005).

88. Gentili, *De legationibus*, 11.

89. Gentili, *De legationibus*, 10. See Virgil, *Aeneid*, 12.75–6.

90. Gentili, *De legationibus*, 11: "Non igitur viro divino assentior Torquato Tasso, qui alios esse pacis legatos, alios belli non fert, sed omnem legatum pacis virum esse contendit. . . . Certe in mandato definito, et bellum indicere iubente, vera Tassi sententia esse non potest" (English trans., 17).

91. Tasso, *Dialoghi*, 3:449–50.

92. Tasso, *Dialoghi*, 3:459–60: "l'ambasciatore, portando e riportando le proposte d'un prencipe e risposte d'un altro, non deve sempre riferirle con le parole istesse con le quali gli sono state scritte o dette: perché, ciò facendo, agevolmente alcuna fiata l'animo d'essi offenderebbe in modo ch'ove è suo fine di generare amicizia, genererebbe odio e mala sodisfazione; ma, conservando pura e intatta nella sua verità l'essenza delle commissioni, può con le parole e con le ragioni mutar loro aspetto e simiglianza; e s'alcuna cosa occorre mai fra' prencipi, fra quali è mezzano, dura e acerba, egli con le dolci e piacevoli parole e co'l destro e cortese modo di negoziare può ammolirla e raddolcirla in modo ch'alcuna mala sodisfazione nell'animo de'prencipi non rimanga."

93. Tasso, *Dialoghi*, 3:450–51: "nella cittadinanza di Romolo vivendo come se nella republica di Platone fosse nato, di molti tumulti fu alcuna volta cagione nella città."

94. Tasso, *Dialoghi*, 3:452–53.

95. Lucretius, *De rerum natura*, 1:936–38; *Liberata*, 1.3. On Tasso as reader of Lucretius, see Prosperi, "*Di soavi licor gli orli del vaso*," 181–265.

96. Baldesar Castiglione, *Il libro del Cortegiano*, ed. W. Barberis (Turin: Einaudi, 1998), 365, English trans. Leonard Eckstein Opdyke (New York: Dover, 2003). See Claudio Scarpati, *Dire la verità al principe: Ricerche sulla letteratura del Rinascimento* (Milan: Vita e Pensiero, 1987), 11–44.

97. Gentili, *De legationibus*, 125–26: "Et sane quidquid excellentissimus distinguat Tassus, ego in ea sententia sum, ne aliquod tale a legatis umquam committi debeat. . . . Nec quidem, si in certo mandato versamur, dubito quin non legatis liceat vel transversum ab illo unguem secedere" (English trans., 175–76).

98. Ermolao Barbaro, *De coelibatu—De officio legati*, ed. Vittore Branca (Florence: Olschki, 1969), 159. See Mattingly, *Renaissance Diplomacy*, 181–206.

99. As cited in Paolo Prodi, *Diplomazia del Cinquecento. Istituzioni e prassi* (Bologna: Patron, 1963), 71.

100. Gentili, *De legationibus*, 125: "Mixta est in legato persona, non duae personae sunt: in qua ius Dei cum sit potentius, trahi ab hoc alterum omnino debet" (English trans., 174). I have slightly modified Laing's translation.

101. Gentili, *De legationibus*, 114–15.

102. Gentili, *De legationibus*, 124: "Itaque nec temporarius legatus audiet, si quid ipsum agere princeps velit, quod fidei Deo devinctae vel tantillum derogare videatur . . . nec alius ullus legatus adeo amens fuerit, qui in divinam fidem peccare, quam in regiam

malit. Is tamen, quicumque erit, aget pessime, si certam suscipit legationem, cui lex Dei sui impedimento est, quominus illam conficiat." (English trans., 195).

103. Gentili, *De legationibus*, 125: "scio, quam ista sint ab usurpatis moribus dissita. Sed ego legatum fingo, non qui esse solet, at qui esse debet" (English trans., 174).

104. George Buchanan's *De iure regni apud Scotos* had been published in 1579 in Edinburgh and immediately reprinted in London in 1580 and 1581. See the new edition edited by Roger A. Mason and Martin S. Smith: George Buchanan, *A Dialogue on the Law of Kingship among the Scots* (Aldershot: Ashgate, 2004). On Sidney's interest in republicanism and tyrannicide, see Blair Worden, *The Sound of Virtue: Philip Sidney's Arcadia and Elizabethan Politics* (New Haven, CT: Yale University Press, 1996). On Gentili's criticism of Buchanan, see Pirillo, *Filosofia ed eresia*, 120–37.

105. On the doctrine of "monarchical republicanism," see Patrick Collinson, "The Monarchical Republic of Queen Elizabeth I," in *The Tudor Monarchy*, ed. John Guy, 110–34 (London: Arnold, 1997), and John F. McDiarmid, ed., *The Monarchical Republic of Early Modern England: Essays in Response to Patrick Collinson* (Aldershot: Ashgate, 2007).

106. Gentili, *De legationibus*, 53. Compare Plato, *Politicus*, 296a–297b.

107. Gentili, *Annotationi*, 66–67, commenting on *Liberata*, 4.80 and alluding to Dante, *Inferno*, 34.

108. Gentili, *De legationibus*, 64 (English trans., 91).

6. Reading Venetian *Relazioni*

1. Willy Andreas, *Staatskunst und Diplomatie der Venezianer im Spiegel ihrer Gesandtenberichte* (Lepizig: Von Quelle & Meyer, 1908), 124; Carlo Morandi, ed., *Relazioni di ambasciatori. Sabaudi genovesi e veneti durante il periodo della Grande Alleanza e della successione di Spagna* (Bologna: Zanichelli, 1935), liii.

2. Benzoni, "Ranke's Favorite Source." On Ranke's "discovery" of the *relazioni*, see also Edward Muir, "Leopold von Ranke, His Library, and the Shaping of Historical Evidence," *Courier* 22, no. 1 (1987): 3–10, and Ugo Tucci, "Ranke and the Venetian Document Market," *Courier* 22, no. 1 (1987): 27–38. On Ranke's library, see Edward Muir, *The Leopold von Ranke Manuscript Collection of Syracuse University: The Complete Catalogue* (Syracuse, NY: Syracuse University Press, 1983). On the meaning of Ranke's famous "wie es eigentlich gewesen," see Grafton, *The Footnote*, 62–93.

3. Paolo Preto, *Venezia e i Turchi* (Florence: Sansoni, 1975), Lucette Valensi, *The Birth of the Despot: Venice and the Sublime Porte* (Ithaca, NY: Cornell University Press, 1993), Eric Dursteler, "Describing or Distorting the 'Turk'? The *Relazioni* of the Venetian Ambassadors in Constantinople as Historical Source," *Acta Histriae* 19, no. 1–2 (2011): 231–48.

4. As noted by De Vivo, "How to Read,". See also De Vivo, *Information and Communication in Venice*.

5. Giacomo Castelvetro, *Album amicorum*, BL, Harley MS 3344, cc. 46v–47r: "alla età di diciotto anni in compagnia di Lelio mio fratello ci partimmo a' 4 di giugno [1564] da la predetta città sopra a un mulo in due ceste, e così andammo a Lione sul Rodano in casa de' magnifici e ricchissimi mercatanti Messer Nicolò e Messer Girolamo Pellic-

ciari. . . . Da detta città andammo a Geneva, ove trovai il letteratissimo Signor Ludovico Castelvetro mio zio paterno." On Castelvetro, see Kathleen T. Blake Butler, "Giacomo Castelvetro 1546–1616," *Italian Studies* 5 (1950): 1–42; H. G. Dick, "A Renaissance Expatriate: Giacomo Castelvetro the Elder," *Italian Quarterly* 7 (1963): 3–19; Luigi Firpo, "Castelvetro, Giacomo," DBI 22, 1–4; Paola Ottolenghi, *Giacopo Castelvetro esule modenese nell'Inghilterra di Shakespeare* (Pisa: ETS, 1982); Maria Luisa De Rinaldis, *Giacomo Castelvetro Renaissance Translator* (Lecce: Milella, 2003); John Martin, "Castelvetro, Giacomo," ODNB; Chiara Franceschini, "Nostalgie di un esule. Note su Giacomo Castelvetro (1546–1616)," in *Questioni di storia inglese tra Cinque e Seicento: cultura, politica e religione*, ed. Stefano Villani, Stefania Tutino, and C. Franceschini, 73–101 (Pisa: Edizioni della Normale, 2006).

6. On Ludovico Castelvetro's library, see Tommaso Sandonnini, *Lodovico Castelvetro e la sua famiglia: Note biografiche* (Bologna: Zanichelli, 1982), 314–34; Giuseppe Cavazzuti, *Lodovico Castelvetro* (Modena: Società tipografica modenese, 1903), appendix 37–39; and more recently Andrea Barbieri, "Castelvetro, i suoi libri, e l'ambiente culturale modenese del suo tempo," in *Ludovico Castelvetro: filologia e ascesi*, ed. Roberto Gigliucci, 57–69 (Rome: Bulzoni, 2007). On Ludovico Castelvetro's religious ideas, see also Massimo Firpo and Guido Mongini, eds., *Ludovico Castelvetro: Letterati e grammatici nella crisi religiosa del Cinquecento* (Florence: Olschki, 2008), and the collection of his religious works edited by Guido Mongini in Ludovico Castelvetro, *Filologia ed eresia: scritti religiosi* (Brescia: Morcelliana, 2011).

7. TCL, R.10.6: *Libretto di varie maniere di parlare della Italica lingua* (Cambridge, August 29, 1613), 156v–157r. On the influence of Erasmus on Italian philo-Protestants, see Seidel Menchi, *Erasmo in Italia*.

8. See Hans Georg Wackernagel, ed., *Die Matrikel der Universität Basel*, 5 vols. (Basel: Verlag der Universitätsbibliothek, 1951–), 2:179; Francesco Petrarca, *Le rime del Petrarca brevemente sposte per Lodovico Castelvetro* (Basel: Pietro Sebadonis [Pietro Perna], 1582).

9. SP 78/4B, c. 163r.: Henry Cobham to Francis Walsingham (Moret, October 4, 1580).

10. On Florio, see Frances Yates, *John Florio*; Wyatt, *Italian Encounter*, 157–254; Warren Boutcher, *The School of Montaigne in Early Modern Europe*, 2 vols. (Oxford: Oxford University Press, 2017), 2:189–271.

11. Alberico Gentili, *De iure belli commentationes tres* (London: John Wolfe, 1589): "expensis I[acobi]C[astelvetri]M[utinensis]." On Gentili's publishers, see Ian Maclean, *Learning and the Marketplace: Essays in the History of the Early Modern Book* (Leiden: Brill, 2009), 291–337. Castelvetro and Gentili both moved within the circle of the Genoese merchant Orazio Pallavicino. On Pallavicino, see Stone, *Elizabethan*, and Villani, "Pallavicino, Orazio," in DBI, 80, 2014.

12. Gentili, *De iure belli*, 562–63.

13. Thomas Erastus, *Explicatio gravissimae quaestionis utrum excommunicatio, quatenus religionem intelligentes & amplexantes, a sacramentorum usu, propter admissum facinus arcet; mandato nitatur divino, an excogitata sit ab hominibus* (Poschiavo: apud Baocium Sultaceterum [London: John Wolfe], 1589). In 1587 Castelvetro had married Erastus's widow Isotta de'Canonici, thus accessing many of Erastus's unpublished manuscripts.

14. On Erastus's ideas on excommunication and the context behind Castelvetro's edition, see Charles D. Gunnoe Jr., *Thomas Erastus and the Palatinate: a Renaissance Physician in the Second Reformation* (Leiden: Brill, 2011), 177–92, 388–93.

15. NLS, MS 23.1.16, *Ragionamento di Carlo V Imperatore tenuto al re Philippo suo figliuolo*. Castelvetro's dedication to James is dated August 16, 1592.

16. Dick, "Renaissance Expatriate," 12. Castelvetro was already a client of Robert Cecil's father William, having translated into Italian Cecil's *Execution of Justice*: William Cecil, *Atto della giustizia d'Inghilterra* (London: John Wolfe, 1584). On Castelvetro's patrons in England, see Eleanor Rosenberg, "Giacopo Castelvetro: Italian Publisher in Elizabethan London and His Patrons," *Huntington Library Quarterly* 2 (1946): 119–48.

17. On the professionalization of intelligencers in the early modern period, see Lisa Jardine and William Sherman, "Pragmatic Readers: Knowledge Transactions and Scholarly Services in Elizabethan England," in Anthony Fletcher and Peter Roberts, eds., *Religion, Culture and Society in Early Modern England: A Festschrift for Patrick Collinson* (Cambridge: Cambridge University Press, 1994), 102–124, and De Vivo, *Information and Communication in Venice*, 74–85.

18. BLC, MS Western 32; NL, Vault Case, MS 5086, vols. 59/2, 69/2, 73/2, 74/2, 75/2, 76/2, 78/2, 79, 116/2. The Newberry Library purchased Castelvetro's miscellanies in 1963 following the suggestion of Hans Baron: see accession number 63-1507. I owe this information to the kindness of Paul Gehl.

19. NL, Vault Case MS 5086, vol. 73/2, cc. 68r–79r. On Castelvetro's years in Denmark, see Giuseppe Migliorato, "Vicende e influssi culturali di Giacomo Castelvetro (1546–1616) in Danimarca," *Critica storica* 19 (1982): 243–96.

20. Various authors, *Thesoro politico* (Cologne [Paris: Denis Cotinet and Léger Delas] 1589), titlepage. On the *Thesoro politico*, see Jean Balsamo, "Les origines parisiennes du Tesoro politico (1589)," *Bibliothèque d'Humanisme et Renaissance* 57, no. 1 (1995): 7–23; Artemio E. Baldini, "Origini e fortuna del *Thesoro politico* alla luce di nuovi documenti dell'Archivio del Sant 'Uffizio,'" in *Cultura politica e società a Milano tra Cinquecento e Seicento*, ed. C. Buzzi and C. Continisio, 155–75 (Milan: Editrice ITL, 2000); Simone Testa, "Did Giovanni Maria Mannelli Publish the *Thesoro politico* (1589)?" *Renaissance Studies* 19 (2005): 380–93.

21. Harold Love, *The Culture and Commerce of Texts: Scribal Publication in Seventeenth-Century England* (Amherst: University of Massachusetts Press, 1993). See also Brian Richardson, *Manuscript Culture in Renaissance Italy* (Cambridge: Cambridge University Press, 2009); Filippo De Vivo and Brian Richardson, eds., *"Scribal Culture in Italy, 1450–1700,"* special issue of *Italian Studies* 66, no. 2 (2011). On the scribal publication of *relazioni*, see De Vivo, "How to Read."

22. Jardine and Grafton, *"Studied for Action."*

23. NL, Vault Case MS 5086, vol. 59/2, cc. 31r–35v. See the full report in Albèri 2.3, 365–416.

24. NL, Vault Case, MS 5086, vol. 69/2, cc. 21r–45r: "quelle Indie . . . le quali, navigando, per l'Oceano verso Ponente, da pochi anni in qua furono trovate, di dove è uscito tanto argento e tanto oro e tante altre novità, che hanno empito l'Europa di ricchezze e di maraviglia." See Albèri 1.5, 1–76.

25. Luciano Canfora, *Il copista come autore* (Palermo: Sellerio, 2002).

26. Richardson, *Manuscript Culture,* 8–9.

27. Virgil, *Aeneid,* 1.203.

28. Muir, *Civic Ritual,* 65–68. For the reception of Virgil in Venetian humanism, see Craig Kallendorf, *Virgil and the Myth of Venice: Books and Readers in the Italian Renaissance* (Oxford: Clarendon Press, 1999).

29. Hampton, *Fictions of Embassy,* 57–59.

30. BLC, MS Western 32, *Selva di varie nobili scritture,* cc. 114r–20r.

31. Jardine and Sherman, "Pragmatic Readers."

32. See Aldo Scaglione, "Giacomo Castelvetro e i conclavi dei papi del Rinascimento," *Bibliothèque d'Humanisme et Renaissance* 28 (1966): 141–49; Eleanor Rosenberg, "Giacopo Castelvetro in Scandinavia," *Columbia Library Columns* 25, no. 2 (1976): 18–27; Palmira Brummett, "The Jacopo Castelvetro Collection: A Renaissance Man with Documents on Istanbul," *Turkish Studies Association Bulletin* 11, no. 1 (1987): 1–8. The only studies that publish some of Castelvetro's annotations to his diplomatic miscellanies are John Tedeschi, "Tommaso Sassetti's Account of the St. Bartholomew's Day Massacre" in *The Massacre of St. Bartholomew: Reappraisals and Documents,* ed. A. Soman, 99–154 (The Hague: Martinus Nijhoff, 1974), and Franceschini, "Nostalgie di un esule."

33. Pirillo, "Republicanism and Religious Dissent.

34. NL, Vault Case, MS 5086, vol. 75/2, cc. 47r–v.

35. NL, Vault Case, MS 5086, vol. 78/2, c. 190v.

36. NL, Vault Case, MS 5086, vol. 78/2, c. 29v.

37. NL, Vault Case, MS 5086, vol. 78/2, c. 14r: "Attribuiscono questa sceleratezza all'onesto Macchiavello, il qual non dice che ciò si convenga al prencipe naturale e buono, ma sí al nuovo prencipe e che voglia tiranneggiare, e 'l libero uomo, nimico mortal d'ogni tirannesca signoria, come quelli che veda nel suo libero commun di Firenze sorgere il tiranno di lei. Questo scrisse acciochè il popolo fiorentino conoscesse quanta differenza sia dal viver libero all'esser sottoposti allo'mperio del Tiranno con magnifica virtú e prodezza, avesse difesa la sua antica e cara libertà."

38. TCL, R.4.5, I 9r–v: "Certo questo buon monaco non ha inteso il Macchiavello, che non chiamerebbe empio, il quale hebbe ottima et santa dottrina, che fa per rendere accorti i suoi liberi cittadini, tra quali egli vedeva nascerne l'usurpator della loro cara libertade. Ben per rendere loro odiosissimo ogni tiranno s'elesse il Borgia, come il più empio, et il crudele, che nascesse giamai su la terra per norma di Prencipe nuovo, acciò che i Fiorentini ciechi tanto più venissero aprir gli occhi e odiassero vie più il vegnente o surgente usurpatore della lor cara libertà. E che ciò sia vero, ecco, che quando parla del Prencipe naturale, e buono, dice che deve seguire e osservare le giuste sue leggi."

39. *Discorsi sopra la prima deca di Tito Livio,* 1.55, in Machiavelli, *Opere,* 1:310: "Vedesi bene nella provincia della Magna questa bontà e questa religione ancora in quelli popoli essere grande; la quale fa che molte repubbliche vi vivono libere;" English translation by Harvey C. Mansfield and Nathan Tarcov, in Niccolò Machiavelli, *Discourses on Livy* (Chicago: University of Chicago Press, 1996), 110.

40. Machiavelli, *Opere,* 1:233: "così come dove è religione si presuppone ogni bene, così, dove quella manca, si presuppone il contrario. Abbiamo, adunque, con la Chiesa e con i preti noi italiani questo primo obbligo di essere diventati sanza religione e cattivi"; English trans., *Discourses,* 38.

41. Machiavelli, *Opere*, 1:233: "E veramente alcuna provincia non fu mai unita o felice, se la non viene tutta alla ubbidienza d'una republica o d'uno principe, come è avvenuto alla Francia ed alla Spagna"; English trans., *Discourses*, 38.

42. NL, Vault Case MS 5086, vol. 59/2, c. 74r: "Rade volte è accaduto che sieno venuti barbari soldati a disturbare la quiete d'Italia, che non sieno stati invitati, o chiamati, anzi sforzati da Papi a venirvi, e poi ardiscono di chiamarsi Vicari di Christo, o successori di Pietro, essendo del Diavolo padre d'ogni dissensione, discordia, o guerra."

43. Machiavelli, *Opere*, 1:148.

44. NL, Vault Case MS 5086, 59/2, cc. 180r–182v. The text is undated. Castelvetro's copy was finalized on July 25, 1595.

45. Ibid., cc. 180r–v: "la più santa, la più nobile, la più illustre"; "vero vicario di Dio, e successor leggittimo di San Pietro, e Patriarca universale, e Signor onnipotente del mondo, a cui tutti noi altri signori o Prencipi, di qualsivoglia stato siamo sudditi;" "Il Papa secondo questo Prencipe e tutti i papeschi, è Signore Onnipotente del mondo. Il che s'è così è seguente che sia il gran Diavolo, havendo la verace bocca di Christo più volte detto, che il Prencipe di questo mondo è il Diavolo."

46. NL, Vault Case MS MS 5086, vol. 59/2, cc. 72r–v: "Ci sono stati alcuni si sfacciati lusinghieri, c'hanno havuto ardire di dire che tutti gli stati, e tutte le signorie mondane sieno sottoposte al Papa, però non è da meravigliarsi se i veraci Catolici Christiani riformati, senza punto temere l'ira, né la tirannesca forza sua gli hanno detto in faccia essere in vero figliuolo del gran Diavolo, il quale tentando Christo disse, che di lui erano le signorie tutte del mondo o che le poteva donare a chi l'adorasse, e a chi gli piacesse."

47. Antonio Rotondò, "Anticristo e Chiesa romana: diffusione e metamorfosi d'un libello antiromano del Cinquecento," in *Forme e destinazione del messaggio religioso: aspetti della propaganda religiosa nel Cinquecento*, ed. Antonio Rotondò, 19–164 (Florence: Olschki, 1991); Lucia Felici, "Il papa diavolo: Il paradigma dell'Anticristo nella pubblicistica europea del Cinquecento," in *La papauté à la Renaissance*, ed. Florence Alazard and Frank La Brasca, 533–69 (Paris: Champion, 2007).

48. Jean-Baptiste Trento and Pierre Eskrich, *Mappe-monde nouvelle papistique*, eds. Frank Lestringant and Alessandra Preda (Geneva: Droz, 2009). I have consulted the copy of the map held at BNCF: Pal.C.B.3.36, str. 982.

49. NL, Vault Case MS 5086, vol. 59/2, c. 2r: "è noto ad ognuno che di questa materia del concilio si cominciò a parlare da molti anni, fin dal tempo di Lione X . . . ma *il timore che si hebbe di vedere col concilio alteratione* si in capite come in membris fu causa che per fuggire questa materia di concilio facilmente fu persuaso essere atto instrumento di provedere al bisogno la persona di questo Reverendissimo San Sisto, legato nelle parti di Germania, il quale, che frutto habbia fatto, il mondo ne può rendere tutto buono testimonio" In this and in the following translated passages, I have indicated the sections highlighted by Castelvetro with underlining and placed his marginal notes in parentheses.

50. NL, Vault Case MS 5086, vol. 59/2, cc. 2r–v: "Il cardinale San Sisto legato nella Magna quantunque letterato fosse, era nondimeno cosí poco destro, che più tosto nocque alle cose papesche, che giovamento alcuno vi recasse" [The cardinal of San Sisto, legate to Germany, despite being very learned, was nonetheless so politically incapable, that he hindered papal interests rather than helping them].

51. NL, Vault Case MS 5086, 59/2, c. 2v.

52. NL, Vault Case MS 5086, 59/2, cc. 15r-v: "ha caminato in questa materia del concilio diversamente da Clemente, perché Clemente haveva timore, nè lo poteva o sapeva tener nascosto. All'incontro Paulo ha proceduto più astutamente, perché non ha mai mostrato di temere il concilio."

53. NL, Vault Case MS 5086, 59/2, c. 16r: "Avegna che Paolo III s'infinga di disiderare il Concilio palesemente, ma nascostamente nondimeno l'haborrisce."

54. NL, Vault Case MS 5086, 59/2, c. 16v: "tiene che, quanto al futuro Concilio, sia da ragionare, ma non da operare; avendo per certo che, se Concilio alcuno ha da succedere, non sia, salvo che in quel modo e forma che ho detto; regolata prima ogni cosa in Roma e determinata secondo il volere del papa (*Questo è un bel concilio*) e dei cardinali, e poi presentata al Concilio per esser da quello approvata, senza disputarla altramente. . . . Occorre poi a chi ben considera, che il Concilio non fa per Sua Santità né forse per quella Sede (*Nota ti prego, il Soriano haver lungo il naso, onde odorare molto in dentro*)."

55. Sarpi, *Istoria del Concilio Tridentino*, 1:121. Sarpi is echoing Tacitus, *Annals*, 4.71.

56. On the relationship between Castelvetro and Sarpi, see chapter 7 of this book.

57. Peter Burke, "Sarpi storico," in *Ripensando Paolo Sarpi*, ed. Corrado Pin, 103–9 (Venice: Ateneo Veneto, 2006).

58. Peter Burke, "Publishing the Private in Early Modern Europe: The Rise of Secret History," in *Changing Perceptions of the Public Sphere*, ed. Christian J. Emden and David Midgley, 57–72 (New York: Berghahn Books, 2012).

59. De Vivo, "How to Read."

60. Paolo Prodi, *Il sovrano pontefice: un corpo e due anime. La monarchia papale nella prima età moderna* (Bologna: Mulino, 1982).

61. NL, Vault Case MS 5086, vol. 59/2, cc. 32r-v: "Si può il Pontefice considerare in due modi, o come Prencipe per lo stato temporale, ch'egli ha, o come Pontefice per la spirituale auttorità." Navagero's relazione from Rome was copied, fragmented, and rearranged by Castelvetro more than once. See, for example, TCL R.4.6.

62. NL, Vault Case MS 5086, vol. 59/2, cc. 58r-v: "non sono punto con gli altri Prencipi communi; poi che essi con la Persona, che rappresentano in terra, pare si levino sopra la conditione humana, onde non solo, come gl'altri Prencipi ne i loro stati hanno autorità sopra la robba e la vita delli huomini, ma ancora per tutto il mondo, anco ne i paesi di tutti li altri pretendono d'haver certa superiorità almeno nelle cose spirituali."

63. NL, Vault Case MS 5086, vol. 59/2, cc. 59r-v: "se vuoi veder di ciò la verità vedi L. Valla de falso [credita et ementita Constantini] donatione"; "Nota come la primitiva chiesa fino a 300 dopo la morte di Christo visse sempre di elemosine, senza già mai possedere cosa alcuna stabile, né proprietà. Tutto quel tempo dunque ella fu buona e vera chiesa, ma così dopo che cominciò ad havere beni subito si corruppe"; "I vescovi di Roma di poveri e miti quanto al mondo, divenuti potenti contendono della signoria d'Italia con gli Imperatori."

64. Giulio Poggiani, *Epistolae et orationes*, ed. Girolamo Lagomarsini, 4 vols. (Rome: G. Salomonio, 1757–66), 4:441–44, cited in Domenico Caccamo, "Commendone, Giovanni Francesco," in DBI 27, 606–13.

65. NL, Vault Case MS 5086, vol. 59/2, cc. 103–173. Along with the one included in Castelvetro's anthology, I have consulted the copy of Commedone's *Discorso* in BLB 92/162 z. For the modern edition of the text, see Giovanni Francesco Commendone, *Discorso sopra la corte di Roma*, ed. Cesare Mozzarelli (Rome: Bulzoni, 1996).

66. NL, Vault Case MS 5086, 59/2, c. 107v.

67. Maria Antonietta Visceglia, "Burocrazia, mobilità sociale e patronage alla corte di Roma tra Cinque e Seicento: alcuni aspetti del recente dibattito storiografico e prospettive di ricerca" *Roma moderna e contemporanea* 3 (1995): 11–55; Wolfgang Reinhard, *Papauté, confessions, modernité*, ed. Robert Descimon (Paris: Editions de l'Ecole des hautes études en sciences sociales, 1998).

68. NL, Vault Case MS 5086, 59/2, c. 112r: "in morte del Papa subito si sente tumultuare ogni cosa e in vita si tumultua nelle scisme"; "Per la morte del papa ogni cosa tumultua, e in vita nascon le scisme."

69. NL, Vault Case MS 5086, vol. 59/2, c. 208r: "siccome avviene nelle repubbliche, che tutti o tardi o per tempo si mutano e passano da una forma di stato in un'altra per una naturale mutazione de' costumi che succede nelle città, così parimente per la cagione istessa avvenga ne' principati ed ancora molto più repentinamente negli elettivi, perché a bello studio si creano li successori di natura differente dal predecessore." In the margin Castelvetro added: "Perché si cerchi per lo più, ne Prencipi elettivi di criare il successore che sia diverso di costumi del morto" [For which reason in the elective principalities it is generally sought to create a successor with different habits from the deceased].

70. NL, Vault Case MS 5086, vol. 59/2, c. 88v: "pare che nissuna cosa possa lungamente conservarsi in uno stato; si che sino all'aere per se incostante pare che a Roma sia più soggetto alla mutatione, che in qual si voglia altro luogo"; "pensino di dover dare tanta maggiore satisfattione di loro, quanto più s'allontanano dell'uso del predecessore suo."

71. NL, Vault Case MS 5086, vol. 59/2, c. 88v.

72. On the victory of the Inquisition over the council, see Tallon, "Le Concile de Trente"; Prosperi, *Tribunali della coscienza*, 117–34. On the trials against Carnesecchi see, Firpo and Marcatto, *I processi inquisitoriali*; Firpo, *Inquisizione romana*, 449–69.

73. NL, Vault Case, MS 5086, vol. 79/2, c. 27v.

74. Giovanni Battista Castrodardo, *L'Alcorano di Macometto, nel qual si contiene la dottrina, la vita, i costumi, et le leggi sue* (Venice: Andrea Arrivabene, 1547). Castelvetro signed his copy, adding his name on the title page: see DKB, 28, 270. On the Alcorano, see Carlo De Frede, *La prima traduzione italiana del Corano sullo sfondo dei rapporti tra Cristianità e Islam* (Naples: Istituto Universitario Orientale, 1960); Pier Mattia Tommasino, *L'Alcorano di Macometto: Storia di un libro del Cinquecento europeo* (Bologna: Il Mulino, 2013).

75. Castelvetro was aware of Botero's work as BL, MS Harley 3344, cc. 18v–19r lists Botero's *Relazioni universali* and *Ragion di Stato*. On the *Relazioni universali*, see Romain Descendre, *L'état du monde: Giovanni Botero entre raison d'État et géopolitique* (Geneva: Droz, 2009).

76. NL, Vault Case, MS 5086, vol. 79/2, c. 194r: "l'importante è leggerli ordinatamente, cominciandoli da più antichi, et seguendo tempo per tempo, luogo per luogo, con una diligente cura, delle tavole del Tolomeo e delle moderne, perché senza questa designatione, et distinzione nulla si profitta."

77. NL, Vault Case, MS 5086, vol. 79/2, cc. 27r–58r, 65r–72r.

78. Valensi, *Birth of the Despot*.

79. NL, Vault Case, MS 5086, vol. 79/2, c. 24r: "che con la prudenza si mantengono gli stati, e con l'astuzia e con gli stratagemmi si assicurano."

80. NL, Vault Case, MS 5086, vol. 79/2, c. 132r: "il seguitare gli esempi passati sia ottima cosa per la conservation dello stato."

81. Barbieri, "Castelvetro, i suoi libri," 69n43. On Bibliander's translation of the Quran, see also for further bibliography, Lucia Felici, "L'Islam in Europa: la traduzione del Corano di Theodor Bibliander (1543)," *Cromohs* 12 (2007): 1–13.

82. Tommasino, *L'Alcorano di Macometto*, 221–55.

83. *L'Alcorano*, IIIv, Vr: "grandi signori, i quali de bassi principii con favore di simolata religione pervennero ad estremo grado," "tutti gli antichi Heroi Re, e governatori da principio del Mondo, non havendo più sicuro modo di signoreggiare che il timore, e spavento della loro simolata religione"

84. NL, Vault Case, MS 5086, vol. 79/2, cc. 129r-v: "Sono osservantissimi della loro religione, guardandosi molto dal romperla, violarla, né disputarla. Del loro profeta ne parlano con somma venerazione"; "è cosa mirabile che non solo non biastemano né meno la loro lingua ha vocabulo da biastema (*Questo si esser degno di lode, e ci dee a noi christiani fare arrossire di perpetua onta le gote*)."

85. NL, Vault Case, MS 5086, vol. 79/2, c. 130r: "Sono ubidientissimi a' loro signori, essendo persuasi che il disubedirgli sia contravvenire alla volontà di Dio (*Et questo è lodevole*)."

86. NL, Vault Case, MS 5086, vol. 79/2, c. 131r: "Permette ai popoli ridotti in servitù l'uso di quella religione che più lor piace, temendo non li disperare forzandoli a una nuova religione, e sperando pur di farli in qualche tempo maomettani (*In questo passa di bontà, e di savere qual si voglia prencipe, o commune christiano, se non se il Polacco ol Transilvano*)."

87. See Adriano Prosperi, "Il 'miles christianus' nella cultura italiana tra '400 e '500," *Critica storica* 26, no. 4 (1989): 685–704, collected in Adriano Prosperi, *Eresie e devozioni: la religione italiana in età moderna* (Rome: Edizioni di Storia e Letteratura, 2010), 147–63; Vincenzo Lavenia, "Non barbari, ma religiosi e soldati: Machiavelli, Giovio e la turcofilia in alcuni testi del Cinquecento," *Storia del pensiero politico* 1 (2014): 31–58.

88. Federico Seneca, *Il doge Leonardo Donà. La sua vita e la sua preparazione politica prima del dogado* (Padua: Antenore, 1959), 263–321; Cozzi, *Venezia barocca*; Preto, *Venezia e i Turchi*, 314–25; Federico Barbierato, *The Inquisitor in the Hat Shop: Inquisition, Forbidden Books and Unbelief in Early Modern Venice* (Farnham: Ashgate, 2012), 118–19. Nicolò Contarini's observations on the Ottoman empire can be read in Federico Barbierato, "Istorie venetiane" in Benzoni and Zanato, eds., *Storici e politici veneti del Cinquecento e del Seicento*, pp. 156–85. See also, in the same volume Fulgenzio Micanzio, "Annotazioni e pensieri," in Benzoni and Zanato, *Storici e politici veneti*, 831–32.

89. De Vivo, "How to Read."

90. Chartier, *Order of Books*, 2.

91. Dooley, *Social History of Skepticism*.

92. Burke, "Publishing the Private."

7. Great Expectations

1. Giovanni Andrea Ugoni, *Discorso della dignità et eccellenza della gran città di Venetia* (Venice: Pietro da Fine, 1562). On Ugoni, see Seidel Menchi, "Protestantesimo a Venezia," and Susanna Peyronel Rambaldi, "Tra *dialoghi* letterari e *ridotti* eterodossi: frammenti di cultura del patriziato veneto nel Cinquecento," in *Per Marino Berengo: Studi degli allievi*, ed. Livio Antonelli, Carlo Capra, and Mario Infelise, 182–209 (Milan: Franco Angeli, 2000).

2. Piccolomini, "Due lettere inedite," 207. For Vergerio's and Altieri's relationship with Ugoni, see ASV, Savi all'eresia (Santo Ufficio), b. 11 fasc. 2, trial against Andrea Ugoni.

3. Martin, *Venice's Hidden Enemies*, 235–47.

4. For the first contacts between Venice and James I, see ASV, Senato, Dispacci ambasciatori, Inghilterra, II, n.12, 91r–93r: Giovan Carlo Scaramelli to the Venetian Senate (March 27, 1603). On James I's views on the myth of Venice, of which he learned during his youth from his tutor George Buchanan, see ASV, Senato, Dispacci ambasciatori, Inghilterra, II, n.29, 156r–158r: Giovan Carlo Scaramelli to the Venetian Senate (June 19, 1603); ASV, Senato, Dispacci ambasciatori, Inghilterra, f. III, n.19, 50r–53vr: Piero Duodo and Niccolò Molin to the Venetian Senate (December 11, 1603). James I's conciliar plans were well-known in Venice. See ASV, Senato, Dispacci ambasciatori, Inghilterra, f. II, n. 21, 128r–129v: Giovan Carlo Scaramelli to the Senate (London, May 8, 1603); ASV, Senato, Dispacci ambasciatori, Inghilterra, f. II, n. 48, 241r–243v: Giovan Carlo Scaramelli to the Senate (Oxford, September 28, 1603). On James I's religious politics, see W. B. Patterson, *King James VI and I and the Reunion of Christendom* (Cambridge: Cambridge University Press, 1997).

5. Paolo Sarpi, *Lettere ai Protestanti*, ed. Manlio Duilio Busnelli, 2 vols. (Bari: Laterza, 1931), 1:215: Paolo Sarpi to Groslot de l'Isle (February 14, 1612); Sarpi, *Lettere ai Protestanti*, 2:207: Sarpi to Philippe Duplessis-Mornay (Venice, December 8, 1609). On Sarpi, James I, and England, see Chiara Petrolini, *"Paolo Sarpi e l'Inghilterra di Giacomo I,"* PhD diss., Istituto Nazionale di Studi sul Rinascimento, Florence, 2010, whom I thank for her many suggestions. On Prince Henry, see Elkin Calhoun Wilson, *Prince Henry and English Literature* (Ithaca, NY: Cornell University Press, 1946); J.W. Williamson, *The Myth of the Conqueror, Prince Henry Stuart: A Study of Seventeenth-Century Personation* (New York: AMS Press, 1978); Roy Strong, *Henry Prince of Wales and England's Lost Renaissance* (London: Thames and Hudson, 1986); Timothy Wilks, ed., *Prince Henry Revived: Image and Exemplarity in Early Modern England* (London: Southampton Solent University-Paul Holberton, 2007); Aysha Pollnitz, *Princely Education in Early Modern Britain* (Cambridge: Cambridge University Press), 344–53.

6. ASV, Senato, Dispacci ambasciatori, Inghilterra, f. III, n. 23, 65r-v: Niccolò Molin to the Venetian Senate (Salisbury, December 15, 1603): "soggetto di ottime conditioni, che è stato in molte corti et in Italia longamente." See also ASV, Senato, Dispacci ambasciatori, Inghilterra, f. III, n. 76, 257r–260v: Niccolò Molin to the Senate (London, November 2, 1604), on Wotton's reception in Venice.

7. HW, 1:280–81: Henry Wotton to Lord Zouche (Florence, June 25, 1592). On Wotton see Mark Netzloff, "The Ambassador's Household: Sir Henry Wotton, Domesticity, and Diplomatic Writing," in *Diplomacy and Early Modern Culture*, ed. R. Adams and

R. Cox, 155–71 (Houndsmills, 2011); Melanie Ord, "Returning from Venice to England: Sir Henry Wotton as Diplomat, Pedagogue and Italian Cultural Connoisseur," in *Books and Travellers in Early Modern Europe*, ed. Thomas Betteridge, 146–67 (Aldershot: Ashgate, 2007); Melanie Ord, "Venice and Rome in the Addresses and Dispatches of Sir Henry Wotton: First English Embassy to Venice, 1604–1610," *Seventeenth Century* 22 (2007): 1–23; Filippo De Vivo, "Francia e Inghilterra di fronte all'Interdetto di Venezia," in *Paolo Sarpi: Politique et religion en Europe*, ed. Marie Viallon, 163–88 (Paris: Éditions Classiques Garnier, 2010); Daniel McReynolds, "Lying Abroad for the Good of His Country: Sir Henry Wotton and Venice in the Age of the Interdict," in *The Image of Venice: Fialetti's View and Sir Henry Wotton*, ed. Deborah Howard and Henrietta McBurney, 115–23 (London: Paul Holberton, 2014); Carol Chillington Rutter, "The English Ambassador Licks His Wounds: Wotton after the Interdict," paper presented at the conference *Global Reformations* (Toronto, Centre for Reformation and Renaissance Studies, Victoria College, September 2017). I thank Carol Rutter for allowing me to read her article before publication.

8. HW, I, p. 281: Henry Wotton to Lord Zouche (Florence, June 25, 1592), HW, I, p. 291: Henry Wotton to Lord Zouche (Siena, November 25, 1592). On Wotton's activity as intelligencer, see Jardine and Sherman, "Pragmatic Readers."

9. On Essex, see Paul E. J. Hammer, "The Uses of Scholarship: The Secretariat of Robert Devereux, Second Earl of Essex, c. 1585–1601," *English Historical Review* 109 (1994): 26–51; Paul E. J. Hammer, *The Polarisation of Elizabethan Politics: The Political Career of Robert Devereux, 2nd Earl of Essex, 1585–1597* (Cambridge: Cambridge University Press, 1999); Janet Dickinson, *Court Politics and the Earl of Essex, 1589–1601* (London: Pickering & Chatto, 2012); Alexandra Gajda, *The Earl of Essex and Late Elizabethan Political Culture* (Oxford: Oxford University Press, 2012).

10. ASF, Mediceo del Principato f. 902 c. 432r-v: Henry Wotton to Marcello Accolti (Florence, April 12, 1601): "benché non le manchino suffitientissimi servidori et istrumenti: tuttavia possino forse intervenire occasioni di valersi della persona d'un forestiero come manco sospetto in alcuni casi: a che m'offerò humilissimamente se le occurra di mandarmi in qualsivoglia parte del mondo. E se in altro non possa esser utile a Sua Altezza . . . almeno in quelle cose che tocheranno alli Regni d'Inghilterra et di Scotia, et alli Principi confederati con essi, servirò d'interprete del vero per quella pratica ed esperientia ch'Io n'ho hauto." On Wotton's stay in Florence and on his letters to the Medici court, see Crinò, *Fatti e figure*, 7–40.

11. ASF, Mediceo del Principato, f. 902, c. 434r: Henry Wotton to Marcello Accolti (Florence, April 12, 1601); ASF, Mediceo del Principato, f. 902, c. 582r–583r: Henry Wotton to Marcello Accolti (Florence, April 28, 1601); ASF, Mediceo del Principato, f. 4185, c. 319r–320r: Henry Wotton to Belisario Vinta (Florence, June 1602?).

12. ASF, Mediceo del Principato, f. 903, c. 3r.: Henry Wotton to Marcello Accolti (Florence, May 1, 1601); ASF, Mediceo del Principato, f. 903, c. 19r. On Sherley, see Subrahmanyam, *Three Ways to Be Alien*, 73–132.

13. ASF, Mediceo del Principato, filza 927, c. 40r–41r: Henry Wotton to Ferdinando I de' Medici (Venice, January 7, 1605). On the English community in Livorno, see Stefano Villani, "Religious Pluralism and the Dangers of Tolerance: the English Nation in Livorno in the Seventeenth-Century," in *Late Medieval and Early Modern Religious*

Dissents: Conflicts and Plurality in Renaissance Europe, ed. Federico Barbierato and Alessandro Veronese, 97–124 (Pisa: Edizioni Il Campano Arnus University Books, 2012).

14. HW, 1:434: Henry Wotton to the Earl of Salisbury (Venice, September 5, 1608).

15. ASV, Collegio, Esposizioni Principi, f. 14: October 1, 1604 (without pagination).

16. HW, II, 101: Henry Wotton to Dudley Carleton (Venice, September 2, 1616).

17. ASV, Collegio, Esposizioni Principi, f. 14: October 18, 1604 (without pagination): "non poteva dire di voler viver senza l'uso de la Religione, ma che prometteva bene, che quest'uso non sarà se non per la sua persona, et famiglia senza ammetter in casa sua perciò mai ne Fiammenghi ne Alemani, ne ancora a pena Inglesi che non siano a suo stupendio"; "lo esercitio suo sarà sempre in lingua Inglese non intesa da chi non è di quella natione."

18. ASV, Senato, Dispacci ambasciatori, Inghilterra, f. II, n. 43, 222r–226v: Scaramelli to the Senate (August 27, 1603).

19. ASV, Senato, Dispacci ambasciatori, Inghilterra, f. II, n. 43, 222r–226v: Scaramelli to the Senate (August 27, 1603): "se ne potevo credere che il Signor Ambasciatore Inglese potrà fare nella sua privata casa quello che vorrà, dovevo nondimeno dire a Sua Signoria che la proportione non è eguale, perché in Londra non vi sono hora Venetiani, se non due fratelli Federici persone molto modeste, et sei, o sette sole altre case d'Italiani, i quali quando non havessero la messa in casa dell'Ambasciatore di Venetia, l'havevano in quella di Francia come l'hanno havuta fin'hora et che all'incontro vi sono a Venetia Inglesi quasi a migliaia, a' quali accostandosi per il più i Fiamenghi anch'esso diversi di Religione da noi, potria il Signor Ambasciatore in questo modo far così gran massa, che dovendo apportar scandolo potesse causar reciproco disgusto."

20. Catherine Fletcher, "'Furnished with Gentlemen': The Ambassador's House in Sixteenth-Century Italy," *Renaissance Studies* 24 (2010): 518–35; Netzloff, "Ambassador's Household."

21. Kaplan, "Diplomacy and Domestic Devotion" and Kaplan, "Fictions of Privacy."

22. Edward R. Adair, *The Extraterritoriality of Ambassadors in the Sixteenth and Seventeenth Centuries* (London: Longmans, 1929); Kaplan, "Fictions of Privacy."

23. Thomas Coryat, *Crudities* (Glasgow: The Macmillan Company, 1905), 380.

24. BNM, Cd. It., Cl. 9, Cod. 28 (6790), cc. 87–118 (c. 95): Antonio Possevino, *Relatione delle cose passate in Venetia coll'ambasciatore del re d'Inghilterra,* published, in Giovanni Soranzo, "Il P. Antonio Possevino e l'ambasciatore inglese a Venezia (1604–1605)," *Aevum* 4 (1933): 385–422.

25. On the French ambassador Canaye de Fresnes, see Gaetano Cozzi, *Paolo Sarpi tra Venezia e l'Europa* (Turin: Einaudi, 1979), 3–133.

26. ASV, Collegio, Esposizioni Roma f. 10, c. 324v: December 13, 1606.

27. BNM, Cd. It., Cl. 9, Cod. 28 (6790), c. 87.

28. BNM, Cd. It., Cl. 9, Cod. 28 (6790), c. 87.

29. BNM, Cd. It., Cl. 9, Cod. 28 (6790), cc. 107–8, 117–18.

30. Teodoro Eugenio di Famagosta [Antonio Possevino], *Risposta all'Avviso mandato fuori dal Signore Antonio Quirino* (Bologna: Archiepiscopal Press, 1606), 6: "somministrate dall'Ambasciatore d'Inghilterra, con chi fra Paolo ha si frequente commercio come si vede; non ostante anco ch'il detto Ambasciatore sia manifesto Calvinista, & faccia in

casa predicare con ogni libertà l'heresia." On the Jesuits and the Venetian Interdict, see Pietro Pirri, *L'interdetto di Venezia del 1606 e i Gesuiti* (Rome: Institutum historicum S.I., 1959); Gaetano Cozzi, "Fortuna e sfortuna, della Compagnia di Gesù a Venezia," in *I Gesuiti e Venezia: Momenti e problemi di storia veneziana della Compagnia di Gesù*, ed. Mario Zanardi, 59–88 (Padua: Gregoriana, 1994); Adriano Prosperi, "'L'altro coltello': *Libelli de lite* di parte romana," in Zanardi, *I Gesuiti e Venezia*, 263–87. On Sarpi's views on the Jesuits, see Vittorio Frajese, "Il mito del gesuita tra Venezia e i gallicani," in Zanardi, *I Gesuiti e Venezia*, 289–345, later developed in Vittorio Frajese, *Sarpi scettico: Stato e Chiesa a Venezia tra Cinque e Seicento* (Bologna: Il Mulino, 1994), 179–246, and Boris Ulianich, "I gesuiti e la Compagnia di Gesù nelle opere e nel pensiero di Sarpi," in Zanardi, *I Gesuiti e Venezia*, 233–62.

31. BAV, Barb Lat 5195: *Raccolta di Alcuni Negotij, e Cause spettanti alla Santa Inquisitione nella Città e Dominio Veneto: Dal principio di Clemente VIII sino al presente Mese di Luglio 1625*, cc. 83r-v: "In Venetia, et altre città del suo Dominio dimorano eretici sotto diverse cause e pretesti. Alcuni vi stanno come familiari, e servitori degli Ambasciatori d'Inghilterra, e di Olanda ivi residenti . . . nelle case loro si fa l'essercitio della loro setta . . . et ultimamente era arrivato a segno che si sonavano campane, si tenevano le porte aperte, vi andavano gente di ogni sorte in gran moltitudine sino le donne, et i putti."

32. ASV, Collegio, Esposizioni Roma f. 10, cc. 322r-v: December 13, 1606.

33. ASV, Collegio, Esposizioni Roma f. 10, c. 322v: December 13, 1606: "perché se nel palazzo del Ambasciator non pubblicamente, et se pubblicamente dunque non nel palazzo dell'Ambasciator."

34. HW, 1:361–63: Wotton to the Earl of Salisbury (Venice, September 22, 1606); HW, 1:377–78: Wotton to Earl of Salisbury (Venice, February 23, 1607); HW, 1:398–99: Wotton to the Earl of Salisbury (Venice, September 13, 1607), where Wotton mentions Bedell as an intermediary between the English embassy and Paolo Sarpi. On Bedell, see E. S. Shuckburgh, ed., *Two Biographies of William Bedell* (Cambridge: Cambridge University Press, 1902) and for further bibliography, see Karl S. Bottigheimer and Vivienne Larminie, "Bedell, William (*bap.* 1572, *d.* 1642)," in ODNB (http://www.oxforddnb.com /view/article/1924, accessed October 16, 2017). On the multiple roles played by embassy chaplains in the early modern period, see William Gibson, *A Social History of the Domestic Chaplain, 1530–1840* (London: Leicester University Press, 1997); Hugh Adlington, "Chaplains to Embassies: Daniel Featley, Anti-Catholic Controversialists Abroad," in *Chaplains in Early Modern England: Patronage, Literature and Religion,* ed. Hugh Adlington, Tom Lockwood, and Gillian Wright, 83–102 (Manchester: Manchester University Press, 2013).

35. ASV, Collegio, Esposizioni Roma f. 10, c. 323r (December 13, 1606): "Ma come di gratia si può dire con verità che si predichi in casa mia, si sono tre mesi che io non ho cappellano in casa! et certo questa è una grassa ignoranza del compositor di questo libro. Et voglio dire, che ritenendosi li Gesuiti tanto vicino a questa città come è Perugia, quando essi sono così mal avisati di quello che si fa in Venetia; non so come si potrà crederli poi le nove del Giapon, di Germania, Polonia, Moscovia, et altri parti lontani. Hora voglio anco dire che il Papa non ha tenuto per iscomunicato il Re di Spagna, ne meno li Arciduchi, per haver ricevuto quei Principi li ambasciatori della Maestà del mio Re." Wotton seems to have had in mind Gentili, *De legationibus*, 64.

36. ASVat, Segreteria di Stato, Venezia, 38, 318v: Berlinghiero Gessi to Scipione Borghese (April 12, 1608).

37. FCM: 6229 b. 3 (National Library of Austria, MS ex Foscarini): Gerolamo Priuli, *Cronaca veneta* c. 277r (February, 23, 1608).

38. ASVat, Segreteria di Stato, Venezia, 38, 318v: Berlinghiero Gessi to Scipione Borghese (April 12, 1608): "se fra le sue robe gli era venuto qualche libro, non era conveniente, che essi lo cercassero, o prohibissero, che saria un violare il *jus gentium*, quando non si portasse rispetto a ministri de principi."

39. ASVat, Segreteria di Stato, Venezia, 38, 302r: Berlinghiero Gessi to Scipione Borghese (March 29, 1608).

40. Gentili, *De legationibus*, 125. On early modern diplomacy and the history of subjectivity, see Hampton, *Fictions of Embassy,* 8–10.

41. HW, 1:462: Wotton to the Earl of Salisbury (Venice, July 3, 1609); Stefano Villani, "Italian Translations of the Book of Common Prayer," in *Travels and Translations*, ed. Alison Yarrington, Stefano Villani, Julia Kelly, 303–19 (Amsterdam: Rodopi, 2013), Stefano Villani, "Uno scisma mancato: Paolo Sarpi, William Bedell e la prima traduzione in italiano del *Book of Common Prayer,*" *Rivista di storia e letteratura religiosa* (2017), 63–112. I thank Stefano Villani for allowing me to read his article before publication.

42. HW, 1:464: Wotton to the Earl of Salisbury (Venice, July 31, 1609); HW, 1:469: Wotton to the Earl of Salisbury (Venice, August 28, 1609).

43. On Biondi, see Gino Benzoni, "Giovanni Francesco Biondi, un avventuroso dalmata del '600'," *Archivio Veneto* 80 (1967): 19–37, and Chiara Petrolini, "Per un regesto delle carte diplomatiche di Giovan Francesco Biondi (1609–1619 ca)," in *Storie inglesi: L'Inghilterra vista dall'Italia tra storia e romanzo (XVII secolo)*, ed. Clizia Carminati and Stefano Villani, 35–42 (Pisa: Edizioni della Normale, 2011).

44. Gabriel Rein, *Sarpi und die Protestanten. Ein Beitrag zur Geschichte der Reformations-Bewegung in Venedig im Anfang des siebzehnten Jahrhunderts* (Helsingfors: Aktiengesellschaft Lilus & Hertzberg, 1904), 210–11: "Nissun luogo più opportuno a si gran principio non v'è di Venetia, per essere le menti Venetiane per li disgusti passati et per causa dell'interesse politico in gran parte chiarite della tirannide papistica; per non vi essere più l'Inquisitione, che di solo nome, parlandosi contro il Papa con ogni libertà et senz'alcun timore; per esservi stati seminati molti libri, li quali faranno buoni effetti a suo tempo et per esservi di già infiniti, li quali hanno il vero lume; tengono il Papa per Antichristo, il suo culto mera Idolatria, e tra questi alcuni principali Cittadini, li quali scoprendosi l'opportunità, procureranno di moltiplicare il loro talento. In somma Venetia è il luogo migliore per essere di già in gran parte disposta a ricevere la fede."

45. Rein, *Sarpi und die Protestanten*, 212.

46. HW, 1:351. See Jean Diodati, *Brève relation de mon voyage a Venise en Septembre 1608* (Geneva: Bonnant, 1863).

47. Fusaro, *Political Economies of Empire*, 151.

48. On the English merchants in early modern Venice, see Fusaro, *Political Economies of Empire*, 202–35, and on their presence in early modern Italy, see Gigliola Pagano de Divitiis, *English Merchants in Seventeenth-Century Italy* (Cambridge: Cambridge University Press, 1997).

49. ASV, Collegio, Esposizioni Principi, f. 14: November 15, 1604 (without pagination).

50. ASV, Senato, Dispacci ambasciatori, Roma, f. 51, n. 35, 222r-v (214r–227r): Francesco Vendramin to the Venetian Senate (Rome, December 6, 1603).

51. Rein, *Sarpi und die Protestanten*, 212–13: "Il terzo mezo è che, per incaminare il servitio di Dio sia necessaria l'assistenza in quella Città d'una persona segretamente trattenuta dalla M.V., la quale habbia cura di seminare libretti, di scoprire gli animi et scoperti di drizzarli sotto l'instruttione de'ministri: facendo egli l'istesso ufficio nell'anime, che fa l'obstetrice ne'corpi de' nascenti fanciulli. Leverà anco l'occasione all'Ambasciatore d'ingerirsi ex professo in questo negotio et gli porgerà modo di affermare et di essere creduto (caso che perciò nascesse incidente alcuno) di non haverne parte caricando ogni colpa sopra quella persona particolare et levando così ogn'ombra, ch'haver si potesse dell'intentione della M.V. o della operatione di esso Ambasciatore."

52. Cozzi, "Il doge Nicolò Contarini," in Cozzi, *Venezie barocca*, 1–245; Cozzi, *Paolo Sarpi tra Venezia e l'Europa*; Stella, *Chiesa e stato nelle relazioni*; William J. Bouwsma, *Venice and the Defense of Republican Liberty: Renaissance Values in the Age of the Counter-Reformation* (Berkeley: California University Press, 1968); De Vivo, *Information and Communication*; Mario Infelise, *I padroni dei libri: Il controllo sulla stampa nella prima età moderna* (Rome: Laterza, 2014); Villani, "Uno scisma mancato."

53. Paolo Sarpi, *Scritti giurisdizionalistici*, ed. G. Gambarin (Bari: Laterza, 1958), 190: "la materia de' libri par cosa di poco momento perché tutta di parole; ma da quelle parole vengono le opinioni del mondo, che causano le parzialità, le sedizioni e finalmente le guerre. Sono parole sì, ma che in conseguenza tirano seco eserciti armati."

54. On the interaction between orality and literacy during the Interdict, see De Vivo, *Information and Communication in Venice*, 121–27, and more generally on early modern Italy, see Luca Degl'Innocenti, Brian Richardson, and Chiara Sbordoni, eds., *Interactions between Orality and Writing in Early Modern Italian Culture* (New York: Routledge, 2016); Stefano Dall'Aglio, Brian Richardson, and Massimo Rospocher, eds., *Voices and Texts in Early Modern Italian Society* (London: Routledge, 2017).

55. Sarpi, *Lettere ai protestanti*, 2:96.

56. Castelvetro mentions Wotton in his *Album amicorum*, BL, Harley 3344, f. 29v (Lo illustrissimo signor Henrigo Wootton, Ambasciator et signor mio spetialissimo), and in his language text book entitled *Libretto di varie maniere di parlare della Italica lingua*: TCL, R.10.6, 7v–8r (dated August 29, 1613), as well as in his letters: SP: 99/6, cc. 182r-v: Giacomo Castelvetro to Robert Cecil (December 31, 1610). For Castelvetro's relationship with Bedell, see SP, 85/3, c. 174r: William Bedell to Giacomo Castelvetro (Venice, Padua, February 13, 1611).

57. SP, 99/8, cc. 38r–39v: Dudley Carleton to the Venetian Senate (August 30, 1611).

58. Warren Boutcher, "Vernacular Humanism in the Sixteenth-Century," in *The Cambridge Companion to Renaissance Humanism*, ed. Jill Kraye, 189–292 (Cambridge: Cambridge University Press, 1996).

59. Sandonnini, *Ludovico Castelvetro*, 350. On Ciotti, see Dennis E. Rhodes, *Giovanni Battista Ciotti (1562–1627?)* (Venice: Marcianum Press, 2013).

60. Angelo Grillo, *Pietosi affetti, et lagrime del penitente* (Venice: Giovanni Battista Ciotti, 1601); Giambattista Marino, *Rime amorose, marittime, boscherecce, heroiche, lugubri, morali, sacre & varie* (Venice: Giovanni Battista Ciotti, 1602).

61. Luigi Firpo, *Il processo a Giordano Bruno*, ed. Diego Quaglioni (Rome: Salerno, 1993), 17–18; Luigi Firpo, "Non Paolo Sarpi, ma Tommaso Campanella," *Giornale storico della letteratura italiana* 158 (1981): 254–74.

62. Sarpi, *Lettere ai protestanti*, 2:54: Sarpi to Francesco Castrino (Venice, October 13, 1609); 2:60: Sarpi to Francesco Castrino (Venice, November 10, 1609); 2:62: Sarpi to Francesco Castrino (Venice, December 9, 1609); Firpo, "Non Paolo Sarpi."

63. Diego Pirillo, "'Questo buon monaco non ha inteso il Macchiavello': Reading Campanella in Sarpi's Shadow," *Bruniana & Campanelliana* 1 (2014): 129–44.

64. Richardson, *Manuscript Culture*; De Vivo and Richardson, *Scribal Culture in Italy*.

65. On Manfredi, see Gino Benzoni, "I teologi minori dell'Interdetto," *Archivio veneto* 91 (1970): 31–108; Roberto Zago, "Manfredi, Fulgenzio," in DBI 68, 683–86; Chiara Petrolini, "*Un salvacondotto e un incendio*: La morte di Fulgenzio Manfredi in una relazione del 1610," *Bruniana & Campanelliana* 1(2012): 161–85.

66. TCL, R.3.42, cc. 147r–148r. See Franceschini, *Nostalgie di un esule*.

67. HW, 1:448: Wotton to James I (Venice, March 20, 1609).

68. Karl Benrath, *Neue Briefe von Paolo Sarpi (1608–1616)* (Leipzig: Rudoplh Haupt, 1909), 97: "se non l'havessi udite—non havendone perduta niuna—che non l'haverei mai creduto ch'egli havesse havuto cotanto ardire, né che cotanto a cuore gli fosse stato l'amor della verità."

69. Benrath, *Neue Briefe von Paolo Sarpi*, 97: "Hoggi gli uomini che l'odono non havessin paura di voler leggere il Vangelio et di ragionarne!"

70. TCL, R.16.23, cc. 47v–55v (which corresponds to Guicciardini, *Storia d'Italia*, 4.12), and cc. 53v–54v (which corresponds to Guicciardini, *Storia d'Italia*, 3.13).

71. Tommaso Campanella, *Del senso delle cose e della magia*, ed. Germana Ernst (Roma-Bari: Laterza, 2007), 165: "per arte del demonio fan cose mirabili a chi non l'intende, e questa senza demonio spesso si fa da cantambanchi in presenza di sciocchi, ma sono cose d'astuzia e non di sapienza." For Wotton's interest in Campanella, see HW, 2:486.

72. Campanella, *Del senso delle cose*: "si stupiva che incontrandosi un sacerdote con l'altro non si ridessero insieme delle burle che al popolo facevano predicando li dei."

73. TCL, R.3.42, 176v: "Vie più si sarebbe, il savio huomo, stupefatto se fino a questi giorni fosse vivuto in veder ciò, che i Preti e i frati a loro popolani fan credere, et bene havrebbe stimato, che tra loro della credulità del popolo si ridano."

74. Edwin Sandys, *A Relation of the State of Religion: and with what hopes and pollicies it hath beene framed, and is maintained in the severall states of these westerne partes of the world* (London, Val. Sims for Simon Waterson, 1605). Theodore K. Raab, *Jacobean Gentleman: Sir Edwin Sandys, 1561–1629* (Princeton, NJ: Princeton University Press, 1998), 22. On the *Relation*, see Gaetano Cozzi, "Sir Edwin Sandys e la *Relazione dello stato della religione*," *Rivista storica italiana* 79 (1967): 1096–121; Theodore K. Raab, "A Contribution to the Toleration Controversy of the Sixteenth Century: Sandys's 'A Relation of the State of Religion,'" in *Renaissance Studies in Honor of Hans Baron*, ed. Anthony Molho and John Tedeschi, 833–47 (Florence: Sansoni, 1971).

75. Edwin Sandys, *Europae Speculum or A View or Survey of the State of Religion in the Western parts of the world* (London: Thomas Basset, 1673), 207–8.

76. Cozzi, "Sir Edwin Sandys"; Sarpi's additions have been republished in Paolo Sarpi, *Opere*, ed. Gaetano Cozzi and Luisa Cozzi (Milan-Naples: Ricciardi, 1969), 295–330.

77. Cozzi, "Sir Edwin Sandys," 1116.

78. TCL, R.4.36, f. 45v: "i Pontefici romani s'assunsero potenza temporale sopra i regni et sopra i prencipati;" "una Gierarchia, che, esclusi i fedeli dal partecipare le cose communi della Chiesa, constituisce nel Pontefice Romano un Imperio assoluto sopra d'ognuno."

79. Edwin Sandys, *Relazione dello stato della religione. E con quali dissegni et arti è stata fabricata e maneggiata in diversi stati di queste occidentali parti del mondo.* Tradotta dall'Inglese del Cavaliere Edoino Sandis in Lingua Volgare con aggiunte notabili [Geneva], 1625.

80. On the controversy over the oath of allegiance, see Michael C. Questier, "Loyalty, Religion and State Power in Early Modern England: English Romanism and the Oath of Allegiance," *Historical Journal* 40 (1997): 311–29; Johann P. Sommerville, "Papalist Political Thought," in *Catholics and the "Protestant Nation": Religious Politics and Identity in Early Modern England*, ed. Ethan H. Shagan, 162–84 (Manchester: Manchester University Press, 2005); Stefania Tutino, *Empire of Souls: Robert Bellarmine and the Christian Commonwealth* (Oxford: Oxford University Press, 2010), 117–58.

81. HW, 1:464: Wotton to the Earl of Salisbury (Venice, July 31, 1609).

82. On Sarpi's reactions to James's *Apology, see* his correspondence with Groslot de l'Isle in Sarpi, *Lettere ai protestanti*, 1:88 (Venice, August 4, 1609); 1:90 (Venice, August 18, 1609); 1:92 (Venice, September 1, 1609), 1:98 (Venice, October 13, 1609); 1:99 (Venice, December 9, 1609); 1:175 (Venice, May 14, 1611); and with Francesco Castrino, in Sarpi, *Lettere ai Protestanti*, 2:37 (Venice, May 26, 1609); 2:44 (Venice, July 7, 1609); 2:45 (July 21, 1609); 2:47 (August 18, 1609); 2:49 (September 1, 1609); 2:52 (September 15, 1609); 2:53 (September 29, 1609); 2:55 (October 13, 1609); with Cristoph con Dohna, in Sarpi, *Lettere ai Protestanti*, 2:153 (Venice, July 21, 1609); 2:158 (Venice, September 1, 1609); 2:161–62 (Venice, September 29, 1609).

83. HW, 1:469: Wotton to the Earl of Salisbury (Venice, August 28, 1609). Same opinion, in Sarpi, *Lettere ai protestanti*, 2:49: Sarpi to Francesco Castrino (Venice, September 1, 1609).

84. TCL, R.10.14, cc. 120r–121v: 120r: "Perché quall è quel Prencipe, che nel suo reame possa tolerare de'sudditi, che nol conoscano punto per Re? o che per esser fedeli al Papa, si stimino tenuti ad infedeltà verso il Re loro? Et non dimeno il Re d'Inghilterra, in questo s'è ritenuto, et non ha già voluto, che la sua clemenza fosse sormontata dalla lor malvagità. Infino là, è venuto, ch'egli ha meglio amato metter la mano alla penna, che al coltello, et ha messo studio d'ammaestrar coloro, ch'egli poteva distruggere. Et ha più tosto voluto convincer con ragione, che vincere con violenza. Maluit sanguinem suffundere quam effundere.... Questo Re adunque per confutare queste lettere papesche, et per giustificar le sue attioni, ha compilato un libro intitolato, Apologia del giuramento di fedeltà, senza nondimeno porvi il suo nome. Perché non si curava punto sotto qual titolo la verità apparisse, purché i suoi nimici riconoscerebbero il lor fatto."

85. Tommaso Campanella, *Discorsi ai principi d'Italia ed altri scritti filo-ispanici*, ed. Luigi Firpo (Turin: Chiantore, 1945), 153–54: "con assolver li vassalli dal giuramento è potentissimo a metter a terra ogni gran principe."

86. TCL, R.4.39, 89v–90r.

87. Campanella, *Discorsi*, 96–97: "pone e depone tutti i principi, e dà legge all'universo"; TCL, R.4,39, 51r-v.

88. BL, MS Royal 14 A XIV: *Dichiaratione del Serenissimo Re della Gran Bretagna . . . per la ragione dei re et per la indipendenza delle loro corone* (1615), cc 1r–150r. Castelvetro also translated into Italian Pierre Du Moulin's *Defence of the Catholicke Faith* against the Dominican Nicolas Coeffeteau: BL, MS Royal 14 A XIV, cc. 150v–151v.

89. BL, MS Royal 14 A XIV: *Dichiaratione del Serenissimo Re della Gran Bretagna*, c.**r: "inanzi a Prencipi et a Sig.ri d'Italia arditamente comparere, accioché ignorando essi ogni altro idioma, che il naturale loro"; "quanto fuori di ragione i Papi s'usurpino l'autorità di potere (a voglia loro) spogliare i Prencipi delle Signorie, e i Re delle corone loro."

90. ASV, Segreteria di Stato, Venezia, 40, 11r (January 3, 1609): "Il Castelvetro, del quale già scrissi a V. S. Illma non è huomo di lettere, e sebbene per l'informatione che ne tengo, é di pessima mente, e poco Cattolico, non è però molto atto con ragionamenti a sovvertire altri, più tosto vi è pericolo che distribuisca qualche libro cattivo de' quali si dice, che egli ne tiene o per heredità del zio, o per l'occasione d'esser stato libraro, o perche in altro modo l'habbia procurati, mi è detto che hora qui attende a assignare la Lingua Italiana a certi forastieri."

91. Sarpi, *Lettere ai protestanti*, 2:96, Sarpi to Francesco Castrino (August 3, 1610): "Castelvetro è uomo da bene compitamente, ma non ha dramma di prudenzia e non vi è in Venezia uomo più osservato da li romani di lui, che mi fa con molto dispiacere temer che qualche male non li succeda."

92. SP, 85/3, c. 174r: William Bedell to Giacomo Castelvetro (Venice, Padua, February 13, 1611).

93. SP, 99/8, cc. 38r–39v: Dudley Carleton to the Venetian Senate (August 30, 1611).

94. ASV, Senato Secreta, Deliberazioni Roma, r. 18 (September 10, 1611).

95. SP, 99/8, cc. 65r–67v: Dudley Carleton to Robert Cecil (Venice, September 6, 1611).

96. ASV, Collegio, Lettere principi, f. 33, n. 103: James to (Westminster, October, 9, 1611). James thanked Venice also in his meeting with the republic's ambassador in England, Antonio Foscarini. See ASV, Senato, Dispacci ambasciatori, Inghilterra, 10, n. 54, c.277v: Antonio Foscarini to the Venetian Senate (London, October 14, 1611).

97. Sarpi, *Lettere ai Protestanti*, 1:193: Sarpi to Groslot de l'Isle (Venice, September 13, 1611): "Già otto giorni, fu imprigionato Castelvetro all'Inquisizione. L'ambasciator d'Inghilterra l'ha dimandato: la repubblica l'ha donato, avendolo cavato di prigione, senza dir niente all'Inquisizione, al nunzio né altro ecclesiastico: ch'è passo maggior che mai sia fatto; perché l'Ufficio sinora è dependuto da Roma, se bene la repubblica ha l'assistenza, e con quella impedito la tirannide. Avergli aperto la prigione senza dir niente è cosa grandissima: ma chi l'ha fatto, non ha pensato la consequenza. Se il papa tacerà, è perduto; se dirà, o vero perderà tanto più, o vero si romperà."

98. SP 99/8, cc. 223r–224r: Biondi to Dudley Carleton (October 1611): "Per consequenza è astretto il Papa cader in uno delli due inconvenienti. O tacendo, permettere a

Venetiani, che godano quell'auttorità, et sopranità, che s'hanno fondata sopra l'Inquisitione con la liberatione del Castelvetro; overo, romereggiando, e strepitando suscitare nuova intelligenza, alle cose intese, le quali prima non s'intendevano, con dar occasione a questi Signori d'aprir gli occhi meglio negl'interessi loro."

99. On Prince Henry, see Wilson, *Prince Henry*; Williamson, *Myth of the Conqueror*; Strong, *Henry Prince of Wales*; Wilks, *Prince Henry Revived*; Pollnitz, *Princely Education*, 344–53.

100. Sarpi, *Lettere ai Protestanti*, 1:215: Paolo Sarpi to Groslot de l'Isle (February 14, 1612); Sarpi, *Lettere ai Protestanti*, 2:207: Sarpi to Philippe Duplessis-Mornay (Venice, December 8, 1609).

101. Paolo Sarpi, *Lettere ai Gallicani*, ed., intro., and notes Boris Ulianich (Wiesbaden: Franz Steiner Verlag GMBH, 1961), 66–67: Sarpi to Jacques Leschassier (Venice, January 5, 1610): "Utinam rex ille regia tantum tractasset, et a theologicis abstinuisset! ... Caelum terrae miscere nolumus, nec humanis divina."

102. See Sarpi's opinion on the marriage negotiations, in Sarpi, *Opere*, 697–98. On prince Henry's first contacts with Venetian and Tuscan diplomacy, see ASV, Senato, Dispacci ambasciatori, Inghilterra, f. III, n.18, 46r–48r: Piero Duodo and Niccolò Molin to the Venetian Senate (December 9, 1603). During his first meeting with the Venetian Collegio Wotton presented a credential letter from Prince Henry (dated July 12, 1604) together with one from James I. See ASV, Collegio, Esposizioni Principi, f. 14: October 1, 1604 (without pagination).

103. Strong, *Henry Prince of Wales*.

104. Bedell, *Two Biographies*, 226–38: William Bedell to Adam Newton (Venice, January 1, 1608).

105. ASV, Senato, Dispacci ambasciatori, Inghilterra, f. 5, n. 40, 114r: Zorzi Giustinian to the Venetian Senate (London, September 26, 1606).

106. Nicolò Molin, *Relazione d'Inghilterra* (1607), in Luigi Firpo, ed., *Relazioni di ambasciatori veneti al Senato*, vol. 1, Inghilterra (Turin: Bottega d'Erasmo, 1965), 529–31: "essendo infine la natura di S.M. piuttosto inclinata a vivere ritiratamente con otto o diece dei suoi, che viver alla libera, come è il costume del paese ed il desiderio del popolo."

107. Sarpi, *Lettere ai Protestanti*, 2:151: Sarpi to Cristoph von Dohna (Venice, July 7, 1609): "Da tutti i canti s'intende la gran virtù del principe [Enrico di Galles] figlio del re d'Inghilterra, ma molto tempo è per aspettar il mondo a riceverne frutto, perché il re d'Inghilterra, si come è compito nella religione riformata, così del rimanente non par vaglia molto: vorrebbe far tutto con parole."

108. See ASV, Senato, Dispacci ambasciatori, Inghilterra, f. 11, n. 80, 395r-v: Antonio Foscarini to the Venetian Senate (London, November 17, 1612): "notabile alteratione ne gl' affari del mondo."

109. Simon Adams, "Spain or the Netherlands? The Dilemmas of Early Stuart Foreign Policy," in *Before the English Civil War: Essays on Early Stuart Politics and Government*, ed. H. Tomlinson, 79–101 (New York: St Martin's Press, 1984).

110. Fulgenzio Micanzio, *Lettere a William Cavendish (1615–1628)*, ed. Roberto Ferrini, intro. Enrico De Mas (Rome: Istituto storico O.S.M., 1987), 130–33 (March 12, 1621).

111. Micanzio, *Lettere a William Cavendish*, 148 (February 1622).

112. Gaetano Cozzi, "Fra Paolo Sarpi, l'anglicanesimo e la *Historia del Concilio Tridentino*," *Rivista storica italiana* 4 (1956): 559–619.

113. Patterson, *King James VI and I*.

114. Infelise, *I padroni dei libri*, 109–24.

115. HW, 1:318: Wotton to Robert Cecil (Venice, May 23, 1603), and Rein, *Sarpi und die Protestanten*, 210–11. On atheism and unbelief in seventeenth century Venice, see Federico Barbierato, *Politici e ateisti: percorsi della miscredenza a Venezia tra Sei e Settecento* (Milan: Unicopli, 2006), Barbierato, *Inquisitor in the Hat Shop*; Edward Muir, *The Culture Wars of the Late Renaissance: Skeptics, Libertines and Opera* (Cambridge, MA: Harvard University Press, 2007).

Conclusion

1. Max Weber, *The Vocation Lectures* (Indianapolis: Hackett, 2004), 38.

2. Garrett Mattingly, *Renaissance Diplomacy* (New York: Dover, 1955).

3. Mattingly, *Renaissance Diplomacy*, 54, 102.

4. Watkins, "Toward a New Diplomatic History," 2; Natalie Rothman, "Afterword: Intermediaries, Mediation and Cross-Confessional Diplomacy in the Early Modern Mediterranean," *Journal of Early Modern History*, 19 (2015): 246.

5. Robert Kingdon, "Garrett Mattingly," *American Scholar* 3 (1982): 398.

6. Mattingly, *Renaissance Diplomacy*, 10.

7. Doran and Richardson, *Tudor England*, 2–3.

8. Kettering, *Patrons, Brokers and Clients*.

9. Franca Leverotti, *Diplomazia e governo dello Stato: I "famigli cavalcanti" di Francesco Sforza (1450–1466)* (Pisa: ETS, 1992); Alison Brown, "Lorenzo de' Medici's New Men and Their Mores: The Changing Lifestyle of Quattrocento Florence," *Renaissance Studies* 2 (2002): 113–42; Lazzarini, *Communication and Conflict*, 123–45.

10. Tallon, *L'Europe au XVIe siècle*, 184–85.

11. Jardine and Grafton, "*Studied for Action*"; Jardine and Sherman, "Pragmatic Readers"; Hammer, "Uses of Scholarship"; De Vivo, *Information and Communication in Venice*.

12. Keck and Sikkink, *Activists beyond Borders*; Riches, *Protestant Cosmopolitanism*.

13. John Watkins, "Introduction: Non-state Actors in Mediterranean Politics," *Mediterranean Studies* 25, no. 1 (2017): 1–8.

14. Enrico De Mas, *Sovranità politica e unità cristiana nel Seicento anglo-veneto* (Ravenna: Longo, 1975); Enrico De Mas, *L'attesa del secolo aureo (1603–1625): saggio di storia delle idee del secolo XVII* (Florence: Olschki, 1982), 73–121; Noel Malcolm, *De Dominis, 1560–1624: Venetian, Anglican, Ecumenist and Relapsed Heretic* (London: Strickland and Scott, 1984), 49–54; Micanzio, *Lettere a William Cavendish*; Petrolini, *Paolo Sarpi e l'Inghilterra*.

15. Watkins, "Toward a New Diplomatic History," 5.

16. Iver B. Neumann, *At Home with the Diplomats: Inside a European Foreign Ministry* (Ithaca, NY: Cornell University Press, 2012), 4.

BIBLIOGRAPHY

Primary printed sources

Alberti, Leon Battista. *I libri della famiglia*. Edited by Ruggiero Romano and Alberto Tenenti. Turin: Einaudi, 1994.

Anonymous. *Thesoro politico*. Cologne [Paris: Denis Cotinet and Léger Delas], 1589.

Aretino, Pietro. *Lettere*. Edited by Paolo Procaccioli. 6 vols. Rome: Salerno, 1997–2002.

———. *Lettere: Libro secondo*. Milan: Guanda, 1998.

———. *Lettere scritte a Pietro Aretino*. Edited by Paolo Procaccioli. 2 vols. Rome: Salerno, 2003–4.

———. *Operette politiche e satiriche*. Edited by Marco Faini. Rome: Salerno, 2012.

Balbani, Niccolò. *The Italian Convert: News from Italy of a Second Moses. Or the Life of Galeacius Caracciolus, the noble Marquis of Vico*. Boston: Thomas Fleet, 1751.

Barbaro, Ermolao. *De coelibatu—De officio legati*. Edited by Vittore Branca. Florence: Olschki, 1969.

Benzoni, Gino and Tiziano Zanato, eds. *Storici e politici veneti del Cinquecento e del Seicento* Milan: Ricciardi, 1982.

Bizzarri, Pietro. *Historia della guerra fatta in Ungheria dall'invittissimo imperatore de christiani, contra quello de Turchi*. Lyon: Rouillé, 1568.

———. *Varia opuscula*. Venice: Paolo Manuzio, 1565.

Blet, Pierre, ed. *Girolamo Ragazzoni évêque de Bergame nonce en France: Correspondence de sa Nonciature 1583–1586.* Paris: Editions E. de Boccard, 1962.

Brucioli, Antonio. *La Biblia quale contiene i sacri libri del Vecchio Testamento, tradotti da la hebraica verità in lingua toscana per Antonio Brucioli.* Venice: Bartolomeo Zannetti, 1539.

Buchanan, George. *A Dialogue on the Law of Kingship among the Scots.* Edited by Roger A. Mason and Martin S. Smith. Aldershot: Ashgate, 2004.

Campanella, Tommaso. *Del senso delle cose e della magia.* Edited by Germana Ernst. Rome: Laterza, 2007.

——. *Discorsi ai principi d'Italia ed altri scritti filo-ispanici.* Edited by Luigi Firpo. Turin: Chiantore, 1945.

Case, John. *Sphaera civitatis.* Oxford: Joseph Barnes, 1588.

Castelvetro, Ludovico. *Filologia ed eresia: scritti religiosi.* Edited by Guido Mongini. Brescia: Morcelliana, 2011.

Castiglione, Baldassarre. *The Courtier.* Translated by Leonard Eckstein Opdyke. New York: Dover, 2003.

——. *Il libro del Cortegiano.* Edited by W. Barberis. Turin: Einaudi, 1998.

Castrodardo, Giovanni Battista. *L'Alcorano di Macometto, nel qual si contiene la dottrina, la vita, i costumi, et le leggi sue.* Venice: Andrea Arrivabene, 1547.

Cecil, William. *Atto della giustizia d'Inghilterra.* London: John Wolfe, 1584.

Cicero, Marcus Tullius. *Le Filippiche di Marco T. Cicerone contra Marco Antonio fatte volgari per Girolamo Ragazzoni.* Venice, 1556.

Commendone, Giovanni Francesco. *Discorso sopra la corte di Roma.* Edited by Cesare Mozzarelli. Rome: Bulzoni, 1996.

Coryat, Thomas. *Crudities.* Glasgow: The Macmillan Company, 1905.

Cotrugli, Benedetto. *Della mercatura et del mercante perfetto.* Venice: Giovanni Franco, 1573.

Diodati, Jean. *Briève relation de mon voyage a Venise en Septembre 1608.* Geneva: Bonnant, 1863.

Elizabeth I. *Translations, 1544–1589.* Edited by Janel M. Mueller and Joshua Scodel. Chicago: University of Chicago Press, 2009.

Erasmus, Desiderius. *Adages.* trans. Margaret Mann Philips. Toronto: University of Toronto Press, 1982–2006.

——. *Opera omnia.* Amsterdam: North Holland, 1969–2017.

Erastus, Thomas. *Explicatio gravissimae quaestionis utrum excommunicatio, quatenus religionem intelligentes & amplexantes, a sacramentorum usu, propter admissum facinus arcet; mandato nitatur divino, an excogitata sit ab hominibus.* Poschiavo: apud Baocium Sultaceterum [London: John Wolfe], 1589.

Firpo, Luigi. *Ambasciatori veneti in Inghilterra.* Turin: Einaudi, 1978.

——, ed. "Inghilterra." In *Relazioni di ambasciatori veneti al Senato.* 14 vols. Turin: Einaudi, 1965–96.

Firpo, Massimo, and Dario Marcatto, eds. *I processi inquisitoriali di Pietro Carnesecchi, 1557–1567.* 2 vols. Vatican City: Archivio Segreto Vaticano, 1998–2000.

Firpo, Massimo, and Sergio Pagano, eds. *I processi inquisitoriali di Vittore Soranzo, 1550–1558.* 2 vols. Vatican City: Archivio Segreto Vaticano, 2004.

Gallucci, Giuseppe. *La vita del clarissimo signor Jacomo Ragazzoni.* Venice: Giorgio Bizzardo, 1610.

Gentili, Alberico. *De iure belli commentationes tres.* London: John Wolfe, 1589.

———. *De iure belli libri tres.* Hanau: Heirs of Wilhelm Antonius, 1612.

———. *De iure belli libri tres.* Translated by John C. Rolfe. Oxford: The Clarendon Press, 1933.

———. *De legationibus libri tres.* London: Thomas Vautrollier, 1585.

———. *De legationibus libri tres.* Translated by G. J. Laing. New York: Oxford University Press, 1924.

Gentili, Scipione. *Annotationi sopra la Gierusalemme liberata di Torquato Tasso.* Leida [London]: John Wolfe, 1586.

———. *Plutonis concilium: ex initio quarti libri Solymeidos.* London: John Wolfe 1584.

———. *Solymeidos.* Venice: Altobello Salicato, 1585.

———. *Solymeidos libri duo priores de Torquati Tassi Italicis expressi.* London: John Wolfe 1584.

Grillo, Angelo. *Pietosi affetti, et lagrime del penitente.* Venice: Giovanni Battista Ciotti, 1601.

Hoby, Thomas. *A Booke of the Travaile and Life of Me Thomas Hoby.* Edited by Edgar Powell. London: Royal Historical Society, 1902.

Lando, Ortensio. *Lettere di molto valorose donne, nelle quali chiaramente appare non essere né di eloquentia né di dottrina alli huomini inferiori.* Venice: Gabriel Giolito de Ferrari, 1548.

———. *Oracoli de moderni ingegni si d'huomini come di donne.* Venice: Gabriel Giolito, 1550.

Luther, Martin. *Werke: Briefwechsel.* Weimar: Hermann Böhlaus, 1947.

Machiavelli, Niccolò. *The Chief Works and Others.* Translated by Allan Gilbert. 3 vols. Durham, NC: Duke University Press, 1989.

———. *Discourses on Livy.* Translated by Harvey C. Mansfield and Nathan Tarcov. Chicago: University of Chicago Press, 1996.

———. "Memoriale a Raffaello Girolami quando ai 23 d'Ottobre partì per la Spagna all'Imperatore." In Machiavelli, *Opere,* 1:731;

Machiavelli, Niccolò. *Opere.* Edited by Corrado Vivanti. 3 vols. Turin: Einaudi, 1997.

Maffei, Paolo Alessandro. *Vita di San Pio V.* Venice: Tommasini, 1712.

Marino, Giambattista. *Rime amorose, marittime, boscherecce, heroiche, lugubri, morali, sacre & varie.* Venice: Giovanni Battista Ciotti, 1602.

Martin, A. Lynn, ed. *Correspondence du nonce en France Fabio Mirto Frangipani (1568–1572 et 1586–1587).* Rome: École Française de Rome, 1984.

Melanchthon, Philipp. *Opera quae supersunt omnia.* 4 vols. Halle: C. A. Schwetschke and Son, 1834–1860.

Mercati, Angelo. *I costituti di Niccolò Franco (1568–1570) dinanzi all'Inquisizione di Roma esistenti nell'Archivio Segreto Vaticano.* Vatican City: Biblioteca Apostolica Vaticana, 1955.

Micanzio, Fulgenzio. *Lettere a William Cavendish (1615–1628).* Edited by Roberto Ferrini. Introduction by Enrico De Mas. Rome: Istituto storico O.S.M., 1987.

Montaigne, Michel de. *Journal de voyage.* Edited by François Rigolot. Paris: Presses Universitaires de France, 1992.

Negri, Francesco. *Della tragedia intitolata Libero Arbitrio*. Basel: Johann Oporin, 1550.

Ochino, Bernardino. *Prediche nomate Laberinti del libero arbitrio o ver servo arbitrio, Prescienza, Predestinatione e libertà divina, e del modo per uscirne*. Basel: [Pietro Perna] 1561.

Pagano, Sergio. *Il processo di Endimio Calandra e l'inquisizione di Mantova nel 1567–1568*. Vatican City: Biblioteca Apostolica Vaticana, 1991.

Paruta, Paolo. *Historia vinetiana*. Venice, 1645.

Pellegrini, Antonio. *I segni de la natura de l'huomo*. Venice: Giovanni de Farri et fratelli, 1545.

Petrarca, Francesco. *Le rime brevemente sposte per Lodovico Castelvetro*. Basel: Pietro Sebadonis [Pietro Perna], 1582.

Poggiani, Giulio. *Epistolae et orationes*. Edited by Girolamo Lagomarsini. 4 vols. Rome: G. Salomonio, 1757–66.

Pole, Reginald. *Pro ecclesiasticae unitatis defensione*. Rome: Antonio Blado, 1538.

Possevino, Antonio. *Risposta all'Avviso mandato fuori dal Signore Antonio Quirino*. Bologna: Archiepiscopal Press, 1606.

Renato, Camillo. *Opere, documenti e testimonianze*. Edited by Antonio Rotondò. Florence: Sansoni, 1968.

Sanders, Nicholas. *De origine ac progressu Schismatis Anglicani*. Rome: Bartolomeo Bonfadini: 1586.

Sandys, Edwin. *Europae Speculum or A View or Survey of the State of Religion in the Western parts of the world*. London: Thomas Basset, 1673.

——. *A Relation of the State of Religion: and with what hopes and pollicies it hath beene framed, and is maintained in the severall states of these westerne partes of the world*. London, Val. Sims for Simon Waterson, 1605.

——. *Relazione dello stato della religione. E con quali dissegni et arti è stata fabricata e maneggiata in diversi stati di queste occidentali parti del mondo. Tradotta dall'Inglese del Cavaliere Edoino Sandis in Lingua Volgare con aggiunte notabili*. [Geneva], 1625.

Sansovino, Francesco. *Del governo et amministratione di diversi regni, et republiche, così antiche, come moderne*. Venice: Altobello Salicato, 1583.

——. *Historia universale dell'origine, guerre, et imperio de' Turchi*. Venice, 1654.

Sanudo, Marin. *I Diarii*. Edited by Rinaldo Fulin, Federico Stefani, Nicolò Barozzi, Guglielmo Berchet, Marco Allegri. 59 vols. Venice: Visentini, 1879–1903.

Sanuto, Livio. *Geografia distinta in XII libri*. Venice: Damiano Zenaro, 1588.

Sarpi, Paolo. *The historie of the Councel of Trent*. London: Robert Baker and John Bill, 1620.

——. *Istoria del Concilio Tridentino*. 2 vols. Edited by Corrado Vivanti. Turin: Einaudi: Turin, 2011.

——. *Lettere ai Gallicani*. Edited, with introduction and notes by Boris Ulianich. Wiesbaden: Franz Steiner Verlag GMBH, 1961.

——. *Lettere ai Protestanti*. Edited by Manlio Duilio Busnelli. 2 vols. Bari: Laterza, 1931.

——. *Opere*. Edited by Gaetano Cozzi and Luisa Cozzi. Milan: Ricciardi, 1969.

——. *Scritti giurisdizionalistici*. Edited by G. Gambarin. Bari: Laterza, 1958.

Scaliger, J. C. *Poetices libri septem*. Lyon: Antoine Vincent, 1561.

Sleidano, Giovanni. *Commentarii overo historie nelle quali si tratta de lo stato de la Repub. e de la religione christiana.* [Geneva: Antoine Davodeau, Jacques Bourgeois, François Jaquy,] 1557.

Tasso, Torquato. *Aminta.* London: John Wolfe, 1591.

——. *Gerusalemme Liberata.* Lyon: Alessandro Marsilij [Petro Roussin] 1581.

——. *Gerusalemme Liberata.* Edited by Lanfranco Caretti. Milan: Mondadori, 1983.

——. "Il forno overo de la nobiltà." In *Dialoghi.* Edited by Ezio Raimondi. 3 vols. Florence: Sansoni, 1958.

——. *Il messaggiero.* Venice: Bernardo Giunti, 1582.

——. *Le lettere di Torquato Tasso.* Edited by C. Guasti. 5 vols. Florence, 1853.

——. *The Liberation of Jerusalem.* Translated by M. Wickert, with introduction and notes by M. Davie. Oxford: Oxford University Press, 2009.

——. *Tre scritti politici.* Edited by Luigi Firpo. Turin: Utet, 1980.

Thomas, William. *The History of Italy.* London: Thomas Berthelet 1549.

Trento, Jean-Baptiste, and Pierre Eskrich. *Mappe-monde nouvelle papistique.* Edited by Frank Lestringant and Alessandra Preda. Geneva: Droz, 2009.

Ugoni, Giovanni Andrea. *Discorso della dignità et eccellenza della gran città di Venetia.* Venice: Pietro da Fine, 1562.

Vergerio, Pier Paolo. *Ad serenissimum Angliae regem, etc. Ecclesiae Christi defensorem, Eduardum VI. De creatione Iulii III pontificis romani, tum quid de eius papatu sperari possit.* Basel: Jean Oporin, 1550.

——. *Al Serenissimo Re d'Inghilterra Edoardo sesto: Della creatione del nuovo Papa, Giulio terzo, & ciò che di lui sperare si possa.* 1550.

——. *Al Serenissimo Re d'Inghilterra Edoardo sesto de' portamenti di Papa Giulio III. Et quale habbia ad essere il concilio, che egli intende di fare.* Poschiavo: Dolfino Landolfi, 1550.

——. *Alla serenissima regina d'Inghilterra del concilio di Trento.* Tübingen: [Morhard] 1562.

——. "Oratione al doge Francesco Donado per il suo ingresso, esortatione alla Riforma della Chiesa." In *Orationi diverse et nuove di eccellentissimi auttori,* edited by Anton Francesco Doni, 7r–12v. Florence: Anton Francesco Doni, 1547.

——. *Risposta ad un libro del Nausea vescouo di Vienna scritto in laude del concilio tridentino.* Poschiavo: Dolfino Landolfi, 1552.

Wicquefort, Abraham de. *L'ambassadeur et ses fonctions.* Cologne: Pierre Marteau, 1715.

——. *The Rights, Privileges and Office of Embassadors and Publick Ministers.* London: Charles Davis, 1740.

Secondary sources

Adair, Edward R. *The Extraterritoriality of Ambassadors in the Sixteenth and Seventeenth Centuries.* London: Longmans, 1929.

Adams, Simon. "Spain or the Netherlands? The Dilemmas of Early Stuart Foreign Policy." In *Before the English Civil War: Essays on Early Stuart Politics and Government,* edited by H. Tomlinson, 79–101. New York: St. Martin's Press, 1984.

Adlington, Hugh. "Chaplains to Embassies: Daniel Featley, Anti-Catholic Controversialists Abroad." In *Chaplains in Early Modern England: Patronage, Literature and Religion*, edited by Hugh Adlington, Tom Lockwood and Gillian Wright, 83–102. Manchester: Manchester University Press, 2013.

Agamben, Giorgio. *Homo Sacer: Sovereign Power and Bare Life*. Stanford, CA: Stanford University Press, 1998.

——. *Means Without End: Notes on Politics*. Minneapolis: University of Minnesota Press, 2000.

Ambrosini, Federica. "'Mestier da donne?' Opinioni su Elisabetta d'Inghilterra e sul governo femminile nella Venezia della Controriforma." *Archivio Veneto* 5, no. 123 (1984): 27–75.

——. *Paesi e mari ignoti: America e colonialismo europeo nella cultura veneziana (secoli XVI–XVII)*. Venice: Deputazione editrice, 1982.

——. *Storie di patrizi e di eresia nella Venezia del '500*. Milan: Franco Angeli, 1999.

——. "Tendenze filoprotestanti nel patriziato veneziano." In *La Chiesa di Venezia tra Riforma protestante e Riforma cattolica*, edited by Giuseppe Gullino, 155–81. Venice: Edizioni Studium Cattolico Veneziano, 1990.

Andreas, Willy. *Staatskunst und Diplomatie der Venezianer im Spiegel ihrer Gesandtenberichte*. Leipzig: Von Quelle & Meyer, 1908.

Anglo, Sydney. *Machiavelli—The First Century: Studies in Enthusiasm, Hostility and Irrelevance*. Oxford: Oxford University Press, 2005.

——. *Storie di patrizi e di eresia nella Venezia del '500*. Milan: Franco Angeli, 1999.

Arbel, Benjamin. *Trading Nations: Jews and Venetians in the Early Modern Mediterranean*. Leiden: Brill, 1995.

Ardissino, Erminia. *Tasso, Plotino, Ficino: in margine a un postillato*. Rome: Edizioni di Storia e Letteratura, 2003.

Arendt, Hannah. *The Origins of Totalitarianism*. New York: Harcourt, 1951.

Armitage, David. *Foundations of Modern International Thought*. Cambridge: Cambridge University Press, 2013.

Bainton, Roland H. *Christian Attitudes toward War and Peace: A Historical Survey and a Critical Re-Evaluation*. Eugene, OR: Wipf and Stock, 1960.

Baldassarri, Guido. "Fra 'dialogo' e 'nocturnales annotationes': Prolegomeni alla lettura del *Messaggiero*," *La rassegna della Letteratura Italiana* 76 (1972): 265–93.

——. "Poema eroico o 'romanzo'? Riscritture della Liberata dal Camilli al Gentili" In *Scritture di scritture: testi, generi, modelli nel Rinascimento*, edited by G. Mazzacurati and M. Plaisance, 439–459. Rome: Bulzoni, 1987.

Baldini, Artemio E. "Origini e fortuna del *Thesoro politico* alla luce di nuovi documenti dell'Archivio del Sant 'Uffizio.'" In *Cultura politica e società a Milano tra Cinquecento e Seicento*, edited by C. Buzzi and C. Continisio, 155–75. Milan: Editrice ITL, 2000.

Balsamo, Jean. "L'Arioste et le Tasse: Des poètes italiens, leurs libraires et leurs lecteurs français." In *L'Arioste et le Tasse en France*, 11–26.

——. *L'Arioste et le Tasse en France au XVIe siècle*. Paris: ENS, 2003.

——. "Les origines parisiennes du Tesoro politico (1589)." *Bibliothèque d'Humanisme et Renaissance* 57, no. 1 (1995): 7–23.

Barbierato, Federico. *The Inquisitor in the Hat Shop: Inquisition, Forbidden Books and Unbelief in Early Modern Venice*. Farnham: Ashgate, 2012.

——. "Istorie venetiane" in Benzoni and Zanato, *Storici e politici veneti*, 156–85.

——. *Politici e ateisti: percorsi della miscredenza a Venezia tra Sei e Settecento*. Milan: Unicopli, 2006.

Barbieri, Andrea. "Castelvetro, i suoi libri, e l'ambiente culturale modenese del suo tempo." In *Ludovico Castelvetro: filologia e ascesi*, edited by Roberto Gigliucci, 57–69. Rome: Bulzoni, 2007.

Barrington, Robert. "Two Houses Alike in Dignity: Reginald Pole and Edmund Harvell." *Historical Journal* 4 (1996): 895–913.

Bayly, Christopher. *Empire and Information: Intelligence Gathering and Social Communication in India, 1780–1870*. Cambridge: Cambridge University Press, 1999.

Bec, Christian. *Les marchands écrivains, affaires et humanisme à Florence, 1375–1434*. Paris: Mouton, 1967.

Beck, Hans Georg, Manoussos Manoussacas, and Agostino Pertusi, eds. *Venezia centro di mediazione tra oriente e occidente (secoli XV–XVI): aspetti e problemi*. 2 vols. Florence: Olshcki, 1977.

Bély, Lucien. *Espions et ambassadeurs au temps de Louis XIV*. Paris: Fayard, 1990.

——, ed. *L'opinion publique en Europe (1600–1800)*. Paris: PUF, 2011.

Benhabib, Seyla. *The Rights of Others: Aliens, Residents and Citizens*. Cambridge: Cambridge University Press, 2004.

Benrath, Karl. *Geschichte der Reformation in Venedig*. Halle: Niemeyer, 1886.

——. *Neue Briefe von Paolo Sarpi (1608–1616)*. Leipzig: Rudolph Haupt, 1909.

Benzoni, Gino. "Giovanni Francesco Biondi, un avventuroso dalmata del '600.'" *Archivio Veneto* 80 (1967): 19–37.

——. "I teologi minori dell'Interdetto." *Archivio veneto* 91 (1970): 31–108.

——. "Ranke's Favorite Source: The Relazioni of the Venetian Ambassadors." *Courier* 22, no. 1 (1987): 11–26.

Berengo, Marino. *Nobili e mercanti nella Lucca del Cinquecento*. Turin: Einaudi, 1965.

Bertolo, Fabio Massimo. *Aretino e la stampa: Strategie di autopromozione a Venezia nel Cinquecento*. Rome: Salerno Editrice, 2003.

Bettoni, Anna. "La dissidence discrète d'Arnaud du Ferrier (1577)." *Les Dossiers du Grihl*: https://journals.openedition.org/dossiersgrihl/5851 accessed December 20, 2015.

Betts, Alexander, and Gil Loescher, eds. *Refugees in International Relations*. Oxford: Oxford University Press, 2011.

Biasiori, Lucio. *L'eresia di un umanista: Celio Secondo Curione nell'Europa del Cinquecento*. Carocci: Rome, 2015.

Biferali, Fabrizio, and Massimo Firpo. *Immagini ed eresie nell'Italia del Cinquecento*. Rome: Laterza, 2016.

Binns, John. "Alberico Gentili in Defense of Poetry and Acting." *Studies in the Renaissance* 19 (1972): 224–72.

——. *Intellectual Culture in Elizabethan and Jacobean England: The Latin Writings of the Age*. Leeds: Francis Cairns, 1990.

Biow, Douglas. *Doctors, Ambassadors, Secretaries: Humanism and Professions in Renaissance Italy*. Chicago: University of Chicago Press, 2002.

Blair, Ann. *Too Much to Know: Managing Scholarly Information before the Modern Age.* New Haven, CT: Yale University Press, 2010.

Blair, Ann, and Jennifer Mulligan, eds. *"Toward a Cultural History of the Archives."* Special issue of *Archival Science* 7 (2007).

Blet, Pierre. "Pio V e la riforma Tridentina per mezzo dei nunzi apostolici." In Fernandez, *San Pio V*, 35–46.

Bolzoni, Lina. "'O maledetto, o abominoso ordigno': la rappresentazione della guerra nel poema epico-cavalleresco." In *Storia d'Italia XVIII: Guerra e pace*, edited by Walter Barberis, 201–47. Turin: Einaudi, 2002.

——. "Osservazioni su Bruno e Ariosto." *Rinascimento* 40 (2000): 19–43.

Bonora, Elena. *Aspettando l'imperatore: Principi italiani tra il papa e Carlo V.* Turin: Einaudi, 2015.

——. "Il sospetto di eresia e i 'frati diplomatici' tra Cinque e Seicento." In Fragnito and Tallon, *Hétérodoxies croisées.* http://books.openedition.org/efr/2823.

——. "Inquisizione e papato tra Pio IV e Pio V." In Guasco and Torre, *Pio V nella società età del suo tempo*, 49–83.

——. "*Ubique in omnibus circumspecti*: Diplomazia pontificia e intransigenza religiosa." In Sabbatini and Volpini, *Sulla diplomazia in età moderna*, 61–76.

Borean, Elisabetta. "Palazzo Ragazzoni." In *Gli affreschi nelle ville venete: Il Cinquecento*, edited by Giuseppe Pavanello and Vincenzo Mancini, 434–35. Venice: Marsilio, 2008.

Bossy, John. *Giordano Bruno and the Embassy Affair.* New Haven, CT: Yale University Press, 1991.

——. *Under the Molehill: An Elizabethan Spy Story.* New Haven, CT: Yale University Press 2001.

Boutcher, Warren. *The School of Montaigne in Early Modern Europe.* 2 vols. Oxford: Oxford University Press, 2017.

——. "Vernacular Humanism in the Sixteenth-Century." In *The Cambridge Companion to Renaissance Humanism*, edited by Jill Kraye, 189–202. Cambridge: Cambridge University Press, 1996.

Bouwsma, William J. *Venice and the Defense of Republican Liberty: Renaissance Values in the Age of the Counter-Reformation.* Berkeley: University of California Press, 1968.

Bowd, Stephen D. *Reform before the Reformation: Vincenzo Querini and the Religious Renaissance in Italy.* Leiden: Brill, 2002.

Braccesi, Simonetta Adorni. *Una città infetta: la Repubblica di Lucca nella crisi religiosa del Cinquecento.* Florence: Olschki, 1994.

Braccesi, Simonetta Adorni, and Carla Sodini, eds. *L'emigrazione confessionale dei lucchesi in Europa.* Florence: Edifir, 1999.

Bracco, Barbara. *Storici italiani e politica estera: Tra Salvemini e Volpe 1917–1925.* Milan: Franco Angeli, 1998.

Branca, Vittore, ed. *Mercanti scrittori: ricordi nella Firenze tra Medioevo e Rinascimento.* Milan: Rusconi, 1986.

Brand, Charles P. *Torquato Tasso: A Study of the Poet and of His Contribution to English Literature.* Cambridge: Cambridge University Press, 1965.

Braudel, Fernand. *The Mediterranean and the Mediterranean World in the Age of Philip II.* 2 vols. Berkeley: University of California Press, 1996.

Brown, Alison. "Lorenzo de' Medici's New Men and Their Mores: The Changing Lifestyle of Quattrocento Florence." *Renaissance Studies* 2 (2002): 113–42.

Brown, Horatio. "The Marriage Contract, Inventory and Funeral Expenses of Edmund Harvel." *English Historical Review* 77 (1905): 70–77.

———. *The Venetian Printing Press 1469–1800.* Amsterdam: Gérard Th. van Heusden, 1969.

Brumbaugh, Barbara. "*Jerusalem Delivered* and the Allegory of Sidney's Revised Arcadia." *Modern Philology* 101 (2004): 337–70.

Brummett, Palmira. "The Jacopo Castelvetro Collection: A Renaissance Man with Documents on Istanbul," *Turkish Studies Association Bulletin* 11, no. 1 (1987): 1–8.

Burke, Peter. "Publishing the Private in Early Modern Europe: The Rise of Secret History." In *Changing Perceptions of the Public Sphere*, edited by Christian J. Emden and David Midgley, 57–72. New York: Berghahn Books, 2012.

———. "Sarpi storico." In *Ripensando Paolo Sarpi*, edited by Corrado Pin, 103–9. Venice: Ateneo Veneto, 2006.

———. "Translations into Latin in Early Modern Europe." In *Cultural Translation in Early Modern Europe*, edited by Peter Burke and R. Po-Chia Hsia, 65–80. Cambridge: Cambridge University Press, 2007.

Burke, Peter, and Ronnie Po-chia Hsia, eds. *Cultural Translation in Early Modern Europe.* Cambridge: Cambridge University Press, 2007.

Buschbell, Gottfried von. *Reformation und Inquisition in Italien: um die Mitte des XVI Jahrunderts.* Padeborn: Schöningh, 1910.

Butler, Kathleen T. Blake. "Giacomo Castelvetro 1546–1616." *Italian Studies* 5 (1950): 1–42.

Campana, Lorenzo. "Monsignor Giovanni della Casa e i suoi tempi." *Studi storici* 1 (1907): 349–580.

Campi, Emidio. "The Italian Convert: Marquis Galeazzo Caracciolo and the English Puritans." In *Church and School in Early Modern Protestantism: Studies in Honor of Richard A. Muller on the Maturation of a Theological Tradition*, edited by Jordan J. Ballor, David S. Sytsma, and Jason Zuidema, 153–63. Leiden: Brill, 2013.

Canfora, Luciano. *Il copista come autore.* Palermo: Sellerio, 2002.

Cantimori, Delio. *Eretici italiani del Cinquecento.* Edited by Adriano Prosperi. Turin: Einaudi, 1992.

———. "Introduzione." In Leopold von Ranke, *Storia dei Papi.* Translated by Claudio Cesa. Florence: Sansoni 1965.

———. "'Nicodemismo' e speranze conciliari nel Cinquecento italiano." In *Studi di storia*, 518–39.

———. "Note sugli studi storici in Italia dal 1926 al 1951." In *Storici e storia*, 268–80.

———. "A proposito di L. Febvre: Au coeur religieux du XVIème siécle." In *Eretici italiani*, 551–52.

———. *Prospettive di storia ereticale.* Rome: Laterza, 1960, republished in *Eretici italiani del Cinquecento*, 421–81.

———. *Storici e storia: Metodo, caratteristiche e significato del lavoro storiografico.* Turin: Einaudi, 1971.

———. *Studi di storia.* Turin: Einaudi, 1959.

Cantù, Cesare. "Spigolature negli archivi toscani." *Rivista contemporanea* 21 (1860): 371–414.

Carrió-Invernizzi, Diana, ed. *Embajadores culturales: Transferencias y lealtades de la diplomacia española de la Edad Moderna*. Madrid: Universidad Nacional de la Educación a Distancia, 2016.

Caponnetto, Salvatore. *La Riforma protestante nell'Italia del Cinquecento*. Turin: Claudiana, 1992.

——. *Melantone e l'Italia*. Turin: Claudiana, 2000.

——. Review of A. Stella, "L'orazione di Pier Paolo Vergerio al doge Francesco Donà sulla riforma della Chiesa (1545)." *Rivista storica italiana* 2 (1971): 466–68.

Caravale, Giorgio. "La polemica protestante contro il Tridentino." *L'uomo del Concilio: il cardinale Giovanni Morone tra Roma e Trento nell'età di Michelangelo*, edited by Roberto Pancheri and Domenica Primerano, 47–61. Trent: Temi, 2009.

——. *Predicazione e inquisizone nell'Italia del Cinquecento: Ippolito Chizzola tra eresia e controversia antiprotestante*. Bologna: Il Mulino, 2012.

——. *Sulle tracce dell'eresia: Ambrogio Catarino Politi (1484–1553)*. Florence: Olschki, 2007.

Casteel, Theodore W. "Calvin and Trent: Calvin's Reactions to the Council of Trent in the Context of his Conciliar Thought." *Harvard Theological Review* 1 (1970): 91–117.

Castelli, Patrizia. "'Ali bianche vestì' la demonologia nel manierismo tassiano." In Moretti and Pepe, *Tasso e l'università*, 389–410.

Catto, Michela, and Adriano Prosperi, eds. *Trent and Beyond: The Council, Other Powers, Other Cultures*. Turnhout: Brepols, 2017.

Cavazza, Silvano. "La censura ingannata: polemiche antiromane e usi della propaganda in Pier Paolo Vergerio." In *La censura libraria nell'Europa del secolo XVI*, edited by Ugo Rozzo, 273–95. Udine: Forum, 1997.

——. "Pier Paolo Vergerio nei Grigioni e in Valtellina (1549–1553): attività editoriale e polemica religiosa." In *Riforma e società nei Grigioni, Valtelllina e Valchiavenna tra '500 e '600*, edited by Alessandro Pastore, 33–62. Milan: Franco Angeli, 1991.

——. "'Quei che vogliono Cristo senza croce': Vergerio e i prelati riformatori italiani (1549–1555)." In Rozzo, *Pier Paolo Vergerio*, 136–41.

Cavazzuti, Giuseppe. *Lodovico Castelvetro*. Modena: Società tipografica modenese, 1903.

Cecchini, Isabella, and Luciano Pezzolo. "Merchants and Institutions in Early Modern Venice." *Journal of European Economic History* 41 (2012): 89–114.

Certeau, Michel de. *The Mystic Fable*. 2 vols. Chicago: University of Chicago Press, 2015.

Chartier, Roger. *The Cultural Origins of the French Revolution*. Durham, NC: Duke University Press, 1991.

——. "Leisure and Sociability: Reading Aloud in Early Modern Europe." In *Urban Life in the Renaissance*, edited by Susan Zimmerman and Ronald F. E. Weissman, 103–20. Newark: University of Delaware Press, 1989.

——. *The Order of Books: Readers, Authors, and Libraries in Europe between the Fourteenth and the Eighteenth Centuries*. Stanford, CA: Stanford University Press, 1994.

Ciliberto, Michele. *Intellettuali e fascismo: Saggio su Delio Cantimori*. Bari: De Donato, 1977.

Cipolla, Carlo. "The Diffusion of Innovations in Early Modern Europe." *Comparative Studies in Society and History* 14 (1976): 46–52.

Clough, Cecil. *The Duchy of Urbino in the Renaissance.* London: Variorum Reprints, 1981.

Cloulas, Ivan. "Les rapports de Jérôme Ragazzoni, évêque de Bergame, avec les ecclésiastiques pendant sa nonciature en France (1583–1586)." *Mélanges d'archéologie et d'histoire* 72 (1960): 509–50.

Cochrane, Eric, ed. *The Late Italian Renaissance.* New York: Harper, 1970.

Cochrane, Eric, and John Tedeschi. "Delio Cantimori: Historian (1904–1966)." *Journal of Modern History* 4 (1967): 438–45.

Collinson, Patrick. "The Monarchical Republic of Queen Elizabeth I." In *The Tudor Monarchy*, edited by John Guy, 110–34. London: Arnold, 1997.

Comba, Emilio. *I nostri protestanti.* 2 vols. Florence: Claudiana, 1897.

Costa, Gustavo. "La dimensione magico-ermetica del sublime nel *Messaggiero* tassiano." In Dutschke et al., *Forma e parola*, 371–88.

Croce, Benedetto. *La storia come pensiero e come azione.* Naples: Bibliopolis, 2002.

Cozzi, Gaetano."Fortuna e sfortuna, della Compagnia di Gesù a Venezia." In Zanardi, *I Gesuiti e Venezia*, 59–88.

———. "Fra Paolo Sarpi, l'anglicanesimo e la *Historia del Concilio Tridentino*." *Rivista storica italiana* 4 (1956): 559–619.

———. *Paolo Sarpi tra Venezia e l'Europa.* Turin: Einaudi, 1979.

———. "Sir Edwin Sandys e la *Relazione dello stato della religione*." *Rivista storica italiana* 79 (1967): 1096–121.

———. *Venezia barocca: Conflitti di uomini e idee nella crisi del Seicento veneziano.* Venice: Il Cardo, 1995.

Craigwood, Joanna. "Shakespeare's Kingmaking Ambassadors." In *Diplomacy and Authority from Dante to Shakespeare*, edited by Jason Powell and William T. Rossiter, 199–217. Aldershot: Ashgate, 2013.

Crimando, Thomas I. "Two French Views of the Council of Trent." *Sixteenth-Century Journal* 2 (1988): 169–86.

Crinò, Anna Maria. *Fatti e figure del Seicento anglo-toscano: Documenti sui rapporti letterari, diplomatici, culturali fra Toscana e Inghilterra.* Florence: Olschki, 1957.

———. "Un altro memoriale inedito di Roberto Ridolfi." In Crinò, *Fatti e figure*, 67–78.

Currin, John M. "Henry VII, France and the Holy League of Venice: The Diplomacy of Balance." *Historical Research* 82 (2009): 526–46.

Currin, John M. "England's International Relations 1485–1509: Continuities amidst Change." In Doran and Richardson, *Tudor England and Its Neighbours*, 14–43.

Curtin, Philip D. *Cross-Cultural Trade in World History.* Cambridge: Cambridge University Press, 1984.

Dall'Aglio, Stefano, Brian Richardson, and Massimo Rospocher, eds. *Voices and Texts in Early Modern Italian Society.* London: Routledge, 2017.

Dall'Olio, Guido. *Eretici e inquisitori nella Bologna del Cinquecento.* Bologna: Istituto per la storia di Bologna, 1999.

D'Amico, Juan Carlos. "Aretino tra Inghilterra e Impero: una dedica costata cara e una lettera non pubblicata." *Filologia e critica* 1 (2005): 72–94.

Daenens, Francine. "Donne valorose, eretiche, finte sante. Note sull'antologia giolitina del 1548." In *La scrittura epistolare femminile tra archivio e tipografia secoli XV–XVII*, edited by Gabriella Zarri, 181–207. Rome: Viella, 1999.

Darnton, Robert. "What Is the History of Books?" In *The Kiss of Lamourette: Reflections in Cultural History*, 107–35. New York: Norton, 1990.

De Bellis, Daniela. "La vita e l'ambiente di Niccolò Leonico Tomeo." *Quaderni per la storia dell'università di Padova* 12 (1979): 37–73.

De Frede, Carlo. *La prima traduzione italiana del Corano sullo sfondo dei rapporti tra Cristianità e Islam.* Naples: Istituto Universitario Orientale, 1960.

———. *La restaurazione cattolica in Inghilterra sotto Maria Tudor: nel carteggio di Girolamo Seripando.* Naples: Libreria Scientifica Editrice, 1971.

Degl'Innocenti, Luca, Brian Richardson, and Chiara Sbordoni, eds. *Interactions between Orality and Writing in Early Modern Italian Culture.* New York: Routledge, 2016.

Del Col, Andrea. "Eterodossia e cultura fra gli artigiani di Porcia nel secolo XVI." *Il Noncello* 46 (1978): 9–76.

———. "Il controllo della stampa a Venezia e i processi di Antonio Brucioli (1548–1559)." *Critica storica* 17 (1980): 457–510.

———. *L'Inquisizione in Italia: dal XII al XXI secolo.* Milan: Mondadori, 2006.

———. "L'Inquisizione romana e il potere politico nella repubblica di Venezia (1540–1560)." *Critica storica* 28 (1991): 189–250.

———. "Organizzazione, composizione e giurisdizione dei tribunali dell'Inquisizione romana nella repubblica di Venezia (1500–1550)." *Critica storica* 25 (1988): 155–67.

De Mas, Enrico. *L'attesa del secolo aureo (1603–1625): saggio di storia delle idee del secolo XVII.* Florence: Olschki, 1982.

———. *Sovranità politica e unità cristiana nel Seicento anglo-veneto.* Ravenna: Longo, 1975.

De Rinaldis, Maria Luisa. *Giacomo Castelvetro Renaissance Translator.* Lecce: Milella, 2003.

Descendre, Romain. *L'état du monde: Giovanni Botero entre raison d'État et géopolitique.* Geneva: Droz, 2009.

De Vivo, Filippo. "Coeur de l'Etat, lieu de tension. Le tournant archivistique vu de Venise (XVe–XVIe siècle)." *Annales: Histoire, Sciences Sociales* 68 (2013): 699–728.

———. "Francia e Inghilterra di fronte all'Interdetto di Venezia." In *Paolo Sarpi: Politique et religion en Europe*, edited by Marie Viallon, 163–88. Paris: Éditions Classiques Garnier, 2010.

———. "How to Read Venetian Relazioni." *Renaissance and Reformation* 34, no. 1–2 (2011): 25–59.

———. *Information and Communication in Venice: Rethinking Early Modern Politics.* Oxford: Oxford University Press, 2007.

———. "Public Sphere or Communication Triangle?" In *Beyond the Public Sphere: Opinions, Publics, Spaces in Early Modern Europe*, edited by Massimo Rospocher, 115–36. Bologna: Il Mulino, 2012.

De Vivo, Filippo, Andrea Guidi, and Alessandro Silvestri, eds. *Archivi e archivisti in Italia tra medioevo ed età moderna.* Rome: Viella, 2015.

De Vivo, Filippo, and Brian Richardson, eds. "*Scribal Culture in Italy, 1450–1700.*" Special issue of *Italian Studies* 66, no. 2 (2011).

Dick, H. G. "A Renaissance Expatriate: Giacomo Castelvetro the Elder." *Italian Quarterly* 7 (1963): 3–19.

Dickinson, Janet. *Court Politics and the Earl of Essex, 1589–1601.* London: Pickering and Chatto, 2012.

Ditchfield, Simon. "In Sarpi's Shadow: Coping with Trent the Italian Way." In *Studi in memoria di Cesare Mozzarelli.* 2 vols., 1:585–606. Milan: Vita e Pensiero, 2008.

——. "Tridentine Catholicism." In *The Ashgate Research Companion to the Counter-Reformation,* edited by Alexandra Bamji, Geert H. Janssen and Mary Laven, 15–31. Farnham, Surrey: Ashgate: 2013.

Dittmer, Jason, and Fiona McConnell. "Introduction: Reconceptualising Diplomatic Cultures." In *Diplomatic Cultures and International Politics: Translations, Spaces, Alternatives,* edited by Jason Dittmer and Fiona McConnell, 1–20. Routledge: New York, 2016.

Divitiis, Gigliola Pagano de. *English Merchants in Seventeenth-Century Italy.* Cambridge: Cambridge University Press, 1997.

Donaldson, Peter S. *Machiavelli and the Mystery of State.* Cambridge: Cambridge University Press, 1988.

Dooley, Brendan. *The Social History of Skepticism: Experience and Doubt in Early Modern Culture.* Baltimore: Johns Hopkins University Press, 1999.

Doran, Susan, and Glen Richardson, eds. *Tudor England and Its Neighbours.* Basingstoke: Palgrave, 2005.

Dursteler, Eric. "Describing or Distorting the 'Turk'? The *Relazioni* of the Venetian Ambassadors in Constantinople as Historical Source." *Acta Histriae* 19, no. 1–2 (2011): 231–48.

——. "Power and Information: The Venetian Postal System in the Early Modern Eastern Mediterranean, 1573–1645." In *From Florence to the Mediterranean: Studies in Honor of Anthony Molho,* edited by Diogo Curto, Eric Dursteler, Julius Kirshner, and Francesca Trivellato, 601–23. Florence: Olschki, 2009.

——. *Venetians in Constantinople: Nation, Identity, and Coexistence in the Early Modern Mediterranean.* Baltimore: Johns Hopkins University Press, 2006.

Dutschke, Dennis J., Pier Massimo Forni, Filippo Grazzini, Benjamin R. Lawton, and Laura Sanguineti White, eds. *Forma e parola: Studi in memoria di Fredi Chiappelli.* Roma: Bulzoni, 1992.

Edwards, John. *Archbishop Pole.* Ashgate: Farnham, 2014.

Elie, Jérôme. "Histories of Refugees and Forced Migration Studies." In *The Oxford Handbook of Refugee and Forced Migration Studies,* edited by Elena Fiddian Qasmiyeh, Gil Loescher, Katy Long, and Nando Sigona, 1–10. Oxford: Oxford University Press, 2014.

Erspamer, Francesco. "Il *pensiero debole* di Torquato Tasso." In *La menzogna,* edited by Franco Cardini. Florence: Ponte alle Grazie, 1989. 120–36.

——. "Introduzione" to Pietro Aretino, *Lettere: Libro secondo,* xxxvi–xxxviii. Milan: Guanda, 1998.

Fernandez, Aniceto, ed. *San Pio V e la problematica del suo tempo.* Alessandria: Cassa di Risparmio di Alessandria, 1972.

Felici, Lucia. "Il papa diavolo: Il paradigma dell'Anticristo nella pubblicistica europea del Cinquecento." In *La papauté à la Renaissance,* edited by Florence Alazard and Frank La Brasca, 533–69. Paris: Champion, 2007.

———. "L'Islam in Europa: la traduzione del Corano di Theodor Bibliander (1543)." *Cromohs* 12 (2007): 1–13.

———, ed. *Ripensare la Riforma protestante: nuove prospettive degli studi italiani.* Turin: Claudiana, 2015.

Fenlon, Dermot. *Heresy and Obedience in Tridentine Italy: Cardinal Pole and the Counter-Reformation.* Cambridge: Cambridge University Press, 1972.

Feo, Roberto de. "Gli affreschi di Francesco Montemezzano in Palazzo Ragazzoni di Sacile ed un inedito." In *Francesco Montemezzano in Palazzo Ragazzoni - Flangini - Billia: Arte, storia e cultura nel Giardino della Serenissima*, edited by Francesco Amendolagine, Roberto De Feo, and Gilberto Ganzer, 35–52. Sacile: Città di Sacile, 1993.

Firpo, Luigi. "La Chiesa italiana di Londra nel Cinquecento e i suoi rapporti con Ginevra." In *Ginevra e l'Italia*, edited by Delio Cantimori, Giorgio Spini, Franco Venturi, Valdo Vinay, 117–94. Florence: Sansoni 1959.

———. "Non Paolo Sarpi, ma Tommaso Campanella." *Giornale storico della letteratura italiana* 158 (1981): 254–74.

———. *Il processo a Giordano Bruno.* Edited by Diego Quaglioni. Rome: Salerno, 1993.

———. *Scritti sulla Riforma in Italia.* Naples: Prismi, 1996.

———. "Un madrigale inedito del Tasso e una testimonianza di Campanella." *Giornale storico della letteratura italiana* 127 (1950): 375–77.

———, ed. *Relazioni di ambasciatori veneti al Senato.* Vol 1. Inghilterra. Torino: Bottega d'Erasmo, 1965.

Firpo, Massimo. *Artisti, gioiellieri, eretici: Il mondo di Lorenzo Lotto tra Riforma e Controriforma.* Rome: Laterza, 2001.

———. *Gli affreschi di Pontormo a San Lorenzo: Eresia, politica e cultura nella Firenze di Cosimo I.* Turin: Einaudi, 1997.

———. *Inquisizione romana e Controriforma: Studi sul cardinal Morone (1509–1580) e il suo processo d'eresia.* Bologna: Il Mulino, 1992.

———. *Juan de Valdés and the Italian Reformation.* Farnham: Ashgate, 2015.

———. *Juan de Valdés e la Riforma nell'Italia del Cinquecento.* Rome: Laterza, 2016.

———. "L'iconografia come problema storiografico: Le ambiguità della porpora e i 'diavoli del Sant'Ufficio. Identità e storia nei ritratti di Giovanni Grimani." *Rivista storica italiana* 3 (2005): 825–71.

———. *La presa di potere dell'Inquisizione romana (1550–1553).* Rome: Laterza, 2014.

———. *Pietro Bizzarri esule italiano del Cinquecento.* Turin: Einaudi, 1971.

———. "Politica imperiale e vita religiosa in Italia nell'età di Carlo V." *Studi storici* 42, no. 2 (2001): 245–61.

———. *Riforma protestante ed eresie nell'Italia del Cinquecento.* Rome: Laterza, 1993.

———. *Storie di immagini, immagini di storia: Studi di iconografia cinquecentesca.* Rome: Edizioni di Storia e Letteratura, 2010.

———. *Tra alumbrados e "spirituali": Studi su Juan de Valdés e il valdesianesimo nella crisi religiosa del '500 italiano.* Florence: Olschki, 1990.

———. *Valdesiani e spirituali: Studi sul Cinquecento religioso italiano.* Rome: Edizioni di Storia e Letteratura, 2013.

———. *Vittore Soranzo vescovo ed eretico.* Rome: Laterza, 2006.

Firpo, Massimo, and Guido Mongini, eds. *Ludovico Castelvetro: Letterati e grammatici nella crisi religiosa del Cinquecento.* Florence: Olschki, 2008.

Firpo, Massimo, and Ottavia Niccoli. *Il cardinale Giovanni Morone e l'ultima fase del concilio di Trento.* Bologna: Il Mulino, 2010.

Fletcher, Catherine. *Diplomacy in Renaissance Rome: The Rise of the Resident Ambassador.* Cambridge: Cambridge University Press, 2015.

———. "'Furnished with Gentlemen': The Ambassador's House in Sixteenth-Century Italy." *Renaissance Studies* 24 (2010): 518–35.

———. *Our Man in Rome: Henry VIII and His Italian Ambassador.* London: Bodley Head, 2012.

———. "War, Diplomacy and Social Mobility: The Casali Family in the Service of Henry VIII." *Journal of Early Modern History* 14 (2010): 559–78.

Fletcher, Catherine, and Jennifer Mara DeSilva. "Italian Ambassadorial Networks in Early Modern Europe: An Introduction." *Journal of Early Modern History* 14 (2010): 505–12.

Forcade, Olivier, and Philippe Nivet, eds. *Les réfugiés en Europe du XVIe au XXe siècle.* Paris: Nouveau Monde, 2008.

Franceschini, Chiara. "La corte di Renata di Francia (1528–1560)." In *Storia di Ferrara.* 7 vols., edited by Adriano Prosperi, 6:185–214. Ferrara: Corbo Editore, 1987–2004.

———. "Nostalgie di un esule: Note su Giacomo Castelvetro (1546–1616)." In *Questioni di storia inglese tra Cinque e Seicento: cultura, politica e religione,* edited by Stefano Villani, Stefania Tutino, and C. Franceschini, 73–101. Pisa: Edizioni della Normale, 2006.

Fragnito, Gigliola. "Evangelismo e intransigenti nei difficili equilibri del pontificato farnesiano." *Rivista di storia e letteratura religiosa* 25 (1989): 20–47.

———. *Gasparo Contarini: Un magistrato veneziano al servizio della Cristianità.* Florence: Olschki, 1988).

———. "Gli *spirituali* e la fuga di Bernardino Ochino." In *Gasparo Contarini,* 251–306.

———. "La terza fase del concilio di Trento, Morone e gli 'spirituali.'" In Firpo and Niccoli, *Il cardinale Giovanni Morone,* 53–78.

———. "Pio V e la censura." In Guasco and Torre, *Pio V nella società,* 129–58.

Fragnito, Gigliola, and Alain Tallon, eds. *Hétérodoxies croisées: Catholicismes pluriels entre France et Italie, XVIe–XVIIe siècles.* Rome: Publications de l'École française de Rome, 2015. http://books.openedition.org/efr/2823.

Frajese, Vittorio. "Il mito del gesuita tra Venezia e i gallicani." In Zanardi, *I Gesuiti e Venezia,* 289–345.

———. *Sarpi scettico: Stato e Chiesa a Venezia tra Cinque e Seicento.* Bologna: Il Mulino, 1994.

Frémy, Édouard. *Un Ambassadeur libéral sous Charles IX et Henri III.* Paris: E. Leroux, 1880.

Friedensburg, Walter. Giovanni Morone und der Brief Sadolets an Melanchthon vom 17. Juni 1537." *Archiv für Reformationsgeschichte* 1 (1903): 372–80.

———. *Nuntiaturberichte aus Deutschland 1533–1559 nebst ergänzenden Actenstücken, I: Nuntiaturen des Vergerio 1533–1536.* Gotha: Friedrich Andreas Perthes, 1892.

Frigo, Daniela. "Prudenza politica e conoscenza del mondo: un secolo di riflessione sulla figura dell'ambasciatore (1541–1663)." In *De l'ambassadeur: Les écrits relatifs à l'ambassadeur et à l'art de négocier du Moyen Âge au début du XIXe siècle*, edited by Stefano Andretta, Stéphane Péquignot, and Jean-Claude Waquet. Rome: École française de Rome, 2015. http://books.openedition.org/efr/2909.

——, ed. *Politics and Diplomacy in Early Modern Italy*. Cambridge: Cambridge University Press, 2000.

——. "Prudence and Experience: Ambassadors and Political Culture in Early Modern Italy." *Journal of Medieval and Early Modern Studies* 38, no. 1 (2008): 15–34.

Furey, Constance M. *Erasmus, Contarini, and the Religious Republic of Letters*. Cambridge: Cambridge University Press, 2006.

Fusaro, Maria. "After Braudel: A Rassessment of Mediterranean History between the Northern Invasion and the Caravane Maritime." In Fusaro, Heywood, and Omri, *Trade and Cultural Exchange*, 1–22.

——. *Political Economies of Empire in the Early Modern Mediterranean: The Decline of Venice and the Rise of England 1450–1700*. Cambridge: Cambridge University Press, 2015.

——. *Uva passa: Una guerra commerciale tra Venezia e l'Inghilterra (1540–1640)*. Venice: Il Cardo, 1996.

Fusaro, Maria, Colin Heywood, and Mohamed-Salah Omri, eds. *Trade and Cultural Exchange in the Early Modern Mediterranean: Braudel's Maritime Legacy*. London: Tauris, 2010.

Gabrieli, Vittorio. "Bernardino Ochino: *Sermo de Christo*: un inedito di Elisabetta Tudor," *La Cultura* 21 (1983): 151–74.

Gaeta, Franco. "La Riforma in Germania nelle *relazioni* degli ambasciatori veneti al Senato." In Beck, Manoussacas, and Pertusi, *Venezia centro di mediazione tra oriente*, 2:571–97.

Gajda, Alexandra. *The Earl of Essex and Late Elizabethan Political Culture*. Oxford: Oxford University Press, 2012.

Gamberini, Andrea, and Isabella Lazzarini, eds. *The Italian Renaissance State*. Cambridge: Cambridge University Press, 2012.

Garavelli, Enrico. *Lodovico Domenichi e i "Nicodemiana" di Calvino*. Introduction by Jean-François Gilmont. Rome: Vecchiarelli, 2004.

Garcia, Stéphane. *Élie Diodati et Galilée: naissance d'un réseau scientifique dans l'Europe du XVII siècle*. Florence: Olschki, 2004.

García-Arenal, Mercedes, and Gerard Wiegers. *Entre el Islam y Occidente: Vida de Samuel Pallache, judío de Fez*. Madrid: Siglo XXI de España Editores, 1999.

——. *A Man of Three Worlds: Samuel Pallache, a Moroccan Jew in Catholic and Protestant Europe*. Translated by Martin Beagles. Baltimore: Johns Hopkins University Press, 2003.

Gardi, Andrea. "Pietro Antonio di Capua (1513–1578): Primi elementi per una biografia," *Rivista di storia e letteratura religiosa* 2 (1988): 262–309.

Gelder, Maartje Van, and Krstić, Tijana, eds. "Cross-Confessional Diplomacy and Diplomatic Intermediaries in the Early Modern Mediterranean." Special issue of the *Journal of Early Modern History* 19 (2015).

Ghezzi, Angelo Giorgio, and Lisa Longhi. *La visita apostolica di Gerolamo Ragazzoni a Milano (1575–1576)*. 2 vols. Rome: Bulzoni, 2010.

Ghobrial, John-Paul. *The Whispers of the Cities: Information Flows in Istanbul, London and Paris in the Age of William Trumbull.* Oxford: Oxford University Press, 2013.

Gibson, William. *A Social History of the Domestic Chaplain, 1530–1840.* London: Leicester University Press, 1997.

Ginzburg, Carlo, ed. *I costituti di don Pietro Manelfi.* DeKalb: Northern Illinois University Press, 1970.

———. *Nessun isola è un'isola: Quattro sguardi sulla letteratura inglese.* Milan: Feltrinelli, 2000.

Ginzburg, Carlo, and Adriano Prosperi. *Giochi di pazienza: Un seminario sul Beneficio di Cristo.* Turin: Einaudi, 1975.

Gleason, Elizabeth G. *Gasparo Contarini: Venice, Rome, and Reform.* Berkeley: University of California Press, 1993.

———. "On the Nature of Sixteenth-Century Italian Evangelism: Scholarship, 1953–1978." *Sixteenth-Century Journal* 9, no. 3 (1978): 3–26.

Gorris, Rosanna. "*Concilii celesti e infernali*: Blaise de Vigenère traduttore della *Gerusalemme Liberata.*" *Studi di letteratura francese* 19 (1993): 385–409.

Gotor, Muguel. "Le vite di San Pio V dal 1512 al 1712 tra censura e storia." In Guasco and Torre, *Pio V nella società,* 207–49

Grafton, Anthony. *The Footnote: A Curious History.* Cambridge, MA: Harvard University Press, 1999.

Graziani, Françoise. "Sur le chemin du Tasse: la fidélité du traducteur selon Vigenère, Baudoin et Vion Dalibray." In Balsamo, *L'Arioste et le Tasse en France,* 203–16.

Grell, Ole Peter. *Brethren in Christ: A Calvinist Network in Reformation Europe.* Cambridge: Cambridge University Press, 2011.

Grendler, Paul F. *Critics of the Italian World, 1530–1560: Anton Francesco Doni, Niccolò Franco and Ortensio Lando.* Madison: University of Wisconsin Press, 1969.

———. *The Roman Inquisition and the Venetian Press, 1540–1605.* Princeton, NJ: Princeton University Press, 1977.

———. "The Tre Savii sopra eresia 1547–1605: A Prosopographical Study." *Studi veneziani* 3 (special issue, 1979): 233–40.

Griffiths, Ralph A., and John E. Law, eds. *Rawdon Brown and the Anglo-Venetian Relationship.* Stroud, Gloucestershire: Nonsuch, 2005.

Guasco, Maurilio, and Angelo Torre, eds. *Pio V nella società e nella politica del suo tempo.* Bologna: Il Mulino, 2005.

Gunnoe, Charles D. Jr. *Thomas Erastus and the Palatinate: A Renaissance Physician in the Second Reformation.* Leiden: Brill, 2011.

Habermas, Jürgen. *The Structural Transformation of the Public Sphere: An Inquiry into a Category of Bourgeois Society.* Translated by Thomas Burger, with Frederick Lawrence. Cambridge, MA: MIT Press, 1991.

———. *Strukturwandel der Öffentlichkeit: Untersuchungen zu einer Kategorie der bürgerlichen Gesellschaft.* Neuwied, Berlin: Luchterhand, 1962.

Haddad, Emma. *The Refugees in International Society: Between Sovereigns.* Cambridge: Cambridge University Press, 2008.

Hammer, Paul E. J. *The Polarisation of Elizabethan Politics: The Political Career of Robert Devereux, 2nd Earl of Essex, 1585–1597.* Cambridge: Cambridge University Press, 1999.

———. "The Uses of Scholarship: The Secretariat of Robert Devereux, Second Earl of Essex, c. 1585–1601." *English Historical Review* 109 (1994): 26–51.

Hampton, Timothy. *Fictions of Embassy: Literature and Diplomacy in Early Modern Europe.* Ithaca, NY: Cornell University Press, 2009.

Hay, Denis. *Polydore Vergil: Renaissance Historian and Man of Letters.* Oxford: Clarendon Press, 1952.

Head, Randolph, ed. "Archival Knowledge Culture in Europe, 1400–1900." *Archival Knowledge* 10 (2010).

Heywood, Colin. "The English in the Mediterranean, 1600–1630: A Post-Braudelian Perspective on the 'Northern Invasion.'" In Fusaro, Heywood, and Omri, *Trade and Cultural Exchange*, 23–44.

Houssaye Michienzi, Ingrid. *Datini, Majorque et le Maghreb (14e–15e siècles): Réseaux, espaces méditerranées et stratégies marchandes.* Leiden: Brill, 2013

Hsia, Ronnie Po-Chia. *The World of Catholic Renewal.* Cambridge: Cambridge University Press, 1998.

Hubert, Friedrich. *Vergerios publizistische Thätigkeit, nebst einer bibliographischen Übersicht.* Göttingen: Vandenhoeck & Ruprecht, 1893.

Huffman, Clifford C. "The Earliest Reception of Tasso in Elizabethan England." *Rivista di Letterature Moderne e Comparate* 32 (1979): 245–61.

———. *Elizabethan Impressions: John Wolfe and His Press.* New York: AMS, 1988.

Ignatieff, Michael. "The Refugees & the New War." *New York Review of Books*, December 17, 2015.

Infelise, Mario. "From Merchants' Letters to Handwritten Political Avvisi: Notes on the Origins of Public Information." In *Correspondence and Cultural Exchange in Early Europe, 1400–1700*, edited by Francisco Bethencourt and Florike Egmond, 33–52. Cambridge: Cambridge University Press, 2007.

———. *I padroni dei libri: Il controllo sulla stampa nella prima età moderna.* Rome: Laterza, 2014.

———. *Prima dei giornali: Alle origini della pubblica informazione.* Rome: Laterza, 2002.

———. "Roman *Avvisi*: Information and Politics in the Seventeenth Century." In *Court and Politics in Papal Rome 1492–1700*, edited by Gianvittorio Signorotto and Maria Antonietta Visceglia, 212–28. Cambridge: Cambridge University Press, 2002.

Jardine, Lisa. "Gloriana Rules the Waves: Or, the Advantage of Being Excommunicated (and a Woman)." *Transactions of the Royal Historical Society* 14 (2004): 209–22.

Jardine, Lisa, and Anthony Grafton. "*Studied for Action*: How Gabriel Harvey Read his Livy." *Past and Present* 129 (1990): 30–78.

Jardine, Lisa, and William Sherman. "Pragmatic Readers: Knowledge Transactions and Scholarly Services in Elizabethan England." In *Religion, Culture and Society in Early Modern England: A Festschrift for Patrick Collinson,* edited by Anthony Fletcher and Peter Roberts, 102–24. Cambridge: Cambridge University Press, 1994.

Jedin, Hubert. "Contarini und Camaldoli." *Archivio italiano per la storia della pietà* 2 (1959): 51–117.

———. "La politica conciliare di Cosimo I." *Rivista storica italiana* 62 (1950): 345–74, 477–96.

———. *Storia del Concilio di Trento.* 4 vols. Brescia: Morcelliana, 1973–81.

Jedin, Hubert, and Paolo Prodi, eds. *Il concilio di Trento come crocevia della politica europea*. Bologna: Il Mulino, 1979.

Kahn, Victoria. *Machiavellian Rhetoric: From the Counter-Reformation to Milton*. Princeton, NJ: Princeton University Press, 1994.

Kallendorf, Craig. *Virgil and the Myth of Venice: Books and Readers in the Italian Renaissance*. Oxford: Clarendon Press, 1999.

Kaplan, Benjamin J. "Diplomacy and Domestic Devotion: Embassy Chapels and the Toleration of Religious Dissent in Early Modern Europe." *Journal of Early Modern History* 4 (2000): 341–61.

——. "Fictions of Privacy: House Chapels and the Spatial Accommodation of Religious Dissent in Early Modern Europe." *American Historical Review* 4 (2002): 1031–64.

Keblusek, Marika, and Badeloch Vera Noldus, eds. *Double Agents: Cultural and Political Brokerage in Early Modern Europe*. Leiden: Brill, 2011.

Keck, Margaret E., and Kathryn Sikkink. *Activists beyond Borders: Advocacy Networks in International Politics*. Ithaca, NY: Cornell University Press, 1998.

Kent, D. V. *Friendship, Love and Trust in Renaissance Florence*. Cambridge, MA: Harvard University Press, 2009.

Kettering, Sharon. *Patrons, Brokers, and Clients in Seventeenth-Century France*. Oxford: Oxford University Press, 1986.

Kingdon, Robert M. "Garrett Mattingly." *American Scholar* 3 (1982): 396–402.

——. "Some French Reactions to the Council of Trent." *Church History* 2 (1964): 149–56.

Kiséry, András. *Hamlet's Moment. Drama and Political Knowledge in Early Modern England*. Oxford: Oxford University Press, 2016.

Kissling, Hans J. "Venezia come centro di informazioni sui Turchi." In Beck, Manoussacas, and Pertusi, *Venezia centro di mediazione tra oriente*, 1:97–109.

Klapisch-Zuber, Christiane. "Parenti, amici, vicini. Il territorio urbano d'una famiglia mercantile nel XV secolo." *Quaderni storici* 33 (1976): 953–82.

Kraye, Jill. "John Bossy on Giordano Bruno." *Heythrop Journal* 33 (1992): 324–27.

Kuntz, Marion Leathers. *Guillaume Postel, Prophet of the Restitution of All Things: His Life and Thought*. The Hague: Kluver Boston, 1981.

Lake, Peter, and Steve Pincus. *The Politics of the Public Sphere in Early Modern England*. Manchester: Manchester University Press, 2007.

——. "Rethinking the Public Sphere in Early Modern England." *Journal of British Studies* 2 (2006): 270–92.

Landi, Sandro. *Stampa, censura e opinione pubblica in età moderna*. Bologna: Il Mulino, 2011.

Laven, Peter J. "The 'causa' Grimani and Its Political Overtones." *Journal of Religious History* 4 (1967): 184–205.

Lavenia, Vincenzo. "Non barbari, ma religiosi e soldati: Machiavelli, Giovio e la turcofilia in alcuni testi del Cinquecento." *Storia del pensiero politico* 1 (2014): 31–58.

Lazzarini, Isabella. *Amicizia e potere: Reti politiche e sociali nell'Italia medievale*. Turin: Einaudi, 2010.

——. *Communication and Conflict: Italian Diplomacy in the Early Renaissance, 1350–1520*. Oxford: Oxford University Press, 2015.

——. "I circuiti mercantili della diplomazia italiana nel Quattrocento." In *Il governo dell'economia: Italia e Penisola Iberica nel basso Medioevo*, edited by Lorenzo Tanzini and Sergio Tognetti, 155–77. Rome: Viella, 2014.

——. "Storia della diplomazia e International Relation studies fra pre- e post-moderno." *Storica* 65 (2016): 9–41.

Lemaitre, Nicole. *Saint Pie V.* Paris: Fayard, 1994.

Leverotti, Franca. *Diplomazia e governo dello Stato: I "famigli cavalcanti" di Francesco Sforza (1450–1466)*. Pisa: ETS, 1992.

Levin, Carole, and John Watkins. *Shakespeare's Foreign Worlds: National and Transnational Identities in the Elizabethan Age*. Ithaca, NY: Cornell University Press, 2009.

Levin, Michael J. *Agents of Empire: Spanish Ambassadors in Sixteenth-Century Italy*. Ithaca, NY: Cornell University Press, 2005.

Loescher, Gil, Katy Long, and Nando Sigona, eds. *The Oxford Handbook of Refugee and Forced Migration Studies*. Oxford: Oxford University Press, 2014.

Lonardi, Simone. "Informazione, spionaggio e segreto di stato a Venezia nella prima età moderna." *Bollettino della Società Letteraria* (2012): 157–74.

Love, Harold. *The Culture and Commerce of Texts: Scribal Publication in Seventeenth-Century England*. Amherst: University of Massachusetts Press, 1993.

Lupprian, Karl-Ernst. *Il Fondaco dei Tedeschi e la sua funzione di controllo del commercio tedesco a Venezia*. Venice: Centro Tedesco di Studi Veneziani, 1978.

MacCulloch, Diarmaid. *Thomas Cranmer: A Life*. New Haven, CT: Yale University Press, 1996.

Maclean, Ian. "Alberico Gentili, His Publishers, and the Vagaries of the Book Trade between England and Germany, 1580–1614." In *Learning and the Market Place*, 291–337.

——. *Learning and the Marketplace: Essays in the History of the Early Modern Book*. Leiden: Brill, 2009.

Maifreda, Germano, ed. *"Mercanti, eresia e Inquisizione nell'Italia moderna."* Special issue of *Storia economica* 17 (2014).

Malcolm, Noel. *De Dominis, 1560–1624: Venetian, Anglican, Ecumenist and Relapsed Heretic*. London: Strickland and Scott, 1984.

Mangoni, Luisa. "Europa sotterranea." In *Politica e storia contemporanea: Scritti (1927–1942)*, edited by Delio Cantimori, xiii–xlii. Turin: Einaudi, 1991.

Mantran, Robert. "Venise, centre d'information sur les Turcs." In Beck, Manoussacas, and Pertusi, *Venezia centro di mediazione tra oriente*, 1:111–16.

Marcatto, Dario. *"Questo passo dell'heresia": Pietroantonio di Capua tra valdesiani, spirituali e inquisizione*. Naples: Bibliopolis, 2003).

Marfleet, Philip. "Refugees and History: Why We Must Address the Past." *Refugee Survey Quarterly* 3 (2007): 136–48.

Martin, John Jeffries. *Myths of Renaissance Individualism*. New York: Palgrave, 2004.

——. *Venice's Hidden Enemies: Italian Heretics in a Renaissance City*. Berkeley: University of California Press, 1993.

Mattingly, Garrett. *Renaissance Diplomacy*. New York: Dover, 1955.

Mayer, Thomas F. *Reginald Pole: Prince & Prophet*. Cambridge: Cambridge University Press, 2000.

Mazzei, Rita. "Convivenza religiosa e mercatura nell'Europa del Cinquecento." In *La formazione storica dell'alterità: studi di storia della tolleranza offerti a Antonio Rotondò*, edited by H. Méchoulan, R.H. Popkin, G. Ricuperati, and L. Simonutti, 395–428. Florence: Olschki, 2001.

———. *Itinera mercatorum: Circolazione di uomini e beni nell'Europa centro-orientale 1550–1650*. Lucca: Fazzi, 1999.

———. *La trama nascosta. Storie di mercanti e altro (secoli XVI–XVII)*. Viterbo: Sette Città, 2011.

McDiarmid, John F., ed. *The Monarchical Republic of Early Modern England: Essays in Response to Patrick Collinson*. Aldershot: Ashgate, 2007.

McEntegart, Rory. *Henry VIII, the League of Schmalkalden, and the English Reformation*. London: The Royal Historical Society, 2002.

McNally, Robert E. "The Council of Trent and the German Protestants." *Theological Studies* 25 (1964): 1–22.

McReynolds, Daniel. "Lying Abroad for the Good of His Country: Sir Henry Wotton and Venice in the age of the Interdict." In *The Image of Venice: Fialetti's View and Sir Henry Wotton*, edited by Deborah Howard and Henrietta McBurney, 115–23. London: Paul Holberton, 2014.

Ménager, Daniel. *Diplomatie et théologie à la Renaissance*. Paris: Presses universitaires de France, 2001.

Micanzio, Fulgenzio. "Annotazioni e pensieri." In Benzoni and Zanato, *Storici e politici venet,i* 733–863.

Migliorato, Giuseppe. "Vicende e influssi culturali di Giacomo Castelvetro (1546–1616) in Danimarca." *Critica storica* 19 (1982): 243–96.

Morandi, Carlo, ed. *Relazioni di ambasciatori: Sabaudi genovesi e veneti durante il period della Grande Alleanza e della successione di Spagna*. Bologna: Zanichelli, 1935.

Moretti, Walter, and Luigi Pepe, eds. *Tasso e l'università*. Florence: Olschki, 1997.

Muir, Edward. *Civic Ritual in Renaissance Venice*. Princeton, NJ: Princeton University Press, 1981.

———. *The Culture Wars of the Late Renaissance: Skeptics, Libertines and Opera*. Cambridge, MA: Harvard University Press, 2007.

———. "Leopold von Ranke, His Library, and the Shaping of Historical Evidence." *Courier* 22, no. 1 (1987): 3–10.

———. *The Leopold von Ranke Manuscript Collection of Syracuse University: The Complete Catalogue*. Syracuse, NY: Syracuse University Press, 1983.

Murrin, Michael. *History and Warfare in Renaissance Epic*. Chicago: University of Chicago Press, 1994.

Netzloff, Mark. "The Ambassador's Household: Sir Henry Wotton, Domesticity, and Diplomatic Writing." In *Diplomacy and Early Modern Culture*, edited by R. Adams and R. Cox, 155–71. Houndmills: Palgrave Macmillan, 2011.

Neumann, Iver B. *At Home with the Diplomats: Inside a European Foreign Ministry*. Ithaca, NY: Cornell University Press, 2012.

Newman, Jane. "'Mediating Amicably?' The Birth of the *Trauerspiel* out of the Letter of Westphalia." In *Early Modern Diplomacy, Theatre and Soft Power: The Making of Peace*, edited by Natalie Rivère de Carles, 69–89. London: Palgrave Macmillan, 2016.

Newman, Karen, and Jane Tylus, eds. *Early Modern Cultures of Translations*. Philadelphia: University of Pennsylvania Press, 2015.

Niccoli, Ottavia. "Il mostro di Sassonia: Conoscenza e non conoscenza di Lutero in Italia nel Cinquecento." In *Lutero in Italia*, edited by Lorenzo Perrone, 5–25. Casale Monferrato: Marietti, 1983.

——. *Rinascimento anticlericale: Infamia, propaganda e satira in Italia tra Quattrocento e Cinquecento*. Rome: Laterza, 2005.

Nigro, Salvatore Silvano. "Il segretario." In *L'uomo barocco*, edited by Rosario Villari, 91–108. Rome: Laterza, 1991.

O'Malley, John. *The Council of Trent: Myths, Misunderstandings and Unintended Consequences*. Rome: Gregorian and Biblical Press, 2013.

——. *Trent: What Happened at the Council*. Cambridge, MA: Belknap Press of Harvard University Press, 2013.

——. *Trent and All That: Renaming Catholicism in the Early Modern Era*. Cambridge, MA: Harvard University Press, 2000.

Ord, Melanie. "Returning from Venice to England: Sir Henry Wotton as Diplomat, Pedagogue and Italian Cultural Connoisseur." In *Books and Travellers in Early Modern Europe*, edited by Thomas Betteridge, 146–67. Aldershot: Ashgate, 2007.

——. "Venice and Rome in the Addresses and Dispatches of Sir Henry Wotton: First English Embassy to Venice, 1604–1610." *Seventeenth Century* 22 (2007): 1–23.

Orgel, Stephen. *The Reader in the Book: A Study of Spaces and Traces*. Oxford: Oxford University Press, 2015.

Osiander, Andreas. "Sovereignty, International Relations and the Westphalian Myth." *International Organization* 2 (2001): 251–87.

Ottolenghi, Paola. *Giacopo Castelvetro esule modenese nell'Inghilterra di Shakespeare*. Pisa: ETS, 1982.

Overell, Ann M. *Italian Reform and English Reformations, c. 1535–1585*. Aldershot: Ashgate, 2008.

——. "Vergerio's Anti-Nicodemite Propaganda and England." *Journal of Ecclesiastical History* 5 (2000): 296–318.

Panizza, Diego. *Alberico Gentili giurista ideologo dell'Inghilterra elisabettiana*. Padua: La Garangola, 1981.

Parekh, Serena. *Refugees and the Ethics of Forced Displacement*. New York: Routledge, 2017.

Paschini, Pio. *Tre illustri prelati del Rinascimento: Ermolao Barbaro, Adriano Castellesi, Giovanni Grimani*. Rome: Lateranum, 1907.

——. *Tre ricerche sulla storia della chiesa nel Cinquecento*. Rome: Edizioni Liturgiche, 1945.

——. *Un amico del card. Polo: Alvise Priuli*. Rome: Lateranum, 1921.

——. *Venezia e l'Inquisizione romana da Giulio III a Paolo IV*. Padua: Antenore, 1959.

Pastor, Ludwig von. *The History of the Popes, from the Close of the Middle Ages*. Translated and edited by Ralph Francis Kerr. London: Kegan Paul, Trench, Trubner & Co., 1929.

Patterson, W.B. *King James VI and I and the Reunion of Christendom*. Cambridge: Cambridge University Press, 1997.

Penzi, Marco. "La politica francese di Pio V: tra riforma cattolica e guerra contro l'eresia." In Guasco and Torre, *Pio V nella società*, 251–76.

Perini, Leandro. "Ancora sul libraio-tipografo Pietro Perna e su alcune figure di eretici italiani in rapporto con lui negli anni 1549–1555." *Nuova Rivista storica* 3–4 (1967): 363–400.

———. *La vita e i tempi di Pietro Perna*. Rome: Edizioni di Storia e Letteratura, 2002.

———. "Spigolature erasmiane." In *Erasmo e la cultura padana nel '500*, edited by Achille Oliveri, 67–74. Rovigo: Minelliana: 1995.

Peter, Rodolphe, and Jean François Gilmont. *Bibliotheca Calviniana: Les oeuvres de Jean Calvin publiées au XVIe siècle*. Geneva: Droz, 1991.

Petitjean, Johann. *L'intelligence des choses: Une histoire de l'information entre Italie et Méditerranée (XVIe–XVIIe siècles)*. Rome: École française de Rome, 2013.

Petrina, Alessandra. *Machiavelli in the British Isles: Two Early Modern Translations of The Prince*. Aldershot: Ashgate, 2009.

Petrolini, Chiara. "*Paolo Sarpi e l'Inghilterra di Giacomo I*." PhD diss., Istituto Nazionale di Studi sul Rinascimento, Florence, 2010.

———. "Per un regesto delle carte diplomatiche di Giovan Francesco Biondi (1609–1619 ca)." In *Storie inglesi: L'Inghilterra vista dall'Italia tra storia e romanzo (XVII secolo)*, edited by Clizia Carminati and Stefano Villani, 35–42. Pisa: Edizioni della Normale, 2011.

———. "*Un salvacondotto e un incendio*: La morte di Fulgenzio Manfredi in una relazione del 1610," *Bruniana & Campanelliana* 1 (2012): 161–85.

Pezzini, Serena. "Dissimulazione e paradosso nelle *Lettere di molto valorose donne* (1548) a cura di Ortensio Lando." *Rivista di letteratura italiana* 1 (2002): 67–83.

Pezzolo, Luciano. "Sistema di valori e attività economica a Venezia, 1530–1630." In *L'impresa: industria commercio banca secc. XIII–XVIII*, edited by Simonetta Cavaciocchi, 981–88. Florence: Le Monnier, 1991.

Piccolomini, Paolo. "Due lettere inedite di Bernardino Ochino." *Archivio della Società romana di storia patria* 28 (1907): 201–7.

Pierce, Robert A. *Pier Paolo Vergerio the Propagandist*. Rome: Edizioni di Storia e Letteratura, 2003.

Pirillo, Diego. *Filosofia ed eresia nel tardo Cinquecento: Bruno, Sidney e i dissidenti religiosi italiani*. Rome: Edizioni di Storia e Letteratura, 2010.

———. "'Questo buon monaco non ha inteso il Macchiavello': Reading Campanella in Sarpi's Shadow." *Bruniana & Campanelliana* 1 (2014): 129–44.

———. "Republicanism and Religious Dissent: Machiavelli and the Italian Protestant Reformers." In *Machiavellian Encounters in Tudor and Stuart England: Literary and Political Influences from the Reformation to the Restoration*, edited by Alessandro Arienzo and Alessandra Petrina, 121–40. Aldershot: Ashgate, 2013.

Pirri, Pietro. *L'interdetto di Venezia del 1606 e i Gesuiti*. Rome: Institutum historicum S.I., 1959.

Plongeron, Bernard. "Unità tridentina e diversità francese: filoromani, giansenisti, gallicani e costituzionali." In *I tempi del concilio: Religione, cultura e società nell'Europa tridentina*, edited by Cesare Mozzarelli and Danilo Zardin, 145–69. Rome: Bulzoni, 1997.

Pollet, J.V. *Martin Bucer: Études sur la correspondence*. 2 vols. Paris: Presses Universitaires de France, 1958.

Pollnitz, Aysha. *Princely Education in Early Modern Britain*. Cambridge: Cambridge University Press.

Potter, Alfred Claghorn. *Catalogue of John Harvard's Library*. Cambridge, MA: John Wilson and Son, 1919.

Potter, David. *Foreign Intelligence and Information in Elizabethan England: Two Treatises on the State of France, 1580–1584*. Cambridge: Cambridge University Press, 2004.

——. "Mid-Tudor Foreign Policy and Diplomacy: 1547–63." In Doran and Richardson, *Tudor England and Its Neighbours*, 106–38.

Preto, Paolo. *I servizi segreti di Venezia: Spionaggio e controspionaggio ai tempi della Serenissima*. Milan: Il Saggiatore, 1994.

——. *Venezia e i Turchi*. Florence: Sansoni, 1975.

Procacci, Giuliano. *Machiavelli nella cultura europea dell'età moderna*. Rome: Laterza, 1995.

Prodi, Paolo. "Controriforma e/o riforma cattolica: superamento di vecchi dilemmi nei nuovi panorami storiografici." In *Crisi e rinnovamenti nell'autunno del Rinascimento a Venezia*, edited by Vittore Branca and Carlo Ossola, 11–21. Florence: Olschki, 1991.

——. *Diplomazia del Cinquecento. Istituzioni e prassi*. Bologna: Patron, 1963.

——. *Il paradigma tridentino: Un'epoca di storia della chiesa*. Brescia: Morcelliana, 2010.

——. *Il sovrano pontefice: un corpo e due anime. La monarchia papale nella prima età moderna*. Bologna: Mulino, 1982.

——. "Structure and Organization of the Church in Renaissance Venice: Suggestions for Research." In *Renaissance Venice*, edited by John R. Hale, 409–30. London: Faber and Faber, 1973.

Prodi, Paolo, and Wolfgang Reinhard, eds. *Il concilio di Trento e il moderno*. Bologna: Il Mulino, 1996.

Prosperi, Adriano. *Eresie e devozioni: la religione italiana in età moderna*. Rome: Edizioni di Storia e Letteratura, 2010.

——. "'Guerra giusta' e cristianità divisa tra Cinquecento e Seicento." In *Chiesa e guerra: Dalla "benedizione delle armi" alla "Pacem in terris,"* edited by Mimmo Franzinelli and Riccardo Bottoni, 29–90. Bologna: Il Mulino, 2005.

——. *Il Concilio di Trento: una introduzione storica*. Turin: Einaudi, 2001.

——. "Il 'miles christianus' nella cultura italiana tra '400 e '500." *Critica storica* 26, no. 4 (1989): 685–704.

——. "'L'altro coltello': Libelli de lite di parte romana." In Zanardi, *I Gesuiti e Venezia*, 263–87.

——. *L'eresia del Libro grande: Storia di Giorgio Siculo e della sua setta*. Milan: Feltrinelli, 2000.

——. *L'Inquisizione romana: Letture e ricerche*. Rome: Storia e Letteratura, 2003.

——. "Lo stato della religione tra l'Italia e il mondo: variazioni cinquecentesche sul tema." *Studi storici* 1 (2015): 29–48.

——. *Lutero: gli anni della fede e della libertà*. Milan: Mondadori, 2017.

——. *Tra Evangelismo e Controriforma: G.M. Giberti (1495–1543)*. Rome: Storia e Letteratura, 1969.

——. *Tribunali della coscienza: Inquisitori, confessori, missionari*. Turin: Einaudi, 1996.

———."Un papato 'spirituale': programmi e speranze nell'età del Concilio di Trento." In *Il Papato e l'Europa*, edited by Gabriele de Rosa and Giorgio Cracco, 239–54. Soveria Mannelli: Rubbettino, 2001.

Prosperi, Valentina. *"Di soavi licor gli orli del vaso": La fortuna di Lucrezio dall'Umanesimo alla Controriforma*. Turin: Aragno, 2004.

Questier, Michael C. "Loyalty, Religion and State Power in Early Modern England: English Romanism and the Oath of Allegiance." *Historical Journal* 40 (1997): 311–29.

Quint, David. *Epic and Empire*. Princeton, NJ: Princeton University Press, 1993.

Raab, Theodore K. "A Contribution to the Toleration Controversy of the Sixteenth Century: Sandys's 'A Relation of the State of Religion.'" In *Renaissance Studies in Honor of Hans Baron*, edited by Anthony Molho and John Tedeschi, 833–47. Florence: Sansoni, 1971.

———. *Jacobean Gentleman: Sir Edwin Sandys, 1561–1629*. Princeton, NJ: Princeton University Press, 1998.

Raimondi, Ezio. *Rinascimento inquieto*. Palermo: Manfredi. 1965.

Rambaldi, Susanna Peyronel. "Tra *dialoghi* letterari e *ridotti* eterodossi: frammenti di cultura del patriziato veneto nel Cinquecento." In *Per Marino Berengo: Studi degli allievi*, edited by Livio Antonelli, Carlo Capra, and Mario Infelise, 182–209. Milan: Franco Angeli, 2000.

———. *Una gentildonna irrequieta: Giulia Gonzaga fra reti familiari e relazioni eterodosse*. Rome: Viella, 2012.

Ray, Meredith K. *Writing Gender in Women's Letter Collections of the Italian Renaissance*. Toronto: University of Toronto Press, 2009.

Reeves, Marjorie. *The Influence of Prophecy in the Later Middle Ages: A Study in Joachimism*. Oxford: Clarendon Press, 1969.

Rein, Gabriel. *Sarpi und die Protestanten: Ein Beitrag zur Geschichte der Reformations-Bewegung in Venedig im Anfang des siebzehnten Jahrhunderts*. Helsingfors: Aktiengesellschaft Lilus & Hertzberg, 1904.

Reinhard, Wolfgang. *Papauté, confessions, modernité*. Edited by Robert Descimon. Paris: Editions de l'Ecole des hautes études en sciences sociales, 1998.

Rhodes, Dennis E. *Giovanni Battista Ciotti (1562–1627?)*. Venice: Marcianum Press, 2013.

———. "La traduzione italiana dei *Commentarii* di Giovanni Sleidano." *La Bibliofilia* 3 (1966): 283–87.

Ricci, Giovanni. *Ossessione turca: In una retrovia cristiana dell'Europa moderna*. Bologna: Il Mulino, 2002.

Richardson, Brian. *Manuscript Culture in Renaissance Italy*. Cambridge: Cambridge University Press, 2009.

Riches, Daniel. *Protestant Cosmopolitanism and Diplomatic Culture: Brandenburg-Swedish Relations in the Seventeenth Century*. Leiden: Brill, 2013.

Romano, Angelo. *Periegesi aretiniane: Testi, schede e note biografiche intorno a Pietro Aretino*. Rome: Salerno, 1991.

Rosenberg, Eleanor. "Giacopo Castelvetro: Italian Publisher in Elizabethan London and His Patrons." *Huntington Library Quarterly* 2 (1946): 119–48.

———. "Giacopo Castelvetro in Scandinavia." *Columbia Library Columns* 25, no. 2 (1976): 18–27.

Rösh, Gerhard "Il Fondaco dei Tedeschi." In *Venezia e la Germania*, 51–72. Milan: Electa, 1986.

Rospocher, Massimo. *Beyond the Public Sphere: Opinions, Publics, Spaces in Early Modern Europe*. Bologna: Il Mulino, 2012.

Rossi, Massimo. *"Io come filosofo era stato dubbio": la retorica dei* Dialoghi *di Tasso*. Bologna: Il Mulino, 2007.

Rossi, Paolo. *Un altro presente: Saggi sulla storia della filosofia*. Bologna: Il Mulino, 1999.

Rossi, Sergio. *Ricerche sull'Umanesimo e sul Rinascimento in Inghilterra*. Milan: Vita e Pensiero, 1969.

Rothman, Natalie. *Brokering Empire: Trans-Imperial Subjects between Venice and Istanbul*. Ithaca, NY: Cornell University Press, 2011.

——. "Afterword: Intermediaries, Mediation and Cross-Confessional Diplomacy in the Early Modern Mediterranean." *Journal of Early Modern History* 19 (2015): 255–259.

Rotondò, Antonio. "Anticristo e Chiesa romana: diffusione e metamorfosi d'un libello antiromano del Cinquecento." In *Forme e destinazione del messaggio religioso: aspetti della propaganda religiosa nel Cinquecento*, edited by Antonio Rotondò, 19–164. Florence: Olschki, 1991.

Rozzo, Ugo. "La lettera al doge Francesco Donà del 1545 e il problema politico della Riforma in Italia." *Acta Histriae* 8 (1999): 29–48.

——, ed. *Pier Paolo Vergerio il giovane, un polemista attraverso l'Europa del Cinquecento*. Udine: Forum, 2000.

Rozzo, Ugo, and Silvana Seidel Menchi. "Livre et Réforme en Italie." In *La Réforme et le livre: L'Europe de l'imprimé (1517–v. 1570)*, edited by Jean-François Gilmont, 327–74. Paris, CERF, 1990.

Ruggiero, Guido. "Constructing Civic Morality, Deconstructing the Body: Civic Rituals of Punishment in Renaissance Venice." In *Riti e rituali nelle società medievali*, edited by Jacques Chiffoleau, Lauro Martines and Agostino Paravicini Bagliani, 175–90. Spoleto: Centro italiano di studi sull'Alto Medioevo, 1994.

Russell, Camilla. *Giulia Gonzaga and the Religious Controversies of Sixteenth-Century Italy*. Turnhout: Brepols, 2006.

Rutter, Carol Chillington. "The English Ambassador Licks His Wounds: Wotton after the Interdict." Paper presented at the conference *Global Reformations*. Toronto, Centre for Reformation and Renaissance Studies, Victoria College, September 2017.

Sabbatini, Renzo, and Paola Volpini, eds. *Sulla diplomazia in età moderna: Politica, economia, religione*. Milan: Franco Angeli, 2011.

Sandonnini, Tommaso. *Lodovico Castelvetro e la sua famiglia: Note biografiche*. Bologna: Zanichelli, 1982.

Scaglione, Aldo. "Giacomo Castelvetro e i conclavi dei papi del Rinascimento." *Bibliothèque d'Humanisme et Renaissance* 28 (1966): 141–49.

Scarpati, Claudio. *Dire la verità al principe: Ricerche sulla letteratura del Rinascimento*. Milan: Vita e Pensiero, 1987.

Schaffer, Simon, Lissa Roberts, Kapil Raj, and James Delbourgo, eds. *The Brokered World: Go-Betweens and Global Intelligence, 1770–1820*. Sagamore Beach, MA: Science History Publications, 2009.

Schilling, Heinz. *Early Modern European Civilization and Its Political and Cultural Dynamism*. Hanover, NH: Brandeis University Press, 2008.

Schmitt, Charles B. *John Case and Aristotelianism in Renaissance England*. Kingston, Ontario: McGill-Queen's University Press, 1983.

Schutte, Anne Jacobson. "Periodization of Sixteenth-Century Italian Religious History: The Post-Cantimori Paradigm Shift." *Journal of Modern History* 61 (1989): 269–84.

———. *Pier Paolo Vergerio: The Making of an Italian Reformer*. Geneva: Droz, 1977.

Scribner, Robert. *For the Sake of Simple Folk: Popular Propaganda for the German Reformation*. Oxford: Clarendon Press, 1994.

Seidel Menchi, Silvana. *Erasmo in Italia, 1520–1580*. Turin: Bollati Boringhieri, 1987.

———. "Characteristics of Italian Anticlericalism." In *Anticlericalism in Late Medieval and Early Modern Europe*, edited by Peter A. Dykema and Heiko A. Oberman, 271–81. Leiden: Brill, 1993.

———. "Chi fu Ortensio Lando?" *Rivista storica italiana* 3 (1994): 501–64.

———. "Les relations de Martin Bucer avec l'Italie." In *Martin Bucer and Sixteenth-Century Europe*, edited by Christian Krieger and Marc Lienhard, 557–69. Leiden: Brill, 1993.

———. "Ortensio Lando cittadino di Utopia: un esercizio di lettura." In *La fortuna dell'Utopia di Thomas More nel dibattito politico europeo del '500*, 95–118. Florence: Olschki, 1996.

———. "Protestantesimo a Venezia." In *La Chiesa di Venezia tra Riforma protestante e Riforma cattolica*, edited by Giuseppe Gullino, 131–54. Venice: Edizioni Studium Cattolico Veneziano, 1990.

———. "Se l'eretico fa testamento." In *La fede degli italiani: Per Adriano Prosperi*, edited by Guido dall'Olio, Adelisa Malena, Pierroberto Scaramella, 33–40. Pisa: Scuola Normale Superiore, 2011.

———. "Spiritualismo radicale nelle opere di Ortensio Lando attorno al 1550," *Archiv für Reformationsgeschichte* 65 (1974): 212–79.

———. "The Age of Reformation and Counter-Reformation in Italian Historiography, 1939–2009," *Archiv für Reformationsgeschicthe* 100 (2009): 193–217.

Senatore, Francesco. *"Uno mundo de carta": Forme e strutture della diplomazia sforzesca* Naples: Liguori, 1994.

Seneca, Federico. *Il doge Leonardo Donà: La sua vita e la sua preparazione politica prima del dogado*. Padua: Antenore, 1959.

Shagan, Ethan H. *Popular Politics and the English Reformation*. Cambridge: Cambridge University Press, 2003.

Sherman, William H. *John Dee: The Politics of Reading and Writing in the English Renaissance*. Amherst: University of Massachusetts Press. 1995.

———. *Used Books: Marking Readers in Renaissance England*. Philadelphia: University of Pennsylvania Press, 2008.

Shuckburgh, E. S., ed. *Two biographies of William Bedell*. Cambridge: Cambridge University Press, 1902.

Simoncelli, Paolo. *Evangelismo italiano del Cinquecento: Questione religiosa e nicodemismo politico*. Rome: Storia e Letteratura, 1979.

———. *Il caso Reginald Pole: Eresia e santità nelle polemiche religiose del Cinquecento.* Rome: Edizioni di Storia e Letteratura, 1977.

———. "Inquisizione romana e Riforma in Italia." *Rivista storica italiana* 1 (1988): 5–125.

Simonetta, Marcello. *Rinascimento segreto: il mondo del segretario da Petrarca a Machiavelli.* Milan: Franco Angeli, 2004.

Solerti, Angelo. *La Vita di Torquato Tasso.* 3 vols. Turin: Loescher, 1895.

Sommerville, Johann P. "Papalist Political Thought." In *Catholics and the "Protestant Nation": Religious Politics and Identity in Early Modern England,* edited by Ethan H. Shagan, 162–84. Manchester: Manchester University Press, 2005.

Soranzo, Giovanni. "Il P. Antonio Possevino e l'ambasciatore inglese a Venezia (1604–1605)." *Aevum* 4 (1933): 385–422.

Sowerby, Tracey A. "Richard Pate, the Royal Supremacy, and Reformation Diplomacy." *Historical Journal* 54, no. 2 (2011): 265–85.

Sowerby, Tracey A., and Jan Hennings, eds. *Practices of Diplomacy in the Early Modern World, c. 1410–1800.* London: Routledge, 2017.

Spini, Giorgio. *Barocco e puritani: Studi sulla storia del Seicento in Italia, Spagna e New England.* Florence: Vallecchi, 1991.

———. "Riforma italiana e mediazioni ginevrine nella Nuova Inghilterra puritana." In *Ginevra e l'Italia: Raccolta di studi promossa dalla Facoltà Valdese di Teologia di Roma,* edited by Delio Cantimori, Luigi Firpo, Giorgio Spini, Franco Venturi, Valdo Vinay, 451–89. Florence: Sansoni, 1959.

———. *Tra Rinascimento e Riforma: Antonio Brucioli.* Florence: La Nuova Italia, 1940.

Stella, Aldo. *Chiesa stato nelle relazioni dei nunzi pontifici a Venezia: Ricerche sul giurisdizionalismo veneziano dal XVI al XVIII secolo.* Vatican City: Biblioteca Apostolica Vaticana, 1964.

———. "Guido da Fano eretico del secolo XVI al servizio del Re d'Inghilterra." *Rivista di storia della Chiesa in Italia* 13, no. 2 (1959): 196–238.

———. "L'orazione di Pier Paolo Vergerio al doge Francesco Donà sulla riforma della Chiesa (1545)." *Atti dell'Istituto Veneto di Scienze, Lettere ed Arti. Classe di scienze morali, lettere e arti* 128 (1969–70): 1–39.

———. "Utopie e velleità insurrezionali dei filoprotestanti italiani (1545–1547)." *Bibliothèque d'Humanisime et Renaissance* 27, no. 1 (1965): 133–61.

Stephens, Walter. "La demonologia nella poetica del Tasso." In Moretti and Pepe, *Tasso e l'università,* 411–32.

Stoler, Ann Laura. *Along the Archival Grain: Epistemic Anxieties and Colonial Common Sense.* Princeton, NJ: Princeton University Press, 2009.

Stone, Lawrence. *An Elizabethan: Sir Horatio Palavicino.* Oxford: Clarendon Press, 1956.

Strong, Roy. *Henry Prince of Wales and England's Lost Renaissance.* London: Thames and Hudson, 1986.

Subrahmanyam, Sanjay. *Three Ways to be Alien: Travails and Encounters in the Early Modern World.* Waltham, MA: Brandeis University Press, 2011.

Šusta, Josef, ed. *Die römishce Kurie und das Konzil von Trient unter Pius IV: Actenstücke zur Geschichte des Konzils von Trient.* 4 vols. Vienna: A. Hölder, 1904.

Tafuri, Manfredo. *Venezia e il Rinascimento: religione, scienza, architettura.* Turin: Einaudi, 1985.

Tallon, Alain. "Diplomate et 'politique': Arnaud du Ferrier." In *De Michel de l'Hospital à l'édit de Nantes: politique et religion face aux églises*, edited by Thierry Wanegffelen, 305–33. Clermont-Ferrand: Presses universitaires Blaise-Pascal, 2002.

———. *L'Europe au XVIe siècle: États et relations internationales*. Paris: Presses Universitaires de France, 2010.

———. "Le Concile de Trente et l'Inquisition Romaine." *Mélanges de l'Ecole Française de Rome* 106 (1994): 129–59.

———. *Le France et le concile de Trente (1518–1563)*. Rome: École française de Rome, 1997.

———. "Le 'parti français' et la dissidence religieuse en France et en Italie." In *La Réforme en France et en Italie: contacts, comparaisons et contrastes*, edited by Philip Benedict, Silvana Seidel Menchi and Alain Tallon, 381–99. Rome: Ecole française de Rome, 2007.

Tateo, Franceso. "I *Dialoghi* del Tasso fra dialettica e retorica." In Moretti and Pepe, *Tasso e l'università*, 199–211.

Tedeschi, John, ed. *The Correspondence of Roland H. Bainton and Delio Cantimori: 1932–1966: An Enduring Transatlantic Friendship between Two Historians of Religious Toleration*. Florence: Olschki, 2002.

———. "The Cultural Contributions of Italian Protestant Reformers in the Late Renaissance." In *Libri, idee e sentimenti religiosi del Cinquecento italiano*, edited by Adriano Prosperi and Albano Biondi, 81–108. Modena: Panini, 1987.

———. "The Dispersed Archives of the Roman Inquisition." In *The Inquisition in Early Modern Europe: Studies on Sources and Methods*, edited by Gustav Henningsen and John Tedeschi, 13–32. Dekalb: Northern Illinois University Press, 1986.

———. "Tommaso Sassetti's Account of the St. Bartholomew's Day Massacre." In *The Massacre of St. Bartholomew: Reappraisals and Documents*, edited by A. Soman, 99–154. The Hague: Martinus Nijhoff, 1974.

Terpstra, Nicholas. *Religious Refugees in the Early Modern World: An Alternative History of the Reformation*. Cambridge: Cambridge University Press, 2015.

Testa, Simone. "Did Giovanni Maria Mannelli Publish the *Thesoro politico (1589)?*" *Renaissance Studies* 19 (2005): 380–93.

Thomas, Keith. *Religion and the Decline of Magic: Studies in Popular Belief in Sixteenth- and Seventeenth-Century England*. London: Weidenfeld and Nicolson, 1971.

Todeschini, Giacomo. Il prezzo della salvezza: Lessici medievali del pensiero economico. Rome: Carocci, 1994.

Tommasino, Pier Mattia. L'Alcorano di Macometto: Storia di un libro del Cinquecento europeo. Bologna: Il Mulino, 2013.

Trivellato, Francesca. *The Familiarity of Strangers: The Sephardic Diaspora, Livorno, and Cross-Cultural Trade in the Early Modern Period*. New Haven, CT: Yale University Press, 2009.

———. "Merchants' Letters across Geographical and Social Boundaries." In Cultural Exchange in Early Modern Europe, edited by Francisco Bethencourt and Florike Egmond, 81–103. Cambridge: Cambridge University Press, 2007.

Trivellato, Francesca, Leor Halevi, and Cátia Antunes, eds. *Religion and Trade. Cross-Cultural Exchanges in World History 1000–1900*. Oxford: Oxford University Press, 2014.

Tucci, Ugo. "Introduzione" to Benedetto Cotrugli, *Il libro dell'arte di mercatura*, 3–128. Venice: Arsenale, 1990.

——. *Mercanti, navi e monete nel Cinquecento veneziano*. Bologna: Mulino, 1981.

——. "Ranke and the Venetian Document Market." *Courier* 22, no. 1 (1987): 27–38.

Tuck, Richard. *The Rights of War and Peace: Political Thought and the International Order from Grotius to Kant*. Oxford: Oxford University Press, 1999.

Tutino, Stefania. *Empire of Souls: Robert Bellarmine and the Christian Commonwealth*. Oxford: Oxford University Press, 2010.

——. *Law and Conscience: Catholicism in Early Modern England, 1570–1625*. Farnham: Ashgate, 2007.

Ulianich, Boris. "I gesuiti e la Compagnia di Gesù nelle opere e nel pensiero di Sarpi." In Zanardi, *I Gesuiti e Venezia*, 233–62.

Valensi, Lucette. *The Birth of the Despot. Venice and the Sublime Porte*. Ithaca, NY: Cornell University Press, 1993.

Vasoli, Cesare. "L'immagine sognata: il 'papa angelico.'" In *Storia d'Italia. Annali 16. Roma, la città del papa. Vita civile e religiosa dal giubileo di Bonifacio VIII al giubileo di papa Wojtyla*, edited by Luigi Fiorani and Adriano Prosperi, 75–109. Turin: Einaudi, 2000.

——. *Profezia e ragione: Studi sulla cultura del Cinquecento e del Seicento*. Naples: Morano, 1974.

Vigezzi, Brunello. "La *nuova storiografia* e la storia delle relazioni internazionali." In *Federico Chabod e la 'nuova storiografia' italiana dal primo al secondo dopoguerra (1919–1950)*, edited by Brunello Vigezzi, 415–77. Milan: Jaca Book, 1984.

——. *Politica estera e opinione pubblica in Italia dall'unità ai giorni nostri*. Milan: Jaca Book, 1991.

Villani, Stefano. "The Italian Protestant Church of London in the Seventeenth Century." In *Exiles, Emigrés and Intermediaries*, edited by Barbara Schaff, 217–36. Amsterdam: Rodopi, 2010,

——. "Italian Translations of the Book of Common Prayer." In *Travels and Translations*, edited by Alison Yarrington, Stefano Villani, Julia Kelly, 303–19. Amsterdam: Rodopi, 2013.

——. "Religious Pluralism and the Dangers of Tolerance: The English Nation in Livorno in the Seventeenth-Century." In *Late Medieval and Early Modern Religious Dissents: Conflicts and Plurality in Renaissance Europe*, edited by Federico Barbierato and Alessandro Veronese, 97–124. Pisa: Edizioni Il Campano Arnus University Books, 2012.

——. "Uno scisma mancato: Paolo Sarpi, William Bedell e la prima traduzione in italiano del *Book of Common Prayer*." *Rivista di storia e letteratura religiosa* (2017), 63–112.

Visceglia, Maria Antonietta. "Burocrazia, mobilità sociale e patronage alla corte di Roma tra Cinque e Seicento: alcuni aspetti del recente dibattito storiografico e prospettive di ricerca." *Roma moderna e contemporanea* 3 (1995): 11–55.

Vivanti, Corrado. *Quattro lezioni su Paolo Sarpi*. Naples: Bibliopolis, 2005.

Wackernagel, Hans Georg, ed. *Die Matrikel der Universität Basel*. 5 vols. Basel: Verlag der Universitätsbibliothek, 1951–.

Warren, Christopher R. "Gentili, the Poets and the Laws of War." In *The Roman Foundations of the Law of Nations: Alberico Gentili and the Justice of Empire*, edited by Benedict Kingsbury and Benjamin Straumann, 146–62. Oxford: Oxford University Press, 2010.

Watkins, John. *After Lavinia: A Literary History of Premodern Marriage Diplomacy*. Ithaca, NY: Cornell University Press, 2017.

——. "Elizabeth through Venetian Eyes." *Explorations in Renaissance Culture* 30 (2004): 121–38.

——. "Introduction: Non-state Actors in Mediterranean Politics." *Mediterranean Studies*, 25, no. 1 (2017), 1–8

——. "Toward a New Diplomatic History of Medieval and Early Modern Europe." *Journal of Medieval and Early Modern Studies* 38, no. 1 (2008): 1–14.

Weber, Max. *The Vocation Lectures*. Indianapolis: Hackett, 2004.

Wilks, Timothy, ed. *Prince Henry Revived: Image and Exemplarity in Early Modern England*. London: Southampton Solent University-Paul Holberton, 2007.

Williams, Megan K. "'Dui Fratelli . . . Con Dui Principi': Family and Fidelity on a Failed Diplomatic Mission." *Journal of Early Modern History* 14 (2010): 579–611.

Williamson, J.W. *The Myth of the Conqueror, Prince Henry Stuart: A Study of Seventeenth-Century Personation*. New York: AMS Press, 1978.

Wilson, Elkin Calhoun. *Prince Henry and English Literature*. Ithaca, NY: Cornell University Press, 1946.

Windler, Christian. "Diplomatic History as a Field for Cultural Analysis: Muslim-Christian Relations in Tunis." *Historical Journal* 1 (2001): 79–106.

Woolfson, Jonathan. *Padua and the Tudors: English Students in Italy*. Toronto: University of Toronto Press, 1988.

——, ed. *Reassessing Tudor Humanism*. New York: Palgrave, 2002.

Worden, Blair. *The Sound of Virtue: Philip Sidney's* Arcadia *and Elizabethan Politics*. New Haven, CT: Yale University Press, 1996.

Wyatt, Michael. *The Italian Encounter with Tudor England: A Cultural Politics of Translation*. Cambridge: Cambridge University Press, 2005.

Yates, Frances A. *Astraea: The Imperial Theme in the Sixteenth Century*. London: Penguin, 1975.

——. *The French Academies of the Sixteenth Century*. London: Warburg Institute, 1947.

——. *John Florio: The Life of an Italian in Shakespeare's England*. Cambridge: Cambridge University Press, 1934.

Zanardi, Mario, ed. *I Gesuiti e Venezia: Momenti e problemi di storia veneziana della Compagnia di Gesù*. Padua: Gregoriana, 1994.

Zanato, Tiziano. "Per l'edizione critica delle 'Istorie veneziane' di Niccolò Contarini." *Studi veneziani* 4 (1980): 129–98.

Zannini, Andrea. *Burocrazia e burocrati a Venezia in età moderna: i cittadini originari (sec. XVI–XVIII)*. Venice: Istituto veneto di scienze, lettere ed arti, 1993.

——. "Economic and Social Aspects of the Crisis of Venetian Diplomacy in the Seventeenth and Eighteenth Centuries." In Frigo, *Politics and Diplomacy*, 109–46.

Zatti, Sergio. "Il linguaggio della simulazione nella *Liberata*." In Dutschke et al., *Forma e parola*, 423–47.

――. *L'uniforme cristiano e il multiforme pagano: Saggio sulla* Gerusalemme Liberata. Milan: Il Saggiatore, 1983.

――. *The Quest for Epic: From Ariosto to Tasso*. Introduction by Albert Ascoli. Edited by Dennis Looney. Toronto: University of Toronto Press, 2006.

Zimmermann, Andreas, ed. *The 1951 Convention Relating to the Status of Refugees and Its 1967 Protocol: A Commentary*. Oxford: Oxford University Press, 2011.

Index

CPSIA information can be obtained
at www.ICGtesting.com
Printed in the USA
LVHW110032171118
596243LV00001B/12/P

9 781501 715310